THE **WHO** INTERNATIONAL CODE OF MARKETING OF BREAST-MILK SUBSTITUTES

To the memory of Sir Robert Jennings,
the inspiring leader in the drafting of The WHO
International Code Of Marketing Of Breast-Milk Substitutes

THE **WHO** INTERNATIONAL CODE OF MARKETING OF BREAST-MILK SUBSTITUTES

HISTORY AND ANALYSIS

2nd edition

Sami Shubber
Lic. en Dr. (Baghdad)
Post-graduate Dip. in Law (London), LL.M. (London)
Ph.D. (Cantab), Barrister-at-law (Gray's Inn),
Member of the Iraqi Bar,
formerly Senior Legal Officer, (WHO)

pinter
&
martin

The WHO International Code of Marketing of Breast-Milk Substitutes
History and Analysis

First published by Kluwer Law International 1998
This second edition published by Pinter & Martin Ltd 2011, reprinted 2024

ISBN 978-1905177-46-2

British Library Cataloguing-in-Publication Data
A catalogue record for this book is available from the British Library

Pinter & Martin Ltd
Unit 803 Omega Works
4 Roach Road
London E3 2PH

www.pinterandmartin.com

TABLE OF CONTENTS

PART II

FOREWORD TO THE FIRST EDITION

It is a privilege to commend this study of an important international social problem. It will interest medical and social workers who are concerned to get a healthy balance between natural breast feeding of infants and the use of manufactured substitutes. It will also interest scholars of international law and relation because this story of a joint endeavour between the WHO and UNICEF is an instructive exemplar of what can be accomplished by hard work and skilled diplomacy.

The social and medical problem that this joint endeavour has been concerned with can be stated simply. It is well established that natural breast feeding is generally medically safer, psychologically superior and a good deal cheaper than the use of manufactured breast milk substitutes; though these substitutes also have their uses in certain exceptional cases where natural feeding is for one reason or another not expedient or not possible. In a developed and relatively well-off society there is probably much to be said for leaving this kind of choice to the individual to make, with the help of such advice as they choose to seek. A complication arises, however, in developing and poor countries when, for instance, commission-driven salesmen are tempted-and one can only hope not instructed-to offer free, or 'special offer' samples of their product, well aware that, after this 'free' or very cheap use for a time, the mother's own milk will dry up so that even in their poverty they become easy victims of 'the market'.

It was to rescue these mothers and their babies that WHO and UNICEF entered upon this joint endeavour. The method was scientific investigation, consultation and co-operation with the manufacturers of formula milk substitute, to get an agreed code of conducts, publicity being the sanction.

The author of this present book, a WHO career international lawyer, has taken a full and dedicated part in this task from the beginning. He has been largely responsible for the actual drafting. He has, since the code was agreed and published, traveled very widely in developing countries, offering advice based on solid experience, helping with local law changes, and much else. This whole operation has been a splendid operation for good. And no-one is better qualified to write about it than Dr. Shubber.

The late Sir Robert Jennings[1]

---

1   Former Whewell Professor of International Law, Cambridge University, and fomer President and Judge of the International Court of Justice.

PREFACE

This is the second edition of my work on the WHO International Code of Marketing of Breast-milk substitutes, 1981. The first edition was published in 1998 by Kluwer Law International. My association with the International Code goes back to the first day of its inception in 1980. On the morning of 4 February 1980, Dr Tejada, the then ADG in WHO, called me to a meeting he held with several senior WHO staff members, and asked me about the legal means available under the WHO Constitution for the formulation of an international code on a health matter. I explained those means to the participants at the meeting. And from that date until my retirement on 28 February 1997 from WHO, I was associated with the preparation of the Code, its drafting and adoption, the provision of legal advice on its various aspects, including implementation at the national level, attendance at consultations, seminars and WHO workshops and meetings on the subject. Moreover, my association with, and keen interest in, the International Code continue until the present time. Therefore, I thought it appropriate to write some of the relevant aspects of my association with the Code, at the preparatory stages, and some of my experience during this period as a Senior Legal Officer of WHO responsible for Code matters, which has not always been very pleasant. I have also offered my objective and impartial interpretation of the provisions of the Code, in the light of their context and the aim of the Code, always bearing in mind the health of infants and mothers.

I have been supported, encouraged and helped, immensely, in the preparation of the first edition of this work, as well as the second edition, by my wife Suzie, to whom I express my deep gratitude and appreciation. I would also like to express my thanks to my daughter Yasmin, who has helped in tidying up the manuscript, according to modern standards of computer usage. I wish also to express my gratitude to my son Hamoudi for steering me around the complexities of wayward computers. Most of all, I wish to express my sincere gratitude and profound appreciation to the late Sir Robert Jennings, who led the drafting group for the preparation of the Code, for his encouragement and support of my efforts during the preparation of the first edition of this work and for his kind words in the Foreword to the first edition, which I have included in the second edition.

Finally, I would like to reiterate my sincere thanks and gratitude for the grant I received from the Swedish International Development Cooperation Agency, (SIDA) for the preparation of the first edition of this work. My thanks go particularly to Eva Wallstrom and Birgitta Rubensen, who have been instrumental in providing this grant from SIDA.

Sami Shubber
Commugny, Switzerland, 27 June 2010

ABBREVIATIONS

ADG	Assistant Director General (WHO)
AFRO	Regional Office for Africa (WHO)
AMRO	Regional Office for the Americas (WHO)
BFHI	Baby Friendly Hospital Initiative
CMC	Christian Medical Commission
EMRO	Regional Office for the Eastern Mediterranean (WHO)
EURO	Regional Office for Europe (WHO)
FAO	Food and Agriculture Organization of the United Nations
FHE	Family Health Division (WHO)
GATT	General Agreement on Tariffs and Trade
GIFA	Geneva Infant Feeding Association
IBFAN	International Baby Food Action Network
ICCR	Interfaith Centre on Corporate Responsibility
ICIFI	International Council of Infant Food Industries
ICJ	International Court of Justice
ICM	International Council of Midwives
INFACT	Infant Formula Action Coalition
IFM	International Association of Infant Food Manufacturers
IGBM	Interagency Group on Breast-feeding Monitoring
INCAP	Institute of Nutrition of Central America and Panama
INF	Information Division (WHO)
IOCU	International Organization of Consumers Union
IPA	International Paediatric Association
ISDI	International Society of Dietetic Industries
IUNS	International Union of Nutritional Societies
LEG	Legal Office (WHO)
MCH	Maternal and Child Health Unit (WHO)
MDGs	Millennium Development Goals
NGO	Non-governmental Organization
NIFAC	Nestlé Infant Formula Commission
NU	News on Health Care in Developing Countries

NUT	Nutrition Unit (WHO)
PAHO	Pan American Health Organization
PCIJ	Permanent Court of International Justice
SEARO	Regional Office for South-East Asia (WHO)
SIDA	Swedish International Development Cooperation Agency
SPARC	Society for the Protection of the Rights of the Child
UN	United Nations
UNCTAD	United Nations Conference on Trade and Development
UNHCR	United Nations High Commissioner for Refugees
UNICEF	United Nations Children's Fund
UNIDO	United Nations Industrial Development Organization
UNU	United Nations University
WHA	World Health Assembly
WFP	World Food Programme
WHO	World Health Organization
WPRO	Regional Office for the Western Pacific (WHO)
WTO	World Trade Organization

LIST OF CASES

INTRODUCTION

Breast-feeding has always been the natural and normal way of feeding an infant. It was not until the 19th century that breast-milk substitutes came into existence, through the efforts of Henry Nestlé, but then only for special cases of infants who could not be breast-fed. It was after the Second World War that the use of breast-milk substitutes became prevalent, and breast-feeding thus suffered from this phenomenon. The WHO Secretariat stated in 2009 that

> Breast-feeding is today the single most effective preventive intervention for improving the survival and health of children[1]

The trend for the use of breast-milk substitutes continued to gather speed, until the realization that its unnecessary and improper use had caused and is still causing health problems, leading to the death of thousands and thousands of infants, particularly in the developing world, and causing great financial strain to families that could ill-afford it.

> It is estimated that more than one million deaths in children under the age of five could be prevented every year with the improvement of breast-feeding practices.[2]

The use of breast-milk substitutes has also deprived the mother and infant from many benefits. For example, it denied the mother the emotional link with her baby, while depriving the infant of the immunity against disease, which breast-milk amply provides to the infant. The economic and social development of any society could suffer from the harmful effects of improper infant feeding.

The increase in the use of breast-milk substitutes has been greatly helped by the marketing practices of the manufacturers and distributors of those products, as well as the manufacturers of feeding bottles and teats. Practices, such as the giving of samples of breast-milk substitutes to mothers, or would-be mothers, providing supplies of such products to hospitals, maternity wards, health centres, and the offering of financial, material inducements and money to health workers and the health care system, have greatly helped to encourage and promote the use of breast-milk substitutes upward in many parts of the world, particularly in the developing world.

WHO and UNICEF have for many years emphasized the importance of breast-feeding for the health and nutrition of infants and young children. Having seen the harmful effects on the health of infants from the unnecessary and improper use of breast-milk substitutes, and the decline in breast-feeding, the

---

1   See Report by the WHO Secretariat on Infant and young child nutrition: quadrennial progress report, *WHO Doc. EB120/9*, 19 November 2009, p. 7, paragraph 33.
2   Ibid.

WHA, twice in the nineteen seventies, called on WHO Member States to take legal and other measures to curb the promotional activities by manufacturers and distributors of breast-milk substitutes and to promote breast-feeding. UNICEF was also concerned about the decline in breast-feeding, together with professional and consumers associations and NGOs. And in 1979, a WHO/ UNICEF meeting was held in Geneva, to which were invited some Member States of WHO, the U.N., several subsidiary bodies of the U.N., several Specialized Agencies, NGOs, the infant-food industry and experts, that gave the impetus for the preparation and the eventual adoption of the WHO International Code of Marketing of Breast-milk Substitutes in 1981.

The aim of the International Code is, essentially, the promotion and protection of breast-feeding, and the use of breast-milk substitutes when necessary. Therefore, it applies to breast-milk substitutes, feeding bottles and teats. In order to achieve its aim, the Code has provided for the provision of objective and consistent information on infant feeding, by governments, for families and persons involved in the area of infant and young child feeding. The Code has also laid down certain particulars which have to be included in informational and educational materials, as well as on labels of products falling within its material scope. Furthermore, it has banned many of the practices that have encouraged the use of breast-milk substitutes, such as the advertising and promotion of those products, giving of samples, gifts and other inducements to health workers, the low-price sales and donations of breast-milk substitutes to the health care system.

The International Code was adopted as a recommendation under Article 23 of the WHO Constitution. Therefore, in order to be effective, the Code has to be implemented at the national level, in its entirety, as well as subsequent relevant WHA resolutions, by legislation, regulations or other suitable measures. Some of those resolutions could be characterized as *de facto* amendments of the Code. The Code has provided for monitoring its application at the State level and the WHA level. It has also given NGOs, professional groups, institutions and individuals, as well as the infant-food industry, a role in the monitoring process.

Even thirty years after the adoption of the International Code, it remains, together with the relevant resolutions of the WHA, the pivot for the protection, promotion, and encouragement of breast-feeding in the world.

The purpose of this work is to survey the historical development of the Code, analyse its provisions, and offer some examples of problems that have arisen in practice, since its adoption, including those involving action on the part of WHO. Reference will also be made, where appropriate, to national measures implementing the Code.

PART I

THE HISTORY OF THE INTERNATIONAL CODE

CHAPTER I

THE HISTORICAL DEVELOPMENT OF THE INTERNATIONAL CODE

INTRODUCTION

The uniqueness of human milk for feeding babies has been known since time immemorial.[1] By contrast, breast-milk substitutes are the products of the twentieth century. Post says that

> Infant formula was developed in the early 1900's in the United States as a medically acceptable alternative form of food supply for new-borns. For thirty years, the product was primarily used in hospital settings. The popularity of formula feeding as a scientific and convenient approach jumped dramatically after World War II....[2]

In Europe, Henry Nestlé invented a mixture of bread and cow milk called "la farine lactée"

> for mothers unable to breast-feed their infants. In September 1867, he tried his invention on a baby born one month premature, because of the mother's serious illness, and who had refused his mother's milk and any other food . The baby took to Nestlé's mixture and survived on it. From 1873, Henri Nestlé sold 500,000 tins of his "farine lactée" a year not only in Europe but also in the U.S., Australia, Argentina, Mexico and the Dutch East Indies. In 1875, Henri Nestlé sold his product and name to a group of businessmen from the French-speaking part of Switzerland, for one million Swiss francs. The company "farine lactée Henry Nestlé" was established, and Henri Nestlé was not even a shareholder.[3]

In 1921, Nestlé launched its first breast-milk substitute lactogène, on the market.[4]

---

1   See Dr. Ghada Hafez and Dr. Kalyan Bagchi, *Promotion of Breast-feeding through MCH Services and Primary Health Care* (1995), p.12; Dr. Hafez was Director, Division of Health Protection and Promotion, WHO Regional Office for the Eastern Mediterranean Region (EMRO), and Dr. Bagchi was Consultant, Reproduction, Family and Community Health, in the latter Regional Office.
2   See James E, Post, "The International Infant Formula Industry", *Marketing and Promotion of Infant Formula in Developing Nations,1978, Hearing Before the Subcommittee on Health and Scientific Research of the Committee on Human Resources, United States Senate, Ninety-Fifth Congress* (hereinafter referred to as the "US Senate Hearing"), 23 May 1978, p. 216.
3   See Jean-Claude Buffle, *Dossier N... Comme Nestlé* (1986), pp. 14, 15 and 16.
4   See Buffle, op. cit., p.20.

The use of breast-milk substitutes in feeding infants has led to a decline in breast-feeding in both developed and developing countries.[5]And yet "breast-milk is clean and free of bacteria so it cannot make a baby ill. It contains anti-infective factors which prevent infection."[6]

By contrast, as the Jelliffes say:

> it has been estimated that some 10 million cases of marasmus and diarrhoea occur annually in infants in developing countries, related in part to inadequate bottle feeding. Also...moves from breast to bottle feeding interferes with biological child spacing and, on a community basis, increase the rate of population growth.[7]

As *The Lancet* put it:

> if a new vaccine became available that could prevent 1 million or more child deaths a year, and that was moreover cheap, safe, administered orally, and required no cold chain, it would become an immediate public health imperative. Breast-feeding would do all this and more....[8]

The position of the World Health Organization (hereinafter referred to as "WHO")

> ...has always been...that breast-feeding is ideally suited to the overall health and well-being of the young infant and that breast milk is the food of choice during early infancy.[9]

This is in line with WHO's objective, namely, "the attainment by all peoples of the highest possible level of health", and the promotion of maternal and child health is one of its functions.[10]Therefore, WHO was concerned about the decline in breast-feeding, and the World Health Assembly (hereinafter referred to as "WHA") adopted a resolution in 1974,

> noting the general decline in breast-feeding, related to sociocultural and environmental factors, including the mistaken idea caused by misleading sales promotion that breast-feeding is inferior to feeding with manufactured breast-milk substitutes.[11]

The WHA also urged Member States to review sales promotion activities on

---

5 See above note 1, pp.12 and 13.

6 See F. Savage King, *Helping Mothers to Breastfeed*, Revised ed. (1992), p.24, (underlining in the original).

7 See D.B. Jelliffe and E.F.P Jeliffe "Feeding Young Infants in Developing Countries", *U.S. Senate Hearing*, op. cit., p. 72, (underlining in the original).

8 *The Lancet*, Vol. 344, No.8932, (5 November 1994), p.1239.

9 See statement by Manuel Carballo before the Subcommittee on Health and Scientific Research, *U.S. Senate Hearing*, p.104. Carballo was a staff member of the Division of Family Health WHO.

10 Art.1 and Art.2 (l) of the WHO Constitution.

11 See Resolution WHA 27.43, second preambular para; the text of the resolution is to be found in *WHO Handbook of Resolutions and Decisions of the World Health Assembly and the Executive Board* (hereinafter referred to as the "*WHO Handbook*"), Vol. II (1985), pp.89-90.

baby foods and to introduce appropriate remedial measures.[12] The WHA, at its Thirty-first session in 1978 again considered the question of breast-feeding and infant health, and recommended that Member States give the highest priority, *inter alia*, to the prevention of malnutrition in infants and young children by

> supporting and promoting breast-feeding by educational activities among the general public; legislative and social action to facilitate breast-feeding by working mothers;...and regulating inappropriate sales promotion of infant foods that can be used to replace breast milk.[13]

However, the break-through, insofar as the development of an international code is concerned, came in October 1979, when the Joint WHO/UNICEF Meeting on Infant and Young Child Feeding (hereinafter referred to as "the October Meeting, 1979"), held in Geneva, recommended the adoption of an international code of marketing of infant formula and other products used as breast-milk substitutes.[14] This recommendation led to the development and adoption of the WHO International Code of Marketing of Breast-milk Substitutes (hereinafter referred to as the "International Code"), by the WHA in May 1981. The following pages cover the various stages of the development of the International Code from October 1979 to May 1981.

I. DEVELOPMENTS BETWEEN OCTOBER 1979–MAY 1980

The October Meeting 1979 was held, thanks to a request from the late Senator Edward M. Kennedy, who wrote to the then Director-General of WHO, Dr. Halfdan Mahler, on 20 July 1978. In his letter, Senator Kennedy referred to the U.S. Senate hearing[15] on the issue of the promotion and marketing of infant formula in developing nations, held on 23 May 1978, in which WHO and infant formula manufacturing companies took part. He also referred to a meeting with officials of more companies, who agreed to join with him

> ...in requesting that the World Health Organization convene a conference of industry representatives, industry critics, nutrition experts, and appropriate government officials and health professionals from developing nations to address the problem [of the promotion and marketing of infant formula in developing nations] on a global basis.

He went on to say:

> the conference might consider, among other things, the adoption of a meaningful uniform code of ethics acceptable to all infant formula manufacturers.[16]

---

12 Ibid., para.3, ibid., p.90.
13 See Resolution WHA 31.47, para.3(1); ibid.,p.85.
14 See *Joint WHO/UNICEF Meeting on Infant and Young Child Feeding, Geneva, 9-12 October 1979, Statement-Recommendations-List of Participants*,p. 28.
15 See above note 2.
16 See letter from Senator Kennedy to the Director-General of WHO dated 23 May 1978.

In his reply to Senator Kennedy, Dr. Mahler accepted the suggestion made by the Senator and referred to the resolutions adopted by WHA on the question of breast-feeding and breast-milk substitutes,[17] in 1974 and 1978. He went on to say that

> the organization of a meeting along the lines suggested in your letter of 20 July would be an important step and would help all concerned to take the necessary action called for to ameliorate the current situation.[18]

Following that exchange of letters, WHO and the United Nations Children's Fund (hereinafter referred to as "UNICEF"), arranged for the convening of a meeting in Geneva from 9 to 12 October 1979, on infant and young child feeding. The meeting was attended by some 150 representatives of governments, organizations of the United Nations system and other intergovernmental bodies, non-governmental organizations (hereinafter referred to as "NGOs"), the infant-food industry, and experts in related disciplines. The October Meeting 1979 was the first meeting organized by WHO and UNICEF, with such representation. It was a constructive meeting, and it succeeded in recommending, *inter alia*, that

> there should be an international code of marketing of infant formula and other products used as breast-milk substitutes. This should be supported by both exporting and importing countries and observed by all manufacturers. WHO/UNICEF are requested to organize the process for its preparation, with the involvement of all concerned parties, in order to reach a conclusion as soon as possible.[19]

This recommendation can be considered as the origin of the International Code, and a signal for WHO and UNICEF to begin work on it.

1. The preparation of the International Code

(i) The First Draft of the International Code

Soon after the end of the October Meeting 1979, the Director-General of WHO wrote a note verbale to all Member States drawing attention to the Meeting and describing it

> as part of the two Organizations' ongoing programmes promoting breastfeeding and the improvement of infant and young child nutrition, and the development of primary health care.[20]

He drew attention to the recommendation of the October Meeting with respect

---

17 See letter from the Director-General of WHO to Senator Kennedy dated 1 September 1978.
18 Ibid.
19 See the October Meeting 1979, above note 14.
20 See circular letter C.L.32.1979, dated 30 November 1979.

to the preparation of an international code of marketing of infant formula and other products used as breast-milk substitutes, and stated that

> a working group composed of all interested parties will be convened immediately to draw up such a code and a progress report on the state of preparation of this code will be presented to the Thirty-third World Health Assembly.[21]

He concluded that

> ...it may be appropriate for national governments to undertake studies and define the situation in their own countries as to formulate better policies and programmes and to develop national legislation in order to regulate and monitor an international code of marketing practices.[22]

He sent copies of the recommendations of the October Meeting to all Member States.

Following the letter of the Director-General to Member States, the secretariats of WHO and UNICEF took the decision to prepare a draft international code, in pursuance of that recommendation. To that end, an American academic, Professor David Kadane, of Hofstra University, New York, U.S.A., was asked by WHO and UNICEF to prepare the text of a draft international code on the question under consideration. In January 1980, Professor Kadane prepared a document entitled "Code for the Marketing of Breastmilk Substitutes". This document became known within WHO and UNICEF as the "First Draft" of the International Code. In February 1980, the Director-General of WHO, on his behalf and that of the Executive Director of UNICEF, dispatched to all Member States of WHO the First Draft of the International Code requesting their comments and suggestions on the text by 31 March 1980.[23] The Director-General also informed Member States that the First Draft was sent to the appropriate specialized agencies of the United Nations, the relevant NGOs, the infant food industry and to scientists. He further stated that informal consultations would be held with those organizations in the near future, in order to expedite the preparation of an international code.[24]The Director-General concluded:

> based on all comments received, a further draft of a Code of Marketing Practices will be prepared for presentation to the Thirty-third World Health Assembly and the Executive Board of the United Nations Children's Fund both to be held in May 1980.[25]

The First Draft was rather detailed, and consisted of a preamble and eight articles with 40 sections. It dealt with issues relating to sales promotion, advertising, product information, samples, relations between companies and their employees and relations between companies and health workers, quality of

---

21 Ibid.
22 Ibid.
23 See circular letter C.L. 2. 80, dated 20 February 1980.
24 Ibid.
25 Ibid.

products and definitions. It also contained a controversial provision providing for the establishment of a "Central Office" by WHO and UNICEF. Infant-food companies were required to submit to the Central Office, for the purpose of reviewing, advertisements, training and educational materials prepared by them and so on. The Central Office was empowered to interpret the code and render opinions as to its applicability to the materials submitted by companies, together with other functions.[26]

(ii) Consultations on the First Draft

WHO and UNICEF held the following consultations during the period February-March 1980, for the purpose of discussing and further developing the First Draft of the International Code:

(1) Consultation with all interested United Nations agencies and selected experts, 14-15 February 1980, WHO Geneva;
(2) Consultation with NGOs and consumer groups, 22 February 1980, WHO, Geneva;
(3) Consultation with bilateral agencies, 25 February 1980, Paris;
(4) Consultation with professional associations and experts, 4 March 1980, WHO, Geneva; and
(5) Consultation with the infant-food industry concerned, 13-14 March 1980, WHO, Geneva.[27]

In consultation No (1), representatives of the United Nations Conference on Trade and Development (UNCTAD) (Dr. S.J. Patel, Director, Technology Division), the United Nations Industrial Development Organization (UNIDO) (Mr. S. Padolecchia, Assistant to the Special Representative of the Executive Director), and the Food and Agriculture Organization (FAO) (Mr. G. Kermode, Chief, Food Standards and Food Science Services), participated in the discussion of the First Draft, in WHO, Geneva. Experts from Belgium, (Professor A. Gerard, Director, Centre de Recherches sur le Droit de l'Alimentation, Brussels), Ethiopia, (Mrs. M. Bekele), Hungary (Professor Ory, Head, Maternal and Child Health, Ministry of Health, Budapest), Malaysia, (Mrs. R. Lin, Nutrition Officer, Institute of Medical Research, Kuala Lumpur and Mr. A. Fazal, President, International Organisation of Consumers Union, (IOUC Penang), Sweden, (Professor B. Wickström, Professor of Business Administration and Marketing, Göteborg University, Göteborg), the United Kingdom, (Mr. J. Braun, Legal Affairs Consultant), and the United States (Professor J. Post, Professor

---

26 See Art. 7 of the First Draft.
27 See memorandum of the late Dr. A. Petro-Barvazian, the then Director, FHE, to Director-General, dated 29 January 1980.

of Management Policy, Boston University, Boston)[28]and Professor Kadane, the author of the First Draft, also took part in the Consultation.

In Consultation No (2), the NGOs concerned with child welfare, women's affairs, family organizations, consumers' welfare, use of infant formula were invited. They were: the International Union for Child Welfare, International Council of Women, International Organization for Consumers Unions, International Union of Food and Allied Workers, Bureau International Catholique de l'Enfance, Christian Medical Commission, OXFAM, La Leche League International, War on Want, Third World Action Group, INFACT, Interfaith Centre on Corporate Responsibility, The Population Council, the NGO's Committee on UNICEF, and the UN Non-governmental Liaison Service.[29] They took part in the proceedings and the discussion of the various parts of the First Draft in Geneva.

In Consultation No (3), staff members of WHO, acting on behalf of their organization, as well as UNICEF, met the representatives of bilateral agencies from Canada (Dr. J. Steckle, Bureau of Nutritional Sciences, Health Welfare, Ottawa), Denmark (Mr. J. Hijman Jensen, Department of Food Preservation, the Royal Veterinary and Agriculture University, Copenhagen), the then Federal Republic of Germany (Dr. W-D Ernest, Ministerial Counsellor, Federal Ministry of Economic Cooperation, Bonn, Professor Dr. C. Leitzmann, Institut für Ernährungswissenschaft, Justus-Liebig Universität, Giessen), Ireland (Mr.Griffin, Head of Development Division in the Department of Agriculture, Dublin) and The Netherlands (Dr. M.I. Cochius, Director, Financial, Economic Development Cooperation, Ministry of Foreign Affairs, The Hague, and Dr. J.G.A.J. Hautvast, Head of Department of Human Nutrition, Agricultural University, Wageningen), Norway, (Ms. E. Helsing, Institute for Nutrition Research, University of Oslo, Oslo), Sweden (Mr. S. Abelin, Head of Division, SIDA, Stockholm), U.K. (Professor J.C. Waterlow, Professor of Human Nutrition, London School of Hygiene and Tropical Medicine, London), U.S.A. (Dr. M. Forman, Director, Office of Nutrition, U.S. Agency for International Development, Department of State, Washington, and Mr. A. Guross (Observer), Agricultural Attaché, U.S.A. Embassy in Rome, Rome).[30] They provided them with information on the First Draft. It would seem that no detailed examination of the First Draft took place at this consultation, because of the shortage of time. However, some general points appear to have been made during that consultation.

In Consultation No (4), representatives of professional associations in the fields of provision of humanitarian assistance in emergencies, various health fields, health education, nutrition, infants' health and so on took part. They

---

28 See WHO internal document entitled *"Consultation on Code of Ethics, Infant and Young Child Feeding*, Geneva, 14-15 February 1980"

29 See memorandum from Dr. De Maeyer and Dr. Sterky, to Dr. Tejada, the then ADG, dated 25 January 1980.

30 See WHO internal document dated 29 February 1980, p.1.

were: League of Red Cross Societies, International Union for Health Education, International Planned Parenthood Federation, International Confederation of Midwives, International Council of Nurses, International Federation of Gynaecology and Obstetrics, International Paediatric Association, International Union of Nutritional Sciences, International Hospital Federation, Centre International de l'Enfance, Medical Women's International Association, The World Medical Association and World Federation of Public Health Associations.[31] Also experts from Egypt (Dr.M Gabre, the then Minister of Health), the then Federal Republic of Germany (Dr. E. Schmidt, Director der Universitäts Kinderklinik, Düsseldorf), France (Professor J. Rey, Professor of Paediatrics, Paris), Ghana (Dr.F. Sai, International Coordinator, WHP/UNU, Accra), India (Dr. M. Mehta, Professor of Paediatrics, LTMG Medical College and Hospital, Bombay), Jamaica (Dr. P. Harland, Senior Lecturer, Child Health, University of the West Indies, Kingston), Malaysia (Dr. A.T. Latiff, Director of Health Services, Kuala Lumpur), Panama (Dr. J. R. Esqiivel, Director, Del Hospital Del Nino, Panama City), Senegal (Mrs. M.A. Savané, President, Associations des Femmes Africaines pour la Recherche sur le Dévelopment, Dakar), Singapore (Professor Wong Hock Boon, Professor of Paediatrics, Singapore), Sweden (Professor S. Sjölin, Professor of Paediatrics, Uppsala), Tanzania (Professor Malentlema, Director, Institute of Nutrition, Dar-es-Salaam), Thailand (Professor A. Valyasevi, Director, Institute of Nutrition and Professor of Paediatrics, Bangkok), and the United Kingdom (Professor Hendrickse, Professor of Paediatrics, Cardiff) took part in the consultation.[32]

Finally, in Consultation No (5), representative of infants and child food industries from Denmark, France, the then Federal Republic of Germany, Japan, the Republic of Korea, The Netherlands, Switzerland, the United Kingdom and the United States, as well as the International Council of Infant Food Industries (ICIFI)[33], were invited. They were: Snow Brand Milk Products Co. Ltd., Meija Milk Products Co. Ltd., Morinaga Milk Industry Co. Ltd., Wakado Co. Ltd., Cow and Gate Ltd., Wyeth International Ltd., Nestlé, Dumex Ltd., B S N Gervais Danone S.A., Coöp Condensenfabtike Friesland, B.V. Lijempf, Nutricia International B.V., Bristol-Myres Co., Mead-Johnson Nutritionals, Gerber Products Company, Ross Laboratories, Division of Abbot Laboratories, C P C International Inc., Unigate Food Ltd, A.B. Semper and Glaxo,[34] who took part in the discussion of the various provisions of the First Draft.

The First Draft was discussed at those Consultations, apart from Consultation No. 3, where lack of time did not allow a serious consideration of the First Draft. Detailed comments and observations were made, but unfortunately, it

---

31 See above note 29, p.2.
32 Ibid. p. 2.
33 ICIFI was an association of a large number of manufacturers of breast-milk substitutes. It has been replaced by the International Association of Infant Food Manufacturers (IFM).
34 See above note 29 pp. 2-3.

would seem that no minutes of all the Consultations were made. The minutes of Consultation No.1, alone, appear to have been made by the WHO secretariat. The First Draft was considered as "a very strong document",[35] a "fairly comprehensive" draft produced in about two months time after the last meeting in October 1979,[36] and generally received support from participants in those Consultations. However, Article 7 of the First Draft on the "Central Office" was criticised by some representatives of the UN agencies. The representative of FAO wondered

> as to whether it is really possible to contemplate a relationship between a central unit of UN agencies dealing directly with industry in many different member countries.

He went on to say that he feels that

> . . . there may be some general hesitation and anxiety having a central unit monitoring and not exactly licensing practices, but expressing opinion on the practices.[37]

Commenting on the "Central Office", a WHO staff member said that

> if you look at the functions assigned, or would be assigned, to this central office, there are too many of them, and some of them are perhaps questionable from a legal point of view .[38]

Another staff member of WHO described the "Central Office" as "a controlling supranational central office, [which] will be absolutely unrealistic."[39] On the other hand, the infant-food industry was not happy with the First Draft. It was described by Abbot Laboratories as

> in many aspects...not faithful to the recommendations of the October Geneva Conference. After evaluation, we find both its concept and specifics to be disappointingly close to the most extreme positions held by the industry critics. Consequently, we do not believe it can serve as a useful starting point for developing guidelines, which could be accepted by the responsible segment of the infant formula industry.[40]

Mead Johnson stated that the First Draft bore no relationship to the recommendations of the October Meeting 1979, and was simply "unacceptable". They made extensive amendments on the text of the First Draft offering the revised text as acceptable to them.[41] ICIFI's view was that

> an attempt to develop <u>one</u> detailed international code is unrealistic in practical

---

35 See statement by Dr. Wickström, above note 28, p.11.
36 See statement by Dr. Patel, representative of UNCTAD, ibid., p.15.
37 See statement by Mr. Kermode, ibid., p.25.
38 See statement by Dr. Shubber, ibid., p.104.
39 See statement by Dr. Behar, ibid., p.109.
40 See a letter from Charles Aschauer, Executive Vice President, Abbot Laboratories, to Dr. De Maeyer, Senior Medical Officer, WHO, dated 3 March 1980. First attachment, p.6.
41 See a letter from Gary W. Mize, Vice President, Mead Johnson, to Dr. De Maeyer, dated 4 March 1980, pp.1 and 2.

terms" and recommended to WHO "to work on a draft code of <u>general principles</u> . . . leaving detailed codes to be worked out between government and industry as required.[42]

The argument that the First Draft was not faithful to the recommendation of the October Meeting 1979, and that it bore no relationship to that recommendation, it is submitted, is untenable, from a legal point of view. The recommendation in question did not lay down any specific framework for an international code of marketing of breast-milk substitutes, nor did it endorse a particular model for the code. Moreover, that recommendation, even assuming that it laid down a specific framework or endorsed a particular model, cannot be considered as binding vis-à-vis WHO and UNICEF, from a legal point of view. The said Meeting was not even composed entirely of Member States of WHO. The participants in it came from some Member States of WHO, as has been mentioned earlier,[43] some organizations of the UN system, NGOs, the infant-food industry and experts.

However, the First Draft of the International Code received general support from Member States, in their replies to the request of the Director-General for comments and suggestions thereon. On the other hand some Member States had some reservations about the formulation, approach or substance of the First Draft. For example, the U.S. government stated that

> ...any document along these lines should be basic, brief and general (avoiding specifics that could make it irrelevant in too many instances), and that it should be sensitive in giving due consideration to the varied health, economic, social and cultural situations in different countries.[44]

The Swiss government made the following observation:

> le code est conçu comme une série d' interdictions alors qu' il devrait énoncer un certain nombre de <u>principes</u> dont découlent <u>des règles de conduite</u> recommandant certaines pratiques et en prevenant d' autres.

They recommended a number of amendments on the text.[45] The Federal Republic of Germany, while expressing understanding for the elaboration of an international code, had some considerable reservations about the "Central Office", in Article 7 of the First Draft.[46] The Danish government thought that the

---

42 See a letter from E. W. Saunders, ICIFI President to Dr.Tejada-de-Rivero, ADG, WHO, dated 20 March 1980, p.1, fourth para., and p.2, third para. (underlining in the original).

43 See above p.8.

44 See letter from Dr. John Bryant, Deputy Assistant Secretary for International Health, Department of Health, Education and Welfare, to the Director-Genearal of WHO, dated 29 March 1980, p.2, first paragraph.

45 See letter from Dr. Frey, Directeur, Office de la Santé Publique, to WHO, dated 31 March 1980. p.2, paragraph 2.2 *et seq.* (underlining in the original)

46 See letter from Mr. Voigtländfr, Head, International Relations Section, Federal Ministry of Youth, Family and Health, to WHO, dated 2 April 1980.

responsibilities and competence of the Central Office, in Article 7 of the First Draft were "very far reaching."[47]

(iii) The Second Draft of the International Code

In the light of the comments and suggestions made in the various consultations, as well as those made by Member States and communicated to the WHO secretariat, a new draft code was prepared by the WHO and UNICEF secretariats, in April 1980. This draft was known within WHO and UNICEF as the "Second Draft". The Second Draft was submitted to the Thirty-third WHA, in May 1980, for information purposes, as an addendum to the Director-General's report on the Follow-up of WHO/UNICEF Meeting on Infant and Young Child Feeding, Draft International Code of Marketing of Breast-Milk Substitutes .[48]

The Second Draft of the International Code covered the same issues contained in the First Draft. It consisted of ten articles, but it was less detailed than the latter. The provision on the "Central Office", contained in the First Draft, was deleted, and a new provision on the scope of the Code was added. Having had the benefits of the comments and suggestions made by Member States and participants in the various consultations mentioned earlier, the wording and presentation of the Second Draft were an improvement on the First Draft. In the words of the New Zealand Delegate, Dr. Barber, to the Thirty-third WHA

> the second draft was a considerable improvement, but still required amendment.[49]

Moreover, while the First Draft was prepared without the involvement of the secretariats of WHO and UNICEF, the Second Draft had the advantage of their participation in its preparation. This participation helped to bring the text more in line with the policies and practices of the two organizations.[50]

2. Action by the World Health Assembly in May 1980

The Second Draft of the International Code was considered by Committee A[51]

---

47 See letter from Mr. Lustrup, Ministry of the Interior, to WHO, dated 2 April 1890, and p.3.

48 See *WHO Doc.* A33/6 Add. 1 (24 April 1980).

49 See *Thirty-third World Health Assembly, Geneva, 5-23 May 1980,Summary Records of Committees, WHO Doc.WHA33/1980/REC/3*, p.70.

50 It is not surprising then that some people who were not familiar with the policies of WHO and UNICEF felt disappointed by the deletion of the provision on the "Central Office". See the letter of the representative of OXFAM, Dr. G. Clugston to Dr. Petros-Barvazian, Director, FHE, WHO, dated 24 July 1980. Dr. Clugston was at the time of the publication of the first edition of this work, Chief, Nutrition, in WHO.

51 According to Rule 34 of the Rules of Procedure of the WHA, "the main Committees of the Health Assembly shall be: a) Committee A – to deal predominantly with programme and budget; b) Committee B – to deal predominantly with administrative, financial and legal matters". For text of the Rules of Procedure of the WHA see *WHO Basic Documents*, 49th ed.

of the Thirty-third WHA, under agenda item 23 entitled "Follow-up of WHO/ UNICEF Meeting on Infant and Young Child Feeding."[52] There was a tremendous reception for the question of promoting breast-feeding in Committee A, and great interest was shown, during the debates, in the formulation of an international code on the marketing of breast-milk substitutes.

Rare are the occasions on which delegates to the WHA showed so much interest and enthusiasm as this session. Fifty-four delegates from developed and developing countries, a representative of an NGO, the Chairman of the October Meeting 1979, the Director-General, the Deputy Director-General, an Assistant Director-General and some senior staff members of WHO took the floor and made their feelings and positions known about the formulation of an international code.[53] A draft resolution sponsored by forty-four Member States[54] on the agenda item, was submitted to Committee A. It might be interesting to point that the U.S. was one of the co-sponsors of the resolution, and the U.S. delegation made a significant contribution to the discussions in Committee A.[55] At the end of the debates, Committee A adopted the draft resolution by 66 votes to none, with two abstentions.[56] The resolution was transmitted to the WHA and was adopted as Resolution WHA 33.32. In that resolution, the Assembly endorsed "in their entirety" the statement and recommendations of the WHO/UNICEF Meeting and requested the Director-General

> (4) to prepare an international code of marketing of breastmilk substitutes in close consultation with Member States and with all other parties concerned....,
>
> (5) to submit the code to the Executive Board for consideration at its sixty-seventh session and for forwarding with its recommendation to the Thirty-fourth World Health Assembly, together with proposals regarding its promotion and implementation, either as a regulation in the sense of Articles 21 and 22 of the Constitution of the World Health Organization or as a recommendation in the sense of Article 23....[57]

By this resolution, the Assembly gave a clear and definite mandate to the Director-General to prepare an international code, in conformity with the Constitution of WHO. The resolution reflected the policy of WHO[58] in this area of health. It may be recalled that the promotion of breast-feeding and the healthy growth and development of infants and young children, and the adoption of a legal instrument in the furtherance of these matters, are issues falling within

---

(2005), pp. 122-149.

52 See above note 49, p.67.

53 See ibid., pp.67-95.

54 Ibid., p.67.

55 See Dr. Bryant's intervention, ibid., pp.81-82. However, in 1981, when the International Code was adopted, the U.S. was the only Member State which voted against it. By 1981, the Reagan Administration was in power, and President Carter was defeated in the 1980 elections.

56 See ibid., p.204.

57 See Resolution WHA 33.32, paras. 6 and 6(4) and (5). *WHO Handbook*, pp. 90-91.

58 In accordance with Art. 18 (a) of the WHO Constitution one of the functions of the WHA is "to determine the policies of the Organization".

the competence of WHO. Article 2 of the WHO Constitution deals with the functions of the Organization, and among them is the promotion of maternal and child health and welfare (Art. 2 (l)). The preamble of the International Code declares that breast-feeding

> forms a unique biological and emotional basis for the health of both mother and child; that the anti-infective properties of breast-milk help to protect infants against disease .[59]

Furthermore, this mandate constituted the legal basis for further action by the Director-General in the development of the International Code.

With this resolution a new phase of development of the International Code was entered, and, as we will see later, more serious and better organized efforts were undertaken by the secretariats of WHO and UNICEF, in order to have the text of the International Code ready for submission to the Executive Board in January 1981.

II. SOME OBSERVATIONS ON THE PROCESS OF THE PREPARATION OF THE INTERNATIONAL CODE

Let us stop for a moment and try to make some observations concerning the action taken by WHO and UNICEF, so far, and the reaction of the other relevant actors in the process.

First, WHO and UNICEF followed a democratic process in the preparation of the International Code, in that they consulted WHO Member States, the relevant UN organizations, the infant-food industry, NGOs and various experts in the field of mother and child health and nutrition. They sought their views and comments on the First Draft, and exchanged views with them during the consultations, prior to the Thirty-third WHA, and took into account comments offered by them, whenever possible and appropriate. In the words of the then Director-General of WHO, Dr. Mahler,

> ...a democratic process had been started – one that went far beyond what WHO had normally been doing; consultation with all parties concerned had been pursued obsessively. [60]

Secondly, during the process of the development of the International Code, WHO was accused of dealing with matters outside the scope of its constitutional authority. The Director-General said during the debates in Committee A that

> ...he had come to the Committee meeting particularly because of accusations that he had been making the Organization play a role it should not be playing and that he

---

59 See fourth preambular para. of the International Code.
60 See above note 49, p.73.

had gone beyond his mandate.[61]

Of course, such accusations are unfounded, as the promotion of breast-feeding and the health of infants are health matters within the constitutional competence of WHO. In the words of Judge Weeramantry, in his Dissenting Opinion in the Advisory Opinion on the *Legality of the Use by a State of Nuclear Weapons in Armed Conflict*, 1996, WHO is the world's leading health authority, and is

> a body charged with the highest responsibility in regard to the health of the global community.[62]

Furthermore, the Director-General refuted those accusations when he said that

> he thought that two World Health Assemblies had instructed the Director-General in unambiguous resolutions to deal with all problems having to do with infant feeding, and particularly the role of breastfeeding.

He went on to say that

> the Organization believed that breastfeeding was a vital concept; if Member States did not think so they should not have passed their previous resolutions on the subject.[63]

The Swedish Delegate, Dr. Alsen, made it clear that it was

> ... natural that WHO should be closely concerned with all aspects of infant feeding, in particular, with the establishment of a framework within which an international code of marketing of infant formulas and other products used as breastmilk substitutes could be elaborated. The code could be regarded as a tool in the primary health care programme consistent with the Declaration of Alma-Ata and the goal of health for all by the year 2000.[64]

Thirdly, the infant-food industry had attempted to influence WHO to adopt their approach in the preparation of the International Code. This is summed up in a letter from the president of ICIFI to WHO, in which he recommended that WHO

> ... work on a draft code of general principles ... leaving detailed codes to be worked out between government and industry as required. May I again repeat the essential importance of working with industry as opposed to being in competition with us....[65]

Moreover, the infant-food industry had tried to have an active role in the formulation of the International Code. This attempt took the form of suggestions made by the industry, through correspondence with WHO, of making available

---

61 See ibid., p. 72.
62 See I.C.J. Reports (1996), p. 25.
63 See above note 49, pp.72 and 73.
64 Ibid., pp.84-85.
65 See letter from Saunders, President of ICIFI, to Dr. Tejada, ADG, dated 20 March 1980, p.2, third paragraph; underlining in original.

their experts for the secretariats of WHO and UNICEF in the preparation of the International Code. It also took the form of proposals by industry of its own codes prepared for use in developing countries. In January 1980, Nestlé wrote to WHO attaching ICIFI's draft code entitled "International Code of Marketing in Developing Countries."[66] Some weeks later, ICIFI wrote to WHO saying that the First Draft of the International Code was

> "unacceptable",

and that

> . . . the draft code which ICIFI submitted informally . . . is a far more realistic basis for discussion and reflects the spirit of the Geneva meeting.[67]

And again, the President of ICIFI wrote to the Director-General of WHO saying:

> I wish to reiterate the readiness of ICIFI to work with WHO and UNICEF in developing a general code of principles for the use of Member States. . . . I wish to confirm the offer I made on behalf of ICIFI to place at your disposal the industry experts in this field who can assist in preparing a realistic and responsible series of principles for approval by the Executive Board and 34th Health Assembly.[68]

WHO and UNICEF declined to accept those offers. WHO as a "neutral forum" and a "neutral institution"[69], used its own resources, staff and consultants, and those of UNICEF, in the preparation of the drafts of the International Code. It took no sides in the controversies that prevailed at the time between the various interested parties.

The fourth observation may be to the effect that, from the outset, the envisaged International Code was intended to apply universally, without any distinction between developed and developing countries, in spite of the attempt by the infant-food industry to make such a distinction.[70] In the words of the Turkish

---

66 See letter from Mr. G. A. Fookes to Dr. Petros-Barvazian, the then Director of Family Health, WHO, dated 22 January 1980.

67 See telex from the President of ICIFI, Mr. Barter, to Dr. Petros-Barvazian, dated 14 February 1980.

68 See telex from Mr. Saunders, ICIFI's President, to the Director-General of WHO, dated 13 May 1980.

69 See the opening statement of Dr. Tejada, ADG, above note 28, p.7.

70 This distinction was alleged by some manufacturers of breast-milk substitutes. For example, in a letter to WHO, dated 29 February 1980, the President of Wyeth International Limited, commenting on the First Draft of the International Code said: "While the deliberations in Geneva focused almost entirely on developing countries, the draft code makes no attempt to distinguish in its application. Obviously such a severe proposal would have virtually no application or acceptance in industrial countries." See p.1, third paragraph of the letter. Further, in a letter from ICIFI to WHO dated 20 March 1980, ICIFI's President said: "...it seemed clear to us that an attempt to develop *one* detailed international code is unrealistic in practical terms, given the large number of countries involved, and their basic economic and

Delegate, the late Professor Dogramaci, "there should not be one code for the privileged and another for all the rest".[71] The Australian Delegate, Dr. Edmondson said:

> the need to promote breastfeeding was possibly more important in industrialized countries than in developing ones. . . .[72]

And the Norwegian Government made it clear in its comments on the First Draft that

> the Norwegian authorities wish to stress the importance of creating one international code for the marketing of substitutes for breast milk....[73]

The fifth observation is that there was overwhelming support for the formulation of the International Code and for the promotion of breast-feeding through it, by Member States, in their comments on the First Draft and at the Thirty-third WHA. As we have seen earlier, fifty-three delegates, representing the various regions of WHO, took the floor during the debates in Committee A, and not a single one objected to the formulation of an international code. In the words of the Director-General of WHO

> there is no doubt that the Thirty-third World Health Assembly will provide the most important consultation with governments on this matter.[74]

Finally, the task of preparing an international code of marketing of breast-milk substitutes was entrusted to the Director-General of WHO, and not to a group of Member States, as was suggested by the U.S. Delegate during the discussions in Committee A, in 1980.[75] Had the latter approach been accepted, it would be reasonable to suggest that the International Code could not have been completed on time for submission to the Executive Board in January 1981. For a

---

social differences." See p.1, fourth paragraph of the letter. In a letter from Ross Laboratories to WHO, dated 27 March 1980, its chairman said: "There seems to be something inherently incorrect about a Code of Marketing which purports to be universal for developed and developing nations...." See p.4, paragraph 6, of the letter.(emphasis in the original).

71 See above note 49, p.72.

72 Ibid., p.80.

73 See letter from Dr. Mork, Director General of the Health Services of Norway, the Norwegian Ministry of Social Affairs to WHO, dated 17 April 1980,(the emphasis is in the original).

74 See a memorandum from the Director-Genersal to the Regional Directors of WHO, dated 1 April 1980.

75 Dr. Bryant, the U.S. Delegate, proposed an amendment to the draft resolution before Committee A (which eventually became Resolution 33.32), to the effect that the words "in close consultation with Member States and", in paragraph 6 (4) of the resolution, be deleted and replaced by the words "by convening a working group of all interested Member States". He explained that "a consultative meeting with Member States would be held prior to the referral of the draft code to the Executive Board." The U.S. amendment was rejected by 42 votes to 11, with 13 abstentions. See above note 49, pp. 202, 203, and 204.

group of Member States would have been free to meet whenever they wished, and the secretariat of WHO would not have been able to influence the holding of such meetings. Furthermore, by the nature of things, it was easier for the WHO secretariat to organize consultations, provide the necessary facilities therefor and contact people than for a group of Member States to do so. And such a group of States could have been subjected to more pressure from the infant-food industry than that brought to bear against the secretariats of WHO and UNICEF, with respect to the contents and formulation of the International Code. The WHO Secretariat, in co-operation with the UNICEF secretariat, had its internal group to deal with the matter, its work plan and a precise time-table, which facilitated the timely accomplishment of the task entrusted to the Director-General by the WHA.

III. DEVELOPMENTS BETWEEN MAY 1980–JANUARY 1981

1. The Establishment of a Steering Committee and Drafting Group

Having been entrusted with the mandate for preparing an international code by the Thirty-Third WHA, the Director-General took certain measures in that direction. First, an internal Steering Committee was formed on 26 May 1980, in order to continue the work on the Second Draft of the International Code. The Steering Committee was composed of the following members:

1. Dr. D. Tejada-de-Rivero, ADG;
2. A member of the Legal Division (the author);
3. A member of the Division of Co-ordination (Dr. O.W. Christensen, Chief, Co-ordination);
4. Dr. A. Petros-Barvazian, Director, Family Health (FHE);
5. Dr. M. Behar/Alternate to Dr. E. M. De Maeyer, Unit of Nutrition (NUT);
6. Dr. G. Sterky, Chief, Maternal and Child Health (MCH); and
7. Dr. R. H. Strudwick, FHE.[76]

The establishment of the Steering Committee was a big step in the direction of the development of the International Code, in that a new body, with various disciplines within WHO represented on it, became responsible for the various steps, plans and actions for the carrying out of the task entrusted to the Director-General by the WHA. The first decision taken by the Steering Committee was the establishment of a "time-table of events"[77], to get the final text of the

---

76 See internal memoranda from Director, FHE, to Chief, NUT., dated 26 May 1980, and to Chief, MCH, dated 26 May 1980.
77 See WHO internal Note for the Record, dated 5 June 1980.

International Code before the Executive Board by January 1981. To that end, the Steering Committee decided that a Third Draft of the International Code should be prepared, in the period 31 July-18 August 1980. This would be done in the light of comments of Member States and all other interested parties on the Second Draft of the International Code. Furthermore, the Steering Committee decided that two consultations should be held, under the auspices of WHO and UNICEF, in Geneva, to consider the Third Draft. The first consultation was scheduled for 28-29 August 1980, and the second for 25-26 September 1980.

Those to be invited to the first consultation were the relevant UN agencies, NGOs, experts and the infant-food industry. Those to be invited to the second consultation were some selected Member States of WHO from its various regions.[78] The Steering Committee, also, decided to establish a drafting group composed of Dr. De Maeyer, Dr. Shubber, Dr. Sterky and Dr. Strudwick. The drafting group was made responsible for the drafting of the Third Draft of the International Code, the late Sir Professor Robert Y. Jennings, Whewell Professor of International law at Cambridge University at the time (former President and Judge of the International Court of Justice) and Mr. Heyward, the then senior Deputy Executive Director, UNICEF, were added to the drafting group.[79]

On 13 June 1980, the Director-General of WHO wrote a letter to Member States on behalf of WHO and UNICEF, attaching the Second Draft of the International Code and Resolution WHA 33.32 and requesting "...their suggestions and comments" thereon, in order to assist him in fulfilling the mandate given to him by the WHA, to reach him by 31 July 1980 at the latest.[80] He also proposed to hold, as requested by the WHA,

> ...further consultations with governments and all other interested parties in August or September 1980, in order that a definitive draft may be with members of the Executive Board six weeks before the sixty-seventh session begins.[81]

---

78 WHO has six Regional Offices: the Regional Office for Africa (AFRO), Brazzaville, Congo; the Regional Office for the Americas (AMRO), Washington D. C., U.S.A.; the Regional Office for the Eastern Mediterranean (EMRO), Alexandria, now in Cairo, Egypt; the Regional Office for Europe (EURO), Copenhagen, Denmark; the Regional Office for South-East Asia (SEARO), New Delhi, India; and the Regional Office for the Western Pacific (WPRO), Manila, Philippines.

79 See above note 77.

80 See WHO, C.L. 10. 1980, p.1 and p.2.

81 Ibid., p.2. In accordance with Rule 5 of the Rules of Procedure of the Executive Board, "notices convening the Board shall be sent by the Director-General, six weeks before the commencement of a regular session, to the members of the Board...." In accordance with Rule 8 of the Rules of Procedure of the Board, the provisional agenda shall also be sent by the Director-General with the notice of convocation. Rule 9 of the same Rules of Procedure states that the provisional agenda shall include "a) all items the inclusion of which has been ordered by the Health Assembly." For the text of the Rules of Procedure, see *WHO Basic Documents*, pp. 153-166.

The Second Draft was also dispatched to all the parties who took part in the consultations of February and March 1980, inviting their comments on it.

2. The Third Draft of the International Code

During the month of July, the WHO secretariat received comments from Member States, the relevant UN agencies, NGOs, the infant-food industry and experts on the Second Draft of the International Code. The drafting group reviewed these comments and used some of them, whenever appropriate, in the preparation of the Third Draft. In the words of Dr. Tejada, the then Assistant Director-General,

> in preparing this third draft, we have given respectful consideration to all the comments and contributions received even though this may not be immediately apparent from an examination of the draft itself. None was ignored even though it is obvious that not every one of them could possibly be incorporated.[82]

By August 1980, the Third Draft entitled "International Code of Marketing of Breastmilk Substitutes and Related Products" was ready. It was dispatched on 14 August to all those invited to the August Consultation, i.e., the relevant UN agencies, NGOs, experts and the infant-food industry. The Third Draft was subsequently sent to those Member States invited to the September Consultation .The Third Draft covered the same issues contained in the Second Draft, with almost the same number of provisions. However, the wording of the preamble of the Third Draft was slightly different from that of the Second Draft, and the headings of its provisions were more accurate than those of the Second Draft. The only significant change in the Third Draft was that it did not contain a provision on the scope of the International Code, which the Second Draft had (Article 1).On the other hand, the substance of the latter provision was reproduced in the Third Draft under Article 9 (Definitions), under the heading "products covered by this Code."

3. The Consultations of August and September 1980

Two consultations were held under the auspices of WHO and UNICEF to consider the Third Draft of the International Code. The first was held in WHO, Geneva, on 28-29 August 1980. Those invited to this Consultation were: FAO, (represented by Mr. Kermode), UNCTAD, (represented by Mr. d'Oliveira e Sousa), and the UN/Non-governmental Organization Liaison, (represented by Mr. Mountain and Mr. Lemarsquier). The following NGOs were invited: IOCU, (represented by Mr. Fazal), International Paediatric Association, (represented

---

82 See opening statement of Dr. Tejada, at the Consultation on the Draft International Code of Marketing of Breast-milk Substitutes, Geneva 28-29 August 1980, (hereinafter referred to as the "August Consultation 1980), p.4.

by Dr. Hallman), International Union of Nutritional Sciences, (represented by Professor Scrimshaw), War on Want, (represented by Mr. Chetley), CMC, (represented by Miss Barrow and Ms Reidy), INFACT, (represented by Mr. Johnson), ICCR, (represented by Ms Margulies) and INFACT/ICCR/IOUC (represented by Mr. Millwood and Ms Visinand). The following infant-food manufacturers were invited: ICIFI, (represented by Mr. Saunders, Dr. Flache, Mr. Bauer of Wyeth International, Mr. Fookes and Mr. Ward of Nestlé, Miss Mann, Professor Jerome, Mr. Braun, Professor Dobbing, Mr. Schipper and Mr. Waters); Mead-Johnson Nutritionals, (represented by Mr. Mize and Mr. Hamel); Ross Laboratories, (represented by Mr. Cox, Mr. McCollough and Mr. Aschauer). The following experts were invited: Professor Gebre,(the then Minister of Health, Egypt), Dr. Hall,(Consultant Obstetrician and Gynaecologist, Aberdeen Teaching Hospital, Scotland), Dr. Mashalaba, (Head, Family Health Division, Ministry of Health, Botswana), Dr. Quamina,(Chief Medical Officer, Ministry of Health, Trinidad and Tobago), Dr. Sai, International Coordinator, WHP/ UN University, Ghana) and Professor Sjölim, (Professor of Paediatrics, University Hospital, Uppsala, Sweden). The Third Draft was the only official WHO/UNICEF document at the Consultation.

The second Consultation was also held in WHO, Geneva, on 25-26 September 1980. Participation in this Consultation was limited to selected Member States of WHO, which were chosen in collaboration with WHO Regional Directors, on the basis of four Member States from each of the six WHO regions. Later on, four additional Member States were invited, upon their request.

The invited Member States were: Algeria, (represented by Dr. Hadj-Lakehal, Ministry of Public Health), Australia (represented by Dr. Booth, Department of Health, and Ms Freeman, Australian Permanent Mission to the UN Office in Geneva), Brazil, (represented by Dr. Grands de Arruda, National Institute of Food and Nutrition, and Dr. Dos Santos, Brazilian Nutrition Society), Canada, (represented by Dr. Smith, Department of National Health and Welfare, Dr. Cheney, Department of National Health and Welfare, and Mr. Sirois, Canadian Permanent Mission to the UN Office in Geneva), the Congo, (represented by Dr. Ondaye, Co-ordinator for WHO Programmes in the Congo), Democratic Yemen (now united with the Republic of Yemen forming the new Member Yemen) (represented by Mr. Bin Gadeem, Ministry of Health), Denmark, (represented by Dr. Rosdahl, National Board of Health, and Ms Poulsen, Ministry of Foreign Affairs), France, (represented by Mr. Vaille, Honorary Inspector General of Public Health), Hungary, (represented by Dr. Ory, Ministry of Health, and Mr.Gaal, Institute of Nutrition), India, (represented by Dr. Reddy, Indian Council of Medical Research), Jamaica, (represented by Dr. Patterson, Ministry of Health), Japan, (represented by Dr. Fukuwatari, Ministry of Health and Welfare, and Mr. Ishimoto, Permanent Mission of Japan to the UN Office in Geneva), Kuwait, (represented by Dr. Buhaimed, and Dr. Al-Dosari, Ministry of Health), Lesotho, (represented by Dr. Marupring, Ministry of Health, and

Mr. Chobokoane, Food and Nutrition Co-ordinating Office), Mozambique, (represented by Dr. Vinhas, Ministry of Health), The Netherlands, (represented by Mr. Loggers, Ministry of Public Health and Environmental Protection, and Mr. van Stigt Thans, Ministry of Agriculture and Fisheries), Niger, (represented by Mrs. Maiga, Ministry of Public Health and Social Affairs), Pakistan, (represented by Dr. Choudri, Ministry of Health and Social Welfare), the Philippines, (represented by Dr. Acosta, Ministry of Health), Singapore, (represented by Mrs. Tan Wei Ling, Ministry of Health), Sri Lanka (represented by Dr. Jayesinghe, Ministry of Health), Sudan (represented by Dr. Ahmed Mohamed, Ministry of Health), Sweden, (represented by Professor Hofvander, University Hospital, Uppsala, Mr. Mathsson, Ministry of Health and Social Affairs, and Mr. Abelin, Swedish International Development Authority), Switzerland, (represented by Dr. Frey, Federal Office for Public Health, and Dr. Cornaz, Federal Department of Foreign Affairs), Thailand, (represented by Dr. Singhapakdi, Ministry of Health), U.K., (represented by Mr. Parker, Department of Health and Social Security, Mr. Harding, Ministry of Agriculture, Fisheries and Food, and Mr. Sturges, Department of Health and Social Security), and the U.S.A, (represented by Dr. Bryant, Department of Health and Human Services, Dr. Rosberg, U.S. Department of State, and Dr. Sanghvi, Agency for International Development).[83] The September Consultation had before it the Third Draft and the proceedings of the August Consultation.

The purpose of both Consultations was to obtain the benefits of the participants' comments, suggestions and proposals in relation to the Third Draft of the International Code. Furthermore, while the previous consultations were general in nature, the August and September Consultations were specific, in that their deliberations concentrated on the contents of the Third Draft. General issues, such as the advantages of breast-feeding and the use of breast-milk substitutes and the possible harm arising from improper use, were not considered at those Consultations. Detailed discussions of the various provisions of the Third Draft took place, and comments and suggestions were made thereon, at those Consultations. And for the first time, selected Member States were invited to a WHO/UNICEF consultation on the International Code, of course, apart from their participation at the WHA. By contrast, the consultations held prior to May 1980 did not include Member States, though they were requested to comment on the First and Second Drafts of the International Code.[84]

4. The Fourth Draft of the International Code

Immediately after the end of the August and September Consultations, the WHO drafting group started the preparation of the text of the Fourth Draft of the International Code, taking into account comments and suggestions made

---

83 Burma (now Myanmar) was also invited, but declined to attend.
84 See above pp.10-13.

on the Third Draft at those Consultations, as well as those made by Member States. By the end of September 1980, the text of the Fourth Draft emerged. It might be interesting to point out that the final touches of the latter text were added on 5-6 October 1980, in the rooms of Professor Jennings, at Jesus College, Cambridge University, Cambridge. The participants at that final drafting session were Dr. G. Sterky, Mr. Heyward, Sir Robert Jennings and the author. However, minor amendments were subsequently introduced into the text finalized at Jesus College. By December 1980, the Fourth Draft entitled "the draft International Code of Marketing of Breast-milk Substitutes", was dispatched by the Director-General to all members of the Executive Board, and to all Member States of WHO, for information purposes.[85] The Fourth Draft was prepared in two versions, one version as regulations in the sense of Articles 21 and 22 of the Constitution of WHO, and the other as a recommendation in the sense of Article 23 of the WHO Constitution, as requested by the WHA.[86] At this point, the Director-General had fulfilled the mandate entrusted to him by the WHA in May 1980, and the matter rested then with the Executive Board.

The Fourth Draft covered all the issues contained in the Third Draft, with improved wording .The provisions of the Third Draft were rearranged in the Fourth Draft, for example Article 9 of the former on Definitions became Article 3 of the latter. Some parts of the Third Draft became independent provisions, e.g., Article 3.1 became Article 9 of the Fourth Draft. Moreover, the Fourth Draft contained a new provision, which did not exist in any of the previous three drafts, namely, Article 1 on the aim of the International Code. Finally, the provision on the scope of the Code, which was included in the Second Draft but deleted in the Third Draft, was reintroduced in the Fourth Draft as Article 2, with improved wording.

It might be appropriate now to survey the implications of the International Code as a regulation and as a recommendation.

5. The Legal implications of an International Code as a Regulation and as a Recommendation

It may be recalled that WHA had requested the Director-General in 1980 to prepare an international code of marketing of breast-milk substitutes and to submit it to the Executive Board

> ... together with proposals regarding its promotion and implementation, either as a regulation in the sense of Articles 21 and 22 of the Constitution of the World Health Organization or as a recommendation in the sense of Article 23, outlining the legal and other implications of each choice.[87]

---

85 See Report of the Director-General to the Executive Board, Infant and Young Child Feeding, *WHO Doc.* EB 67/20, 10 December 1980.
86 See Resolution WHA 33.22, operative paragraph 6 (4) and (5).
87 See ibid.

What are the legal implications arising from the adoption of a code as a regulation or as a recommendation? There is no doubt, as has been mentioned earlier, that the issue of the promotion of breast-feeding and the healthy growth and development of infants and young children falls within the competence of WHO. WHO has three possibilities under its Constitution insofar as the preparation of the International Code is concerned. They are: treaties, regulations and recommendations.[88] The first possibility, i.e. treaties, had been discarded by the WHA, when it requested the Director-General to prepare the International Code. It is worthwhile mentioning that the only treaty adopted by WHO so far is the Framework Convention on Tobacco Control 2003, which entered into force in 2005.

So, now an attempt to explain the legal implications of the regulations and recommendations shall be made.

(a) Regulations

In accordance with Article 21 of the WHO Constitution,

> the Assembly shall have authority to adopt regulations concerning:
>
> ...
>
> (d) standards with respect to the safety, purity and potency of biological, pharmaceutical and similar products moving in international commerce;
>
> (e) advertising and labelling of biological, pharmaceutical and similar products moving in international commerce.[89]

In accordance with Article 22 of the Constitution of WHO,

> regulations adopted pursuant to Article 21 shall come into force for all Members after due notice has been given of their adoption by the Health Assembly except for such Members as may notify the Director-General of rejection or reservations within the period stated in the notice.[90]

Consequently had the International Code been adopted as a regulation, it

---

88 On a discussion of these possibilities, see Shubber, "The International Code of Marketing of Breast-milk Substitutes", 36 *International Digest of Health Legislation* (1985), No 4, pp. 880-885.

89 Two instruments have, so far, been adopted by the WHA under Article 21 of the WHO Constitution, namely, the Nomenclature Regulations 1967, and the International Health Regulations 1969, replaced by the International Health Regulations 2005; the text of the former is to be found in Resolution WHA 20.18, see *WHO Handbook*,Vol.I, pp.175-176, and the text of the latter is to be found in the *International Health Regulations (2005),*2nd edn. 2008.

90 Under the International Health Regulations 1969, the notice period is 9 months; see Art. 87 (1) of the Regulations; under the 2005 version, the notice period is 18 months; see Art. 59 (1).

would have had a binding effect vis-à-vis Member States without the need for ratification, acceptance or approval by each Member, except those rejecting it or attaching reservations to it. Any rejection or reservation received by the Director-General after the expiry of the notice period would have no effect. Furthermore, the wording of the International Code as a regulation would have contained specific rules intended to impose specific obligations and using a mandatory language. In addition, in accordance with Article 62 of the Constitution of WHO, Member States are required to report annually on the action taken with respect to regulations adopted by the WHA. Moreover, had the Code been adopted as a regulation, then it would have had to contain final clauses dealing with its entry into force, the notice period for making reservations or rejection, withdrawal of such reservations or rejection, notification by the Director-General to Member States of the adoption of the code as a regulation or any amendment thereof, and so forth.[91]Furthermore, the need would, probably, have arisen for a machinery for the settlement of disputes concerning the interpretation or the application of the code.[92] Finally, as a regulation, the International Code, following the practice of WHO, would have been registered with the United Nations Secretariat in accordance with Article 102 of the United Nations Charter, as an international agreement.[93] The United Nations Secretariat publishes such instruments in the United Nations Treaty Series.

The WHO practice of registering regulations under Article 102 of the UN Charter as treaties, it is submitted, is open to question. For, according to Article 19 of the WHO Constitution,

> the Health Assembly shall have authority to adopt conventions or agreements with respect to any matter within the competence of the Organization.

On the other hand, Article 21 of the Constitution gives the WHA the authority to adopt regulations, while Article 23 gives it the authority to adopt recommendations. If the drafters of the WHO Constitution had intended the regulations to be on a footing of equality with treaties, they would not have dealt specifically with regulations in a separate article. The specific enumeration of these three instruments shows that the intention of the drafters was probably to have

---

91 As an illustration of this point, see Arts. 59-63 of the International Health Regulations, 2005.

92 There is such a machinery under Article 56 of the International Health Regulations, 2005.

93 A member of the Executive Board, Dr. Kruisinga, raised the question whether the Fourth Draft of the International Code could be adopted under Article 21 of the WHO Constitution. He asked for a legal opinion on the subject. See *Executive Board, Sixty-Seventh Session, Geneva, 14-30 January 1981, Summary Records, WHO Doc.EB67/1981/REC/2*, p.312. The then legal adviser, Mr. Vignes, replied that breast-milk substitutes fell precisely under Article 21 of the Constitution. The Health Assembly itself had taken that position since, in its resolution WHA 33.32, operative paragraph 6 (5), it had requested that a text be drafted either as a regulation in the sense of Articles 21 and 22 of the Constitution or as a recommendation. See ibid., p.319. For a discussion of the question of WHO's competence to adopt the International Code as a regulation, see Shubber, above note 88, pp.881-884.

regulation as an independent category of legal instrument not covered by treaties. Article 31, paragraph 1, of the Vienna Convention on the Law of Treaties provides that

> a treaty shall be interpreted in good faith in accordance with the ordinary meaning to be given to the terms of the treaty in their context and in the light of its object and purpose.

(b) Recommendation

The legal implications which may arise from the adoption of the International Code as a recommendation under Article 23 of the Constitution are as follows: first, recommendations of the WHA are not legally binding on Member States *per se*. However, they carry some moral or political weight, as they constitute the judgement of the collective membership of the Organization. On the other hand, some recommendations of the WHA may have some binding effect vis-à-vis Member States.[94] Unlike regulations, Member States do not have to notify WHO of their reservations or rejection of the recommendations of the WHA. Furthermore, as a recommendation, the International Code would lay down (which is the case now) general principles and advice to Members on certain practices, technical matters and similar questions, using a recommendatory language. In view of the legal nature of the recommendation, there would be no need for final clauses to be incorporated in the Code, nor for a machinery for the settlement of disputes, and no registration with the United Nations Secretariat, in accordance with Article 102 of the United Nations Charter. However, as is the case with regulations, Members of WHO are required to report annually to the Organization on the action taken with respect to the Code, in accordance with Article 62 of the Constitution of the Organization.

---

94 On the question of the legal effect of the resolutions of the WHA, see below pp. 200-203.

CHAPTER II

THE FINAL PHASE OF THE PREPARATION OF THE INTERNATIONAL CODE (JANUARY–MAY 1981)

With the formulation of the Fourth Draft of the International Code, and its dispatch to all Member States and all members of the Executive Board in December 1980, as we have seen earlier, the final phase of the preparation of the Code was reached. This phase was a decisive one, as it required action on the part of two organs of WHO, namely the WHA and the Executive Board, i.e., the plenary and executive organs. This process involved all Members States and all members of the Board of the Organization. Needless to say that without that action, the International Code could not have come into existence, from a legal point of view.

We shall now survey the actions of the Executive Board and the WHA in this respect.

I. THE ACTION OF THE EXECUTIVE BOARD IN JANUARY 1981

The Executive Board considered the Fourth Draft of the International Code under the heading "Infant and Young Child Feeding", item 20.2 of its agenda. The crucial decision facing the Executive Board was whether to recommend to the WHA the adoption of the Fourth Draft of the International Code as a regulation or as a recommendation. As a member of the Board, Dr. Mork put it:

> the Board must consider whether, in the context of "Health for all", a regulation or a recommendation would best serve the aim of promoting breast-feeding and infant and child health.[1]

There was a difference of opinion among members of the Executive Board as to whether the Fourth Draft of the International Code should be recommended to the WHA for adoption as a regulation or a recommendation. Some members of the Board preferred a regulation (Article 21 of the Constitution of WHO). One member of the Board, Dr. Al-Ghassani

---

1   See *WHO Doc.EB 67/1981/REC/2*, p.307.

considered that the code should be adopted in the form of regulations in accordance with Articles 21 and 22 of the Constitution.[2]

Another member of the Board, Dr. Lisoba Ramos, stated that

he was in favour of adopting the draft code as regulations as it would be more binding on Member States, even though some might not accept it or might make reservations.[3]

Another member of the Board, Dr Adandé Menest, stated that

the basic purpose of the draft international code was to be an instrument for the protection of infants and young children, and as such it warranted unanimous support. Regulation form would make that support more forceful, and would ensure a greater degree of protection against undesirable practices.[4]

On the other hand, some members of the Board favoured a recommendation (Article 23 of the Constitution of WHO). One member, Dr. Hiddlestone, was of the view that

...the code's contents could be far more detailed and significant in the form of a recommendation.[5]

Another member, Dr. Law, thought that

...it would be better to adopt [the draft international code as] a recommendation; a recommendation was easier to monitor and revise.[6]

Another member, Dr. Oldfield, stated that

ideally he would have liked to see the code as a regulation, but realism required him to accept it as a recommendation, bearing in mind that...the requirements laid down in it were the minimum.[7]

Some other members of the Board took the position that, while supporting the regulations approach, they were nevertheless willing to opt for the recommendation approach. One member, Dr. Alvarez Gutierrez said

from the point of view of developing countries the code should have the force of a regulation; a unanimous decision of the World Health Assembly could carry greater weight, and if that could not be assured for a regulation then a unanimous recommendation would be desirable.[8]

---

2   See ibid., p.313. See to the same effect the views of Dr. Rezai, ibid., p.311, and Dr.Al-Saif, ibid., p.314.
3   See ibid., p.312.
4   See ibid., p.314. 21.
5   See ibid., p. 310.
6   See, ibid., pp.314-315.
7   See ibid.,p.315.
8   See ibid., p.306. See to the same effect the position of Dr. Reid and that of Professor Dogramaci, ibid, pp.309 and 310.

Finally, it would seem that there was general agreement among the members of the Board that, for the sake of maintaining unanimity within the membership of WHO, the Fourth Draft of the International Code should be forwarded for adoption by the WHA in the form of a recommendation, in the sense of Article 23 of the WHO Constitution. The draft resolution for its adoption was therefore suitably amended for that purpose, and was adopted unanimously on 28 January 1981 (Resolution EB 67.R12).[9]

However, the Executive Board left the door open for the possibility of adoption of the International Code as a regulation, some time later, if the Code was not effective in its operation as a recommendation. In its resolution of 28 January 1981, (Resolution EB 67.R12), the Board recommended for adoption by the Assembly a resolution containing the International Code. In that resolution, the Director-General was requested to report to the Thirty-sixth WHA in May 1983 on the status of compliance with and implementation of the International Code, and

> based on the conclusions of the status report, to make proposals, if necessary, for revision of the text of the Code and for the measures needed for its effective application.[10]

While it is not clear as to what is meant by the phrase "to make proposals...for the measures needed", it would appear from the discussions of the Board that what was probably intended was that if the International Code, as a recommendation, did not prove to be effective, then WHO would have to move to a regulation. As one member of the Board, Dr. Hiddlestone, put it:

> If the recommendation did not prove sufficiently effective, the Organization would have to move to a regulation.[11]

However, the Director-General, in his report to the Thirty-sixth WHA considered that it was premature to propose any revision of the International Code, either in its form or content,[12] and the position has not changed since. However, it should be interesting to point out that twenty years after the adoption of the International Code, the regulation approach was raised, by implication, by one of the delegates to the 54th WHA. The Thai Delegate, Professor Jongjit Ang-

---

9   See ibid., p.321.

10 See Resolution WHA 34.22, paragraph 5 (4).

11 See above note 1, p.310.

12 See Report of the Director-General entitled Infants and Young Child Nutrition, including the Nutritional Value and Safety of Products specifically intended for Infants and Young Child Feeding and the Status of Compliance with and Implementation of the International Code of Marketing of Breast-milk Substitutes (WHO Doc. A 36/7, dated 15 March 1983), p. 39, paragraph 130. The Thirty-sixth WHA took note of the Director-General's report, see *Thirty-sixth World Health Assembly, Geneva, 2-16 May 1983, Summary Records of Committees, WHO Doc. WHA36/1983/REC73*, p.304.

katavanich, referring to the problem of non-compliance with the International Code raised in the draft resolution proposed by the Executive Board to the WHA, stated that

> ... it was timely to redress the issue and to reinforce the International Code of Marketing of Breast-milk Substitutes. She suggested the addition of the words "and initiate research to identify the underlying causes of non-compliance both from the government and the commercial sectors and to find ways to alleviate the problem, such as making the Code mandatory in nature....[13]

The expression "making the Code mandatory in nature", it is submitted, can only refer to regulations under the WHO Constitution, for the treaty option was discarded by the WHA in its Resolution WHA 33/32, paragraph 6 (6). The Thai amendment was not considered by Committee A, probably because it came too late.[14]

With the adoption of Resolution EB67.R.12 on 28 January 1981 by the Executive Board, the process of preparing the International Code was completed and the only issue left was the decision to be taken by the WHA in May 1981. Of course, from a legal point of view, the WHA could have taken a different stand on the matter, because it is the plenary organ of WHO, is composed of representatives of Member States and has the authority to determine the policies of WHO.[15]By contrast, the Executive Board is composed of persons "technically qualified in the field of health"[16] and can only advise the WHA "on questions referred to it by that body".[17] Indeed, the Executive Board, in its Resolution EB67.R12, recommended to the WHA the adoption of the text of a resolution, which eventually became Resolution WHA34.22, to which the International Code was annexed.

II. SOME OBSERVATIONS ON THE PROCESS OF THE PREPARATION OF THE INTERNATIONAL CODE UNTIL JANUARY 1981

Some observations may be made with respect to the process of preparation of the International Code during the period May 1980 to January 1981.

The first observation is that, like the previous period, i.e. prior to May 1980, WHO and UNICEF had followed a democratic process in the preparation of the International Code. The Second and Third Drafts of the International Code were sent to Members States and to all those involved in the consultations of February-March 1980. Moreover, two consultations were held under the aus-

---

13 See Fifty-Fourth World Health Assembly, Geneva, 14-22 May 2001, *WHO Doc., A54/A/ SR/3*. 16 May 2001, p. 3.
14 See the statement of the Botswana Delegate, ibid. p. 7.
15 See Art. 18 (a) of the WHO Constitution.
16 See ibid., Art. 24.
17 See ibid., Art. 28 (d).

pices of WHO and UNICEF in August and September 1980. As has been seen earlier, participation in the August consultation was open to the relevant UN organizations, NGOs, infant-food industry and experts, whereas participation in the September Consultation was limited to selected Member States of WHO.[18] Comments and suggestions made by Member States during this consultation and outside it, as well as those made by NGOs, the infant-food industry and experts were taken into account, whenever possible, in the preparation of the Third and Fourth Drafts. However, the involvement of Member States in the process of preparation of the International Code was greater during the period under consideration than during the previous period. Member States had more opportunities to comment on the Second and Third Drafts, by correspondence, at the Thirty-third WHA and in the September Consultation 1980. In the words of the then Director-General of WHO, Dr. Mahler

> ... the [Executive] Board had indicated that the draft international code was a highly respectable democratic product....[19]

The U.S. Delegate to the Thirty-ninth WHA (Mr. Boyer) made a relevant observation, in this context, though some time after the adoption of the Code. Commenting on a draft resolution under consideration by Committee A

> he contrasted the current haste and pressure with the careful, deliberate process relating to the writing of the Code itself in 1981 that had endured for more than a year with opportunities for Member governments to consult with each other, with industry, with consumer groups, with experts in paediatrics, and with the Director-General and his staff.[20]

Secondly, accusations in the press and elsewhere continued to be levelled against WHO, that its action was an "anti-industry" exercise. In an article published in *The Wall Street Journal*, Mr. Ernest Lefever, the then President of the Ethics and Public Policy Centre in Washington said

> ... The WHO-UNICEF staff ... decided to draft a highly restrictive and detailed international code for adoption by the World Health Assembly next May. Behind the facade of democratic and representative procedures that should govern the drafting of a code, a major power play is taking place. Reports of successive drafts indicate that an unrepresentative coalition of anti-industry critics and UN bureaucrats sympathetic to them has prevailed over a rational and more representative process....The UN drafters see adoption of this code as a precedent for controlling the pharmaceutical industry and multinational operations generally.

He went on

> this will be an unprecedented attempt at international legislation by ideological in-

---

18 See above pp. 23-25.

19 See above note 1, p.319.

20 See *Thirty-Ninth World Health Assembly, Geneva, 5-16 May 1986, Summary Records of Committees, WHO Doc. WHA39/1986/REC/3*, (hereinafter referred to as "WHO Doc.39/1986/REC/ 3") pp.207-208.

timidation.[21]

The International Code was also described as "highly restrictive", "irrelevant and unworkable".[22] Of course, this was not the case, and as one member of the Executive Board, Dr. Ridings, put it:

> The Director-General and the Secretariat, together with UNICEF, had taken a tolerant and reasoned approach.[23]

The Director-General, commenting on the press accusations, said that

> he realized that freedom of expression involved the right to be as far from the truth as possible; that included doing harm to children's health and consequently to WHO. He had hoped, however, that the Board would defend the Secretariat and see the proposals not as the Secretariat's policy but as the high degree of participatory democracy for which the Organization had been able to provide a platform in developing protection for children throughout the world.[24]

In reply, one member of the Board, Dr. Kruisinga, assured the Director-General that

> ...the Secretariat had the Board's fullest support, and that the Board had the greatest admiration for the work of the Director-General and the Secretariat in the face of all the accusations they had had to endure."[25]

The third observation is to the effect that both the infant-food industry and some NGOs had attempted to have an active role in the formulation of the Third and Fourth Drafts of the International Code. This was expressed in offers made by the industry and the NGOs for the use of their own draft codes and efforts in the preparation of the Third Draft. In June 1980, the then President of ICIFI wrote a letter to WHO saying that they had studied the Second Draft of the International Code and the minutes of Committee A covering the discussion of the issue of the preparation of an international code. He went on:

> the main purpose of this letter, however, is again to urge you to involve us fully in the process of developing what will presumably become a third draft. I repeat my offer made at the March consultation, namely that ICIFI is prepared to put its technical experts at your disposal to work out with your experts, the basis of a code of principles that we can accept and work with in a practical way.

---

21 See *The Wall Street Journal*, 14 January 1981.

22 See a letter from Saunders, president of ICIFI to members of WHO Executive Board, dated 13 January 1981.

23 See above note 1, p.315.

24 Ibid., p.319.

25 See ibid., p.320. Dr. Mork associated himself with the remarks of Dr.Kruisinga, ibid. Professor Aujaleu, another member of the Board stated that "...the best defence of the Secretariat and the Director-General was the unanimity with which the Board was prepared to adopt the text with only minor drafting changes." Ibid.

He went on:

> surely, it would be preferable for an ICIFI expert to be part of the drafting team so that we can play a full and constructive part in the process."[26]

Furthermore, some individual companies offered their own codes, for example, Ross Laboratories offered

> a Suggested WHO/UNICEF Code for the Marketing of Infant Foods and Related Products, July 1,1980.[27]

On the other hand, IBFAN wrote to WHO suggesting that

> ...[the Director-General of WHO] call on our expertise in preparing future drafts of the code. We envision involvement that goes beyond routine consultations currently planned for NGOs, industry, UN agencies and experts. We have experience that could help WHO avoid some of the liabilities that the first draft codes may have caused.[28]

WHO and UNICEF declined to accept the offers from both the infant-food industry and the NGOs, and used their own staff members and consultants for the purpose of preparing the Third and Fourth Drafts of the International Code. It is, indeed, amazing to see that, twenty years after the adoption of the International Code, Dr. Bronner, speaking on behalf of the International association of Infant Food Manufacturers (IFM) alleges before the WHA in 2001 that the IFM had taken an active part in formulation of the International Code. He said that

> IFM was proud to have taken an active part in the formulation of the International Code of Marketing of breast-milk Substitutes ....[29]

According to *The Concise Oxford Dictionary*, "formulate" means "2. express clearly and precisely".[30] The IFM (the successor of ICIFI), took neither an active part in the preparation of the International Code, nor did it "express clearly and

---

26 See a letter from Saunders to Dr. Tejada, Assistant Director-General, dated 10 June 1980, (underlining in the original). On 12 June 1980, two days later, Saunders wrote to the Director-General of WHO saying that "...we feel that a small expert working group drafting committee comprised of WHO staff, Industry representatives, and other experts with relevant professional experience representing third parties, is the best way to arrive at a successful solution". See a letter from the President of ICIFI to Dr. Mahler, Director-General of WHO, dated 12 June 1980, p.2,(emphasis in the original).

27 See attachments to the letter of Chairman of Ross Laboratories Division, David Cox, Abbott Laboratories, to Dr. Petros-Barvazian, Director, FHE, WHO, dated 10 July 1980.

28 See a letter from Mrs. Allain, IBFAN, to the Director-General of WHO dated 27 May 1980. IBFAN is "a network of independent non-governmental organizations working on the issue of baby foods; it is a means of coordinating activities." See a letter from Mrs. Allain, IBFAN, to Dr. Tejada, ADG, dated 10 June 1980.

29 See *WHO Doc. A54/A/SR/3*, 6 May 2001, p. 12.

30 See 9th edn., p. 533.

precisely" any wording of any of the provisions of the International Code. As has just been mentioned, ICIFIC's offer to send "an ICIFI expert to be part of the [WHO] drafting team" was not accepted by the WHO Secretariat. However, it is surprising that the WHO Secretariat did not feel called upon to challenge the allegation of the representative of the IFM.

IBFAN also claimed that it took part in the drafting of the International Code. Mrs. Allain before Committee A of the Thirty-ninth WHA 1986: commenting on the agenda item before the Committee (the report of the Director-General on the International Code), said :

> The agenda item before the Committee was of great importance to consumers everywhere. IOCU had participated in the joint WHO/UNICEF Meeting...in 1979, as well as in the drafting of the International Code.[31]

It is submitted that the refusal of the WHO Secretariat to accept the offers from the infant food industry and the NGOs, is in line with the neutrality and impartiality of the two Organizations on the issue. It is well-known that the infant-food industry and the NGOs have different views and positions on the nature and contents of the drafts of the International Code in question, motivated by their interests. There was confrontation and controversy between the infant-food industry and some NGOs, which began in 1974, with the publication by War on Want, an NGO, of *The Baby Killer*.[32] The latter publication dealt with problems relating to infant feeding, largely in Africa. Nestlé brought a libel case in Bern, Switzerland, in 1974, against the Third World Action Group, an NGO, which had translated *The Baby Killer* into German and gave it the title *Nestlé Kills Babies*. In 1977, INFACT, an NGO, launched a boycott of Nestlé.[33]

It must be stated for the record that, so far as WHO and UNICEF are concerned, there were no negotiations with the infant-food industry on the formulation of the International Code, at any stage of the preparation of the Code. The author recalls clearly that attempts were made at that time by the infant-food industry to negotiate with the WHO and UNICEF Secretariats about the drafting of the texts of the Code. But they were told by those secretariats, in no uncertain terms, that there was no question of negotiation, consultations yes, but negotiations no.

The fourth observation is to the effect that the Third and Fourth Drafts of the International Code maintained the universality of its application, in spite of the repeated stand of the infant-food industry[34]that there should be two codes,

---

31 See *Thirty-Ninth World Health Assembly, Geneva, 5-16 May 1986, Summary Records of Committees*, WHO Doc. *WHA39/1986/REC/3*, p.101.

32 See Chetley, *The Politics of Baby Foods—Successful Challenges to an international marketing Strategy (1988), p. 43.*

33 Ibid., p. 52.

34 See August Consultation 1980, p.3, para. 2.1(b). In its comments on that statement ICIFI suggested changes, in hand-writing, altering the statement to read: "...therefore, the distinction to be drawn is between social and economic strata in communities and between

one for developing and the other for developed countries. For example, in its comments on the Second Draft of the International Code, Wyeth said:

> despite the enormous differences among the countries of the world...this draft ignores all such differences and provides for world-wide application. We submit that this is unrealistic, impractical and unnecessary.[35]

As one member of the Executive Board, Dr. Mork, put it:

> It had also been suggested – though not in the Board – that the sociocultural differences between developing and industrial countries demanded separate codes. Such double standards were not admissible in matters of health; the code represented minimum requirements for all countries....[36]

The fifth observation is to the effect that the Executive Board added its unanimous support to that of Member States for the formulation of an international code for the promotion of breast-feeding and the regulation of marketing practices relating to breast-milk substitutes. There were differences, as we have seen earlier, as to whether the International Code should be adopted as a regulation under Article 21 of the WHO Constitution, or as a recommendation under Article 23 thereof.[37] But there was agreement on the basic issue of adopting an international code and the resolution adopted by the Board recommending to the WHA the adoption of the International Code as a recommendation, was adopted unanimously.

Finally, it must be stated that the Director-General succeeded in fulfilling the task entrusted to him by the WHA, on time and against many odds. This was made possible by the tremendous efforts of the secretariats of WHO and UNICEF, who worked under sever pressure of time and difficult circumstances.

III. THE ADOPTION OF THE INTERNATIONAL CODE BY THE WORLD HEALTH ASSEMBLY IN MAY 1981

The Fourth Draft of the International Code and Resolution EB 67. R 12 of the

---

industrial and developing countries." See ICIFI's Annotated Copy of the report of the August Consultation 1980, attached to the letter to WHO of 23 September 1980, p.3, para. 2.1(b).

35 See a letter from Steven Bauer, Vice President of Wyeth, to Dr. Petros-Barvazian, dated 11 July 1980, comments on WHO Code Draft 2 on Infant and Young Child Feeding, p.1.

36 See above note 1. One member of the Executive Board, Dr. Kruisinga, came near questioning the notion of one code for both developed and developing countries. "He asked whether the Secretariat considered that there should be flexibility to take account of circumstances in different areas. The situation in developing countries was undoubtedly very serious, but there were also problems in developed countries." See ibid., p.312. A number of speakers at the September Consultation emphasised that "...it was essential that a single code be developed which was applicable in all countries...." See the September Consultation 1980, p.3, paragraph 1.1.

37 See above pp. 30-32.

Executive Board were considered by the Thirty-fourth WHA in May 1981. It was discussed by Committee A under agenda item 23.2. However, the Committee's discussions were preceded by a hostile campaign against WHO, UNICEF and the International Code, carried out, basically, by the infant-food industry. According to *The Washington Post*,

> ...three American manufacturers of infant formula publicly launched a joint campaign yesterday to defeat a proposed international marketing code for breast-milk substitutes. Executives of Bristol-Myers Co., Abbott Laboratories and American Home Products Corp. began a two-week series of visits to officials of all affected federal agencies and key legislators to urge that the United States oppose adoption of the draft code....The {World Health} Assembly's more than 150 other member governments are being pressed by foreign formula-makers to reject the draft....[38]

Keller, writing in *The International Herald Tribune* and referring to the International Code and the Specialized Agencies said :

> ...a trend persists towards turning these UN organizations into supranational instruments....More and more, these codes infringe on the rights and responsibilities of sovereign nations.

He went on to refer to the Fourth Draft and said:

> even though its purported goal on the promotion of infant breast-feeding is universally accepted, this is clearly a matter over which each member state has exclusive jurisdiction – and which thus falls outside the legal competence of WHO....Its elevation to a WHO regulation or recommendation would directly undercut the national sovereignty, and be in conflict with member states' prerogatives, laws and interests.[39]

Furthermore, *The International Herald Tribune*, referring to the future discussion of the Fourth Draft at the WHA, said

> ...U.S. companies are now crying foul, complaining that the code is too restrictive.[40]

The Wall Street Journal described the Fourth Draft in the following terms:

> ...the proposed WHO-UNICEF code is both foolish and insidious....The WHO-UNICEF code now looks like a power grab to regulate all baby food sales in the U.S. as well as the "Third World".[41]

The Reagan Administration also openly declared its opposition to the adoption of the International Code. The deputy press secretary of the White House, Mr. Larry Speakes said that

> ...a consensus had been reached within the administration -including officials of the State Department, the Department of Health and Human Services, UN Ambassa-

---

38 See M. Mintz, *The Washington Post*, (18 March 1981).
39 See *The International Herald Tribune*, (17 April 1981).
40 See I. Guest, *The International Herald Tribune*, (30 April 1981).
41 See *The Wall Street Journal*, (4 May 1981), (emphasis in the original).

dor Jeane J. Kirkpatrick and the president himself- to caste a negative vote [at the WHA].[42]

Moreover, before the beginning of discussions on the Fourth Draft, ICIFI's Secretary-General wrote a circular letter to all Permanent Missions to the United Nations and Specialized Agencies in Geneva, expressing reservations about the Fourth Draft. He said:

> ICIFI has explicitly stated...in detail to the World Health Organization...its position and the reasons for expressing reservations on a number of major provisions of the [International] Code should those provisions be considered for strict universal application.

He concluded by stating that

> ...for the purpose of information of those [to the WHA] Delegates who wish to know more about ICIFI's position on the Code and the reasons for it, ICIFI established a Centre at the Intercontinental Hotel..., which will be at...their disposal throughout the World Health Assembly.[43]

It may be recalled that in April 1981, ICIFI issued a position statement to the effect, *inter alia*, that it

> ...has criticized the form and content of the successive code drafts which were found to contain unacceptable provisions being too detailed, counter productive, and in parts, incompatible with the constitutional requirements of a number of countries.[44]

It was reported that some members of ICIFI

> the "hawks" hoped...that if the United States. spoke out against the code, the... [WHA] would react by adopting it as a regulation. At that point, other industrialized countries would also speak out against the code...[One industrialized country] would then take WHO to the International Court of Justice on procedural irregularities in the development of a regulation.[45]

The only way possible to involve the ICJ in this context would have been through a request from the WHA to the Court for an advisory opinion.[46]On the other

---

42 See *International Herald Tribune* (19 May 1981).

43 See a letter from ICIFI's Secretary-General, Dr. S. Flache, to Dr. Tejada, ADG, WHO, dated 6 May 1981 with a copy of the circular letter sent to all Permanent Missions to the United Nations and the Specialized Agencies in Geneva. Dr. Flache was himself a former ADG of WHO, before his retirement.

44 See ICIFI's *Summary Position Statement re proposed WHO International Code for the Marketing of Breast-milk Substitutes*, dated April 1981, p.2, para. 3.

45 See Chetley, op. cit. p.93.

46 Article 76 of the WHO Constitution authorizes WHO to request an advisory opinion from the ICJ, upon authorization by the General Assembly of the UN. In the Agreement between WHO and the UN, bringing WHO into relations with the UN, in conformity with Article 57 of the Charter, the General Assembly has authorized WHO to request advisory opinions from the ICJ on legal questions arising within the scope of its competence. See Art. X, para. 2, of the Agreement, which is reproduced in the *WHO Basic Documents*, pp. 41-49. In fact,

hand, it would appear that some NGOs were not entirely happy with the Fourth Draft. In its commentary on the Fourth Draft, IBFAN, while describing it as "an important document which is fully supported by IBFAN", still considered that "certain provisions of the Code remain weak" and that there were "loopholes and inconsistencies" in it.[47]

However, the International Code and resolution EB 67. R 12 were considered by Committee A of WHA, against a tense background, as mentioned earlier, under agenda item 23.2.[48] The item was introduced by Dr. Mork, the representative of the Executive Board to the WHA. He said that

> two issues were before the Committee, namely, the content of the Code and the question whether it should be adopted as a regulation in the senses of Articles 21 and 22 of the WHO Constitution, or as a recommendation in the sense of Article 23.[49]

He went on to say:

> few, if any, issues before the Board and the Assembly had been the object of such extensive consultations. During the process, the Director-General and the Secretariat had been subjected to a variety of pressures and counter-pressures, in addition to accusations and allegations, from some quarters, which had sought to compromise their integrity...That activity had regrettably continued....[50]

He concluded

> with a plea for consensus

on the draft resolution recommended, unanimously, by the Executive Board to the WHA. He went on to state that

> the Committee was not considering an economic issue of particular importance to only one or a few Member States; it was considering a health issue of essential importance to developing countries and the children of the whole world – and, thus, to all future generations.[51]

When the debate was opened, more than fifty speakers were on the list of the

---

WHO has so far requested two advisory opinions from the ICJ, the first was on the transfer of the EMRO from Egypt to another State, see *Interpretation of the Agreement of 25 March 1951 between the WHO and Egypt*, ICJ Report (1980), p. 73. The second was about the use of nuclear weapons by a State in war or other armed conflict in relation to international law and the WHO Constitution." See Resolution WHA 46.40, adopted on 14 May 1993, *WHA 46/1993/REC/1*, pp. 43-44. The ICJ declined to give an advisory opinion, arguing that WHO's activities do not include such matters. See *Legality of the Use by a State of Nuclear Weapons in Armed Conflict*, ICJ Report (1996,p.16, paragraph 31).

47 See IBFAN's Commentary on the International Code of Marketing of Breast-milk Substitutes, undated but after the adoption of EB 67. R 12, p.1.

48 See *Thirty-Fourth World Health Assembly,Geneva, 4-22 May 1981,WHA 34/1981/REC/3*, p. 187.

49 Ibid.

50 Ibid., p.188.

51 Ibid.,p.189.

Chairman of Committee A.[52] But after only ten delegates had spoken, the Belgian Delegate, Professor Halter, moved the closure of the debate[53], and the motion was carried out.[54] Finally, the draft resolution proposed by the Executive Board in its resolution EB 67. R 12, i.e., the resolution adopting the International Code as a recommendation, was approved in a roll-call vote in Committee A by 93 votes to 3, with 9 abstentions.[55] The resolution was transmitted to the WHA in Committee A's second report, and was adopted by the WHA, by a roll-call vote by 118 votes in favour, one against and 3 abstentions[56], on 21 May 1981. This was Resolution WHA 34-22, to which the International Code was annexed. And thus the work of the WHO and UNICEF on the preparation of the International Code, which started in January 1980, came successfully to an end on that date.

It is touching to note that the President of the WHA at the adoption of the International Code in 1981, the Greek Delegate, Professor Violaki-Paraskeva, made the following statement in 2001, twenty years after the adoption of the Code:

> some 20 years ago after she had held the office of President of the Health Assembly, she was pleased to note renewed progress in discussion of breastfeeding issues within the framework of the WHO.[57]

IV. SOME OBSERVATIONS ON THE ADOPTION OF THE INTER-

---

52 See ibid., p.189.

53 Ibid., p. 197. The relevant rule of the Rules of Procedure of the WHA on the closure of debate is Rule 63; see *WHO Basic Documents*, pp.136-137. While the Delegate of the Netherlands, Dr. Sibbel, spoke on behalf of the members of the then European Economic community (now the European Union), the Delegate of Sweden, Dr. Alsen, spoke on behalf of the five Nordic States. See ibid.,p.190, and p.192.

54 The motion was carried by 59 votes to 14, with 21 abstentions. See above note 84.

55 Ibid., p.199. However, because of the confusion which prevailed during the discussion of the procedural motion for closure of the debate, some delegates did not know whether they were voting for the closure of the debate or the adoption of the International Code. Several delegates corrected the position during the consideration of the report of Committee A by the plenary meeting of the WHA; for example, see the statements of the Delegates of Bangladesh, Romania, Malawi, Chad and Yugoslavia. See *WHA 34/1981/REC/2*, pp. 262 and 263.

56 The negative vote was cast by the U.S., and the abstaining States were Argentina, Japan, and the Republic of Korea. See ibid., p.266. It is curious to see a cryptic statement issued by Nestlé U.K. in February 1997, in reply to the IGBM Report on the monitoring of the International Code. Nestlé claimed that the Code was adopted by a negotiated consensus, which included the infant-food industry. The statement runs thus: "The 1981 Code is important because it was preceded by extensive consultation with all parties, ending in a negotiated consensus which included industry". See "A *Missed Opportunity*" – *Nestlé Comments on the IGBM Report "Cracking the Code*", p. 5. For details about the IGBM Report, see below Chapter V. As has been seen above, the Code was not adopted by consensus; a roll call voting on it took place and the U.S voted against the Code.

57 See *WHO Doc. A54/A/SR/3*, p. 4.

NATIONAL CODE BY THE WORLD HEALTH ASSEMBLY

The first observation worth making is that the International Code was adopted by the WHA by an overwhelming majority. As we have seen earlier, only one Member State voted against it,[58]and three other Member States abstained. There was a clear understanding that the Assembly was dealing with a health issue and not a commercial matter[59], which was not directed against the manufacturers of breast-milk substitutes.[60] There may be some commercial aspects in the question of the use of breast-milk substitutes vis-à-vis the protection and promotion of breast-feeding, but they cannot alter its character as a health issue. As the ICJ said in the case of *Legality of the Use by a State of Nuclear Weapons in Armed Conflict*: commenting on the political aspects of a legal question submitted to it for an advisory opinion,

> the fact that this question also has political aspects, as, in the nature of things, is the case with so many questions which arise in international life, does not suffice to deprive it of its character as a "legal question...."[61]

That health issue was "one of the most important issues before the Assembly".[62] In the words of the Kuwaiti Delegate,

> ...the drafting of this Code is an historic event for all the children of the world, and especially those of the developing world.[63]

Secondly, the International Code was adopted by the WHA as a recommendation, in order to maintain unanimity, and to avoid dissent within the membership of the Organization. However, it was adopted as "a minimum requirement"[64]and as "a minimum compromise."[65] The WHA described the adoption and adherence to the International Code as "a minimum standard".[66]This notion becomes

---

58 See above note 56. In explaining its reasons for voting against the International code, the U.S. Delegate, Mr. Helman said: "...the apparent flexibilities provided to governments by paragraph 11.1 did not, in {the U.S.} view, overcome the overall effect of prescribing a rigid set of rules applicable to companies, health workers, and health care systems in all parts of the world....Moreover, the United States was seriously concerned about WHO's involvement in commercial codes, and that was a central basis for its inability to support the code." See above note 48, p.200.

59 See the statement of the representative of the Executive Board, Dr. Mork, above note 111; see also the statement of the Algerian Delegate, Dr. Hadj-Lakehal, see above note 48, p.190.

60 See the statement of the Turkish Delegate, Professor Dogramaci, see ibid., p.194.

61 See ICJ Reports (1996), p.8. The ICJ made a similar remark in the case of *Legality of the Threat or Use of Nuclear Weapons*, ICJ Reports (1996), p.9.

62 See the statement of the Swedish Delegate, Dr. Alsen, on behalf of the five Nordic States, note 48, p.190.

63 See the statement of Dr. Al-Saif, see above note 55, p.264.

64 See the statement of the Samoa Delegate, Dr. Ridings, see ibid., p.262.

65 See the statement of the Swedish Delegate, see above note 62, and the statement of the Tunisian Delegate, ibid., p.197.

66 See resolution WHA 34.22, last preambular paragraph.

relevant and meaningful when the question of implementation of the International Code is considered[67]. The International Code was adopted for the whole world and for all the membership of WHO, and there was no question of any distinction between developed and developing countries.

Thirdly, the International Code was adopted against the background of a hostile press campaign against WHO and UNICEF and their Secretariats, with pressures and counter-pressures.[68] Member States of WHO were convinced of the importance of the International Code for the promotion of breast-feeding and its relevance to the development of infants' health. In the words of the Swiss Delegate, Dr. Frey, in Committee A,

> his government attached so much importance to breast-feeding because infant and young child feeding played a key role in the health and in the physical and mental development of the child, and indirectly influenced the socio-economic development of society as a whole.[69]

And as a health matter, it fell within the constitutional functions of WHO "to promote maternal and child health and welfare".[70] The WHA clearly declared in the resolution adopting the International Code that it was

> convinced that the protection of infant feeding, including the regulation of marketing of breast-milk substitutes, affect infant and young child health directly and profoundly, and are a problem of direct concern to WHO.[71]

Since these pages constitute an attempt to survey the historical development of the International Code, it would be fair to mention, as part of that development, the role played by Dr. Tejada, the then Assistant Director-General of WHO, in the process of the preparation and development of the International Code. While the said process was the result of team work from WHO and UNICEF, Dr. Tejada, in all fairness, can be considered as the hero of the International Code, for his courage, flexibility, reasonableness, dedication to the cause of breast-feeding and his leadership. He stood fast against pressures from various sides, he was flexible enough to take into account the views and comments from various parties, and he provided excellent leadership at all the various stages of the preparation of the International Code.

---

67 See below, Chapter XIII.
68 See the statement of the representative of the Executive Board Dr. Mork, before Committee A, see above p. 41.
69 See above note 48, p.192.
70 See Article 2, paragraph (1), of the WHO Constitution.
71 See resolution WHA34.22, fifth preambular paragraph; for the text of the resolution see *WHO Handbook*, Vol. II, pp.91-92.

PART II

THE INTERNATIONAL CODE OF MARKETING OF BREAST-MILK SUBSTITUTES

CHAPTER III

THE AIM OF THE INTERNATIONAL CODE

The aim of an international instrument could be described as the raison d'être[1] of that instrument, be it in the area of health, drug-trafficking, or in the area of terrorism.[2] For example, the WHO Constitution declares that

> the objective of the World Health Organization … shall be the attainment by all peoples of the highest possible level of health.[3]

The aim of a legal instrument therefore is to give the reader an idea about what the drafters of the instrument had in mind when formulating it. The aim of the International Code is laid down in Article 1, which reads as follows:

> The aim of this Code is to contribute to the provision of safe and adequate nutrition for infants, by the protection and promotion of breast-feeding, and by ensuring the proper use of breast-milk substitutes, when these are necessary, on the basis of adequate information and through appropriate marketing and distribution.

The provision on the aim of the International Code was introduced in the Fourth Draft after some Member States participating in the September Consultation of 1980[4] referred to the absence, or lack, of a clear reference to the aim of the International Code. The Swiss Delegate said

> …we regret that the draft text [Third Draft] does not explicitly define the aim of the

---

1   With reference to the U.N. Charter, the Rapporteur of Committee I made the following statement: referring to the "Preamble", "Purposes" and "Principles" of the Charter, he said: "(b) the Purposes" constitute the raison d'être of the Organization. They are the aggregation of the common ends on which our minds met." See Report of the Rapporteur of Committee I to Commission I (U N Conference on International Organization, Document 944, I/134), quoted by H. Kelson, *The Law of the United Nations* (1950), p. 10. n.3. According to Kelson, "'ends' or 'aims', means the same as 'purposes'". Ibid., p. 10.

2   See Art. 2, paragraph 1, of the United Nations Convention against Illicit Traffic in Narcotic Drugs and Psychotropic Substances, 1988; the text of the Convention is reproduced in *International Legal Materials* (ILM) xxvii, (1988), pp. 672-684. See also the preamble to the European Convention on the Suppression of Terrorism, 1977, UN General Assembly Doc. *A/AC.188/L.2*, 10 August 1977, p. 33.

3   See Art. 1 of the WHO Constitution.

4   On the September Consultation 1980, see above pp. 23-26.

Code, the objective of the Code, that is to say to promote breast-feeding....[5]

The Swedish Delegate said that

> in the first place we would wish the preamble to state more clearly than it does now the purpose, the aim of the Code. We think this is necessary...to set the direction right from the start.[6]

Moreover, when the WHA, at its thirty-third session in 1980, requested the Director-General to prepare an international code of marketing of breast-milk substitutes, it specifically requested him to bear in mind that

> (b) the aim of the code should be to contribute to the provision of safe and adequate nutrition for infants and young children, and in particular to promote breast-feeding and ensure ... the proper use of breast-milk substitutes, if necessary.[7]

It is clear that there is one aim for the International Code, as both the title and the wording of the provision are in the singular "aim". The aim "is to contribute to the provision of safe and adequate nutrition for infants". This end is to be achieved in two ways: a) the protection and promotion of breast-feeding; and b) ensuring the proper use of breast-milk substitutes when they are necessary. It may be appropriate, again, to quote the Swiss Delegate at the September Consultation; he said

> there are three essential points which we feel are lacking in this preamble [of the Third Draft]....The first point is the most important, that is outlining the purpose of the code, and we should make an explicit mention of the double aim to promote breast-feeding, and second to ensure that in cases where breast-milk substitutes are necessary to ensure that the quality of the product is adequate, that correct use is made of the product, and that the products are accessible....[8]

Therefore, it would be reasonable to suggest that the aim of the International Code consists of two elements, namely, the protection and promotion of breast-feeding and the proper use of breast-milk substitutes, when necessary, though they differ in importance. It would seem from the context of the International Code that the protection and promotion of breast-feeding is the more important, or the principal element, of its aim, while the proper use of breast-milk substitutes is the subsidiary one. This standpoint can derive support from some parts of the preamble, where it is stated that "breast-feeding is an unequalled way of providing ideal food for the healthy growth and development of infants."[9] By contrast, the preamble treats breast-milk substitutes as an alter-

---

5   See September Consultation 1980, Transcription of Tapes, tape 3, p.4.

6   Ibid., tape 4, p.3. see to the same effect the statement of the U.S. Delegate, ibid., tape 9, p.3.

7   See Resolution WHA33/32 (23 May 1980), operative paragraph 6(4)(b), for text of the resolution, see *WHO Handbook*, Vol. II, pp.90-92.

8   See above note 4, tape 8, p.4.

9   See fourth preambular paragraph of the International Code.

native only "when mothers do not breast-feed or only do so partially"[10]. Furthermore, while the protection and promotion of breast-feeding is the normal rule, as it were, the proper use of breast-milk substitutes may be considered as the exception to be resorted to "when these are necessary", as stated in Article 1 of the Code. Therefore, it is only in cases of compulsion that such use is permissible. "Necessary" according to *The Concise Oxford Dictionary* means: "thing without which life cannot be maintained....".[11] Moreover, the Cuban Delegate to the Thirty-third WHA, 1980, Professor Tejeiro said:

> The draft marketing code [the Second draft] should be amended to give greater emphasis to the promotion of breast-feeding and to the proper use of breast-milk substitutes when, and *only when, their use was unavoidable.*[12]

On the other hand, breast-milk substitutes should be used on the basis of "adequate information and through appropriate marketing and distribution". No such qualification exists *vis-à-vis* breast-feeding. Therefore, it is submitted that "the protection and promotion of breast-feeding" is intended to be the principal part of the aim of the International Code,[13] while "the proper use of breast-milk substitutes" is the subsidiary part thereof. The American Delegate at the Thirty-fourth WHA, 1981 (Mr. Helman) stated that

> the United States recognized that one of the important aims of the code...was to encourage breast-feeding.[14]

The two elements of the aim of the International Code will be surveyed now.

1. The protection and promotion of breast-feeding

It is logical that the protection and promotion of breast-feeding is the principal element in the aim of the International Code, for its Preamble declares that

> breast-feeding is an unequalled way of providing ideal food for the healthy growth and development of infants; that it forms a unique biological and emotional basis for the health of both mother and child; that the anti-infective properties of breast-milk help to protect infants against disease.[15]

Deborah Kaplan and Kristina Graff are of the opinion that

> breast-milk is the gold standard for infant nutrition and the only necessary food for the first 6 months of an infant's life. No formula preparation comes close to breast-milk in meeting the nutritional needs of infants....[16]

---

10 Ibid., sixth preambular paragraph.
11 See 6th edn. (1976), p.728.
12 See *WHO Doc. WHA33/1980/REC/3*, p. 90.(emphasis added).
13 See ibid., p.200.
14 See ibid.
15 See fourth preambular paragraph of the International Code.
16 See "Marketing Breastfeeding-Reversing Corporate Influence on Infant Feeding Practices",

Breast-feeding is also beneficial to the health of the mother, and to the economy of the family and the country concerned. Thus, the Innocenti Declaration of 1990 on the Protection, Promotion and Support of Breast-feeding declares that breast-feeding

> ...contributes to women's health by reducing the risk of breast and ovarian cancer, and by increasing the spacing between pregnancies; [and] provides social and economic benefits to the family and the nations.[17]

The participants in the international meeting "1990-2005 CELEBRATING THE INNONCETI DECLARATION on the Protection, Promotion and Support of Breastfeeding" stated that:

> Research has shown that breastfeeding may already be saving about 6 million lives every year from common infectious diseases, and recent findings have clarified that early, exclusive breastfeeding for six months and continued breast-feeding with complementary feeding for two years or beyond could save more than 2 million additional lives every year.[18]

The WHO Executive Board recognized in January 2010 that

> the improvement of breastfeeding practices could save annually the lives of about one million children under five years and that each year the deaths of more than half a million such children could be prevented by adequate timely complementary feeding along with continual breastfeeding for up to two years or beyond.[19]

Furthermore, in a new study published in the Archives of Internal Medicine, Dr. Alison Stuebe has found that breast-feeding is associated with a lower incidence of breast cancer among a group of younger women, who are at particularly high risk, those with breast cancer in the family. The study was carried out from 1997 to 2005, and involved 60,075 participants. Dr. Stuebe suggested that

---

Journal of Urban Health: Bulletin of the New York Academy of Medicine, June 2008, p. 1.

17 The Innocenti Declaration was adopted at a meeting held by WHO and UNICEF, at Florence, Italy, on 30 July-1 August 1990. There were 40 participants from the various WHO regions, as well as representatives of US AID, UNFPA, UNDP, UNICEF National Committees, SIDA, UKODA, FAO, WFPA, and the World Bank, besides the secretariats of WHO and UNICEF. The following States were represented at the meeting: Bangladesh, Brazil, Chile, China, Colombia, Ecuador, Ethiopia, Guatemala, Honduras, India, Indonesia, Iran, Italy, Ivory Coast, Jordan, Kenya, Mali, Mauritius, Mexico, Nigeria, Pakistan, Poland, Swaziland, Tanzania, Thailand, Turkey, U.K., USA, Zaire and Zimbabwe.

18 See UNICEF Innocenti Research Centre, 1990-*2005 CELEBRATING THE INNOCENTI DECLARATION ON THE PROTECTION, PROMOTION AND SUPPORT OF BREASTFEEDING,* 2nd edn., November 2006, p. 45. This meeting was hosted by the Regional Authority of Tuscany, in collaboration with WHO, UNICEF, USAID, the World Alliance for Breastfeeding Action, the International Baby Food Action Network, La Leche League International, the International Lactation Consultant Association, and the Academy of Breastfeeding Medicine, with the support of the Meyer Hospital. Ibid.

19 See Resolution EB 126.R5, 21 January 2010, twelfth preambular paragraph.

breast-feeding may prove just as effective a strategy for high-risk women as the use of Tamoxifen, a drug that interferes with estrogen activity and is often used in high-risk women to reduce breast cancer risk.[20]

These studies have also found that women who breast-fed are less likely to develop osteoporosis and ovarian cancer, as well as high-blood pressure and heart disease decades later.[21]

Dr. Hafez and Dr Bagchi summarized the benefits of breast-feeding as follows:

> ...reviews of the recent literature show that breast-feeding can save more infant lives and prevent more morbidity than any other intervention strategy. Breast-feeding currently saves six million infant lives each year by preventing diarrhoea and acute respiratory infections alone, is responsible for between a quarter and a third of the observed fertility suppression, and can provide high quality nutrition at a fraction of the cost of high-risk substitutes. Breast-feeding is a natural resource that is too valuable to lose; to ignore it is to promote mortality, suffering, and personal and national economic stress.[22]

A former Director-General of WHO, Dr Mahler, said that

> children are a priceless resource, and that any nation which neglects them would do so at its peril.[23]

Moreover, it has been said that

> the intellectual development of breastfed children is slightly but significantly better than that of children fed artificially.[24]

Breast-feeding has also some social and economic relevance to any society. As the Swiss Delegate to the Thirty-fourth WHA (Dr Frey) put it:

> his government attached so much importance to breast-feeding because infant and young child feeding played a key role in the health and in the physical and mental development of the child, and indirectly influenced the socioeconomic development of society as a whole.[25]

The financial saving that can be achieved from breast-feeding to any Member State of WHO, as well as for any mother, cannot be ignored. It is estimated that in 1980 developing countries spent more than US$ 1000 million on the import

---

20 See the *International Herald Tribune*, August 13 2009, p. 8. Dr. Alison M. Stuebe is an Assistant Professor of obstetrics and gynaecology at the University of North Carolina, Chapel Hill, USA.
21 Ibid.
22 See *Promotion of Breast-feeding*, op.cit., p.14.
23 See message from the Director-General of WHO for World Heath Day 1984, "Children's health is tomorrow's wealth", *World Health*, January-February 1984, p. 3.
24 *The Lancet*, Vol. 344, 5 November, 1994, p.1239.
25 See above note 12, p.192.

of breast-milk substitutes.[26] And Deborah Kaplan and Kristina Graff, quoting US sources in 2006, say

> according to the US Department of Agriculture, the USA would save a minimum of $3.6 billion per year in health care and indirect costs if at least 75% of mothers initiated breastfeeding, and 50% breastfed until the infant is at least 6 months old.[27]

The Tunisian Delegate to the Thirty-fourth WHA (Professor Hamza) pointed out, long ago, that

> quite apart from the scientific evidence...on the biological, immunological and emotional advantages of mother's milk, the economic aspect was becoming progressively more important in view of the adverse effect of the increasing costs of breast-milk substitutes on the family budget of poorer families.[28]

Breast-feeding could also contribute to the Millennium Development Goal of eradicating extreme poverty and hunger (MDG 1). It has been said that

> if breast-milk were prioritised as a high-quality source of infant food, households (especially those without land and headed by women),could withstand some of [the] burden [of high food prices] Moreover, through saving lives, breast-feeding obviates many health-care expenses and lost work hours.[29]

These qualities, benefits and advantages of breast-feeding render it more than "safe and adequate nutrition for infants", as stated in Article 1 of the International Code.

The protection and promotion of breast-feeding is dealt with in the International Code in several ways, and takes several forms, such as the provision of information and education to the mother about breast-feeding,[30] and the protection of the mother from the influences, or temptations of advertising of breast-milk substitutes, which might discourage her from feeding her infant with her own milk. The WHA in 1982 recognized

---

26 See the late M. Nashat, "Le Code International de Commercialisation des Substituts du Lait Maternel", *Annuaire français de droit international* 27 (1981), p. 490. The total value of nominal sales for 1980 in the baby-food market in Denmark, France, the then Federal Republic of Germany (now Germany), Ireland, and the U.K. had been estimated at over US$ 746 million. See *The Economist* (31 January 1981), p.66. Prakash Sethi estimates the total 1990 Third World sale of major brand of infant formula products at approximately US$ 1,150 million, and for the total world market at US$ 3,850 million. See Prakash Sethi, *Multinational Corporations and the Impact of Public Advocacy on Corporate Strategy: Nestlé and the Infant Formula Controversy*, 1994, p.133. The Financial Times estimates the worldwide market for breast-milk substitutes at US$ 6 BN (£3.5 BN). See *The Financial Times* (9 January 1997).

27 See "Marketing Breastfeeding-Reversing Corporate Influence on Infant Feeding Practices", op. cit, p. 17.

28 See above note 12, p.196.

29 See Anna Coutsoudis, Hoosen M. Coovadia, Judith King "The breast-milk brand: promotion of child survival in the face of formula-milk marketing", *The Lancet*, Vol. 374, August 1, 2009, p. 424.

30 See below Chapter VI.

...that commercial marketing of breast-milk substitutes for infants has contributed to an increase in artificial feeding[31]

The would-be mother needs advice and encouragement about breast-feeding from her family, community, health workers[32] and the health care system.[33] Hence, the International Code affirms that

...health care systems, and the health professionals and other health workers serving in them, have an essential role to play in guiding infant feeding practices, encouraging and facilitating breast-feeding, and providing objective and consistent advice to mothers and families about the superior value of breast-feeding....[34]

The International Code also recognizes that families, communities, women's organizations and other NGOs have "...a special role to play in the protection and promotion of breast-feeding...."[35] It also affirms that the educational system and social services in a given country should be involved in the protection and promotion of breast-feeding.[36]

All these measures and roles attributed to various entities, it is submitted, are intended to achieve the principal element of the aim of the International Code and are intended, it would appear, to complete each other. It might be appropriate to conclude this part by reference to the U.N. Convention on the Rights of the Child.[37] In accordance with Article 24 of the Convention:

1) States Parties recognize the right of the child to the enjoyment of the highest attainable standard of health....
2) States Parties shall pursue full implementation of this right and, in particular, shall take appropriate measures:
(a) To diminish infant and child mortality;

(e) to ensure that all segments of society, in particular parents and children, are informed, have access to...the advantages of breast-feeding....

If these provisions are read together it would seem that the States Parties to the Convention have recognized the need to take appropriate measures to diminish infant mortality. Furthermore, they have undertaken to provide information on, and access to, the advantages of breast-feeding. In these undertakings one

---

31 See Resolution WHA 35.26, fourth preambular paragraph; the resolution is reproduced in *WHO Handbook*, Vol. II (1985), p.92. See also below Chapter VII.
32 The "health worker" is defined in Article 3 of the International Code, see also below Chapter IX.
33 The "health care system" is defined in Article 3 of the International Code, see also below Chapter VIII.
34 See tenth preambular paragraph of the International Code.
35 Ibid., twelfth preambular paragraph.
36 Ibid., eleventh preambular paragraph.
37 The Convention was adopted by the General Assembly of the U.N. on 20 November 1989; see General Assembly Resolution 44/25 (20 November 1989), *General Assembly A44/49 (Supplement 49)*, p.174. The Convention entered into force on 2 September 1990.

can easily imply an intention to promote breast-feeding, for, as we have seen earlier, breast-feeding is one of the most important measures to reduce infant mortality. Therefore, the aim of the International Code, here, has received significant support, albeit not express, from the U.N. Convention on the Rights of the Child.

2. The proper use of breast-milk substitutes when necessary

It is known that there are cases where the mother is unable to breast-feed her infant, for health or other reasons. Although these numbers of cases are small, nevertheless the International Code recognizes that in such cases breast-milk substitutes have to be used for the survival of the infant. The French Delegate said the following in the September Consultation 1980:

> what should be done in other cases, which are, fortunately, very rare but are real cases, where the mother cannot breast-feed...we must give these mothers every possibility of raising their infants satisfactorily. What should be done in the case of breast-abscess in France...we immediately stop breast-feeding in the case of an abscess.[38]

Hence, the subsidiary element of the aim of the International Code is there to show this recognition. Furthermore, the International Code says that

> ...when mothers do not breast-feed, or only do so partially, there is a legitimate market for infant formula...; that all these products should accordingly be made accessible to those who need them through commercial or non-commercial distribution systems.[39]

The International Code also affirms the "essential role" of the health care systems and health workers to provide objective and consistent advice to mothers and families "on the proper use of infant formula", where needed.[40]

It should be pointed out, at the outset, that when the International Code refers to "infant formula", this does not necessarily exclude other breast-milk substitutes, because it applies to all breast-milk substitutes, of which "infant formula" is but one. Mr. Heyward, the then Senior Deputy Executive Director, UNICEF, made the following statement at the September Consultation 1980:

> I think that the concern that we have is with whatever is marketed or handled in a way that may lead mothers to believe that the products may be used as a substitute for breast-milk in the early months of life. Infant formula is one of those products....[41]

This occasional reference to "infant formula", instead of "breast-milk substitutes", in the International Code is probably due to an oversight on the part of

---

38 See above note 4, tape 3, p.1.
39 See sixth preambular paragraph of the International Code.
40 See ibid., tenth preambular paragraph.
41 See above note 4, tape 13, p.1; see also definition of "infant formula" in Article 3 of the International Code; see below p. 88.

the drafters. This standpoint may be supported by the wording of Article 4.2 of the Code and the clarification provided by the WHA with respect to Article 6.6 of the Code. So far as Article 4.2 is concerned, the provision lays down certain requirements to be included in informational and educational materials on infant feeding. One of these requirements is to the effect that

> when such materials contain information about the use of infant formula,they should include...the health hazards of inappropriate...feeding methods; and, in particular, the health hazards of unnecessary or improper use of infant formula and other breast-milk substitutes (Article 4.2(e)).

This shows how the drafters used the term "infant formula" at the beginning of this part of the provision and ended up with the use of the expression "infant formula and other breast-milk substitutes". On the other hand, Article 6.6 permits the donation or low price of "supplies of infant formula", to institutions and organizations under certain conditions. In a resolution adopted in 1994, the WHA urged Member States to take measures

> to ensure that there are no donations of free or subsidized supplies of breast-milk substitutes . . . in any part of the health care system.[42]

The Assembly used the term "breast-milk substitutes", instead of the term "infant formula" used by Article 6.6. Moreover, some members of the Executive Board suggested that the term "breast-milk substitutes" should replace the term "infant formula" in WHO texts.[43] The Swedish Delegate to the Forty-seventh WHA (Mr Örtendahl) stated that

> the International Code covered a wider area than "infant formula", and it was unfortunate that WHO statements sometimes employed that term where it would be more appropriate to speak of "breast milk substitute".[44]

The Swaziland Delegate (Dr Dlamini) speaking on behalf of the Africa Group, said

> the term "breast-milk substitutes" should be used instead of "infant formula" throughout the documentation.[45]

The Iranian Delegate (Dr. Mirandi) supported the retention of the term "breast-milk substitutes" in preference to the term "infant formula", as the use of the former "avoided any ambiguity on the subject."[46]

---

42 See Resolution WHA 47.5, (9 May 1994), operative paragraph 2(2); for the text of the resolution, see *Forty-Seventh World Health Assembly 2-12 May 1994, WHO document WHA 47/1994/REC/1,* (hereinafter referred to as "WHO DOC. WHA47/1994/REC/1"), pp.3-5.

43 See statement by the representative of the Executive Board (Professor Mbade) to the Forty-seventh WHA, 1994; see *WHO Doc. WHA47/1994/REC/3,* p.29 .

44 Ibid., p.30.

45 Ibid., p.33.

46 Ibid., p.37.

It should be pointed that the International Code contains no provision for its amendment. But the absence of such a provision does not prevent the WHA from providing clarification with respect to some provisions of the Code. Indeed, from a legal point of view, the WHA is competent to amend the Code, even in the absence of a provision expressly providing for such a measure. After all, the WHA is the plenary organ of WHO, which determines the policies of the Organization, in accordance with the WHO Constitution,[47] and it was the organ which adopted the Code in 1981. The position of the WHO Secretariat is that resolutions of the WHA do not modify[48] the provisions of the International Code. However, there is no reason in law why such resolutions of the WHA could not amend the Code. The position of the WHO Secretariat may be justified on the basis that they want to maintain the role of good offices of the Director-General in this area, a role which the WHA entrusted to him in a resolution it adopted in 1981.[49] This role, the Secretariat fear, might be impaired if they took the position that resolutions of the WHA could amend the Code.

Article 1 of the Code stipulates that the proper use of breast-milk substitutes is to be made on the basis of adequate information. This stipulation is given effect to in the Code in several ways, and takes several forms, such as the requirement to state, "the health hazards of unnecessary or improper use of infant formula and other breast-milk substitutes", on informational and educational matters[50], and a statement in the label, or on the container, that breast-milk substitutes "should be used only on the advice of a health worker as to the need for its use and the proper method of use."[51] The WHA declared in 2002 that

> every year as much as 55% of infants deaths from diarrhoeal disease and acute respiratory infections may be the result of inappropriate feeding practices.[52]

Furthermore, the International Code requires that the ingredients and composition of breast-milk substitutes be made known on the label, as well as the storage conditions and date before which the product is to be consumed.[53] The International Code also insists on the quality of breast-milk substitutes and requires them to

---

47 See Art. 18 (a) of the WHO Constitution.
48 See WHO Press Release WHO/36 (14 October 1988), p.2; see also the report of the Director-General to the Forty-third WHA, 1990, on Infant and Young Child Nutrition (Progress and Evaluation Report; and Status of Implementation of the International Code of Marketing of Breast-milk Substitutes), *Forty-Third World Health Assembly, Geneva, 7-17 May 1990, WHO Doc. WHA43/1990/REC/1* (hereinafter referred to as "WHO Doc. WHA43/1990/REC/1"), p.76, paragraph 215.
49 See Resolution WHA34.22, operative paragraph 5(2); for the text of the resolution see above note 12, pp.91-92.
50 See Art. 4.2 (e) of the International Code.
51 See ibid. Art. 9.2 (c).
52 See Resolution WHA55/25, third preambular paragraph, 18 May 2002
53 See Article 9.4 of the International Code.

meet applicable standards recommended by the Codex Alimentarius Commission and also the Codex Code of Hygienic Practice for Foods for Infants and Children.[54]

After all, the overall aim of the Code is to contribute to the provision of safe and adequate nutrition for infants.

In addition, Article 1 of the Code also stipulates that the proper use of breast-milk substitutes be "through appropriate marketing and distribution". This expression means that any marketing of such products, as the term is defined in the Code,[55] has to be appropriate, which simply means that it has to be in conformity with the Code. Any marketing activity, e.g., the giving of samples of such products, for promotional purposes, which is banned by the Code,[56] will not be in conformity with the Code. Therefore, it will not constitute "appropriate marketing". The same applies to the distribution of breast-milk substitutes.

It must be stated that the inclusion of the proper use of breast-milk substitutes in the aim of the International Code refutes the allegations made during the preparatory stages of the Code that it was directed against the infant food industry.[57] Indeed, the International Code itself recognizes that

> ...manufacturers and distributors of breast-milk substitutes have an important and constructive role to play in relation to infant feeding....[58]

In the words of the Swiss Delegate to the Thirty-fourth WHA (Dr Frey),

> there should be no misunderstanding on the subject: the Code recognized objectively that breast-milk substitutes fulfilled a need and it did not set out to prevent such products from being sold or used when necessary."[59]

However, the International Code allows the use of breast-milk substitutes *only* when they are *necessary*,[60] for one reason or another. The wording of Article 1, Article 4.2, and that of Article 6.6, support this proposition. So far as Article 1 is concerned, it clearly states that the aim of the Code is to contribute to the provision of safe and adequate nutrition for infants, *inter alia*, "by ensuring the proper use of breast-milk substitutes, when these are *necessary*", (emphasis added).Therefore, there is a qualification in the provision ("necessary"). The provision does not give a *carte blanche* for the use of such products. It is only when their use is "necessary" that they can be properly used for infant feeding. As regards Article 4.2, it requires that informational and educational materials, which contain information on the use of infant formula, to include "the

---

54 See ibid., Art. 10, see below Chapter XII.
55 Art. 3 of the Code defines "marketing" as "product promotion, distribution, selling, advertising, product public relations, and informational services." On definitions see below Chapter V.
56 See below Chapter VII.
57 See Chapter II above pp.73-74.
58 See fifteenth preambular paragraph of the International Code.
59 See above note 12, p.193.
60 For the dictionary meaning of "necessary", see above p.49.

health hazards of unnecessary ... use of infant formula and other breast-milk substitutes"

So far as Article 6.6 is concerned, it allows the donations or low-price sales of supplies of, *inter alia*, breast-milk substitutes to institutions or organizations, which "should only be used or distributed for infants who have to be fed on breast-milk substitutes". Accordingly, the Code allows this practice only in cases of necessity and compulsion[61] ("infants who have to be fed on breast-milk substitutes").

Of course, the mother, alone, decides whether to breast-feed her infant or use breast-milk substitutes. But the mother has to have all the relevant and objective information on breast-feeding and bottle-feeding, and without interference, or influence, through advertising or promotion, in order to make her decision. The Turkish Delegate (the late Professor Dogramaci) put it eloquently in 1981, in Committee A, when he said:

> it was argued that mothers had a right to choose whether or not they wanted to breast-feed; no one would deny that...provided [that the mother] was properly informed about the facts.[62]

3. Breast-feeding and HIV

Concern has been expressed about the possible transmission of HIV from HIV-infected mothers to their infants through breast-feeding. In such cases, the question of the use of breast-milk substitutes to feed infants arises. Under such circumstances it becomes necessary for the mother to decide whether to breast-feed her infant, or use breast-milk substitutes to that end. Therefore, it is essential to weigh the advantages of breast-feeding vis-à-vis the risks which may arise from the use of breast-milk substitutes. According to the WHO Global Strategy for Infant and Young Child Feeding

> there is continued concern that 10% to 20% of infants born to HIV-positive mothers may acquire HIV through breast-feeding, and recent studies indicate a heightened risk of transmission during the early months. However, evidence from one study show that exclusive breast-feeding in the first three months of life may carry a lower risk of HIV transmission than mixed feeding does....[63]

However, the WHO Strategy advises the avoidance of breast-feeding, and recommends the use of breast-milk substitutes ("replacement feeding") but under strict conditions. It says:

> when replacement feeding is acceptable, feasible, affordable, sustainable and safe, avoidance of all breastfeeding by HIV-positive women is recommended; otherwise

---

61 For details, see below Chapter VIII.
62 See above note 12, p.194.
63 See WHO Doc. A54/7, 9 April 2001, p. 4, paragraph 13.

exclusive breastfeeding is recommended during the first months of life.[64]

These conditions and recommendations were adopted by the WHA in 2001.[65]Accordingly, the WHO recommends two options in cases of HIV-positive mothers for feeding their infants, namely, "replacement feeding", i.e., not breast-feeding implying the use of breast-milk substitutes, under specific conditions, or breast-feeding. And the final decision as to which one of these options to choose "should be the mother's and she should be supported in her choice".[66]

However, the WHO Global Strategy emphasises that

> all HIV-infected mothers should receive counselling that includes information about risks and benefits of different feeding options, and specific guidance in selecting the option most likely to be suitable for their situation.[67]

The "replacement feeding", i.e., the use of breast-milk substitutes, recommended by the WHO Strategy to an HIV-infected mother is subject to the following conditions:

(i)   The replacement feeding is acceptable to the mother;
(ii) The replacement feeding is feasible, from the mother's point of view;
(iii) The replacement feeding is affordable to the mother, or her family;
(iv) The replacement feeding is sustainable; and
(v)   The replacement feeding is safe.

These conditions are cumulative, and in the absence of any one of them, the recommendation for "replacement feeding" does not apply. In that case, WHA recommends exclusive breast-feeding during the first months of life, which now means the first six months, "as a global public health recommendation", as stated by the WHA.[68]

Let us now deal with these conditions.

(i) The replacement feeding is acceptable to the mother

This condition means that the mother must find the use of breast-milk substitutes an acceptable option to feed her infant. But in her decision to resort to this option, the mother should receive counselling that includes information about the risks and benefits of the different feeding options and specific guidance, so as to facilitate her informed decision-making, as required by the WHO Global

---

64 See ibid.
65 See Resolution WHA54.2, operative paragraph 2 (10), 18 May 2001.
66 See above note 63.
67 See ibid.
68 Resolution WHA 54.2, operative paragraph 3 (3), 18 May 2001.

Strategy and the WHA resolution.[69] The question then arises is this: if the HIV-infected mother has received no such information and guidance, or has been misled to believe that the option for the use of breast-milk substitutes is the right one for her infant, does this constitute acceptability?

It is submitted that the answer should be in the negative, because the WHO Strategy, which was endorsed by the WHA, requires counselling and the provision of information, which should be objective and accurate. Therefore, the absence of such counselling and information or the lack of objectivity and impartiality render such acceptance by the mother not one based on "informed" decision. It is interesting to point out that one of the problems identified by UNICEF in some countries in the context of HIV and breast-feeding is that

> Counsellor's lack of adequate knowledge and skills led to poor outcomes, advising mothers to use formula without taking their circumstance into account.[70]

(ii) The replacement feeding is feasible, from the mother's point of view

This condition means that the mother (or her family) is in such circumstances which allow her adequate time, with the knowledge, skills and other resources to prepare the replacement food and feed the infant adequately. It also suggests that the mother can understand and follow instructions for preparing breast-milk substitutes, which may not be the case in many developing countries. In this case, the mother's better option is to breast-feed her infant.

(iii) The replacement feeding is affordable to the mother, or her family

This condition requires that the mother and/or her family, have the financial means to meet the cost of buying and preparing breast-milk substitutes. This can be a heavy burden on poor families in the third world. This financial element should be part of the information and counselling to be given to the mother, in order to decide which option of feeding her infant to choose.

(iv) The replacement feeding is sustainable

This means the availability of a continuous and uninterrupted supply and dependable system of distribution for all ingredients and products needed for safe breast-milk substitutes, for as long as the infant needs them. This again constitutes a heavy burden, which not many families in the third world can afford. According to UNICEF, one of the problems faced in this context in some

---

69 See above p. 59.
70 See UNICEF Innocenti Research Centre, op. cit., p. 22.

countries is that

> many women were unable to obtain constant supply of formula, leading to inferior replacements or mixed-feeding.[71]

(v) The replacement feeding is safe

This condition requires the breast-milk substitutes to be correctly and hygieni-cally prepared and stored, and fed to the infant in nutritionally adequate quan-tities with clean hands and using clean utensils. This means access to a reliable supply of safe water, that the breast-milk substitute is nutritionally sound and free from pathogens, and is stored in a clean environment. This condition im-plies that the mother is educated and thus capable of following all the measures that ensure the safety of the infant food. Such mothers are to be found mostly in developed countries, where the standards of education are much higher than those in developing countries.

These conditions cover the health, emotional, financial, and the practical as-pects relating to the use of breast-milk substitutes by an HIV-infected mother. All the five conditions have to be met in order to apply the recommendation concerning the use of breast-milk substitutes by an HIV-infected mother. And this will be compatible with Article 1 of the International Code, which allows the use of breast-milk substitutes when they are "necessary", which is probably the case when the mother is HIV-infected. However, if one of them is not met, then exclusive breast-feeding becomes the applicable mode of feeding infants.

It may be interesting to point out that the WHA, in endorsing the WHO Strategy, it could be argued, has clarified the notion of "necessity" in Article 1 of the International Code, insofar as HIV-infected mothers are concerned. This is perfectly acceptable, from a legal point of view, for the WHA is the plenary organ of WHO, which adopted the Code in 1981, and as such, it can clarify any of its provisions in the interest of the health of the infant and mother. This clarification, it could be argued, might amount to a *de* facto amendment of the International Code. On the other hand, the WHO Secretariat is not entitled, from a legal point of view, to clarify the provisions of the Code.

It is worth noting that on 30 November 2009, WHO adopted a new recom-mendation in the context of HIV-infected mothers and breast-feeding. This recommendation calls

> for early initiation of antiretroviral therapy (ART) for adults and adolescents, the delivery of more patient-friendly antiretroviral drugs (AVR), and prolonged use of ARVs to reduce the risk of mother-to-child transmission of HIV. And for the first time, WHO recommends that HIV-positive mothers or their infants take ARVs while breast-feeding to prevent transmission... WHO also now recommends that breast-feeding continue until the infant is 12 months of age, provided the HIV-pos-itive mother or baby is taking ARVs during that period. This will reduce the risk of

---

71 Ibid.

HIV transmission and improve the infant's chance of survival.[72]

4. Breast-feeding and emergencies

Emergencies arising from man-made or natural disasters can, and do, lead to the displacement of populations, including mothers and infants. In cases of civil wars, civil strife, and political upheavals, a certain section of the population is forced to leave their homes and go either to a foreign country, or to refugee camps. The same applies in cases of earthquakes, or tidal waves. In such emergencies, the WHO Global strategy for infant and young child feeding declares that

> the best hope for averting the disability and death that are so common among infants and young children in exceptionally difficult circumstances is to ensure that they are adequately cared for and fed.[73]

Ensuring that infants are adequately fed in an emergency raises the question of breast-feeding or the use of breast-milk substitutes, in the context of the International Code. It is common knowledge that the conditions in refugee camps, or shelters, in emergencies are difficult and may not provide the right environment for the use of breast-milk substitutes, because of the lack of clean and safe water, the lack of washing facilities, the absence of facilities for sterilization of feeding utensils. Therefore, as is the case with HIV-infected mothers, the question will be weighing the advantages of breast-feeding vis-à-vis the risks of the use of breast-milk substitutes. A WHO Press Release on the Kosovo Crisis in 1999 sums up the situation with respect to the options of breast-feeding vis-à-vis the use of breast-milk substitutes. It says:

> infant formula is unsafe and likely to be the main source of infection and cause of diarrhoea in infants during an emergency. This is because there is usually a lack of: clean water; facilities to boil water and detergents to clean bottles and teats. Therefore breast-feeding should be promoted, protected and supported amongst the refugees as a life-saving source of nutrition and the main protection against infections in infants and young children.[74]

It goes on to say that

> Indeed during emergencies the hormones produced in breast-milk can help to sooth both the mother and her baby. Even if women have lost weight, have not eaten properly for days or are anaemic they can breast-feed. What they need, more than anything, is the confidence that breast-feeding is the best choice.[75]

---

72 See *New WHO recommendation on infant feeding in the context of HIV*, 30 November 2009, available at http://www.who.int/child_adolescent_health/news/archive/2009/30.

73 See WHO Doc. A54/7, 9 April 2001, p. 3, paragraph 12.

74 See WHO Press Release, 21 April 1999 concerning the Kosovo Crisis.

75 Ibid.

Furthermore, the joint statement of WHO, UNICEF, ICRC, and the International Federation of Red Cross and Red Crescent on appropriate infant and young child feeding in the Asian emergency (the Tsunami) in 2004, reiterated that

> … no food or liquid other than breast-milk, not even water, is normally needed to meet an infant's nutritional requirements during the first six months of life.[76]

These principles have been reiterated in the UNICEF, WHO and WFP call for support for appropriate infant and young child feeding in Haiti in January 2010.[77]

Therefore, it would be reasonable to state that breast-milk substitutes may be resorted to in emergencies to feed infants, provided that it is "necessary" for the survival of the infant. However, when breast-milk substitutes are donated as "supplies" as defined in the International Code, the donors must comply with Article 6.6 of the Code, as well as the requirement of Resolution WHA 47.5,1994.[78]On the other hand, the promotion, protection and support of breast-feeding in emergencies is the most important factor in the feeding and protection of infants against infections. And this is in line with the aim of the International Code, as stated in its Article 1.

5. Conclusion

The aim of the International Code represents a public health policy declared by the highest health authority in the world, namely WHO. This policy is intended to protect the health of infants from infections and diseases, and their healthy development, through the promotion, protection, and support of breast-feeding. At the same time, the policy admits the need for the use of breast-milk substitutes, when such use is necessary for the survival of infants. The aim of the Code is to take an appropriate approach to the question of infant feeding and health, in that it provides the rule for the most important source of nutrition for infants, i.e., breast-feeding, and allows the use of breast-milk substitutes, as the exception, in well-defined circumstances. This is the case, even in situations of HIV-infected mothers and emergencies. For even in such situations, breast-milk is the best option for feeding infants, due to the risks which are likely to arise from using breast-milk substitutes.

It is not surprising then to see that, in the implementation of the International Code by Member States, the general trend is towards following the

---

76 See *WHO, UNICEF, the International Committee of the RED Cross and the International Federation of Red Cross and Red Crescent Societies call for support for appropriate infant and young child feeding in the current Asian emergency, and caution about unnecessary use of milk products*, 2004, p.1, second paragraph.

77 See Press Release by UNICEF, WHO, and WFP, dated 21 January 2010, p.1, fourth paragraph.

78 On the question of "supplies", see below pp.139-149.

approach of the Code, i.e., providing a provision on the aim of the national measures in question. A survey of national measures giving effect to the Code, whether in legislation or regulations and whether they are in force or not yet in force, in 20 Member States, reveals that a large majority of them contain a provision, describing the aim of the instrument in question. Some of these national measures contain provisions identical with Article 1 of the Code, in wording and/or substance[79], while others use the two elements of Article 1, alone, in the formulation of their aim[80]. Other national measures, which are the minority, contain no provision on their aim[81], even though their contents demonstrate their concern for the protection and promotion of breast-feeding and the regulation of the use of breast-milk substitutes. It is worth mentioning that, twenty years after the adoption of the International Code, WHA declared the following:

---

79 See for examples: Art. 1 of the Brazilian Marketing Regulations for Infant's Foods, 1992, (hereinafter referred to as the "Brazilian Marketing Regulations"), the sixth paragraph of the Preface to the Kenyan Code for Marketing of Breast-milk Substitutes, 1983, (hereinafter referred to as the "Kenyan Code 1983"), the first paragraph of the Preamble of the Nepalese Breast-milk Substitution Substances (Sales, Distribution and Control) Act 1992, (hereinafter referred to as the "Nepalese Breast-milk Substitution Act"), Art. 2 of the Philippines Code of Marketing of Breast-milk Substitutes, 1986, (hereinafter referred to as the "Philippines Code of Marketing"), the penultimate paragraph of the Preambule of the Sri Lankan Code for the Promotion of Breast-feeding and Marketing of Breast Milk Substitutes and Related Products, 1983, (hereinafter referred to as the "Sri Lankan Code for the Promotion of Breast-feeding") and Art. 2 of the Peruvian Standards for the Marketing of Breast-milk Substitutes and Complementary Infant Foods, 1982, (hereinafter referred to as the "Peruvian Standards for the Marketing of Breast-milk Substitutes"). See also the Preambule to IBFAN's Model Law on the Protection of Breast-feeding, for text, see E. J. Sokol, *The Code Handbook- A Guide to Implementing the International Code of Marketing of Breast-milk Substitutes* (1997), pp.134-147.This work contains a useful collection of some national measures giving effect to the International Code, see Appendix A thereof.

80 See for examples: Art. 1 of the Guatemalan Law on Marketing of Breast-milk Substitutes, 1983, (hereinafter referred to as the "Guatemalan Law 1983"), the Preambule of the Indian Infant Milk Substitutes, Feeding Bottles and Infant Foods (Regulations of Production, Supply and Distribution) Act, 1992, (hereinafter referred to as the "Indian Infant Milk Substitutes Act 1992"), Art. 1 of the draft Jordanian Code for the Protection and Promotion of Breast-feeding, 1994, (hereinafter referred to as the "draft Jordanian Code 1994"), Art. 1 of the draft Omani Code on the Protection and Promotion of Breast-feeding, 1995 (hereinafter referred to as the "draft Omani Code 1995"), and Art. 1 of the United Arab Emirates draft Code on the Protection and Promotion of Breast-feeding, 1995, (hereinafter referred to as the "draft UAE Code 1995").

81 See Bahraini Law concerning the Regulation of the Marketing, Promotion and Use of Breast-milk Substitutes, 1995, (hereinafter refered to as the "Bahraini Law 1995"), the Iranian Law on the Promotion of Breast-feeding and Supporting Lactating Mothers, 1996, (hereinafter referred to as the "Iranian Law 1996"), the Papua New Guinea Baby Feed Supplies (Control) Act, 1977 and Baby Feed Supplies (Control) (Amendment) Act, 1984, (hereinafter referred to as the "Papua New Guinea Legislation 1977 and 1984"), and the Tunisian Law on the Quality Control, Marketing and Information Concerning the Use of Breast-milk Substitutes and Related Products, 1983, (hereinafter referred to as the "Tunisian Law 1983").

Mindful that 2001 marks the twentieth anniversary of the adoption of the International Code of Marketing of Breast-milk Substitutes, and the adoption of the present resolution provides an opportunity to reinforce the International Code's fundamental role in protecting, promoting and supporting breastfeeding.[82]

---

82 See Resolution WHA54.2, 9th preambular paragraph, 18 May 2001.

CHAPTER IV

THE MATERIAL SCOPE
OF THE INTERNATIONAL CODE

The material scope of the International Code is to be found in Article 2 thereof entitled "Scope of the Code". It is one of the most important provisions of the International Code, because it determines whether or not a particular marketing activity, practice, or product is subject to the Code's regime. Article 2 reads as follows:

> The Code applies to the marketing, and practices related thereto, of the following products: breast-milk substitutes, including infant formula; other milk products, foods and beverages, including bottle-fed complementary foods, when marketed or otherwise represented to be suitable, with or without modification, for use as a partial or total replacement of breast-milk; feeding bottles and teats. It also applies to their quality and availability and to information concerning their use.

The First Draft of the International Code contained no specific provision on the material scope. By contrast, the Second Draft contained such a provision[1], which was deleted in the Third Draft. Article 2, in its present form, was incorporated in the Fourth Draft after a request for a specific provision on the scope of the International Code was made by some Member States participating in the September Consultation 1980.[2] The Swiss Delegate stated that

> ... it is regrettable...that the field of application [of the Code] is not clearly...and explicitly defined. This must be remedied.[3]

The Swedish Delegate added his support for a scope provision when he said

> we feel fairly strongly that in the transition between the [preamble and the articles of the code] we need a statement which spells out the scope of the code.[4]

---

1 See Art. 1 of the Second Draft, (Scope).
2 On the September Consultation 1980, see Chapter I above, pp.24-25.
3 See September Consultation 1980, Transcription of Tapes., tape 3, p.5.
4 Ibid., tape 17, p.1. The Canadian and U.K. Delegates supported the need for a scope article; see ibid., tape 5, p.3, and tape 17, p.2. The U.K. Delegate proposed a wording for the scope article, which was not as wide as the wording of Article 2 of the International Code. See ibid., p.6. At the August Consultation 1980, it was suggested and accepted that the provisions of the Code could begin with an article describing the scope of the Code. See the August Consultation 1980, p.7, paragraph 16.1. It might be interesting to note that ICIFI wanted

The International Code applies to the marketing, and practices related thereto, of the following products:

a) breast-milk substitutes;
b) milk products, foods and beverages, including bottle-fed complementary foods, when marketed or otherwise represented to be suitable, for use as a partial or total replacement of breast-milk; and
c) feeding bottles and teats.

It also applies to the quality, availability and to information relating to those products.

The following aspects of the material scope of the International Code shall be dealt with.

1. MARKETING AND PRACTICES RELATED THERETO

The International Code applies to the marketing, and practices related thereto of breast-milk substitutes, other food products marketed or represented as breast-milk substitutes and feeding bottles and teats. Marketing is defined in Article 3 of the Code as

> product promotion, distribution, selling, advertising, product public relations, and information services.

Accordingly, any of these activities is subject to the regime of the International Code if it relates to a product considered as a breast-milk substitute under the International Code, or relates to feeding bottles and teats. In conformity with Article 2 of the International Code, any activity of "marketing", i.e., promotion, distribution, selling, advertising, product public relations and information services, has to comply with the requirements of the International Code. For example, no company can promote breast-milk substitutes in a facility of a health care system, because this practice is not allowed by the Code.[5] Nor can such a company provide donations or low-price sales of supplies of breast-milk substitutes to an institution or organization for use for feeding infants, *routinely*[6], or to be given to a health care facility, because this is not possible under the Code.[7]

---

the scope article, which was deleted from the Third Draft, to be "reinstated". See ICIFI's Comments and Recommendations on the Third Draft, September 1980, p.13. ICIFI also proposed the following text for the Scope provision: "This Code defines the conditions under which products, appropriate for use as breast milk substitutes, are to be marketed". See ibid.

5   See Art.6.2 of the International Code.
6   Art.6.6 of the International Code allows such supplies, but they "should only be used or distributed for infants who have to be fed on breast-milk substitutes", i.e., in cases of compulsion and not routinely. For a discussion of this subject, see below Chapter VIII.
7   The WHA has disallowed the donations of free or subsidized supplies to any part of the

The same applies to all the marketing activities enumerated in the definition of "marketing" in the Code.

While "marketing" is defined by the International Code, "practices related thereto" are not defined. Therefore, it would be reasonable to interpret the term according to its plain meaning.[8]Accordingly, any practice related to any of the activities covered by the definition of marketing, would, in general, be subject to the International Code, whether or not it is mentioned in the Code, as long as it concerns a product covered by the Code. For example, any practice related to the provision of information for any infant food, which qualifies as a breast-milk substitute, has to comply with the requirements of the International Code. It is, however, difficult to enumerate such practices, therefore, in order to determine whether or not any practice falls within the orbit of the International Code, one has to look at the relationship between that practice and the activities mentioned in the Code as "marketing" activities, against the background of the products covered by the Code. One example of a relevant practice, which is mentioned in the Code, is "sales incentives" for employees of companies, insofar as the sale of breast-milk substitutes is concerned.[9]

It has to be stated that the International Code is not designed against the infant food industry, nor is it intended to ban the sale of breast-milk substitutes, or the other products covered by it. It is intended as a measure to regulate certain marketing activities, which may be harmful to, discourage or are likely to discourage, breast-feeding. Indeed, as has been mentioned earlier, the preamble of the International Code, expressly recognizes that "there is a legitimate market for infant formula", when mothers do not breast-feed or do so partially, and that

> manufacturers and distributors of breast-milk substitutes have an important and constructive role to play in relation to infant feeding.[10]

It is now proposed to survey the products covered by Article 2 of the International Code.

---

health care system. See Resolution WHA 47.5 (9 May 1994), operative paragraph 2 (2).

8   See Art.31, paragraph 1, of the Vienna Convention on the Law of Treaties 1969, which can apply by analogy. It reads: "A treaty shall be interpreted in good faith in accordance with the ordinary meaning to be given to the terms of the treaty in their context and in the light of its object and purpose".

9   See Art.8.1 of the International Code.

10 See sixth and fifteenth preambular paragraphs of the International Code. Indeed, ICIFI recognized that some of its proposals were reflected in the preamble of the Fourth Draft of the International Code. See ICIFI's Summary Position Statement Re WHO International Code for the Marketing of Breast Milk Substitutes, April 1981, p.2, paragraph 5. Furthermore, the August Consultation 1980 concluded that "... the preamble [of the International Code] should reflect the positive role of industry as a collaborator in this field". See August Consultation 1980, p.3, paragraph 2.1(a).

(i) Breast-milk substitutes

A breast-milk substitute is defined in Article 3 of the Code as

> any food being marketed or otherwise represented as a partial or total replacement for breast-milk, whether or not suitable for that purpose.

Accordingly, the test as to whether a given food product is a breast-milk substitute or not appears to be a functional one, i.e., the marketing or representing of such a product "as a partial or total replacement of breast-milk". If the function attributed to the product is the "partial or total replacement" of mother's milk, then the product will be caught by the provision, irrespective of the name or description of the product. If otherwise, then the product is not subject to the International Code. Therefore, in order to determine whether a particular food product is a breast-milk substitute or not, one has to look at the way it is being marketed in the sense of the definition of marketing under the Code, i.e., whether it is being promoted, distributed, sold, or advertised...etc., as a breast-milk substitute, in the relevant context. Moreover, for the same purpose, one has to look at the way in which the product is being represented. Representation is not defined in the Code, but according to *The Concise Oxford Dictionary*,

> to "represent" means 6. a) state by way of expostulation or persuasion; b) try to bring (the facts influencing conduct) home (to).[11]

Accordingly, if a given cereal product is being portrayed to the mother, with a view to influencing her conduct, to use it to replace her milk in feeding her infant, then the product will be considered as a breast-milk substitute under the regime of the International Code, whatever name might have been given to that product. If, for example, (and this is an extreme example), Coca Cola is described as suitable to feed infants between the age of 2-3 months, it is submitted that it becomes a breast-milk substitute, and as such it would be subject to the requirements of the International Code.

However, there may be some grey areas where it is difficult to decide with certainty whether a particular product is a breast-milk substitute or not. For example, "follow up milks" have been produced after the adoption of the International Code in 1981, and it may be difficult to decide, in the abstract, whether or not they are breast-milk substitutes. Even the WHA, when it considered the question of the use of "follow-up milks" for infant feeding in 1986, did not say whether or not they should be treated as breast-milk substitutes. It merely stated that

> the practice being introduced in some countries of providing infants with specially formulated milks (so-called "follow-up milks") is not necessary.[12]

---

11 See 9th edn. (1995), p.1167.
12 See Resolution WHA39.28 (May 1988), operative paragraph 3(2)(b); the text of the resolution

Nevertheless, one has to look at the way in which the product is being represented to the user, in the relevant context. If the mother, or the would-be mother, is being targeted with a view to influencing her to believe that the product can be used as a breast-milk substitute, then the Code applies to the product. If otherwise, then the Code would not apply. At any rate, in case of doubt, the benefit of the doubt should be given to the promotion of breast-feeding and the applicability of the Code, as this attitude would be in line with the spirit and intent of the Code.

It should be pointed out that Nestlé has provided some qualification with respect to Article 2 of the International Code. In its Instructions to its personnel for the Implementation of the WHO International Code of Marketing of Breast-milk Substitutes, the reproduction of Article 2 of the International Code contains the following:

> N.B. The scope is clarified in Annex 3 (p. 33) of the Code.

Then the Nestlé Instructions go on to cite part of the statement made by the then representative of the WHO Executive Board to the Thirty-fourth WHA, Dr. Mork, in 1981, that

> during the first four to six months of life, breast-milk alone is usually adequate to sustain the normal infant's nutritional requirements.[13]

Furthermore, the Nestlé Instructions concerning Article 2 of the International Code read as follows:

> These Instructions apply to the marketing of infant formula covered by Codex (FAO/WHO Food Standards Programme, Recommended International Standard)....[14]

The first point to be made is that the period of "four to six months" is no longer the position of WHO since the WHA declared

> exclusive breast-feeding for six months as a global public health recommendation.[15]

Therefore, six months exclusive breast-feeding must be considered as having altered the statement of Dr. Mork. Furthermore, Dr. Mork's statement is his personal point of view, for members of the Executive Board of WHO are persons "technically qualified in the field of health,"[16] therefore, their statements represent their personal views and not necessarily those of WHO. By contrast, the WHA is the policy-making organ of WHO, therefore, its pronouncements

---

is to be found in *WHO Handbook*, Vol.III, pp.61-62.

13 See Nestlé Implementation of the WHO Code (International Code of Marketing of Breast-milk Substitutes) – Official Response to the Directory-General of the World Health Organization, July 1999, p. 25.

14 See ibid.

15 See Resolution WHA 54.2, operative paragraph 2 (4), 18 May 2001, *WHO Doc. A54/DIV/9.*

16 See Art. 24 of the WHO Constitution.

represent the views of the Organization. It is to be noted that the insertion of the "N.B." by Nestlé as a clarification of the scope of Article 2 of the International Code is misleading, for it may convey the impression that Annex 3 of the Code (i.e., Dr. Mork's statement) constitutes part of the provision, which is not the case.

The second point to be made with respect to Nestlé's Instructions is that, according to Nestlé, these Instructions apply to infant formula only. It should be pointed out that "infant formula" is only one of the breast-milk substitutes covered by Article 2 of the International Code. Thus Nestlé's Instructions restrict the scope of Article 2 considerably. Moreover, in the Note under the Instructions relating to the scope of Article 2, Nestlé itself excludes the application of Article 2 to a number of its products, e.g., "follow-up formulae, Sweetened Condensed Milk, Skimmed Milk,…etc."[17] without regard to the qualification mentioned in Article 2, namely, the marketing or representation of such products as partial or total replacement of breast-milk. This qualification is a very important test as to whether or not a milk product could be subject to Article 2 of the International Code. As Dr. Mork said in the other part of his statement cited by the Nestlé Instructions,

> products other than bona fide breasts-milk substitutes, including infant formula, were covered by the Code only when they were ' marketed or otherwise represented to be suitable for use as a partial or total replacements for breast-milk'.[18]

It would be worthwhile mentioning here what an IBFAN Consultant said on this point. Referring to Nestlé's Instructions, the Consultant said:

> (a) Article 2 of the International Code applies to breast-milk substitutes, including infant formula, as well as other milk products, foods and beverages, which would fall under the heading of breast-milk substitutes when marketed or otherwise represented as a partial or total replacement of breast-milk. The Nestlé Instructions apply to infant formula only. This considerably narrows the scope of the Instructions.[19]

Consequently, any such product would be subject to the provisions of the International Code, whatever may be said by their producers, as long as they are marketed or otherwise represented to be suitable for use as a partial or total replacement of breast-milk.

(ii) Milk products, foods and beverages, including bottle-fed complementary foods

This is the second category of food products covered by the International Code. This category includes cow's milk, fruit juices, cereals and vegetables and so on,

---

17 See above note 13, p. 25.
18 See the International Code, Annex 3, p. 34.
19 See *Does the Nestlé Report Comply with the International Code – A legal Evaluation of the Nestlé Report by a Consultant for IBFAN and GIFA, 2000*, p. 15.

which are considered as breast-milk substitutes only under certain conditions. These conditions are that such products are "marketed or otherwise represented to be suitable...for use as a partial or total replacement of breast-milk." If, for example, a milk product is promoted, sold or represented as suitable to replace mother's milk, then it becomes a breast-milk substitute covered by the International Code. This is so, irrespective of whether or not it is a partial or total replacement, and with or without modification, and by implication, whether or not it is actually suitable for that purpose. If they are not represented or marketed as such, then the International Code will not apply. The same applies to foods, beverages, and bottle-fed complementary foods. This point was made clear by the representative of the Executive Board, Dr. Mork, to the WHA during the discussion of the Fourth Draft in May 1981. He said that

> products other than *bona fide* breast-milk substitutes, including infant formula, were covered by the Code only when they were "marketed or otherwise represented to be suitable for use as a partial or total replacement for breast milk". Thus the Code's reference to products used as partial or total replacements for breast milk was not intended to apply to complementary foods <u>unless</u> those foods were actually marketed (as breast-milk substitutes, including infant formula) as suitable for the partial or total replacement of breast-milk. So long as the manufacturers and distributors of the products did not promote them as being suitable as partial or total replacements for breast -milk, the Code's provisions concerning limitations on advertising and other promotional activities did not apply to those products.[20]

The use of the qualifying term "bottle-fed" insofar as complementary foods are concerned, seems to be intended to distinguish between spoon-fed and "bottle-fed" complementary foods. The latter are caught by Article 2 of the Code, because they interfere with breast-feeding and can be mistaken for breast-milk substitutes, which is not the case with the former. During the discussions of the September Consultation 1980, the Philippine Delegate asked about "those supplements which were not given through bottle". Mr. Heyward, UNICEF, replied that

> ... in general supplements or complements that were not fed through the bottle would not be mistaken for use as a breast-milk substitute and therefore in the interest of not going too far could be left out.[21]

What is the position when such foods are not marketed or represented as a partial or total replacement of breast-milk, but are *perceived* and used as such? For example, if a certain fruit juice has a baby picture on the container and is placed, intentionally, on a shelf containing breast-milk substitutes, a mother may perceive it to be one of those products and may buy it to use in feeding her infant because of that. The position is not clear under the International Code, as the latter speaks only of marketing or representation of such products as suitable breast-milk substitutes. Therefore, it could be argued that in the

---

20 See *WHO Doc. WHA 34/1981/REC/3*, p.188, (emphasis in the original).
21 See September Consultation 1980, tape 18, pp.1-2.

absence of marketing or representation, the fruit juice in the above example would not be subject to the Code. On the other hand, it could be argued that the intentional placing of a fruit juice, with a baby picture on the container, on a shelf, normally used to display breast-milk substitutes, could be considered as a measure designed to represent it as one belonging to that group of products. And as such, it could amount to a representation of that product as a breast-milk substitute. If so, then it would be subject to the International Code. However, it might be advisable for States implementing the International Code to cover the notion of "perceived and used as a breast-milk substitute", in their legal instruments if they intend to include this notion. After all, the International Code was adopted as a "minimum requirement."[22]It would be appropriate here to refer to the Hague Meeting, held under the auspices of WHO in 1991. The participants in that Meeting recommended that

> when adopting measures to give effect to the International Code, national authorities should use clear definitions.... The scope of these measures should include all products that are perceived and used as breast-milk substitutes, whether or not suitable for this purpose, and whatever the age of children concerned.[23]

The question may be raised: Does Article 2 of the International Code place an age-limit for its application? This question is raised because of the reference in the Code's preamble to "four to six months of age"[24] of the infant and a similar reference in the statement of the representatives of the Executive Board[25] to the

---

22 See above pp.43-44.
23 See In-depth Review and Evaluation of National Action Taken to Give Effect to the International Code of Marketing of Breast-milk Substitutes, held at the Hague, 30 September–3 October 1991, *WHO Doc. WHO/NUT/MCH/91.2*, p.4, paragraph 11. The recommendations of the Hague Meeting are also reproduced in Forty-Fifth World Health Assembly, Geneva, 4-14 May 1992, WHO Doc. *WHA45/1992/REC/1* (hereinafter referred to as" WHO Doc.WHA45/1992/REC/1"), p.230, paragraph 124 *et seq.* In fact, some national measures do include the notion of "perceived as a breast-milk substitute"; see for examples, Art.2 of the draft Jordanian Code, Art.2 of the draft Omani Code 1995 and the Tanzanian The Food (Control of Quality) (Marketing of Breast-milk Substitutes and Designated Products) Regulations 1994 (hereinafter referred to as the "Tanzanian Regulations 1994"), sec.3.
24 See eighth preambular paragraph of the International Code: "...It is important for infants to receive appropriate complementary foods, usually when the infant reaches four to six months of age..."
25 Dr. Mork said: "During the first four to six months of life, breast-milk alone was usually adequate to sustain the normal infant's nutritional requirements....Any other food...intended for infants, and given after this initial period, could no longer be considered as a replacement for breast milk....Such foods only complemented breast-milk...and were thus referred to in the draft Code as complementary foods." See above note 20, p.188. It might be interesting to point out that in two resolutions adopted by the WHA in 1992 and 1994, and again in the context of complementary food for infants, the Assembly used the expression "from the age of about six months". See Resolution WHA 45.34 (May 1992), fifth preambular paragraph, and Resolution WHA 47.5 (9 May 1994), operative paragraph 2(1) (d). See also the statement of Dr. Behar, former Chief of Nutrition unit in WHO: "...after the age of 4-6 months, foods that supplemented breast-milk became necessary, though breast-feeding should, of course,

Thirty-fourth WHA. As stated earlier, six months exclusive breast-feeding is the health policy declared by the WHA in Resolution 54.2, in 2001. It is submitted that there is nothing in Article 2 that can be read as placing any age-limit to its application to the marketing and related practices of breast-milk substitutes and other products covered by it. The Code applies as long as any particular food product is marketed, or represented for use as a breast-milk substitute, without any age-limit. This approach is reasonable and is in line with the spirit and policy of the International Code. It is, also, practical, for it is difficult to decide the age-limit of the period of breast-feeding in a legal instrument of this nature for all societies. Each society has its own way of determining the period of breast-feeding, for example, in a Muslim society this period is two years, according to the Holy Koran.[26] The references to four to six months mentioned above have to be understood in their context. They were made in connection with the age at which complementary food may be introduced. The position of WHO and UNICEF is that Article 2

> ...applies regardless of the age of the infant.[27]

It might be appropriate to mention that the WHO Secretariat, on another occasion, repeated its position that the International Code places no age-limit to its applicability to the marketing and distribution of breast-milk substitutes.[28]

Further support for this standpoint can be derived from the decision of the Supreme Court of the Philippines in 2007. In a dispute between the health authorities and some infant-food manufacturers concerning the implementation of the Philippines Milk Code in national regulations (implementing the International Code), after quoting Section 3 of the Philippines Milk Code (Scope of the Code, which is identical with Article 2 of the International Code), the Court held that

> Clearly, the coverage of the Milk Code is not dependent on the age of the child but on the kind of product being marketed to the public.

The Court went on to say that

> Evidently, as long as what is being marketed falls within the scope of the Milk Code as provided in Section 3, then it can be subject to regulation pursuant to [the] said law, even if the product is to be used by children over 12 months .[29]

---

be continued." See *WHO Document WHA 33/1980/REC/3*, p.93.

26 The Holy Koran says: "the mothers shall give suck to their offspring for two complete years, for those who desire to complete the term". Sura II, Al-Baquarah, verse 232.

27 See WHO/UNICEF *Notes on the International Code of Marketing of Breast-milk Substitutes*, WHO/UNICEF/IC July 1982, (hereinafter referred to as the "WHO/UNICEF Notes 1982") p.2, paragraph 7, (emphasis in original).

28 This position of the WHO Secretariat is reflected in a Note for the Record of a meeting held in WHO with representatives of Nutricia (a Dutch infant-food manufacturer), dated 16 November 1984, p.2, second paragraph.

29 See Decision of the Supreme Court of the Republic of the Philippines, EN BANC, G.R. No.

(iii) Feeding bottles and teats

Feeding bottles and teats are the third category of products, whose marketing and other practices related thereto, are governed by the International Code. Feeding bottles and teats are not food products, but they are tools which are used for, or may be identified with, bottle-feeding. Any of the activities which constitutes marketing under the International Code relating to feeding bottles or teats is subject to the requirements of the Code. For example, a producer of feeding bottles can sell his products in the market, but he cannot promote them in a health care facility, because Article 6.2 of the Code does not allow this practice.[30] The rationale for this attitude is that such a practice may harm breast-feeding, in that the free marketing of such a product would draw attention to, or may encourage, bottle-feeding. It may be interesting to refer to a case of advertising, which actually took place a few years ago. There was an advertisement for a microwave oven, with a feeding bottle next to it, presumably to show that it can be used for warming the breast-milk substitute without harming the bottle. The distributor wrote to WHO asking if such an advertisement would be in conformity with the International Code. The Director of the WHO Legal Office had no difficulty in describing it as a form of promotion of bottle-feeding. Referring to Articles 2 and 5 of the International Code, he said:

> ... The publication of a feeding bottle, next to a micro-wave oven constitutes a form of promotion of a product within the scope of the International Code, to the detriment of breast-feeding.[31]

It may be concluded that the reason for regulating the marketing of products covered by Article 2 of the International Code is the special circumstances surrounding their use, and the impact thereof on breast-feeding and the harmful effect from their improper use on the health of infants. As the drafters of the International Code clearly stated:

> ... in view of the vulnerability of infants in the early months of life and the risks involved in inappropriate feeding practices, including the unnecessary and improper use of breast-milk substitutes, the marketing of breast-milk substitutes requires special treatment, which makes usual marketing practices unsuitable for these products.[32]

173034, October 9, 2007, pp. 25 and 26.

30 On Article 6.2, see below Chapter VIII.

31 See a WHO internal memorandum from Director, LEG, to Director, INF, dated 13 February 1991, attachment, second paragraph.

32 See penultimate preambular paragraph of the International Code.

2. QUALITY OF PRODUCTS COVERED BY THE INTERNATION-AL CODE

The quality of products covered by the International Code is of concern to it and is subject to its requirements, because of its importance to the protection of the health of infants. Therefore, the Code requires those products to be of high quality, and it particularly requires food products covered by it to meet standards recommended by the Codex Alimentarius Commission and also the Codex Code of Hygienic Practice for Foods for Infants and Children, when sold or otherwise distributed.[33]

> Codex standards contain requirements for food aimed at ensuring for the consumer a sound, wholesome food product free from adulteration correctly labelled and presented.[34]

On the other hand, the Codex Code of Hygienic Practice contains the minimum hygienic requirements for the handling (including production, preparation, processing, packaging, etc.) of infant foods to ensure a safe, sound and wholesome product.[35] These requirements are intended to provide a reasonable measure of protection for the health of the consumer (the infant). Furthermore, an importing country of infant formula can insist that the imported infant formula should meet the Codex standards, and if otherwise it could reject the products.[36]

It is significant to point out that in 2004, powdered infant formula was contaminated with E. sakazakii and salmonella, which caused infection and illness in infants. The WHA was very much concerned about the situation and adopted a resolution requesting the Codex Alimentarius Commission

> urgently to complete work currently under way on addressing the risk of microbiological contamination of powdered infant formula and establish appropriate microbiological criteria or standards related to E. Sakazakii and other relevant microorganisms in powdered infant formula; and to provide guidance on safe handling and on warning messages on product packaging.[37]

Furthermore, in 2008 in China 50,000 children were admitted to hospital suffering from contamination of infant formula, with some cases of death. According to Professor Anna Coutsoudis, Professor Hoosen M. Coovadia, and Judith King,

---

33 See Art. 10 of the International Code. On the Codex Alimentarius Commission, see below Chapter XII..

34 See paragraph 3 of the General Principles of the Codex Alimentarius, *Codex Alimentarius Commission, procedural Manual,* 15th edn. (2005), p.31.

35 See *CAC/RCP21-1979,* paragraph 1, see also Sections I and II of the Code of Hygienic Practice for Powdered Formulae for Infants and Young Children, *CAC/REC66-2008.*

36 For details see below Chapter XII.

37 See Resolution WHA 58.32, operative paragraph 2 (3), 25 May 2005, WHO Doc. *WHA58/2005/REC/3* p.136.

> ... mothers in China unwittingly [fed] their babies formula milk that was con-
> taminated by a potentially toxic chemical, melamine.... The epidemic has spread
> to neighbouring countries in Southeast Asia, and melamine has been detected in
> formula milks... in the USA and South Africa. The source of the epidemic is the de-
> liberate adulteration of formula milks with melamine by commercial firms in China
> to mislead consumers into believing that the product is rich in proteins.[38]

It would seem that

> the full extent of the epidemic might not yet be known, since toxic effects are often
> difficult to detect. The clinical effects are mainly gastrointestinal and renal (leading
> to obstructive uropathy and acute renal failure).[39]

So far as feeding bottles and teats are concerned, it would appear that no international standards exist regarding their quality, though there may be some national regulations in some countries. So far as teats are concerned, some trace
elements of potentially cancerous substances may be present in both rubber
and silicone teats.[40] In the summer of 1997, 30,000 teats (tétines Rémond) were,
discreetly, withdrawn from the French market, because a French consumers
organization (Que choisir) had tested the teats and found them to contain some
cancerous substances.[41] Subsequently, the French secrétaire d'Etat en charge de
la consommation ordered the seizure of four models of teats (tetines Rémond),
suspected of being contaminated by a cancerous substance, and their withdrawal from the market.[42] As regards feeding bottles, it has been reported that
a group of major producers of those products announced in 1991 the creation
of the World Association of Bottles and Teats Manufacturers (WBT). "The objectives of WBT are to oversee the quality and design of [their] products ...."[43]
But nothing appears to have been developed yet. WBT seems to distinguish between developing and developed countries, where the marketing policies and
distribution practices of their members are concerned.[44] Of course, neither the
International Code nor the WHA has made, or accepted, such a distinction.

---

38 See "The Breastmilk brand : promotion of child survival in the face of formula-marketing",
    The Lancet, Vol. 374 August 1, 2009, p. 423. The families of four children poisoned in China
    by tainted milk in 2008 have sued Fonterra, a cooperative based in New Zealand, which is
    said to be responsible for the contamination of the milk, in Hong Kong for compensation,
    but the case was rejected largely on jurisdictional grounds. See *The Economist*, June 5th-11th
    2010, p.72.
39 Ibid.
40 See *J'achète mieux*, (November 1996), p.10.
41 See *Le Monde* (24-25 August 1997).
42 See ibid.(2 September 1997).
43 See Report of the Director-General on Infant and Young Child Nutrition (Progress and
    Evaluation Report; and Status of Implementation of the International Code of Marketing of
    Breast-milk Substitutes) (A45/28 – 6 April 1992), *WHO Doc., WHA45/1992/REC/1*, p.234,
    paragraph 139.
44 See ibid., paragraph 140.

3. AVAILABILITY OF PRODUCTS COVERED BY THE INTERNATIONAL CODE

So far as the availability of products covered by the International Code is concerned, they are also of concern to the Code, because of their impact on breast-feeding and possible harm to it, if they are left unregulated. For example, the International Code does not permit the distribution of samples of breast-milk substitutes to mothers[45] and restricts the donation or low-price sales of breast-milk substitutes.[46] In addition, the Code requires a statement on the label of each container of breast-milk substitutes to the effect that the product should be used only on the advice of a health worker as to the need for its use and the proper method of use[47]. Thus, the Code regulates the availability of breast-milk substitutes in the manner specified in its provisions.

The free availability of breast-milk substitutes would, probably, promote their use to the detriment of breast-feeding. A case in point may be worthwhile mentioning. While the author was on a mission, some years ago, to a Member State of WHO, the Islamic Republic of Iran, with a predominantly Muslim population, for the implementation of the International Code, he visited the head of the medical administration of a large province in the south-west of the country, which has a large rural population. He asked him about the prevalence and duration of breast-feeding in his province. The head of the medical administration replied that breast-feeding was very poor, because the great majority of mothers come to his health centres and ask, and obtain easily and without charge, breast-milk substitutes. This easy availability, said the head of the administration, has done a great deal of harm to breast-feeding in that province. This shows that even in a predominantly Muslim society, whose teachings enjoin mothers to breast-feed their infant for two full years, the easy availability of breast-milk substitutes can do a great deal of harm to breast-feeding. Another example is the situation in Iraq during the 1990s, when Iraq was under UN economic sanctions, after the invasion of Kuwait.[48] In that situation, the availability of powdered milk, as part of the family ration under the regime of Oil-for-Food Programme,[49] did a great deal of harm to breast-feeding.

---

45 See Art. 5.2 of the International Code; see also below Chapter VII.

46 See Art. 6.6 of the Code; see also below Chapter VIII.

47 See Art. 9.2(c) of the International Code; see also below Chapter XI.

48 See Security Council Resolution 661(1990), UN Dc. S/RES7661 (1990), 6 August 1990. Most of the resolutions of the Security Council concerning the Iraq-Kuwait crisis are to be found in *The Kuwait Crisis: Basic Documents* (1991), *Cambridge International Documents Series*, Vol. I, and *The United Nations Iraq-Kuwait Conflict* 1990-1996, United Nations Department of Public Information, New York, (1996).

49 Security Council Resolution 687 (1991), 3 April 1991, and Resolution 706 (1991), 15 August 1991.

4. INFORMATION CONCERNING THE USE OF PRODUCTS COVERED BY THE INTERNATIONAL CODE

Article 2 of the Code applies to information concerning the use of products covered by it. It follows that any information relating to the use of a product covered by the Code has to comply with the requirements of its provisions. For example, if a manufacturer of a breast-milk substitute produces a pamphlet relating to its use, which is intended to reach health professionals, this pamphlet should contain only "scientific and factual matters", as required by Article 7.2. If it contains some promotional matters, then it would be incompatible with Article 7.2.

The International Code regulates the question of information relating to the use of breast-milk substitutes, and insists that information on infant and young child feeding should be objective and consistent.[50] Furthermore, the Code requires informational and educational materials to contain a number of points relating to the use of breast-milk substitutes and warning about the danger to health from improper or unnecessary use.[51] Moreover, the Code allows manufacturers and distributors of products covered by it to provide health professionals with information of "scientific and factual nature" relating to those products.[52] In addition, the labelling of those products is another area where the Code specifies the type of information required on each container of the product.[53] Those requirements are designed to ensure correct and appropriate use of breast-milk substitutes, and to avoid unnecessary and improper use. They also contain information regarding the superiority of breast-feeding, the health hazards of improper or unnecessary use of breast-milk substitutes, and the financial implications thereof. This information is intended to protect the health of infants, and to enable the mother to decide whether to breast-feed, or bottle-feed, her infant. All this is in line with the aim of the Code and for its achievement.

Some Member States of WHO have enlarged the material scope of the International Code, in its implementation at the national level, to include complementary foods,[54] infant foods,[55] and infant milk foods[56]. Some other Members,

---

50 See Art. 4.1 of the International Code; see also below Chapter VI.

51 See Art. 4.2 of the International Code.

52 See Art.7.2 of the International Code; see also below Chapter VIII.

53 See Art. 9.2; see also below Chapter XI.

54 See Bahraini Law 1995, Art.2, Bangladeshi Breast-Milk Substitutes (Regulations of Marketing) Ordinance, 1984, (hereinafter referred to as the "Bangladeshi Ordinance 1984"), sec. 2(a); and the Nepalese Breast-milk Substitution Act, 1992, sec.2 (d).

55 See the Indian Infant Milk Substitutes Act, 1992, sec. 2(f) and (g); and the Tanzanian Food Regulations 1994, Part I, sec.3(a).

56 See the Sri Lankan Code for the Promotion of Breast-feeding, sec. 1; the IBFAN Model Law does not contain a scope provision. However, the products intended to be covered by it are included in Sec. 2, on Definitions; its paragraph 5 reads: "Designated Products", means (a) infant formula; (b) any other product marketed or otherwise represented as suitable

in preparing national measures implementing the International Code, followed the scheme of its material scope,[57] while others did the same, but gave the Minister of Health the authority to add a new category of breast-milk substitutes, if the need arose, to those already mentioned in the national measures.[58] Of course, every State Member is entitled to widen the scope of its national legislation, regulations or any other measure, when it implements the International Code, for two reasons: (a) as a sovereign State, it can do so, in the absence of any constraints imposed by international law or accepted by it, nor are there constraints in the International Code and subsequent WHA resolutions. (b) The International Code, as we have seen earlier, was adopted as a "minimum requirement" and was the result of a compromise reached under difficult conditions. Therefore, Member States can certainly go beyond that "minimum requirement" in their implementation of the International Code. But caution should be exercised in this respect, as too wide a scope may cause long delays in the adoption of the national measures, open the instrument to criticism, and perhaps even opposition, from the infant-food industry and may not necessarily serve the cause of breast-feeding. A pragmatic approach, based on Article 2 of the International Code, with some new breast-milk substitutes added to the

---

for feeding infants; (c) follow-up formula; (d) feeding bottles, teats, pacifiers; and (e) such other product as the Minister of Health may, by Notice in the Official Gazette, declare to be a "designated product" for purposes of this Act". See Sokol, op. cit., p.134.. In a training seminar on the implementation of the International Code, organized by IBFAN for some Member States of EMRO, the definition of "designated products", contained in the Model Law, adopted at the seminar, goes even further in enlarging its scope. It reads:
"Section 2 – Definitions
For purposes of this Act
(5)   "Designated product" means
(a)   any milk food promoted for the use of a child below two years of age;
(b)   any packaged food or drink promoted for the use of a child below two years of age, or which is commonly used for the feeding of such a child;
(c)   feeding bottles, teats, pacifiers and nipple shields;
(d)   such other products of a similar nature as the Government may, by Notice in the Official Gazette, declare to be a "designated product" for purposes of this Act."

57 For examples see Brazilian Marketing Regulations Art. 2; Guatemalan Law 1983, Art.1. The Guatemalan Rules for the Marketing of Breast-milk Substitutes, 1987, (hereinafter referred to as the "Guatemalan Rules 1987"), enlarged the scope to cover "foods and dairy and non-dairy products which are used as complementary foods to feed infants...." See Art. 1(b) of those Rules; see also the Kenyan Code 1983, Art. 2; and the Philippines Code of Marketing, sec. 3. The European Directive has a narrow scope; it applies to the compositional and labelling of infant formulae and follow-on formulae, see Commission Directive of 14 May 1991 on infant formulae and follow-on formulae, Art. 1. The Directive is to be found in the *Official Journal of the European Communities*, L 175/37 (4.7.91), pp.35-39.

58 See the draft Jordanian Code 1994, Art. 2; the draft Syrian Code on the Protection and Promotion of Breast-feeding 1993 (hereinafter referred to as the "draft Syrian Code 1993"), Art. 2; the draft Moroccan Code on the Protection and Promotion of Breast-feeding, 1993, (hereinafter referred to as the "draft Moroccan Code 1993") Art.2; and the draft Omani Code 1995, Art. 2.

list, coupled with the authority given to the ministry of health, or another competent authority, to add new categories of breast-milk substitutes, as and when developed, would be the preferred approach. After all, the International Code has been intended to deal with breast-milk substitutes, only.

CHAPTER V

DEFINITIONS OF THE INTERNATIONAL CODE

I. DEFINITIONS

The International Code contains its own definitions, which cover certain important terms frequently used in its various provisions. Definitions in a legal instrument can be described as agreed meanings of the terms used in that instrument and for its own purposes. The drafters of an instrument at the international plane are free to choose the meanings they wish to attribute to the terms of the instrument, and thus can make them applicable specifically to that instrument alone. For that purpose, expressions such as, "for the purposes of the International Health Regulations",[1] or "for the purposes of the present Convention"[2] may be used. The International Code follows that pattern in its Article 3, which reads as follows:

> "For the purposes of this Code:
>
> "Breast-milk substitute" means any food being marketed or otherwise represented as a partial or total replacement for breast-milk, whether or not suitable for that purpose.
>
> "Complementary food" means any food, whether manufactured or locally prepared, suitable as a complement to breast-milk or to infant formula, when either becomes insufficient to satisfy the nutritional requirements of the infant. Such food is also commonly called "weaning food" or "breast-milk supplement".
>
> "Container" means any form of packaging of products for sale as a normal retail unit, including wrappers.
>
> "Distributor" means a person, corporation or any other entity in the public or private sector engaged in the business (whether directly or indirectly) of marketing at the wholesale or retail level a product within the scope of this Code. A "primary distributor" is a manufacturer's sales agent, representative, national distributor or broker.

---

1   See Art. 1 of the WHO *International Health Regulations* (2005), 2nd edn., p. 6, which have replaced the International Health Regulations (1969), 3rd Annotated Edition (1983); for details concerning the legal nature of these Regulations see above pp.27-29.

2   See Art. 2(1) of the Vienna Convention on the Law of Treaties, 1969, and Art. 2(1) of the Vienna Convention on the Law of Treaties between States and International Organizations or between International Organizations, 1986.

"Health care system" means governmental, non-governmental or private institutions or organizations engaged, directly or indirectly, in health care for mothers, infants and pregnant women; and nurseries or child-care institutions. It also includes health workers in private practice. For the purposes of this Code, the health care system does not include pharmacies or other established sales outlets.

"Health worker" means a person working in a component of such a health care system,whether professional or non-professional, including voluntary, unpaid workers.

"Infant formula" means a breast-milk substitute formulated industrially in accordance with applicable Codex Alimentarius standards, to satisfy the normal nutritional requirements of infants up to between four and six months of age, and adapted to their physiological characteristics. Infant formula may also be prepared at home, in which case it is described as "home-prepared".

"Label" means any tag, brand, mark, pictorial or other descriptive matter written, printed, stencilled, marked, embossed or impressed on, or attached to, a container (see above) of any products within the scope of this Code.

"Manufacturer" means a corporation or other entity in the public or private sector engaged in the business or function (whether directly or through an agent or through an entity controlled by or under contract with it) of manufacturing a product within the scope of this Code.

"Marketing" means product promotion, distribution, selling, advertising, product public relations, and information services.

"Marketing personnel" means any persons whose functions involve the marketing of a product or products coming within the scope of this Code.

"Samples" means single or small quantities of a product provided without cost.

"Supplies" means quantities of a product provided for use over an extended period, free or at a low price, for social purposes, including those provided to families in need.

The four drafts of the International Code contained a provision on definitions, although their number and the place of the provision containing them differed from one draft to another.[3] However, the Third and Fourth Drafts contained the largest number of definitions (13 definitions).[4]

---

3   See Art. 8 of the First Draft, Art. 10 of the Second Draft, Art. 9 of the Third Draft, and Art. 3 of the Fourth Draft.

4   It might be interesting to note that the IBFAN Model Law contains 21 definitions (Sec. 2), the Bangladeshi Ordinance 1984, contains five definitions (Sec. 2), the Brazilian Regulations 1992, contain 13 definitions (Art. 3), the Directive of the Commission of the EEC (now EU) 1991, contains four definitions (Art. 1(2)), the Guatemalan Law 1983, contains six definitions (Art. 2), the Indian Infant Milk Substitutes Act 1992, contains nine definitions (Sec. 2), to give but a few examples. ICIFI proposed, in its comments on the Third Draft, the inclusion of 16 definitions in the Fourth Draft; see ICIFI, *Draft 3 – Comments and Recommendations*, September 1980, pp.6-13. The Nestlé Instructions, as mentioned earlier, limit breast-milk substitutes to infant formula only; see above pp.70-71.

An attempt to explain the definitions of the International Code shall now be made.

1. Breast-milk substitute

The Code defines "breast-milk substitute" as

> any food being marketed or otherwise represented as a partial or total replacement for breast-milk, whether or not suitable for that purpose.

This is a very important definition, because the application or otherwise of the International Code turns on whether the product in question is, or is not, a breast-milk substitute. Accordingly, any food product, when sold, distributed, advertised or promoted, or otherwise represented[5] as a partial or total replacement for mother's milk, becomes a breast-milk substitute, and as such will be subject to the Code. This is so irrespective of the name or designation of the product, and irrespective of whether or not the product is suitable for use as a replacement of mother's milk. There is also no age-limit to the application of the definition. For example, if mineral water is advertised by anybody as a partial replacement for mother's milk, to be used for infant feeding whatever the age of the infant, it will be considered as a breast-milk substitute subject to the Code.

What is decisive in the definition is the function attributed to the food product in question. Therefore, the test is functional. If the function is to replace mother's milk (breast-milk), whether partially or totally, then the product falls within the definition of breast-milk substitute, regardless of whether or not the product can, in reality, do so.

This definition is rather wide, and is intended to protect breast-feeding, in that the Code governs any marketing activity or practice relating to any food product which may be represented as an alternative to breast-milk and thus divert the mother from using her own milk. During the discussions of the definitions of the Code at the August Consultation 1980, there was some disagreement between the representatives of the infant-food industry and those of some of the NGOs concerning the definition of the term "breast-milk substitute." A working group was established, with representation from the industry and NGO's, in order to harmonize the divergent points of view, but no agreement could be reached on the question.[6]

---

5   On representation of products as breast-milk substitutes, see above Chapter IV.

6   See August Consultation 1980, p.15, paragraph 52.2 .The working group was composed of representatives of ICIFI, the International Union of Nutritional Sciences and ICCR, with the assistance of two senior staff members of the WHO and UNICEF Secretariats.

2. Complementary food

The Code defines "complementary food" as

> any food, whether manufactured or locally prepared, suitable as a complement to breast-milk or to infant formula, when either becomes insufficient to satisfy the nutritional requirements of the infant. Such food is also commonly called "weaning food" or "breast-milk supplement".

Accordingly, any food, whether produced in a factory or home-made, which is suitable to complement mother's milk or a breast-milk substitute, when the latter is being used, is considered as complementary food under the Code. It is to be noted that the definition requires the food to be "suitable", as a complement to breast-milk or breast-milk substitutes; whereas in the definition of breast-milk substitute, suitability of the product for the purpose is not relevant. Therefore, if a food product is *not suitable* to complement breast-milk or breast-milk substitutes, it cannot qualify as complementary food under the Code.

Here again the test is functional. Does the food product in question complement breast-milk or its substitutes? If the answer is yes, then it is a complementary food, and if the answer is no, then it is not a complementary food. Furthermore, the definition does not contain an age-limit as regards the introduction of complementary foods. However, the definition, by implication, suggests that such foods can be introduced when either breast-milk or a breast-milk substitute "becomes insufficient to satisfy the nutritional requirements of the infant."

It is to be noted that complementary foods are not subject to any particular restrictions under the Code, except when they are bottle-fed and are marketed or otherwise represented to be suitable for use as a replacement of breast-milk.[7]

3. Container

The Code defines "container" as

> any form of packaging of products for sale as a normal retail unit, including wrappers.

This definition relates to the exterior of the products covered by the Code, and the form used to cover such products. It is relevant to the labelling of the product, as Article 9 of the Code requires a number of points to be put on the container, or a label attached to it[8]. This definition is borrowed from the Codex Alimentarius, with a slightly different wording[9]. It covers tins, packets, wrap-

---

7   See Art. 2 of the International Code; see also Dr. Mock's statement above, p.72.

8   On labelling, see below Chapter XI.

9   See the Codex International Standard for the Labelling of Prepackaged Foods (1969), *CAC/RS1-1969*, p.5, paragraph 1. States participants at the September Consultation 1980 were aware of the fact that some of the Code's definitions were borrowed from the Codex Alimentarius; see for example the statement of the Canadian Delegate, September

pers, boxes, cartons, cans and any form, used in whatever size or shape to cover a breast-milk substitute offered for sale as an ordinary retail unit.

4. Distributor

The Code defines "distributor" as

> a person, corporation or any other entity in the public or private sector engaged in the business (whether directly or indirectly) of marketing at the wholesale or retail level a product within the scope of this Code. A "primary distributor" is a manufacturer's sales agent, representative, national distributor or broker.

This definition is wider than the dictionary definition of "distributor", which reads:

> "distributor" means a person or thing that distributes; an agent who supplies[10].

It is intended, it would appear, to be so wide, in order to cover various types of persons and entities engaged in the marketing of products covered by the Code, whether at the wholesale or retail level. Therefore, it applies to any ordinary person, a company and any other entity, whether in the public or private sector, or public/private sector, as long as it is engaged in the marketing of any product covered by the Code. The term marketing has to be understood in the meaning of the term given by the Code[11].

The test under the definition is therefore the engagement in the business of any activity which constitutes marketing under the Code, be it direct or indirect, at the retail or wholesale level, e.g., selling breast-milk substitutes, promoting them, distributing them and so on. The definition also covers, specifically, sales agents of the manufacturers, their representatives, as well as national distributors or brokers. Such persons would be covered by the definition, in any case, without any specific reference to them, as long as they are engaged in one of the marketing activities subject to the Code. Perhaps the specific reference to such persons might have been intended to avoid leaving any gap in the definition, since the Code regulates some of the activities of distributors and imposes certain obligations on them.[12]

5. Health care system

According to the Code "health care system" means

> governmental, non-governmental or private institutions or organizations engaged, directly or indirectly, in health care for mothers, infants and pregnant women; and

---

Consultation 1980, Transcription of Tapes, tape 36, p.1.

10 See The *Concise Oxford Dictionary*, 9th edn., p.394.

11 See below p.89.

12 For details, see below Chapter VII.

nurseries or child-care institutions. It also includes health workers in private practice. For the purposes of this Code, the health care system does not include pharmacies or other established sales outlets.

The definition is very wide, indeed, and covers any institution or organization, be it governmental, non-governmental or private, which provides health care for the mother, the pregnant woman or the infant. Accordingly, the definition covers hospitals, health centres, clinics, maternities, paediatric wards, obstetric centres and out-patient departments, and so on, as long as they provide health care to the mother, pregnant woman or infant. The test therefore is whether or not such an institution or organization provides health care to any of the persons just mentioned, directly or indirectly. If it does, then it is a health care system, whatever name might have been given to it, and as such it will be subject to all the provisions of the Code. If not, then it is not a health care system, and as such it falls outside the scope of the Code.

Health care includes treatment, advice, check ups, tests and so on. It might be interesting to point out that IBFAN's Model Law includes in its definition of "health care facility" institutions or organizations providing "health care education".[13] This definition is much wider than the Code's definition, and could include schools and educational institutions, if their curricula provide health care education to their students.

It is to be noted that while the definition of health care system includes a general reference to institutions and organizations, it refers, at the same time, to specific facilities, namely, nurseries, child-care institutions and surgeries of health workers in private practice, which the Code describes as " health worker in private practice." The definition also excludes certain types of facilities from its scope, namely, pharmacies and other established sales outlets, such as shops.

6. Health worker

The Code defines "health worker" as

a person working in a component of such a health care system, whether professional or non-professional, including voluntary, unpaid workers.

Accordingly, any person working in any component of an organization or institution providing health care to mothers, pregnant women or infants, as well as those facilities specifically mentioned in the definition of health care system, is a health worker. This is so whether or not he is a professional health worker, e.g., a doctor, or a chemist, non-professional, e.g., a ward attendant, and whether paid or unpaid. Therefore, such persons are subject to the provisions applicable to health workers.[14] Health workers are subject to certain obligations under

---

13 See Sec. 2(8), see Sokol, op. cit., p.135.
14 See below Chapter IX.

the International Code, and they can play an important role in the promotion of breast-feeding, or its discouragement.

7. Infant formula

The Code defines "infant formula" as

> a breast-milk substitute formulated industrially in accordance with applicable Codex Alimentarius standards, to satisfy the normal nutrional requirements of infants up to between four and six months of age, and adapted to their physiological characteristics. Infant formula may also be prepared at home, in which case it is described as "home-prepared".

Accordingly, infant formula is one category of breast-milk substitutes, prepared in accordance with the applicable Codex [15] standards or at home. The definition covers, and the Code applies to, infant formula satisfying the nutritional needs of infants up to six months, irrespective of designation or name. The expression "between four and six months of age" has now been clarified by the WHA in 2001, when it urged Member States

> to strengthen activities and develop new approaches to protect, promote and support exclusive breastfeeding for six months as a global public health recommendation....[16]

The wording of the definition contains nothing to suggest a distinction between a certain type of infant formula and another, or between a certain infant and another.

As mentioned earlier there was some disagreement between the representatives of the infant-food industry and those of some NGOs at the August Consultation 1980 in relation to the definition of infant formula.[17]

8. Label

The Code defines "label" as

> any tag, brand, mark, pictorial or other descriptive matter, written, printed, stencilled, marked, embossed or impressed on, or attached to, a container (see above) of any products within the scope of this Code.

This is a very wide definition of label and is borrowed from the Codex Alimentarius[18], with slight modification. This may be justified by the importance attached by the drafters to the labelling of products covered by the Code, and what should be put on the label. Any picture, brand, mark, tag or any descriptive matter, irrespective of the way it is made, on a container of any breast-milk

---

15 On the Codex Alimentarius standards, see below Chapter XII.

16 See Resolution WHA54.2, operative paragraph 2 (4), 18 May 2001.

17 See above note 6.

18 See above note 9.

substitute, feeding bottle or teat, in whatever form, constitutes a label, which has to comply with the provisions of the Code.[19]

9. Manufacturer

The Code defines "manufacturer" as

> a corporation or other entity in the public or private sector engaged in the business or function (whether directly or through an agent or through an entity controlled by or under contract with it) of manufacturing a product within the scope of this Code.

Accordingly, any company or other entity, whether in the public or private sector, engaged in the business or function of producing breast-milk substitutes, feeding bottles or teats is a manufacturer. The definition appears to exclude individuals from its scope, unlike the definition of "distributor", which covers individuals. On the other hand, there is no reason why individuals cannot be manufacturers of a product covered by the Code, even though in practice, manufacturers of products covered by the Code are companies. For an individual could be covered by the term "entity", which means, according to *The Concise Oxford Dictionary* "1. a thing with distinct existence, as opposed to a quality or relation".[20] Furthermore, the definition covers products made by an agent or an entity controlled by the corporation in question, or under its control, which amounts to an indirect business or function. Therefore, the principal corporation would be considered as a "manufacturer" and as such, would be subject to the provisions of the Code.

The test applied by the definition contains two elements i.e., whether or not the company or entity is engaged in "the business or function" of manufacturing a product within the scope of the Code, directly or indirectly. The "business" element refers to companies (the private sector), whereas the "function" element refers, presumably, to the public sector. If there is such an engagement, then the entity or company is a manufacturer, subject to the applicable provisions of the Code. The Code's definition of "manufacturer" is wider than the dictionary definition.[21]

10. Marketing

The Code defines "marketing" as

> product promotion, distribution, selling, advertising, product public relations, and information services.

---

19 On labelling see below Chapter XI.
20 See 9th edn. p.451.
21 According to *The Concise Oxford Dictionary*, to "manufacture" means "make (articles), esp. on an industrial scale." See ibid., p. 831.

This is, again, a very wide definition of the term marketing, and is justified by the special circumstances of the Code and the role which marketing of breast-milk substitutes could play to the detriment of breast-feeding. The Code is essentially intended to regulate the commercial practices of products covered by it, which were prevalent at the time of its adoption, and which were doing a great deal of harm to breast-feeding. Therefore, it was necessary to adopt a definition of the term "marketing" that went beyond the dictionary meaning of marketing. According to *The Concise Oxford Dictionary*,

> to "market" means ... sell, ...offer for sale, ...buy or sell goods in the market.[22]

Therefore, all the activities which constitute marketing under the definition, be they promotion of products covered by the Code, their distribution[23] or sale[24] are subject to the applicable provisions of the Code.

11. Marketing personnel

The Code defines "marketing personnel" as

> any persons whose functions involve the marketing of a product or products coming within the scope of this Code.

Accordingly, any person who sells, advertises, distributes and so on breast-milk substitutes, and/or feeding bottles or teats, is a marketing person subject to the applicable provisions of the Code[25]. Here again the test is functional: Do the person's functions involve marketing a product covered by the Code? If the answer is yes, then he is subject to the Code, and if the answer is no, then he is outside the scope of the Code.

12. Samples

The Code defines "samples" as

> single or small quantities of a product provided without cost.

Accordingly, any single or small quantity of a product covered by the Code, and given free of charge, is a sample under the Code, irrespective of the motive. The Code is intended to ban, *inter alia*, the marketing practice of giving samples of products covered by it, which was used by the infant-food industry to promote their products. What is meant by a single quantity can be easily defined, but what constitutes "small quantities" may be difficult to define, and may lead

---

22 Ibid., p. 834.
23 See below Chapter VII.
24 See below Chapter VIII.
25 See below Chapter X.

to abuse. However, the ordinary meaning of the term should be used in it interpretation. According to *The Concise Oxford Dictionary*, "quantity" means 1. that property of things that is (in principle) measurable".[26] Therefore, "small quantities" should be interpreted to mean small measurable products. Furthermore, the definition speaks of a single or small quantity provided without cost; therefore, if a price is paid for such a quantity, then presumably it would no longer be a sample. But if the price is merely derisory and is intended to meet the formal requirement of the Code, is it sufficient to meet the price test? Two answers may be given: The first is to the effect that according to a literal interpretation of Article 3 of the Code, if a price is paid for the product, no matter how insignificant it may be, then it would cease to be a sample or small quantity. The second is to the effect that, taking into account the intent and purpose of the Code, it could be argued that, if the price of the product is derisory then it would be characterised as a device to avoid the application of the Code. It is submitted that the first interpretation should be rejected and the second one should be preferred, because it is more in line with the intent and policy of the Code. Thus such cases would be subject to the provisions of the Code.

It should be pointed out that the wording of the definition does not make a link between the single or small quantity and the products covered by the Code. It merely says "of a product", without qualification. It is submitted that there is probably an oversight here, as the drafters must have meant the products covered by the Code, and not any other products. This standpoint is confirmed by the wording of Article 5.2 of the Code, which bans the giving of "samples of products within the scope of this Code."

13. Supplies

The Code defines "supplies" as

> quantities of a product provided for use over an extended period, free or at a low price, for social purposes, including those provided to families in need.

Accordingly, the definition consists of three elements:

1. The quantities of products provided should be for use over an extended period of time;
2. the products should be provided free of charge or at a low price; and
3. the products should be provided for non-commercial purposes (social purposes).

However, here again, there is no link between the products and the Code, i.e., the definition speaks of "quantities of a product" in general. There is probably

---

26 See 9th edn., p. 1120.

an oversight by the drafters, here too. Support for this standpoint can be found in Article 6.6, which deals with supplies, and uses the expression "infant formula or other products within the scope of this Code."

It should be observed that if any of the three elements of the definition of "supplies" is missing, then the quantities of the product in question cease to be supplies. This is very important, because Article 6.6 of the Code allows the provision of supplies, under certain conditions[27]. Therefore, such supplies have to meet the conditions laid down in the definition of the term under the Code. And this may be the reason why the definition is wider than the dictionary meaning of the term. According to *The Concise Oxford Dictionary*,

> "supplies" means a stock. Store, amount etc., of something provided or available....[28].

2. CONCLUSION

It might be appropriate to conclude this chapter with some observations. The first observation is that the definitions of the International Code are not exhaustive, and since the Code is "a minimum requirement", Member States implementing it are free to add to those definitions any others they deem necessary for their internal needs. Secondly, those definitions are given special meanings "for the purposes" of the International Code, which may not necessarily be their ordinary meanings[29]. The special meanings are applicable within the context and the regime of the Code, because the drafters considered it advisable to do so in view of the special needs and circumstances of the Code. It is submitted that it is permissible and perfectly lawful for the drafters of the International Code to do so. States participants at the September Consultation 1980

> ...were reminded that the definitions arrived at in this context were not intended for universal acceptance; rather, they were being formulated for the purposes of the code and should, therefore, be adapted to its specific needs.[30]

Thirdly, these definitions cover important terms used frequently in the Code, which were the subject of agreement at the WHO/UNICEF Consultations held in August and September 1980. They are also intended to provide some understanding and consistency in the Code, even vis-à-vis the infant-food industry. As ICIFI pointed out in its comments on the Third Draft:

> Unless there is clear understanding of the terms used in the Code, and unless these are used consistently, there will continue to be confusion both on the products cov-

---

27 See below Chapter VIII.
28 See 9th edn., p.1400.
29 Walker says that "statutes define many terms and concepts, frequently assigning meanings narrower or more extensive than the dictionary...would give to the particular word or phrase." See *The Oxford Companion to Law* (1980),p.346.
30 See September Consultation 1980, Summary of Discussions, p.22, paragraph 50.4.

ered by the Code and the methods used to market them[31].

The Dutch government clearly stated in its comments on the Second Draft of the Code that

> the Code can only be properly understood and applied when the definitions are clear and unambiguous.[32]

However, there was some disagreement in both Consultations concerning certain terms in the International Code. For example, as mentioned earlier, in the August Consultation there was no agreement on the definitions of the terms "breast-milk substitutes", and "infant formula" among the participants. A working group was established to harmonize the divergent points of view, but no agreement could be reached on any of those definitions.[33] There was also disagreement at the September Consultation in relation to certain terms. For example, the Canadian Delegate suggested that there was a need for definitions of the terms marketing, promotion, information and advertising.[34] The U.K. Delegate thought that there should be a distinction between educational promotion and sales promotion.[35] The Swedish Delegate did not go along with that, arguing that "...the object of all promotion is sales".[36] However, at the end the delegates decided to provide the WHO/UNICEF Secretariats with "food for thought"[37] to refine and develop the definitions in the Fourth Draft.[38]

Fourthly, some of the definitions of the International Code were borrowed from the Codex Alimentarius, while the rest were formulated by the drafters of the Code, in order to meet the special needs of Code. It is axiomatic to say that Codex standards and the work of the Codex Alimentarius Commission are well-known to the infant-food industry, therefore the drafters of the Code did not have to re-invent the wheel.

Finally, the definitions cannot be claimed to be perfect, or without ambiguity, at times, as they were adopted as a result of compromise, at the international

---

31 See ICIFI's Comments and Recommendations, above note 4, p.6.
32 See Comments of The Netherlands on the Draft International Code of Marketing of Breast-Milk Substitutes, p.1, paragraph 1.1, attached to a letter from the Ministerie van Volksgezondheid en Milieuhygiëne to the Director-General of WHO, dated 23 July 1980.
33 See above note 6.
34 See September Consultation 1980, Transcription of Tapes, tape 36, p.2. The French Delegate agreed with the Canadian Delegate; ibid., p.2. Canada took the same position in its comments on the Second Draft of the International Code. See Canadian Comments on Draft International Code of Marketing of Breast-milk Substitutes, p.6, attached to the letter of the Canadian Ambassador and Permanent Representative to the U.N. Office in Geneva, D.S. McPhail, to the Director-General of WHO, dated 18 August 1980.
35 See September Consultation 1980, tape 36, p.3.
36 Ibid., p.4.
37 See the statement of the Dutch Delegate, ibid., tape 36, p.1.
38 See the statements of the Swedish and Canadian Delegates, ibid., tape 35, p.6, and tape 36, p.1.

plane, between various views and under very difficult circumstances. But they do provide an adequate framework, for the purposes of the International Code, and reasonable guidance for Member States in the implementation of the Code at the national level.

CHAPTER VI

INFORMATION AND EDUCATION UNDER
THE REGIME OF THE INTERNATIONAL CODE

The provision of information to the mother, or would-be mother, and her education about infant feeding and the benefits of breast-feeding are very important elements in the promotion and protection of breast-feeding. They are also needed for the proper use of breast-milk substitutes. The more the mother, or would-be mother, knows about the health benefits and other advantages of breast-feeding, the more she is likely to breast-feed her infant. It has been said that

> in contrast to developing countries, in industrialized countries extended breast-feeding is more common among educated, economically advantaged mothers. Breast-feeding prevalence is higher in cities than in rural areas in many developed countries. This increase may simply be due to more access to breast-feeding information in general, and lactation management in particular.[1]

Furthermore, it has been said that

> there has been a noticeable improvement in the prevalence and duration of breast-feeding in a number of industrialized countries where a combination of public education, social support, and a greater awareness on the part of health care workers has made breast-feeding both more attractive and more feasible. Examples of this are found in Australia, Canada, the Netherlands, Sweden and the United Kingdom.[2]

On the other hand, lack of information and education may cause mothers to stop breast-feeding too early. As the Managing Director of Nestlé in Norway said:

> I heard one of the paediatricians in our company saying...that insufficient production of breast-milk is the most important reason why mothers stop breast-feeding their babies .... One reason why this happens is lack of information and education.[3]

The Nigerian Delegate to the Thirty-ninth WHA, 1986 (the late Professor Ran-

---

1   See Hafez and Bagchi, *Promotion of Breast-Feeding through MCH Services and Primary Health Care,* op.cit. p.20.
2   See Saadeh, Labbok, Cooney, and Koniz-Booker, *Breast-feeding – The technical basis and recommendations for action,* (1993), p.16.
3   See Lennart Svensson, "The role of the infant food industry: Today and tomorrow", *NU,* op.cit., p.24.

some Kuti), made a very important point when he said:

> When women were given the opportunity to make an informed choice, they regularly opted for breast-feeding.[4]

Furthermore, according to Deborah Kaplan and Kristina Graff,

> most women decide how they will feed their baby by the last trimester of pregnancy. Information given during prenatal care is extremely influential, and it is well documented that both advertising and provider attitudes influence women's choice of infant-feeding methods.[5]

The International Code recognizes the importance and role of information and education for the promotion and protection of breast-feeding in its Article 4, which reads as follows:

> 4.1 Governments should have the responsibility to ensure that objective and consistent information is provided on infant and young child feeding for use by families and those involved in the field of infant and young child nutrition. This responsibility should cover either the planning, provision, design and dissemination of information, or their control.

> 4.2 Informational and educational materials, whether written, audio, or visual, dealing with the feeding of infants and intended to reach pregnant women and mothers of infants and young children, should include clear information on all the following points:

> (a) the benefits and superiority of breast-feeding;
> (b) maternal nutrition, and the preparation for and maintenance of breast-feeding;
> (c) the negative effect on breast-feeding of introducing partial bottle-feeding;
> (d) the difficulty of reversing the decision not to breast-feed; and
> (e) where needed, the proper use of infant formula, whether manufactured industrially or home-prepared. When such materials contain information about the use of infant formula, they should include the social and financial implications of its use; the health hazards of inappropriate foods or feeding methods; and, in particular, the health hazards of unnecessary or improper use of infant formula and other breast-milk substitutes. Such materials should not use any pictures or text which may idealize the use of breast-milk substitutes.

> 4.3 Donations of informational or educational equipment or materials by manufacturers or distributors should be made only at the request and with the written approval of the appropriate government authority or within guidelines given by governments for this purpose. Such equipment or materials may bear the donating company's name or logo, but should not refer to a proprietary product that is within the scope of this Code, and should be distributed only through the health care system.

---

4   See *Thirty-Ninth World Health Assembly, Geneva, 5-16 May 1986, WHO Doc. WHA39/1986/REC/3*, (hereinafter referred to as "WHO Doc. WHA39/1986/REC/3") p. 100.
5   See "Marketing Breastfeeding-Reversing Corporate Influence on Infant Feeding Practices", *Journal of Urban Health: Bulletin of the New York Academy of Medicine*, June 2008, available on doi:10.1007/s11524-008-9279-6, 2008, p.3.

The four drafts of the International Code contained a provision on information and education,[6] but only the Fourth Draft contained an entire article on the subject. A call for a provision on information and education was made at the August Consultation 1980. At the latter Consultation

> ... there was agreement that an appropriate provision should be introduced in ...[Article 3 of the Third Draft] to deal with education, information and training ...[7].

This call was repeated more clearly at the September Consultation 1980. The Swedish Delegate commented that

> we ...should like to see the whole of Section 2.5 [of the Third Draft] shifted into either Article 3 or Article 4 as it relates more properly to those Articles.[8]

This was supported by the US Delegate, who suggested that the paragraph in question (Article 2.5) should be

> ...made part of more substantial provisions on education and information, which should be the responsibility of governments ....[9]

The following aspects of Article 4 shall now be surveyed.

1. RESPONSIBILITY FOR THE PROVISION OF INFORMATION ON INFANT FEEDING

Article 4.1 of the International Code makes it the responsibility of the government of a Member State of WHO to provide information on infant feeding. It reads as follows:

> Governments should have the responsibility to ensure that objective and consistent information is provided on infant and young child feeding for use by families and those involved in the field of infant and young child nutrition. This responsibility should cover either the planning, provision, design and dissemination of information, or their control.

The provision consists of the following elements:

1. It is the responsibility of the government of each Member State of WHO to provide information on infant and young child feeding.
2. The information should be objective and consistent.
3. The information should be intended for use by families and others involved

---

6 See Art.2.7 of the First Draft, Art 3.4 of the Second Draft and Art. 2.5 of the Third Draft.
7 See August Consultation 1980, p.10, paragraph 27.1.
8 See September Consultation 1980, Transcription of Tapes, tape 27, p.1.
9 Ibid.

in the field of infant and young child nutrition.

The government's responsibility should cover the planning, provision, design and dissemination of information or their control.

So far as the first element is concerned, the responsibility of the government is to ensure that information is provided on infant and young child feeding. It is to be observed that the government responsibility is "to ensure" the provision of information. This means that the government can produce such information, itself, or the information may be produced by someone else, be it a company or an NGO. This choice is to be made by the government concerned, in the light of its health, economic and social conditions

So far as the second element is concerned, irrespective of the producer or provider of such information, the government has to make sure that it is objective and consistent. This requirement is necessary and logical, for information on infant feeding has to be produced, always in the light of the aim and principles of the International Code. Such information, for example, on the promotion of breast-feeding, has to be consistent in that direction. If, in one part of a pamphlet designed to promote breast-feeding for use by families, the use of breast-milk substitutes is promoted, such a pamphlet would not contain "consistent" information. This is so because it would not be reasonable to encourage breast-feeding and explain its usefulness and advantages, and in the same document promote the use of breast-milk substitutes. The two methods of feeding infants are not complementary, and the aim of the Code is to allow the use of breast-milk substitutes only when necessary. Furthermore, such information has to be "objective", therefore, if it is produced by a manufacturer of breast-milk substitutes, there would be a presumption of subjective information, as it would be logical that such a company would want to promote its interests,[10] hence the responsibility of the government to make sure that such information is objective, besides being consistent.

According to Kaplan and Graff,

> in a randomized controlled trial studying the impact of educational packs on infant feeding, women who received formula company-produced infant feeding materials at their first prenatal visit were more likely than those who received non-commercial materials to stop breastfeeding before hospital discharge and before 2 weeks postpartum. Women with an uncertain decision to breastfeed, or with a plan to breastfeed 12 weeks or less, who received the commercial materials also had notably lower rates of

---

10 In Sweden, "... all parents of three months old babies receive pamphlets about infant feeding from the baby-food industry directly to their homes". See E. Kylberg, "The Swedish Code", *NU* op.cit., p.10. In the U.K., Alexandra Frean writes in *The Times* that the supermarket Tesco launched the Tesco Baby Club in January 1997, "...a glossy magazine offering baby-food recipes, advice on weaning and general articles on parenting....*TESCO Baby Club* is an example of the growing tactic of using magazines or "information" packs to influence how pregnant women and new mothers shop." She went on: "The babyfood manufacturer Heinz also produces a free guide for mothers, with information about weaning babies from milk to solid food". See *The Times* (5 February 1997), p.21.

exclusive breastfeeding and overall duration.[11]

Families, no matter how well educated they might be, need objective and consistent information, on infant feeding, from the Ministry of Health, or any other competent authority in the country concerned. This need is specially acute when there is much non-objective information, advertising and all sorts of promotion, in favour of breast-milk substitutes and other related products, particularly in developing countries.

The third element requires that the information provided should be for use by families and those involved in the field of infant and young child nutrition. In other words, such information should be directed at families and those involved in the field of nutrition for infants and young children. In both situations, it would seem that the Code intended to provide correct and appropriate information, on the best nutrition for infants, to reach families and nutritionists, health workers and any person involved in this area, for the purpose of using such information for infant feeding, in particular, for the promotion of breast-feeding.

The fourth element of the provision covers the responsibility of a government with respect to the planning, provision, design and dissemination of the information, or their control. Therefore, there are two components:

a) the planning, provision, design and dissemination of such information, or
b) the control of these processes.

So far as a) is concerned, it seems clear that the government concerned is directly involved in the planning, provision, design and dissemination of the information on infant and young child feeding. Any of these activities is intended to be done by the government alone. Therefore, if a producer of breast-milk substitutes, or an NGO, for example, plans, or disseminates information on infant and child feeding, without the involvement of the competent authorities of the Member State concerned, even if such information was objective and consistent, it would appear that such an action would not be in conformity with the International Code.

The planning, provision, design and dissemination of information need no labouring to explain, and their ordinary meaning should be given to them, in their context.[12] However, these activities cover the production of books, papers, pamphlets, as well as radio or television programmes, the internet and SMS messages and so on, containing information on the importance and necessity of breast-feeding for the healthy growth and development of infants. Informa-

---

11 See above note 5.
12 See Art. 31 (1) of the Vienna Convention on the Law of Treaties, 1969, which may apply by analogy; it reads : "A treaty shall be interpreted in good faith in accordance with the ordinary meaning to be given to the terms of the treaty in their context and in the light of its object and purpose."

tion provided in this way may, also, contain information about the importance of adequate nutrition for the pregnant and lactating mother, and how to achieve that, in the community in question. It may be recalled that the International Code affirms

> . . . the right of every child and every pregnant and lactating woman to be adequately nourished as a means of attaining and maintaining health.[13]

Information on the proper use of breast-milk substitutes, and the danger to health from incorrect or inappropriate use, should also be provided. The Japanese Delegate to the September Consultation 1980 said:

> I think that the health care systems should encourage breast-feeding and that at the same time they must have the responsibility to give those mothers who need breast-milk substitutes full information and instructions regarding the correct and safe use of these substitutes.[14]

So far as b) is concerned, it would seem that the government concerned can authorize any third-party to plan, provide, design and disseminate the type of information required by Article 4.1 of the Code. This appears to be the intent of the term "their control", used in the provision. It is possible that in some Member States, the governments, as such, have no or limited means of producing information on infant and young child feeding, or they may not have the means of dissemination of such information to families and those involved in the area of infant nutrition. In that case, the Code provides the possibility for such governments to ask any entity, be it an individual, a manufacturer of breast-milk substitutes, an NGO, or a UN agency to carry out such activities. Here the government would be involved, in that it authorizes, or agrees to allow, such an entity to carry out the activities in question. Furthermore, it would be reasonable to assume that the government would lay down certain conditions under which such activities may be carried out. However, it has to be borne in mind that such arrangements have to be compatible with the aim and principles of the Code.

It should be stated that the purpose of Article 4.1 is not to interfere in the freedom of publication of information, but rather to put an end to a practice that existed before the adoption of the Code. This practice allowed the publication, design and distribution of information on the subject of infant and young child feeding, which might not be objective and consistent, and might have been issued without any reference, or involvement, of the competent health authorities of a Member State. The involvement of the latter is a guarantee that public health interests, rather than commercial interests, would be served by the issue of such information. It might be interesting to mention that, at the Cairo Workshop on the Implementation of the International Code (17-23 September 1993),

---

13 See first preambular paragraph of the International Code.
14 See above note 8, tape 27, p.3.

organized by EMRO and WHO Headquarters, one of the participants from a State in the region showed the other participants an informational pamphlet produced by a manufacturer of breast-milk substitutes, on infant feeding, and intended to reach mothers. Some parts of the pamphlet were clearly intended to promote bottle-feeding and the use of breast-milk substitutes. Furthermore, the problem of breast-feeding, as the French Delegate (Professor Senault) said in the WHA in 1980, is "basically one of health education".[15] And the promotion of breast-feeding would not succeed without proper education.[16]

It might be interesting to point out that in some national legislations implementing the International Code, responsibility for the provision of information and education on infant feeding is put on the shoulders of governments.[17] It would be interesting to cite a Belgian Order of the Regent, dated 15 July 1946, for its clarity and significance. According to that Order,

> The Ministry of Public Health had the task of distributing leaflets and other publicity material designed to promote breast-feeding or stressing the dangers of giving it up without valid reasons, in maternity establishments and clinics and in prenatal consultation centres for infants.[18]

2. INFORMATIONAL AND EDUCATIONAL MATERIALS AND THEIR CONTENTS

Article 4.2 of the Code requires that certain informational items to be included in any informational and educational material, intended to reach pregnant women and mothers of infant and young children. It reads as follows:

> Informational and educational materials, whether written, audio, or visual, dealing with feeding of infants and intended to reach pregnant women and mothers of infant and young children, should include clear information on all the following points:
> a) the benefits and superiority of breast-feeding;
> b) maternal nutrition, and the preparation for and maintenance of breast-feeding;
> c) the negative effect on breast-feeding of introducing partial bottle-feeding;
> d) the difficulty of reversing the decision not to breast-feed; and

---

15 See *WHO Doc. WHA 33/1980/REC/3*, p.85.
16 See statement of the Congolese Delegate (Dr. Ondaye), ibid., p.91.
17 To give but some examples: under the Brazilian Marketing Regulations 1992, it is the responsibility of the "public health and educational agencies", see Art. 15 thereof; under the Guatemalan Rules for the Marketing of Breast-milk Substitutes 1987, it is the responsibility of the Ministry of Health and Social Welfare, General Directorate of Health Services, see Arts. 4 and 6; under the draft Omani Code 1995, it is the responsibility of the Ministry of Health, see Art. 5(1); under the EEC (now EU) Directive 1991, it is the responsibility of Member States, see Art. 9(1). By contrast, under the Indian Infant Milk Substitutes Act 1992, the responsibility is not specified, see Sec. 7(1); the same applies to the IBFAN Model Law 1996, see Secs. 12 and 13.
18 See WHO Working Paper, by the late Dr. De Moerloose, the then Chief of Health Legislation (1972), p. 3

> e) where needed, the proper use of infant formula, whether manufactured industri-
> ally, or home-prepared. When such materials contain information about the
> use of infant formula, they should include the social and financial implications
> of its use; the health hazards of unnecessary or improper use of infant formula
> and other breast-milk substitutes. Such materials should not use any pictures or
> text which may idealize the use of breast-milk substitutes.

This requirement is very important because of its impact on the decision of the mother or would-be mother as to whether or not to breast-feed her infant. If the mother knows, or has read or seen, all the relevant points and advantages of breast-feeding, it is hardly likely that she would use breast-milk substitutes to feed her infant, unless she has a health problem which prevents her from doing so.

Whether or not a mother should breast-feed her infant is her own decision, but it should be done on the basis of adequate information and advice, which Article 4.2 is intended to achieve. In the words of the New Zealand Delegate to the Thirty-third WHA (Dr. Barker):

> the decision whether or not to breast-feed a child should rest with the mother; such
> a decision should be informed, in that the mother should be aware of all the implica-
> tions of whichever decision she made ....[19]

This was echoed by the Turkish Delegate to the Thirty-fourth WHA (Professor Dogramaci) who said :

> it was argued that mothers had a right to choose whether or not they wanted to
> breast-feed; no one would deny that ..., provided [the mother] was properly informed
> about the facts.[20]

The informational and educational materials covered by Article 4.2, should in-clude clear information on *all* the following points:

a) the benefits and superiority of breast-feeding;
b) maternal nutrition, and the preparation for and maintenance of breast-feeding;
c) the negative effect on breast-feeding of introducing partial bottle-feeding;
d) the difficulty of reversing the decision not to breast-feed; and
e) where needed, the proper use of infant formula, whether manufactured industrially or home-prepared.[21]

Unlike Article 4.1, Article 4.2 does not expressly state who is responsible for the production or preparation of the informational and educational materials.

---

19 See above note 15, p. 70.
20 See *WHO Doc. WHA 34/1981/REC/3*, p.194.
21 Art. 9.2 of the International Code requires certain items to be mentioned on the label, some of which are similar to those mentioned in Article 4.2. For details see below Chapter XI.

It would therefore seem reasonable to suggest that the responsibility here is, implicitly, that of the government concerned and no others. It could be maintained that since Article 4.1 mentions, expressly, the responsibility of governments for the planning, provision, design and dissemination of information on infant and young child feeding, its paragraph 2 could be considered as an illustration of the sort of information to be provided. Therefore, since the responsibility for the main activity lies with governments, then *a fortiori* the responsibility for the illustration should lie with governments, as well. At the September Consultation 1980, the U.S. Delegate agreed with the Swedish suggestion to have a separate article dealing with information and education in the Code, and said that it should be

> ... made part of more substantial provisions on education and information, which should be the responsibility of governments ....[22]

Items a) to d) of Article 4.2 are relevant to the protection and promotion of breast-feeding, while item e) relates to the proper use of infant formula, which should be read to include all breast-milk substitutes.[23] As mentioned earlier, the purpose of giving information on all points a) to d) is to enable the mother or would-be mother to decide what is the best method of feeding her infant, and to warn her about some difficulties arising from a decision to bottle-feed. And a mother who has no particular health problem and is concerned about the healthy growth and development of her infant will certainly choose to breast-feed her infant, rather than use breast-milk substitutes. The mother and would-be mother, who is made aware, through such informational and educational materials, of the unique biological and emotional basis for her health and her child's, arising from breast-feeding, as well as the anti-infective properties of breast-feeding, will opt for the latter. But when the information given is not complete or accurate, or when the advantages of breast-feeding are not known to the mother or would-be mother, then she may not be able to make the right decision about the best feeding method for her infant.

Some examples of promoting breast-feeding under Article 4.2 may be given:

Campaigns of information and education promoting breast-feeding have been carried out, successfully, in Brazil, the Islamic Republic of Iran, Australia and Kenya, using written, audio and visual materials and messages for the purpose.[24] Information, education and communication, it has been said, provide

> ... the tools and techniques, messages, and materials that are necessary to address the various obstacles affecting breast-feeding, including:

---

22 See above note 8. See also the comment of the representative of the Christian Medical Commission to the Thirty-third WHA (Dr. Kingma): "...Education in the field of infant feeding should be the province of governments in cooperation with health care providers, educators, and community...workers." See above note 15, p. 80.

23 See on this point Chapter III, pp. 54-55.

24 See *Breast-feeding – The technical basis and recommendations for action,* op. cit., pp.77-78.

a) negative cultural beliefs and practices;

b) social norms that tend to create stigma against breast-feeding;

c) lack of current information on or knowledge of specific breast-feeding issues and skills, such as correct positioning and techniques for increasing milk production; and

d) the pervasive availability and marketing of breast-milk substitutes and bottles, and their misrepresentation as a desirable alternative to breast-feeding.[25]

It is to be noted that Article 4.2 uses the term "when needed", in relation to the use of breast-milk substitutes, whereas Article 1 (the Aim of the Code) uses the term "when these are necessary". The former should be interpreted in the sense of necessity and should not be understood to allow more flexibility for the use of breast-milk substitutes. The Aim of the Code should provide the guiding principle for the intent of the provisions of the Code generally. Furthermore, Article 6.6 of the Code allows donations or low-price sales of supplies of breast-milk substitutes to institutions or organizations. But it insists that they "should only be used or distributed for infants who *have to be fed* on breast-milk substitutes" (emphasis added). Therefore, the provision emphasizes situations where there is compulsion and the absence of any choice, for the use of such supplies.

Moreover, when informational and educational materials contain information about the use of breast-milk substitutes, there are other requirements to mention. They are:

1. the social and financial implications of the use of breast-milk substitutes;
2. the health hazards of inappropriate foods or feeding methods; and
3. the health hazards of unnecessary or improper use of breast-milk substitutes.

Those elements appear to be intended to warn the mother, or would-be mother, about the financial, social or health hazards and implications, which may arise from the use of breast-milk substitutes. Again, those elements are designed to complete the picture the mother, or would-be mother, should have before deciding whether to breast-feed or use breast-milk substitutes, for feeding her infant.

A final, and very important, point to be made with respect to Article 4.2, is that any informational or educational material cannot use "any pictures or text which may idealize the use of breast-milk substitutes". It is clear that the intention here is to disallow the use of such materials for promoting[26] breast-milk substitutes, for it is known that pictures of healthy-looking infants are used by manufacturers of breast-milk substitutes to encourage the sale of their products. Such pictures or texts may tempt a mother to use the product in question, or may mislead her into believing that bottle-feeding could be the equivalent,

---

25 Ibid., p.76.

26 Art. 5 of the International Code bans the advertising and promotion of breast-milk substitutes; for details see below Chapter VII.

or superior, to her own milk. Attention should be drawn to the use of the term "may"[27], which is a permissive term, to indicate the possible effect of the use of pictures or texts in relation to breast-milk substitutes. It has to be stated that the provision bans the use of *any picture*, be it of an infant, animal, bird or object, as long as it "may idealize" the use of breast-milk substitutes. The same applies to any text of the same nature. The competent authorities of the States implementing the Code, alone, can decide whether or not a picture or a text may, or may not, idealize [28] the use of breast-milk substitutes.

3. DONATIONS OF INFORMATIONAL AND EDUCATIONAL EQUIPMENT OR MATERIALS

It is not unknown that in some Member States of WHO, the financial resources of the health authorities may not be so great or plentiful. Therefore, those authorities may feel the need to seek some assistance, or accept offers of assistance, from the private sector, in particular the infant-food industry, or NGOs, for the production, preparation or the possession of informational or educational materials or equipment. This area covers the production of booklets, books, posters, slides, video machines, televisions and so on, which the appropriate health authorities, or other competent authorities, may need for the purpose of informing and educating the public, health workers, community workers or any section of the society in the State concerned. The drafters of the International Code, understandably, intended to maintain this practice because of the obvious need for it, in some parts of the world. Furthermore, the drafters intended to show that there is a role for the infant-food industry to play in this area. The US Delegate to the September Consultation 1980, made this point quite clear during the discussion of the issue of informational and educational materials and equipment. He said:

> The responsibility for the orientation, development and use of training materials lies with governments, that governments can request manufacturers to collaborate with them in the production of materials.... We concur with this provision. It deals with an important problem, namely providing a responsible role for industry in the educational process at the same time ensuring that education is not used for promotional purposes.[29]

Accordingly, Article 4.3 of the Code allows the donations of informational or

---

27 In the case of the *International Status of South-West Africa*, 1950, the ICJ interpreted the expression "as may be placed thereunder", contained in Articles 75 and 77 of the U.N. Charter. It said: "The language used in both articles is permissive ("as may be placed thereunder")". See ICJ Rep. (1950),p. 138. According to *The Concise Oxford Dictionary*, "may" means "1) Expressing possibility (it may be true...)", 9th edn., p. 842.

28 "Idealize" means "1) regard or represent (a thing or person) in ideal form or character. 2) Exalt in thought to ideal perfection or excellence." See ibid., p. 674.

29 See above note 8, tape 27, p.2.

educational equipment or materials by manufacturers or distributors of products covered by the Code. It reads as follows:

> Donations of informational or educational equipment of materials by manufacturers or distributors should be made only at the request and with the written approval of the appropriate government authority or within guidelines given by governments for this purpose. Such equipment or materials may bear the donating company's name or logo, but should not refer to a proprietary product that is within the scope of the Code, and should be distributed only through the health care system.

Such donations are subject to the following conditions:

1. The donation is made only at the request and written approval of the competent authority of the Member State concerned, or within guidelines laid down for this purpose.
2. The donation cannot refer to a proprietary product within the scope of the International Code.
3. Any donation must be distributed only through the health care system.

So far as condition 1 is concerned, the donation of such materials or equipment by manufacturers or distributors of products within the scope of the Code should be made "only at the request and with the written approval of the appropriate government authority, or within guidelines" given by the government concerned for that purpose. Accordingly, if company X produces educational materials on infant feeding, without a request from the appropriate government authority, shall we say the Ministry of Health; this action by X would not be in conformity with the International Code. The same applies, even if there was a request for such materials, but without the written approval of the Ministry of Health, in our example. On the other hand, if company X has been requested, in writing, by a department of the Ministry of Health, and the request has been approved by the appropriate department, then X's action would be in conformity with Article 4.3 of the Code. The same applies, if a written request is made, and the request falls within guidelines formulated by the Ministry of Health, for this kind of activity. In this situation, it would seem that the guidelines would provide the legal basis for the request, in lieu of the "approval of the appropriate government authority". This approach provides a flexible means for requesting such materials and equipment, but it could be abused if special care is not paid to the strict observance of the guidelines in question. Moreover, this condition prevent unsolicited donations of this nature by the infant food industry or any NGO.

As regards condition 2, the donated equipment or materials cannot refer to a proprietary product that is within the scope of the International Code. For example, if company X has donated informational materials, in conformity with condition 1) above, it is not allowed to refer to a breast-milk substitute, or a feeding bottle, produced and patented by it, or it would appear, produced by any other company. The wording of the provision permits this interpretation, for while it refers expressly to the "donating company's name or logo", there is no such link insofar as the proprietary products within the scope of the Code are concerned. The reference to the latter is general, therefore, it would be reasonable to interpret it in this broad way, which is, at any rate, in line with the intent and aim of the Code. Any such reference would be incompatible with Article 4.3 of the Code. However, such materials or equipment could bear the name or the logo of the donating company. The reason for banning the reference to proprietary products, and allowing it for the name or logo of the donating company is that, in the former this reference may amount to advertising or promotion of such products, whereas in the latter case there is no possibility for such a promotion.

Condition 3 stipulates that any donated informational materials or equipment can only be distributed through the health care system.[30] Accordingly, if the Ministry of Health of State A requests company X, or NGO Y, to give it some educational materials on infant feeding, and X or Y does so, without any reference to a proprietary product within the scope of the Code, X or Y, cannot distribute such material, itself, to health professionals, mothers and would-be mothers. Such distribution is restricted by Article 4.3 to the health care system. It would be reasonable to assume that the distribution is done by the health care system itself, without any role for the donor in this respect. The aim, it would seem clear, is to prevent promotion of breast-milk substitutes, which could otherwise occur, if entities other than the health care system were allowed to distribute such materials.

These three conditions are cumulative in effect, therefore, if one of them is missing, the action in question will be in breach of Article 4.3 of the Code.[31]

The importance of information and education on infant and child feeding has been reiterated by the Convention on the Rights of the Child, Article 24 of which reads as follows:

> 1. States Parties recognize the right of the child to the enjoyment of the highest at-

---

30 Health care system is defined in Article 3 of the International Code as: "governmental, non-governmental or private institutions or organizations engaged, directly or indirectly, in health care for mothers, infants and pregnant women; and nurseries or child care institutions. It also includes health workers in private practice. For the purposes of this Code, the health care system does not include pharmacies or other established sales outlets."

31 A number of Member States implementing the Code have included a provision similar to Article 4.3. For examples, see Art.4.7 of the Ghanaian Law; Art.4 of the Guatemalan Law 1983; Sec.5 (b) and Sec. 8 (1) (a) of the Indian Infant Milk Substitutes Act 1992; Art.5 (3) of the draft Omani Code 1995, and Art.5 (3) of the draft UAE Code 1995; see also to the same effect Art. 9 3 of the European Union's Directive, 1991. Other Member States implementing the Code have not included in their national measures a provision similar to Article 4.3 of the Code. For examples, see the Brazilian Law 1992, the Kenyan Law 1983, the Philippine's Code 1986 and the Tunisian Law 1983.

tainable standard of health....

2. States Parties shall pursue full implementation of this right and, in particular, shall take appropriate measures:

- – -

(e) To ensure that all segments of society, in particular parents and children, are informed, have access to education and are supported in the use of basic knowledge of child health and nutrition, the advantages of breast-feeding....

Breaches of Article 4 of the International Code have been reported. A research on the state of the Code, commissioned, some years ago, by the Interagency Group on Breast-feeding Monitoring (IGBM), a group composed of NGOs, academic institutions and churches in the UK[32], was carried out in Bangladesh, Poland, South Africa and Thailand. The researchers discovered evidence that some manufacturers of breast-milk substitutes were violating Article 4 of the Code. The companies involved were: Nestlé, Nutricia, Dumex, Mead Johnson and Snow. For example, it was found that a Cerelac care book, published by Nestlé in Bangladesh,

> deals with infant feeding, but meets none of the requirements of Article 4.2 of the Code."[33]

The Cerelac book shows on the cover a picture of a healthy-looking infant, with a happy smiling face. Another example is a Nutricia leaflet entitled "Mummy I'm Hungry", found by the researchers in a health care facility in Poland. It is said that this leaflet

> contains pictures which idealise the use of breast-milk substitutes, with the caption "Mummy, if at hospital I was given a particular formula milk, don't change it to a different one at home.[34]

The IGBM report also shows a drawing of a smiling infant, who appears to be skipping happily and carrying a basket with something like a bottle on top of the basket.[35] The only company which has replied to this report is Nestlé, as far as can be ascertained. Nestlé does not deny the publication of the Cerelac care book, but says

> it is outside the scope of the Code.[36]

In another context, Nestlé expressly admits using pictures of babies in informational and educational materials, but gives a different justification. Nestlé, in

---

32 See *Cracking the Code*, op. cit., p.1.
33 See ibid., p. 18.
34 Ibid.
35 Ibid.
36 See *A Missed Opportunity" – Nestlé Comments on the IGBM Report "Cracking the Code"* (hereinafter referred to as "A Missed Opportunity"), published by Nestlé UK in February 1997, p. 10.

its Instructions mentioned earlier, commenting on Article 4.2 of the Interventional Code, says that

> baby pictures may be used only to enhance the educational materials value of information.[37]

It would seem to an impartial and neutral observer that the situation is as follows: Article 4.2 of the Code applies to any written, audio or visual informational and educational materials, which are intended to reach pregnant women and mothers of infants and young children. Furthermore, the provision requires clear information on points (a) to (e).[38] Finally, the provision declares that

> such materials should not use any pictures or text which may idealize the use of breast-milk substitutes.

In addition, Article 4.1 places on governments the responsibility or control over the provision, design and dissemination of information on infant and young child feeding. The Nestlé Cerelac book is said to deal with infant feeding. Nestlé does not seem to deny this description, but claims that it is outside the scope of the Code. ("This is a Cerelac care book which is outside the scope of the Code," says Nestlé,[39] whereas in its Instructions, it claims that such baby pictures enhance the value of the information provided.

But Nestlé does not say why the Cerelac book is outside the scope of the Code, presumably because it does not consider the product in question as a breast-milk substitute. Even if one assumes that this is the case, Article 4.2 speaks of informational and educational materials "dealing with the feeding of infants and intended to reach pregnant women and mothers of infants and young children." Therefore, if the Cerelac book deals with infant feeding and is addressed to, at least, mothers of infants and young children, then it is subject to Article 4 of the Code. In that case, it has to comply with all the requirements of Article 4.2. Failure to do so constitutes a breach of the provision. The same applies to Nestlé's Instructions. However, whether or nor a particular picture "may idealize" the use of breast-milk substitutes is a matter of interpretation, using objective criteria in the relevant context.

On the other hand, it is not clear whether the Cerelac baby care book was published by Nestlé with, or without, the agreement of the Bangladeshi government. If the latter has given its consent to the publication, then there is no problem, but in the absence of such consent, Nestlé's action is not in conformity with Article 4.1 of Code. It is submitted that what has been said with respect to the Cerelac baby care book also applies to Nutricia's leaflet "Mummy I'm Hungry."

It has been reported that an infant food manufacturer in Lebanon, called

---

37 See the *Nestlé Report to the Director-General of WHO*, op. cit, p. 25.
38 See above pp. 101-103.
39 See above note 36.

Blédina, promotes, in a booklet, Blédina cereals

> for use from four months and describes the products as the ideal food for small infants since its gluten free composition 'does not disturb the digestive system of babies'.[40]

Another example is reported in The Netherlands, where Friesland, an infant food manufacturer, distributes a colourful information brochure, Friso Kinder-voeding Nutrition Guide to health workers in a hospital.

> The information in the brochure claims that Friso formula products are 'inspired by the positive effects of breastfeeding, Friso infant foods contain nutrients for natural growth and development'[41]

The pamphlet appears to contain a picture of a mother with her infant on the cover. These two examples appear to violate Article 4.2 of the International Code, in that they contain texts and/or pictures which may be characterised as "may idealize the use of breast-milk substitutes". For, to say the products is "the ideal food for small infants", and the product is "inspired by the positive effects of breastfeeding... for natural growth and development" of infants, constitutes a language that could be easily described as an attempt to idealize and not only "may idealize" the use of such products. And since they are promoted for use by infants as breast-milk substitutes, then they are caught by Article 4.2 of the Code.

---

40 IBFAN, *Breaking the Rules – Stretching the Rules*, 2007, p. 19.
41 Ibid., p. 26.

CHAPTER VII

ADVERTISING AND PROMOTION OF PRODUCTS COVERED BY THE INTERNATIONAL CODE

The advertising and promotion of breast-milk substitutes, and their representation as equivalent to, or better than breast-milk, have caused a decline in breast-feeding. As early as 1974, the WHA adopted a resolution in which it noted

> ...the general decline in breast-feeding, related to socio-cultural...factors, including the mistaken idea caused by misleading sales promotion that breast-feeding is inferior to feeding with manufactured breast-milk substitutes.[1]

It is common to find in advertising and promotional materials, or on containers of breast-milk substitutes, pictures of healthy-looking infants,[2] or texts, designed to give the impression that such products have the same benefits, or can produce the same if not better results, as breast-milk, or offer a viable option to the latter. Another negative effect of advertising and promotion of breast-milk substitutes is that they seem to cause anxiety and doubt in mothers about their ability to breast-feed. The Jelliffes, leading authorities on breast-feeding, say that

> also, and underappreciated, successful breast feeding literally depends physiologically on confidence. Advertising can have the subtle and unique side-effect of causing anxiety and doubt, and thus undermining the production of the rival product,

---

1 See Resolution WHA27.43, (May 1974), second preambular paragraph, *WHO Handbook*, Vol.II, pp.89-90.
2 "...In most Middle Eastern cities, 20 to 50 different brands of infant formulas and supplementary foods are available. These are marketed to be as attractive as possible to the general public, usually with pictures of smiling healthy Western...babies on the labels". See *Infant Feeding in the Middle East*, Report by James Firebrace, IBFAN Consultant, March/April 1983, p.42. It is reported that "to encourage sales in Pakistan, Abbott offers a free tin of Similac for every ten tins bought....In South Africa, promotional brochures for Isomil, Similac and Similac PM 60/40 are given to parents in pharmacies. The cover of one such brochure has a photograph of a sleeping baby behind a graphic of the Abbott bear growing from a sitting baby into a standing, talking bear, effectively equating the bear on the labels with a baby". See IBFAN, *Breaking the Rules*, 1994, p.8. The Kiribati Delegate to the 38th WHA (Dr Tira) said: "...his delegation would be glad if Member States would adhere to the clauses of [the International] Code and prohibit the use on [breast-milk substitute] products of pictures of healthy babies, which held great appeal for the young mothers of his country". See *Thirty-eighth World Health Assembly, Geneva, 6-20 May 1985, WHA38/1985/REC/3,* (hereinafter referred to as "WHO Doc. WHA38/1985/REC/3")p.71.

human milk.[3]

The International Code addresses this problem in its Article 5, which reads as follows:

> 5.1 There should be no advertising or other form of promotion to the general public of products within the scope of this Code.

> 5.2 Manufacturers and distributors should not provide, directly or indirectly, to pregnant women, mothers or members of their families, samples of products within the scope of this Code.

> 5.3 In conformity with paragraphs 1 and 2 of this Article, there should be no point-of-sale advertising, giving of samples, or any other promotion device to induce sales directly to the consumer at the retail level, such as special displays, discount coupons, premiums, special sales, loss-leaders and tie-in sales, for products within the scope of this Code. This provision should not restrict the establishment of pricing policies and practices intended to provide products at lower prices on a long-term basis.

> 5.4 Manufacturers and distributors should not distribute to pregnant women or mothers of infants and young children any gifts of articles or utensils which may promote the use of breast-milk substitutes or bottle-feeding.

> 5.5 Marketing personnel, in their business capacity, should not seek direct or indirect contact of any kind with pregnant women or with mothers of infants and young children.

Article 5 is one of the salient provisions of the International Code simply because of the harmful effects which result, or are likely to result from, the advertising and promotion of breast-milks substitutes on breast-feeding. All the four drafts of the International Code contained a provision on the subject-matter, though the wording differed from one to another.[4] During the consideration of those drafts of the International Code by the WHA and the Executive Board, much concern was expressed by delegates and members of the Board about the negative impact of advertising and promotion of breast-milk substitutes on breast-feeding. The Cape Verde Delegate (Dr Fermino Pina) observed at the WHA, in 1980, that

> encouragement of breast feeding for as long as possible and the introduction of supplementary feeding from the age of 4-6 months...were of key importance. At the same time, advertising and promotion of breast milk substitutes had to be rigorously

---

3   See D. Jelliffe and E.F. Jelliffe, "Feeding Young Infants in Developing Countries", *US Senate Hearing*, p.74. Firebrace says, in relation to advertising and promotion of breast-milk substitutes: "No warning of the health hazards involved is given, and the advertisements and labels are often couched in a way that introduces doubts about the mother's ability to breast-feed (of the type – 'Breast feeding is best for baby, but if you are unable...'). The effect of this exposure has therefore been...(b) to undermine the 'confidence factor' which is crucial to successful breast feeding". See above note 2, pp.42-43.

4   See Art. 1.3 of the First Draft; Art. 2.1 of the Second Draft; Art. 1.1 of the Third Draft, and Art. 5 of the Fourth Draft.

controlled if maternal and child health was to be ensured.[5]

A member of the Executive Board, (Dr. Yacoub), said the following, during the discussion of the Fourth Draft of the International Code:

> mothers were often persuaded by advertisements to use [breast-milk substitutes] instead of breast feeding their infants.[6]

The Swiss Delegate to the Thirty-fourth WHA (Dr Frey) clearly stated that

> any code governing the advertising of breast-milk substitutes should be designed to offer better protection and to improve the health of the child.[7]

One year after the adoption of the International Code, the WHA reiterated that

> ... commercial marketing of breast-milk substitutes for infants has contributed to an increase in artificial feeding.[8]

It is well-known that improper use of breast-milk substitutes may lead to sickness and mortality in infants. The Jelliffes say that

> it has been estimated that some 10 million cases per year of marasmus and diarrhoea occur annually in infants in developing countries, related in part to inadequate bottle feeding.[9]

Therefore, the advertising and promotion of breast-milk substitutes could be a danger to the health of infants. The New Zealand Delegate (Dr. Barker) stated at the Thirty-third WHA that

> in certain countries firms were following promotional practices which represented a danger to the health and life of infants and were therefore clearly unacceptable.[10]

The Executive Board stated in 2010 that it was

> Aware that inappropriate feeding practices and their consequences are major obstacles to attaining sustainable socioeconomic development and poverty reduction.[11]

---

5   See *WHO Doc.WHA 33/1980/REC/3*, p.77.
6   See *Executive Board, Sixty-seventh session, Geneva, WHO Doc. EB 67/1981/REC/2*, p.306. Another member of the Board, Mr. Al-Sakaaf, stated that "excessive use of breast milk substitutes was brought about by uncontrolled advertising ..." Ibid., p.311. Dr. Reid, another member of the Board observed that "there was need both to foster breast-feeding and to protect mothers from influences which might discourage this, and the Code clearly had an important part to play in the latter process." Ibid., p.309.
7   See *WHO Doc.WHA 34/1981/REC/3*, p.193.
8   See Resolution WHA 35.26, fourth preambular paragraph, *WHO Handbook*, Vol.II, p.92.
9   See *US Senate Hearing*, p.72. A member of the Executive Board went so far as to state that "because of artificial baby-foods millions of infants died from diarrhoeal diseases every year in the developing countries". See statement by Dr Rezai above, note 6, p.311.
10 See above note 5, p.70.
11 See Resolution EB126.R5, 21 January 2010, 9th preambular paragraph, WHO Doc. *EB126/2010/REC/1*.

The following aspects of Article 5 shall now be surveyed.

1. BAN ON ADVERTISING AND OTHER FORM OF PROMOTION TO THE GENERAL PUBLIC

In accordance with Article 5.1 of the International Code, the advertising, or any other form of promotion, of any product covered by the Code, and addressed to the general public, is prohibited. It reads as follows:

> There should be no advertising or other form of promotion to the general public of products within the scope of this Code.

This prohibition is very wide and covers mass media, e.g., television, radio and newspapers and electronic transmission, posters, pictures, as well as any other means of advertising of such products. This prohibition is general and without any qualification, for the wording of the provision contains no limitations, or exceptions, concerning its application. This standpoint also derives support from the WHA, which urged Member States in 2001

> to strengthen national mechanisms to ensure global compliance with the International Code of Marketing of Breast-milk Substitutes and subsequent relevant Health Assembly resolutions, with regard to ... all form of advertising and commercial promotion in all types of media....[12]

Furthermore, the prohibition applies to direct and indirect advertising and promotion, and includes brand and non-brand names.

However, the International Code does not define the terms "advertising" and "promotion"[13], and this seems to be deliberate on the part of the drafters. As mentioned earlier, there was a call at the September Consultation 1980 for the definition of these terms, without any result. Therefore, these terms should be given their ordinary meaning.[14] According to *The Concise Oxford Dictionary*,

> "advertise" means draw attention to or describe favourably (goods, services ...) in a

---

12 See Resolution WHA54.2, 18 May 2001, operative 2 (9).

13 Some Member States implementing the International Code in national measures have defined advertising and promotion, for examples see Brazilian Regulations for Marketing of Infant Foods 1992, Art.3, Sec. XI; Indian Infant Milk Substitutes Act 1992, Sec. 2(a); draft Jordanian Code 1993, Art. 4(1); and draft Omani Code 1995, Art. 4(1); See also IBFAN's Model Law (1996), Sec. 2(1).

14 In accordance with Art.31, paragraph 1, of the Vienna Convention on the Law of Treaties "a treaty shall be interpreted in good faith in accordance with the ordinary meaning to be given to the terms of the treaty in their context and in the light of its object and purpose". While the International Code is not a treaty, it is submitted that Art.31, paragraph 1, could apply by analogy.

public medium in order to sell, promote sales ...; and "promote" means publicize and sell (a product).[15]

Of course, Member States implementing the International Code can adopt a wider definition of those terms than the dictionary meaning, as they see fit.[16]

The test as to whether a particular statement, picture or text is an advertisement or promotion of a product covered by the Code, would be to see whether or not it is intended to describe favourably, or draw attention to, such a product with a view to promoting its sales; or whether or not it is intended to publicize that product and sell it, taking into account all relevant circumstances. This is to be done, always against the background of the aim and principles of the Code. However, there may be some situations where it is not clear, or some doubt may exist, as to whether or not a particular statement or picture amounts to advertising or constitutes a form of promotion. It is submitted that in this kind of situation the benefit of the doubt should be given in favour of breast-feeding. This approach would be more in line with the intent and aim of the Code.[17]

It is interesting to note that the Parties to the WHO Framework Convention on Tobacco Control 2003 recognize that a comprehensive ban on advertising and promotion reduce the consumption of tobacco products.[18]Furthermore, the Convention provides that

> 2. Each Party shall, in accordance with its constitution or constitutional principles, undertake a comprehensive ban of all tobacco advertising, promotion and sponsorship.[19]

It might be interesting to point out that, during the preparatory stages of the International Code, the infant-food industry tried to introduce a qualifying phrase, namely "to the detriment of breast-feeding", on the wording of Article 5.1 of the Code. This phrase was used in the recommendation of the WHO/UNICEF Meeting of 1979.[20] The representative of ICIFI at the August Consul-

---

15 See 9th edn. (1995), pp.20, and 1095.
16 According to Sec. 2(a) of the Indian Infant Milk Substitutes Act 1992 "advertisement" includes any notice, circular, label, wrapper and other documents and also includes any visible representation or announcement made by means of any light, sound, smoke or gas". According to Art.4(1) of the draft Omani Code 1995, "advertisement means every form of statement:
(a) in a publication of any sort, by television, radio or telephone;
(b) by display of notices, signs, labels, show cards or display of goods;
(c) by the distribution of circulars, catalogues or any other material;
(d) by the display of pictures, samples or films; or
(e) the advertising in any other manner."
17 See above p. 75.
18 See Art. 13 (1) of the Convention.
19 See ibid., Art. 13 (2).
20 See Joint WHO/UNICEF Meeting, Geneva, 9-12 October 1979, p.28, which reads: "There should be no sales promotion, including promotional advertising* to the public of products to be used as breast milk substitutes or bottle-fed supplements and feeding bottles. (*This

tation 1980 voiced his disagreement with the wording of Article 1.1 of the Third Draft (the origin of Article 5.1 of the International Code)

> ... because, according to ICIFI's interpretation, the provision did not reflect the wording of the recommendation on this issue made at the WHO/UNICEF October Meeting (page 28 of the Statement and Recommendations, last paragraph and footnote).[21]

ICIFI repeated its objection to the wording of Article 5.1, for the reason just mentioned, as well as other reasons, e.g., it is "unprecedented", it is "likely to encourage the use of inferior substitutes" and is "illegal" in some countries.[22] Had the qualification in question been accepted, it would have led to the introduction of difficulties, and a great deal of uncertainty, in the application of the provision. For who would decide whether a particular advertisement is to the "detriment of breast-feeding" or not. What criteria are to be applied? And how do you assess the anxiety and doubt that can be caused to the mind of the mother or would-be mother about her ability to breast-feed from such advertisements? The WHO/UNICEF Secretariats took the position that the International Code was prepared on the basis of the mandate given to the Director-General of WHO by the WHA, rather than the recommendations of the WHO/UNICEF October Meeting, and that there was no legal obligation on the part of WHO and UNICEF to adhere to the precise wording of the Statement and Recommendations of the latter Meeting. They said

> ...The Secretariat stated that what was at issue was not whether the first part of Article 1 reproduced literally what was said in the last paragraph and footnote on page 28 of the Statement and Recommendations of the October Meeting, but rather whether Articles 1 and 2, taken as a whole, faithfully translated into code form the intent of the Statement and Recommendations of the October Meeting and the overall purpose of the code. Further, the Secretariat stated that from a legal point of view, the preparation of the code should be based on the mandate given to the Director-General by Member States in resolution WHA33.32 of the Thirty-third World Health Assembly, while taking into consideration the underlying principles expressed in the Statement and Recommendations of the October Meeting. There was, therefore, no obligation to adhere to the precise wording of the Statement and Recommendations which had been prepared in a manner not necessarily suitable for a legal instrument as an international code.[23]

The nature of the prohibition on advertising and promotion, and the extent

---

includes the use of mass media and other forms of advertising directly to the mother or general public, designed to increase sales of breast milk substitutes, to the detriment of breast feeding").

21 See August Consultation 1980, p.7, paragraph 17.2. Other participants in the Consultation disagreed with ICIFI. The representatives of IOCU, IUNS and some experts "...expressed the view that the first part of paragraph 1.1 [Art. 5.1 of the Code] was a better and clearer interpretation of the ideas expressed in the October Meeting than that contained in the Statement and Recommendations". Ibid. On the October Meeting see above Chapter I, p.5.

22 See ICIFI Observations on the Shortcomings of the Proposed WHO International Code of Marketing for Breast-milk Substitutes, March 1981, p.7, paragraphs 1-3.

23 See above note 21, pp.7-8, paragraph 17.3.

thereof, contained in Article 5.1 of the Code, can be justified, as has been mentioned earlier, by the adverse effect which they have, or can have, on the decision of the pregnant woman, or the mother of an infant, as to whether or not
she should breast-feed her infant. According to Kaplan and Graff

> the infant formula industry has had a significant adverse impact on breastfeeding
> rates through strategic marketing, targeting women with direct adverting and with
> the implicit and explicit endorsement of health providers.[24]

Furthermore, it has been pointed out, in the context of the contamination of
infant formula in China in 2008, that

> ... in China, television marketing of infant formula has a pronounced influence on
> the population, such that infant formula has become a standard gift for new parents;
> expectant parents save to purchase these products.[25]

The tempting texts and/or pictures of healthy-looking infants and happy mothers in glossy magazines, on television or in other means of advertising, accom-
panying advertisements and promotion of breast-milk substitutes, could easily
influence mothers to use them, instead of their own milk. In the words of the
Togolese Delegate to the Thirty-third WHA (Dr Houénassou-Houangbé)

> every effort should be made to eliminate the kind of advertising that left a mother
> with the impression that a given type of breast-milk substitute was the best one for
> her particular child.[26]

The Hungarian Delegate (Dr Elias) shared the view that

> ... willingness to breast-feed could be adversely affected by uncontrolled advertising
> and promotion of breast-milk substitutes.[27]

Moreover, the Nigerian Delegate (Dr Smith) saw a link between advertising
and the decline in breast-feeding. He said:

> The aggressive and uncontrolled advertisement of breast-milk substitutes and the
> trend towards a breakdown in traditional culture...had contributed to the decline.[28]

It might be appropriate to conclude this part with the position of WHO on the
health implications of direct advertising of breast-milk substitutes to the gen-

---

24 See "Marketing Breastfeeding-Reversing Corporate Influence on Infant Feeding Practices",
    Journal of Urban Heath: Bulletin of the New York Academy of Medicine, doi:10.1007/s11524-
    008-9279-6, 2008, p.3.
25 See Anna Coutsoudis, Hoosen M Coovadio, Judith King, "The breastmilk brand:
    promotion of child survival in the face of formula-milk marketing", *The Lancet*, Vol. 374,
    August 1, 2009., p.423, quoting Xu F, Liu X, Binns CW, Xiao C, Wu J, Lee AH, " A decade of
    change in breastfeeding in China's north-west", *Int Breastfeed J* 2006.
26 See above note 5, p.79.
27 Ibid.
28 Ibid., p.88.

eral public. This position was expressed by the Director-General, in his report to the Forty-fifth WHA, 1992, when he said:

> Even viewed from the perspective of fostering competition, WHO considers that direct advertising to mothers with infants in the first four to six months of life is singularly inappropriate because:
>
> – advertising infant formulas as a substitute for breast milk competes unfairly with normal, healthy breast-feeding, which is not subject to advertising, yet which is the safest and lowest-cost method of nourishing an infant; advertising infant formulas as a substitute for breast milk favours uninformed decision-making, by-passing the advice and supervision of the mother's physician or of health workers.[29]

It has been reported that advertising and promotion to the general public of products within the scope of the Code are still continuing in many parts of the world. The IGBM research found that in the four countries where it was carried out, namely, Bangladesh, Poland, South Africa and Thailand, media advertising of products covered by the Code in magazines had taken place,[30] as well as other forms of promotion of breast-milk substitutes in Armenia, France, Germany, Lebanon, Switzerland and the UK.[31]

It is worthwhile pointing out that Nestlé has attempted to narrow the scope of Article 5.1 of the International Code, in that it stated in its Instructions, mentioned earlier, in the context of Article 5.1.

> 5.1 Information relating to infant formula must not be communicated directly to mothers or the general public.[32]

Accordingly, the Nestlé Instructions ban the communication of "information", whereas the International Code bans the "advertising or other form of promo-

---

29 See Report of Director-General on Infant and Young Child Nutrition (Progress and Evaluation Report; and Status of Implementation of the International Code of Marketing of Breast-milk Substitutes). [A45/28 – 6 April 1992], WHO Doc. WHA45/1992/REC/1, p.229, paragraph 123.

30 See *Cracking the Code*, op. cit., pp.20-21.The researchers found magazine advertisement for feeding bottles by Cannon in Poland and by Pur in Thailand, and magazine advertisement for complementary foods for infants from 4 months of age, with a picture of a very young infant, by Gerber in South Africa. See ibid., p.21. Examples of other reported advertisements of products covered by the Code may be given: feeding bottles of Bagel company are widely advertised in magazines to the South African public; Cannon's bottles and teats are advertised in magazines in Brazil, Ireland, Malaysia, and Pakistan, and on television in Malaysia and in cinemas in Pakistan; Gerber advertises its infant formula to mothers in Colombia, Peru and the USA; Humana's infant formula and bottles are advertised to mothers in magazines in Germany and Luxemburg; Migros (a Swiss supermarket chain) advertised its infant formula in Famina magazine in 1994; Nestlé advertises its infant formula directly to mothers on television in the USA and in magazines in Canada, Germany, Spain and the USA; see *Breaking the Rules*, pp.10, 11, 17, 19, 23 and 27.

31 See IBFAN's *Breaking the Rules Stretching the Rules 2007*, pp 16 and 44.

32 See the Nestlé Report to the Director-General of WHO, op. cit., p.26

tion." These is therefore a considerable difference between "information" and "advertising" and "promotion". "To advertise", according to *The Concise Oxford Dictionary* means

> 1. draw attention to or describe favourably (goods, services…) in a public medium in order to sell, promote sales….[33]

On the other hand, "to promote" means

> 3. publicise and sell (a product).[34]

By contrast, "to inform" means

> 1. Tell (informed them of their rights).[35]

Furthermore, the Nestlé Instructions ban the direct communication of information to mothers or the general public, only, whereas the International Code bans advertising of the products covered by it directly and indirectly. Therefore, it seem clear that the manner in which Nestlé intends to implement Article 5.1 of the Code is significantly narrower than that intended by the Code.

A problem may arise in the case of cross-border advertising and promotion of products covered by the International Code, in the context of its Article 5.1 Supposing State A bans such advertisements and promotion in its territory, but Company X advertises and promotes such products from the territory of State Y into State A. What is the legal position? Is Company X violating Article 5.1? And what can State A do in this case? It could be argued that Company X's advertising and promotion, though done from outside the territory of State A, still has effect in the latter. As such, it could be considered as advertising and promotion of those products in State A. Since the law of State A bans these practices, it is submitted, it should apply to those practices of Company X. Consequently, State A would be entitled to impose whatever its law provides as a penalty in such cases of violation.

2. BAN ON THE GIVING OF SAMPLES

The practice of giving samples of products within the scope of the International Code, e.g., samples of infant formula, to pregnant women, or mothers, was prevalent in many parts of the world at the time of the adoption of the Code. It is believed that this practice still exists today. It is known that free samples of breast-milk substitutes are given to "all mothers discharged from maternity units" in the USA.[36] Kaplan and Graff state that

---

33 See 9th edn., p. 20.
34 Ibid., p. 1095.
35 Ibid., p. 697.
36 See the Jelliffes above note 3, p.73.

most US hospitals provide discharge packs containing free formula to mothers when they leave the hospital.[37]

Article 5.2 of the International Code is intended to ban this practice; it reads as follows:

> 5.2 Manufacturers and distributors should not provide, directly or indirectly, to pregnant women, mothers or members of their families, samples of products within the scope of this Code.

The term "samples", is defined by the International Code as

> single or small quantities of a product provided without cost.[38]

Accordingly, the provision bans the giving of samples of products covered by the Code, namely, breast-milk substitutes, other products considered as such by the Code and feeding bottles and teats, by manufacturers and distributors[39] to mothers or members of their families. The ban is general and applies to direct and indirect giving of such samples to the persons mentioned in the provision. Direct giving means, directly, by a manufacturer or distributor of such samples to a pregnant woman, a mother, a husband, a child or any other member of the family, whereas indirect giving means using a third party to carry out the action. For example, a manufacturer uses a mothercraft nurse or a nurse, to give the mother samples of breast-milk substitutes. It is to be noted that, if a member of the family of a pregnant woman, or a mother, happens to be a health worker, he or she cannot be given samples of, for example, breast-milk substitutes, for the ban is general and applies irrespective of the profession of the person concerned.[40] Furthermore, the ban applies without any geographical limitation, i.e., it applies to the home of those persons, the market place, health care system[41], a pharmacy or any other institution. Finally, the ban applies to all products within the scope of the International Code, i.e., all products covered by Article 2 of the Code, namely, breast-milk substitutes, other products considered as such by the Code, feeding bottles and teats.[42]

The rationale for the ban on the giving of samples is the promotional nature of this practice[43] and the adverse effect it may have on the decision of the

---

37 See above note 23, p. 4.

38 See Art. 3 of the International Code.

39 For the definition of the terms "distributor" and "manufacturer" see ibid.

40 Art. 7.4 permits the giving of samples, for professional evaluation or research, to health workers; see below Chapter IX.

41 For the definition of health care system, see Art. 3 of the International Code.

42 On the scope of the International Code, see above Chapter IV.

43 During the August Consultation 1980, one of the invited experts stated that "...any sample, by virtue of brand identification, was by its very nature promotional, and therefore should not be allowed." See August Consultation 1980, p.10, paragraph 23.2. The representative of one of the infant food manufacturers, Ross Laboratories, at that consultation said that "...

mother of an infant, or the pregnant woman, as to whether to breast-feed or use breast-milk substitutes. As the Turkish Delegate to the Thirty-fourth WHA (the late Professor Dogramaci) pointed out:

> ... if the expectant mother was showered with clever publicity and sometimes even free samples of breast-milk substitutes, she could not always be expected to make a wise decision in the best interests of the health of her baby. The aim of the Code was precisely to protect mothers and future mothers from unethical marketing practices.[44]

The New Zealand Delegate (Dr Barker), commenting on the mother's choice of breast-feeding or otherwise, said that

> in making her decision she should not be subjected to commercial pressure of any kind.[45]

An authority on breast-feeding, Dr. Savage King, has made the point very clearly:

> We know that [giving samples] and advertisements are one of the factors that make women stop breast-feeding. Mothers are persuaded that breast milk substitutes are as good as breast milk, or better....[46]

Moreover, samples of breast-milk substitutes cannot provide adequate quantities for feeding the infant. They are, as defined by the Code, "single or small quantities of a product". Therefore, their giving can only be motivated by the desire to promote breast-milk substitutes and influence the mother on their use. The Swiss Delegate to the September Consultation 1980 used very clear terms to describe the motive behind the giving of samples. He said:

> samples are clearly sales promotion and samples can never be sufficient,...either for short term or long term, for the infant feeding.[47]

It might be appropriate to conclude by referring to a successful example of how the banning of advertising and the distribution of samples can lead to the promotion of breast-feeding. In a health care facility in the Philippines, the International Code was applied, some years ago, on a trial basis, where advertisements for breast-milk substitutes and the distribution of samples thereof to mothers were banned. This is reported to have led to a 60% increase in breast-

---

it would be practically impossible to discontinue the use of samples given the high demand for them among paediatricians and physicians in general." Ibid. It is interesting to note that ICIFI, in its Observations on the International Code, made no objection to the ban on the giving of samples of products covered by the Code. See ICIFI's Observations, above note 22, pp.6-7.

44 See above note 7, p.194.
45 See above note 5, p.70.
46 See Dr Savage King, op.cit., pp.167-8.
47 See September Consultation 1980, tape 26, p.2.

feeding.[48]

It has been reported that the practice of giving samples of products within the scope of the Code is still continuing in many parts of the world. The IGBM researchers have found that in all the four countries where the research was carried out, mothers and pregnant women received samples of products covered by the Code.[49] Similar practices have recently been reported in Croatia, Lebanon and the Netherlands, to give but a few examples.[50]

3. BAN ON ADVERTISING, PROMOTION AND THE GIVING OF SAMPLES AT THE RETAIL LEVEL

As a form of elaboration of the principle of the prohibition on advertising and other forms of promotion and the giving of samples, the International Code, in Article 5.3, specifies what is not allowed at the retail level. It reads as follows:

> in conformity with paragraphs 1 and 2 of this Article, there should be no point-of-sale advertising, giving of samples, or any other promotion device to induce sales directly to the consumer at the retail level, such as special displays, discount coupons, premiums, special sales, loss-leaders and tie-in sales, for products within the scope of this Code. This provision should not restrict the establishment of pricing policies and practices intended to provide products at lower prices on a long-term basis.

Accordingly, the Code bans any advertisement at any point-of-sale, be it a shop, pharmacy, supermarket, stall and so on. Moreover, it bans the giving of samples of any product covered by it, as well as the use of any promotional device mentioned in Article 5.3, in order to induce sales of such products, directly to the consumer, at the retail level. It has to be stated that the provision only gives some examples of these promotional devices, i.e., special displays, discount coupons, tie-in-sales and so on. It should be pointed out that the mention of these promotional devices is by way of giving examples and is *not meant to be*

---

48 See *New Scientist*, Vol. 94, No. 1310 (17 June 1982), p.799.

49 See *Cracking the Code*, op. cit., p. 12. The researchers found Nestlé gave samples of breast-milk substitutes in Poland and South Africa; Curity gave samples of feeding bottles in South Africa; Mead Johnson, Snow and Dumex, gave samples of breast-milk substitutes in Thailand, to give but a few examples. Ibid., p. 13. Nestlé's reply to this finding is that they were unable to check the validity or otherwise of the finding and that the report contained allegations relating to products outside the scope of the Code. See "*A Missed Opportunity*", op. cit., p. 11. Examples of other reported giving of samples may be given :in Pakistan, Abbott-Ross offers a free tin of Similac for every ten tins bought; Friesland sends samples of its infant formula Frisolac to Dutch mothers; samples of Maeil's infant formula Mamma are given to mothers in shops in the Republic of South Korea; samples of Milupa's infant formula are sent by post to mothers in Switzerland, and future mothers in Canada and the USA are mailed samples of Nestlé's infant formula Good Start. See *Breaking the Rules*, op. cit., pp. 8, 15, 20, 24 and 27.

50 See *Breaking the Rules Stretching the Rules, op..cit.*, pp. 30,36, and 52.

exhaustive. The Code will apply to any promotional device, whether it is mentioned in the Code or not, as long as it is intended to induce sales directly to the consumer, at the retail level. The test is therefore this: is the device intended to persuade the consumer to buy the product in question? If the answer is yes, then the Code applies, and if the answer is no, the Code will not apply. It is known that where people are offered discount coupons on certain products, the intention is to attract the buyer and sell more of such products. Therefore, when any of the products covered by the Code is being sold with this device, the intention is likely to be to induce people to buy such products, and thus promote the product in question. Since the Code bans any form of promotion of breast-milk substitutes, feeding bottles and teats, this ban applies to this particular form of promotion. Indeed, Article 5.3 begins with the phrase "in conformity with paragraphs 1 and 2 of this Article", and goes on to refer to advertising, giving of samples and the other activities which are subject to the ban.

The specific situation dealt with in Article 5.3 is the retail level. This appears to be intended to complete the picture, insofar as the ban on advertising, promotion and giving of samples are concerned. For Article 5.1 deals with the general public while Article 5.2 deals with pregnant women, mothers and members of their families, whereas Article 5.3 deals with the consumer, in general at the retail level. Therefore, if any category of persons is not caught by paragraphs 1 or 2 of Article 5, then it must be caught by paragraph 3 of the provision, as the term "consumer" is so general that it can apply to any person. According to *The Concise Oxford Dictionary*

> "consumer" means "1) a person who consumes, especially one who uses a product. 2) A purchaser of goods or services.[51]

It must be stated that Article 5.3 is not intended to interfere with sales and pricing policies of manufacturers and distributors of products within the scope of the International Code. This is clearly stated in the provision:

> this provision should not restrict the establishment of pricing policies and practices intended to provide products at lower prices on a long-term basis.

This wording can be interpreted to mean that a manufacturer of a breast-milk substitute can offer his product at a reduced price, provided that it is on a long-term basis. For in this case, the assumption of promotional intent, which exists if the reduced price is on a short-term basis, would not apply when sales are on a long-term basis. This is in line with the policy and spirit of the International Code on advertising, promotion and the giving of samples of products covered by it.

It has been reported that the practice of point-of-sale advertising, giving of samples and the use of the promotional devices mentioned in Article 5.3, in

---

51 See 9th edn. (1995), p.287.

order to induce sales at the retail level, is continuing in many parts of the world. The IGBM researchers found that, in all the four countries where the research was carried out, advertising and promotion of products within the scope of the Code at the retail level is continuing.[52]

4. BAN ON GIFTS OF ARTICLES AND UTENSILS

Following its aim of encouraging breast-feeding and its policy of banning any form of promotion of breast-milk substitutes, Article 5.4 of the International Code bans another promotional device, namely the giving of gifts of articles and utensils, which *may* promote the use of breast-milk substitutes or bottle-feeding. It reads as follows:

> Manufacturers and distributors should not distribute to pregnant women or mothers of infants and young children any gifts of articles or utensils which may promote the use of breast-milk substitutes or bottle-feeding.

It is known that manufacturers and distributors of breast-milk substitutes or feeding bottles and teats distribute gifts, such as calendars, attractive posters, booklets, product samples,[53] cups and so on, to pregnant women or mothers of infants, in order to promote their products. This practice is banned by Article 5.4 of the International Code. It is to be noted that the provision uses the term "may", which is a permissive term and expresses the possibility of something happening (I may have been wrong).[54]

---

52 See Cracking the Code, op. cit., p. 20. The researchers found flyers on the counter by Coberco Omefa for their breast-milk substitute product, in Bangladesh; Nestlé's Nan 1 leaflets in retail outlets in Poland; Curity's posters for teats at a supermarket in South Africa; Pur's special display cabinet in a shop in Thailand; and Nutricia's billboards for their products in Bangladesh. See ibid., p. 21. Nestlé's reply to this finding is that two of the Nestlé promotions remain unidentified by IGBM, while the identified one relates to Nan 1 and Nan 2, which are prepared for the medical profession. See *"A Missed Opportunity"*, op. cit., p. 13. Other reported examples of promotion at the retail level may be given : special displays of Chicco's bottles and teats are used in shops in Colombia, Côte d'Ivoire, the Czech Republic, Mauritius, Mexico, Peru, Portugal and Spain; Evenflo's feeding bottles are advertised at the point-of-sale in Colombia, Mexico and Peru; in the Republic of Korea, mothers are given samples of Maeil's infant formula Mamma, discounts and promotional literature in shops; in the Philippines, Mead Johnson representatives promote their products directly to mothers at the milk shelves in supermarkets, while a chain of pharmacies has filled the windows of its shops with desplays of Mead Johnson's infant formula; Morinaga promotes its infant formula at the point-of-sale and tie-in sales in Pakistan; and in Côte d'Ivoire, shops give gifts to mothers if they buy Nestlé's infant formula Guigoz; and in South Africa, shops sell Nestlé's infant formula at a special price. See *Breaking the Rules*, op. cit., pp. 11, 13, 20, 21, 25 and 27. See also *Breaking the Rules Stretching the Rules,* op. cit., pp. 37, 45, and 52.

53 See the Jelliffes above, note 3, p.73.

54 See *The Concise Oxford Dictionary,* 9th edn. (1995), p.842; see also above Chapter VI, p.105.

The expression "any gifts of articles or utensils" applies generally and without any qualification as long as they "may" promote the use of breast-milk substitutes or bottle-feeding. Moreover, the ban applies without any geographical limitations, i.e., it applies to the distribution of such gifts in hospitals, health centres, homes, shops, pharmacies and so on. Therefore, if the mere possibility of promotion exists, the action is covered by the provision. However, in determining whether or not promotional intent exists, logic and reasonableness have to be applied, even though the provision speaks of "any gift of articles or utensils". For example, if a manufacturer of breast-milk substitutes offers the pregnant wife of one of his clients a bunch of roses, common sense suggests that this cannot be considered as a promotion of breast-milk substitutes. Therefore, the Code would not apply. But if, in this example, the offer was a package of literature on infant feeding, with a calendar showing an infant being bottle-fed, this package suggests a promotional intent. Therefore, it would be covered by the International Code.

As we have seen, the provision applies to the distribution to pregnant women or mothers of infants and young children of gifts of articles or utensils. Now, supposing the distribution of such gifts is made to the husbands, or daughters, of pregnant women or mothers of infants and young children, does Article 5.4 apply ? If the provision is interpreted literally, then it would not apply, because the wording speaks of "pregnant women or mothers of infants and young children". Therefore, in our example above, the distribution of such gifts would fall outside the scope of Article 5.4. On the other hand, it could be argued that the intent of the Code and its policy favour the promotion of breast-feeding. And one of its major principles is the banning of advertising and all sorts of promotion and promotional devices of breast-milk substitutes and other products covered by it. Therefore, it would not be logical to allow the form of promotion mentioned in our example above. Nor would it be compatible with the spirit of the Code to do so. Accordingly, it is submitted that any gift of article or utensil, distributed to any person closely related to the pregnant woman or the mother of an infant or young child, should be subject to the Code, as long as it "may" promote the use of breast-milk substitutes or bottle-feeding. Therefore, the expression "members of their families" should be implied in the provision, and their non-mention maybe due to an oversight by the drafters. Article 5.2 refers expressly to the members of the family of pregnant women and mothers.

It has been reported that the practice of giving gifts to mothers is continuing in several parts of the world.[55]

---

55 For examples, see the giving of diaries to mothers by Maeil in the Republic of Korea; the giving of carrier bags to mothers by Nutripharm/Diepal in Gabon; and the giving of baby health record books to parents by Wyeth in Chile, Colombia, Nicaragua, Pakistan, the Philippines and Thailand. See *Breaking the Rules*, op. cit., pp.20, 32 and 38; also *Breaking the Rules Stretching the Rules,* op. cit., pp.52, 56, and 66.

5. BAN ON CONTACT BETWEEN MARKETING PERSONNEL AND PREGNANT WOMEN AND MOTHERS

Article 5.5 of the International Code bans marketing personnel from contacts with pregnant women or mothers of infants and young children, as part of its policy to remove the influences and pressures on them, regarding the decision as to the method of feeding their infants. It reads as follows:

> Marketing personnel, in their business capacity, should not seek direct or indirect contact of any kind with pregnant women or with mothers of infants and young children.

The term "marketing personnel" is defined in Article 3 of the Code as

> any persons whose functions involve the marketing of a product or products coming within the scope of this Code.[56]

This ban applies to the seeking of direct and indirect contact of any kind, by such personnel with pregnant women, mothers of infants and young children. Furthermore, it applies to any means used to effect such contact, be it by personal contact, telephone, post, internet, and so on. In addition, the ban applies wherever the contact takes place, be it in the street, health centre, clinic, hospital, the home and so forth. This standpoint is based on the wording of the provision, which contains neither limitations, nor qualifications, with respect to the means used for, and the venue of, such contact.

It would seem that Article 5.5 of the Code implies an action on the part of any marketing personnel vis-à-vis pregnant women or mothers of infants and young children. For seeking[57] contact implies an effort on the part of the former towards the latter. Therefore, if a mother of an infant, herself, seeks the contact with a person employed by a manufacturer of breast-milk substitutes to sell those products, then Article 5.5 would not apply. This is so, because the contact was initiated by the mother and not by the seller of the breast-milk substitutes. But if the latter pursues the pregnant woman, or tempts her, to seek contact subsequently, in order to sell her those products, then his action would be caught by Article 5.5.

It is to be noted that the provision applies to contacts between the marketing personnel and pregnant women and mothers of infants "in their business capacity". Therefore, any other contact, which is not in a business capacity, would not offend against the provision. The qualification just mentioned seems reasonable, as the intent of the provision is to remove any possible influence, which may be exerted by such personnel, on the pregnant woman and the mother, for

---

56 The term "marketing" is also defined in Article 3 of the Code.

57 According to *The Concise Oxford Dictionary* "seek" means "make a search or inquiry for,... try or want to find or get." See 9th edn. (1995), p 1251.

the purpose of promoting and selling the products they are employed to sell. This kind of influence and promotion would be to the detriment of breast-feeding, which is the principal element of the aim of the Code,[58] and would not be compatible with Article 5.1 of the International Code.

It has been reported that contacts between representatives of producers of breast-milk substitutes and mothers, in their business capacity, are still continuing, in several parts of the world. The IGBM *Cracking the Code* report has found that in all four countries where the research was carried out, personnel employed by manufacturers of products covered by the Code visited health care facilities, unrequested, in order to give product information to mothers.[59]

In the process of implementation of the International Code, the ban on advertising and other forms of promotion of breast-milk substitutes and other products covered by the Code is the most widely implemented part of the Code. Some Member States have followed the approach of the Code, as laid down in Article 5,[60] while others have enlarged the ban to include infant foods other than breast-milk substitutes.[61] And yet, there are others, which, while not adopting any national measures to implement the Code, or doing so only in part, have banned the advertisement and promotion of breast-milk substi-

---

58 See above p.48.

59 See *Cracking the Code*, op. cit. p.17. Examples of the manufacturers in question are Mead Johnson in Thailand and Bangladesh, Nestlé in Poland, Thailand and Bangladesh, Milco in Bangladesh, and Gerber in South Africa. See ibid. Nestlé's reply to this finding is that such visits would be against company policy. See "*A Missed Opportunity*", op. cit., p.13. Examples of other reported visits of company personnel may be given: Mead Johnson's representatives visit hospitals in Pakistan to "help" mothers with breast-feeding and to show them how to use their products, health care facilities in Brazil, Chile, and Pakistan; Milupa's representatives visit hospitals in Côte d' Ivoire to "help" mothers with breast-feeding; representatives of Nutricia/Cow & Gate visit mothers in hospitals in Côte d' Ivoire, Netherlands and Pakistan; and representatives of Nutripharm/ Diepal have a considerable level of contact with mothers in Côte d' Ivoire. See *Breaking the Rules*, op. cit., pp. 21, 24, 31 and 32. See also *Breaking the Rules Stretching the Rules, op.cit.*, p. 56.

60 For examples, see Art. 6 of the Bahraini Law 1995, Art. 5 of the Brazilian Marketing Regulations, Arts. 5, 6 and 7 of the Guatemalan Law, 1983, Sec. 9 of the Kenyan Code 1983, Sec. 6 of the Philippines Code of Marketing 1986, Art. II (2.1 and 2.2) and Art. III (3.1-3.3) of the Sri Lankan Code for the Promotion of Breast-feeding, Art. 6 of the Tunisian Law 1983, Art. 6 of the draft Syrian Code 1993, Art. 6 of the draft Jordanian Code1994, Art. 6, of the draft Omani Code1995 and Art. 6 of the draft UAE Law 1995. Art. 8, paragraph 1, of the European Directive 1991, restricts advertising of infant formulae to publications specializing in baby care and scientific publications. It goes on to say: "Member States may further restrict or prohibit such advertising". It thus gives Member States the legal basis for enlarging the scope of the ban. Art. 8, paragraphs 2 and 3 of the Directive, ban the point-of-sale advertising, the giving of samples, other promotional devices and gifts to the consumer, the general public, or to pregnant women or members of their families, directly or indirectly.

61 For example, see Sec. 3(c) of the Indian Infant Milk Substitutes Act 1992, and Art. 2 of the Guatemalan Rules 1987; see also Sec. 4(1) of IBFAN's Model Law.

tutes.[62] This demonstrates clear recognition on the part of Member States that this marketing practice causes harm to breast-feeding, which should not be allowed to continue. For even those Member States which took no particular action to promote breast-feeding, or adopt any of the principles of the Code, felt the need to ban, specifically, this practice.

---

62 For examples, see the ban on advertising of breast-milk substitutes in Algeria, Central African Republic, Gabon, Liberia, Cuba, Panama, Bulgaria, Turkey, Egypt, Yemen, Brunei Darussalam, the Cook Islands, Japan and Malaysia. See the International Code of Marketing of Breast-milk Substitutes: Synthesis of Reports on Action Taken (1981-1990), *WHO Doc. WHO/MCH/NUT/90.1*, p.4, paragraph 13, p.5, paragraphs 18 and 22, p.6, paragraph 28, p.11, paragraph 58, p.13, paragraph 71, p.19, paragraph 101, p.26, paragraph 132, p.30, paragraph 152, p.33, paragraph 169, p.35, paragraphs 178 and 181, p.36, paragraph 185 and p.37, paragraph 190.

CHAPTER VIII

THE POSITION OF THE HEALTH CARE SYSTEM UNDER THE INTERNATIONAL CODE

Article 3 of the International Code defines the health care system as

> governmental, non-governmental or private institutions or organizations engaged, directly or indirectly, in health care for mothers, infants and pregnant women; and nurseries or child-care institutions. It also includes health workers in private practice. For the purposes of this Code, the health care system does not include pharmacies or other established sales outlets.

These institutions, organizations, nurseries and surgeries can play a very important role in the promotion, encouragement and support of breast-feeding, as well as in the proper use of breast-milk substitutes, when their use is necessary. One need look no further than the Code's preamble for the recognition of this role, which reads as follows:

> The Member States of the World Health Organization:
>
> - - -
>
> Affirming that health care systems, and the health professionals and other health workers serving in them, have an essential role to play in guiding infant feeding practices, encouraging and facilitating breast-feeding, and providing objective and consistent advice to mothers and families about the superior value of breast-feeding, or, where needed, on the proper use of infant formula ....[1]

It is for these reasons that the Code attributes several tasks to the health care systems and regulates certain activities in those systems. These are laid down in Article 6 of the Code, which reads as follows:

> 6.1 The health authorities in Member States should take appropriate measures to encourage and protect breast-feeding and promote the principles of this Code, and should give appropriate information and advice to health workers in regard to their responsibilities, including the information specified in Article 4.2.
>
> 6.2 No facility of a health care system should be used for the purpose of promoting infant formula or other products within the scope of this Code. This Code does not, however, preclude the dissemination of information to health professionals as provided in Article 7.2.

---

1   See tenth preambular paragraph of the International Code.

6.3 Facilities of health care systems should not be used for the display of products within the scope of this Code, for placards or posters concerning such products, or for the distribution of material provided by a manufacturer or distributor other than that specified in Article 4.3.

6.4 The use by the health care system of "professional service representatives", "mothercraft nurses" or similar personnel, provided or paid for by manufacturers or distributors, should not be permitted.

6.5 Feeding with infant formula, whether manufactured or home-prepared, should be demonstrated only by health workers, or other community workers if necessary; and only to mothers or family members who need to use it; and the information given should include a clear explanation of the hazards of improper use.

6.6 Donations or low-price sales to institutions or organizations of supplies of infant formula or other products within the scope of this Code, whether for use in the institutions or for distribution outside them, may be made. Such supplies should only be used or distributed for infants who have to be fed on breast-milk substitutes. If these supplies are distributed for use outside the institutions, this should be done only by the institutions or organizations concerned. Such donations or low-price sales should not be used by manufacturers or distributors as a sales inducement.

6.7 Where donated supplies of infant formula or other products within the scope of this Code are distributed outside an institution, the institution or organization should take steps to ensure that supplies can be continued as long as the infants concerned need them. Donors, as well as institutions or organizations concerned, should bear in mind this responsibility.

6.8 Equipment and materials, in addition to those referred to in Article 4.3, donated to a health care system may bear a company's name or logo, but should not refer to any proprietary product within the scope of this Code.

All the drafts of the International Code contained a provision on the health care system and its role in the promotion and protection of breast-feeding, though the wording, the order and the contents of the provision varied from one draft to another.[2]

The following aspects of the provision shall now be surveyed:

1. MEASURES TO ENCOURAGE AND PROTECT BREAST-FEEDING

Article 6.1 of the International Code calls on the health authorities of Member States to take appropriate measures to encourage and protect breast-feeding and to promote the principles of the International Code. It reads as follows:

> The health authorities in Members States should take appropriate measures to encourage and protect breast-feeding and promote the principles of this Code, and should give appropriate information and advice to health workers in regard to their responsibilities, including the information specified in Article 4.2.

---

2   See Art. 3 of the First Draft, Art. 4 of the Second Draft, Art. 3 of the Third Draft and Art. 6 of the Fourth Draft.

It is clear from the wording of the provision that no specific measures are suggested to achieve the desired end. Although the wording of the provision is general, it would seem that it was intended to be so, in order to enable Member States to take whatever measures they consider appropriate to encourage and protect breast-feeding. There is, therefore, a large measure of flexibility provided in the provision. Moreover, the preamble of the Code calls on governments to develop social support systems to protect, facilitate and encourage breast-feeding.[3] Accordingly, a State implementing the International Code could take various measures to this end. For example, it could require that the subject of breast-feeding and lactation management should be included in the training and curricula of doctors, nurses, mid-wives, nutritionists and so on. Such a measure would equip those persons with the scientific and practical knowledge to promote breast-feeding. A nurse or a midwife, well versed with the advantages of breast-feeding and lactation management, could play a very important role in explaining to the mother the advantages of breast-feeding to her baby and herself, thus encouraging her to breast-feed. It has been said that

> The training of physicians includes little on infant feeding, and the information that is included (rarely more than two hours of lectures) is more likely to be on artificial feeding than breast-feeding.[4]

Kaplan and Graff gave a good example of training of health workers on breast-feeding. They say that in the USA, the New York City Department of Health (DOHMH)

> in May 2007 ... trained 50 providers from its own staff anf from the public hospital system (Health and Hospitals Corporation) as Certified Lactation Coordinators (CICs), increasing the capacity of both agencies to provide skilled support to breast-feeding women. Four more courses will train 200 additional providers in 2008.[5]

Moreover, the health authorities of a State implementing the International Code can impose on a health worker the duty to encourage, advise and inform mothers and would-be mothers of the health benefits of breast-feeding to them and their infants. Such a measure would be an incentive to the health worker to do so, and, at the same time, makes him accountable to the health authorities, if he fails to do so. It might be interesting to mention that in Belgium, an Order of the Regent prescribed that the staff of maternity establishments and clinics

> ... had the obligation of ensuring that mothers did not elude the natural duty to breast-feed their infants except on adequate grounds and with the approval of the attending physician.[6]

---

3   See ninth preambular paragraph of the International Code.
4   See *Breast-feeding – The technical basis and recommendations*, op. cit.,p. 50.
5   See "Marketing Breast-feeding-Reversing Corporate Influence on Infant Feeding Practices", op. cit., p.14.
6   See Sec. 3 of the Order of the Regent, dated 15 July 1946; see the late Dr. De Moerloose,

Furthermore, in South Africa, national regulations prescribe that

> ... midwives must take all possible steps to promote breast-feeding, unless there is medical advice to the contrary.[7]

In Austria, professional rules lay down that

> ... the midwife must emphasize to the mother the importance of breast-feeding for the healthy development of the infant. If there are difficulties in this regard, the midwife must arrange for a physician to be called in.[8]

In the land of Hamburg (in the then Federal Republic of Germany), an Ordinance of 25 July 1961 prescribes, in Sec.32, that

> ... the midwife must in all cases insist that the mother breast-feed her own child. If the woman is ill, a physician is required to decide whether recourse should be had to artificial feeding.[9]

Another appropriate measure that can be taken by the health authorities under Article 6.1, which is of special importance to the working mother, is the question of maternity leave[10] and other measures to facilitate breast-feeding, at or near, the work place. A working mother, who is keen and determined to breast-feed her infant, may hesitate to do so, if her job is at risk. If she cannot be absent from her job, on maternity leave, she will not be in a position to breast-feed, because she will not want to risk losing her job. Or, if her maternity leave is limited to, shall we say, two months, she would not be encouraged to breast-feed her infant beyond that two months period. But if she knows she has a maternity leave, of a reasonable duration, the mother will certainly be encouraged to breast-feed her infant. Therefore, maternity leave provides an important incentive to the working mother to breast-feed, and thus achieve the aim of Article 6.1 for the promotion of breast-feeding.

Sweden offers an excellent example of this facility, which is named parental leave. When a child is born in Sweden, the parents can take up to 390 days of paid leave, up to the child's eighth birthday. This period is shared between the

---

"Maternity and Child Health: Legislation on the Promotion of Breast-feeding", op. cit., p.3.

7 See Regulation 19 concerning the conduct of midwives promulgated by the 1963 Government Notice, ibid., p.4.

8 See Sec.44 of the Professional Rules for Midwives, issued by an ordinance of 3 April 1970. Ibid. In the UK, the Midwives Rules of 1955 laid down that a practising midwife, or a midwife acting as a maternity nurse, must forthwith notify the local authorities of each case in which artificial feeding is adopted in addition or in place of breast-feeding. However, since 1960, this is no longer required. Ibid.

9 Ibid.

10 There is an ILO Convention and a Recommendation providing for 12 or 14 weeks maternity leave for breast-feeding mothers; see ILO Convention No.103, Convention concerning Maternity Protection (Revised 1952) Art.3.2; and Recommendation No.95, Recommendation concerning Maternity Protection, Art. I,1(1).

father and the mother of the child by agreement between them. The State pays 80% of their salary for 13 months, and parents' jobs are guaranteed during parental leave, which can be taken monthly, weekly, daily and even hourly.[11]

Other facilities at or near the work place, such as crèches, nurseries, feeding intervals provided by law, could also be provided by the health authorities for the encouragement of breast-feeding. If the mother is able to bring her infant to the work place, or near it, she will be encouraged to breast-feed him. Even if the maternity leave is too short, the provision of such facilities would encourage the mother to continue breast-feeding her infant. The preamble of the Code calls upon governments to "create an environment that fosters breast-feeding."[12] It might be worthwhile mentioning a successful example of a facility for breast-feeding at the work place. When the author was on a mission for WHO in Guatemala in 1992, he visited the offices of the Institute of Nutrition of Central America and Panama (INCAP) [13] in Guatemala city. He was shown a reasonably-sized room, on the premises, where mothers of infants and young children left them during working hours. Breast-feeding mothers would come at regular intervals to that room to feed their infants. This arrangement provided satisfaction to both the mothers and the employer.

Of course, it is not always possible to provide adequate maternity leave, or facilities for breast-feeding at, or near the work place. But if there is a political commitment to encourage and promote breast-feeding in a given State, and if the health benefits to society and its economic development resulting from the healthy growth of infants are taken into account, ways can be found to accommodate the needs of the working mother in this respect.

Article 6.1 also calls on the health authorities to take appropriate measures to promote the principles of the Code. It is difficult to see what specific measures are envisaged here, for the principles of the Code cover several areas. However, it could be argued that the wording in question should be considered as a general recommendation to Member States to take whatever measures they deem appropriate for the promotion of any and every principle contained in the Code. That is to say, Member States may adopt any measure, though not included in the provisions of the Code, for the purpose of promoting its principles. For example, the Code does not refer to the holding of workshops in Member States for the promotion of its principles. Under Article 6.1 a State implementing the Code in a national statute could hold such workshops in its territory, for the purpose of launching its statute. The holding of such workshops amounts to a measure intended to promote the principles and aim of the

---

11 See *International Herald Tribune*, June 10,2010, p. 4.

12 See ninth preambular paragraph of the International Code.

13 INCAP was established in 1948 by the Ministers of Health of Costa Rica, El Salvador, Guatemala, Honduras, Nicaragua and Panama and the Director of the Pan American Health Organization (PAHO). Its headquarters are in Guatemala city. See pamphlet issued by INCAP on its origins and organization...etc. p.1.

statute. As such, it would be considered as a measure envisaged under Article 6.1 of the Code.

It may be interesting to point out that some Member States implementing the International Code have provided for the inclusion of breast-feeding and lactation management in the curricula of health workers, and provided for maternity leave and breast-feeding periods during working hours.[14]

2. INFORMATION AND ADVICE TO HEALTH WORKERS

Article 6.1 of the International Code calls on the health authorities of Member States to provide appropriate information and advice to health workers, with respect to their responsibilities under the Code. The responsibilities of the health workers are dealt with in Article 7 of the Code, and they include the encouragement of breast-feeding, non-acceptance of financial or material inducements and so on.[15] It is, therefore, very important for the health workers to know what their responsibilities are under the Code, and how to exercise them. For, given their work commitments, they may not be aware of such responsibilities. It has been said that

> lack of information and lack of support from health professionals, particularly physicians and nurses, for mothers who are considering, who wish to, or who are breast-feeding have been identified as major obstacles to successful breast-feeding. Although health professionals generally have positive attitudes towards breast-feeding, they are often misinformed about the basic physiology and lack of the skills necessary for the management of lactation.[16]

Furthermore, the Code has brought about a new situation and a new regime, which is intended to disallow certain previous marketing practices. If the health worker is not aware of such a change, her or she may continue to accept, for example, samples of breast-milk substitutes from manufacturers or distributors, and thus harm breast-feeding, unintentionally. Thus, the provision of advice and appropriate information to the health worker can be a very useful tool to guide, educate and alert him, or her, to their essential role in encouraging and facilitating breast-feeding, or where necessary, on the proper use of breast-milk substitutes. Article 6.1 makes a specific reference to the information contained in Article 4.2, which has to be provided. The latter provision requires informa-

---

14 See for examples, Art. 7(a), paragraphs 1-3 of the draft Jordanian Code 1994; Art. 7, paragraphs 1-3 of the draft Omani Code 1995; and Art. 7, paragraphs 1-3 of the draft Code of the UAE 1995. The Iranian Law 1996, grants breast-feeding mothers maternity leave for four months, for up to three children, in the government and private sectors; see Art. 3 thereof. It also provides for one hour leave every day for mothers to breast-feed their infants and job security, ibid, Art. 3, Notes 1 and 2.

15 For details see below Chapter IX.

16 See *Breast-feeding – The technical basis and recommendations for action*, op.cit., pp.49-50.

tion regarding the superiority of breast-feeding, the negative effect on breast-feeding from the introduction of partial bottle-feeding and so on.[17] This reference is not exclusive of other information, but is intended to provide a specific example of information to be provided.

3. BAN ON PROMOTION IN THE HEALTH CARE SYSTEM

Article 6.2 of the International Code does not permit the use of any facility of a health care system, for the purpose of promoting breast-milk substitutes, feeding bottles and teats. It reads as follows:

> No facility of a health care system should be used for the purpose of promoting infant formula or other products within the scope of this Code. This Code does not, however, preclude the dissemination of information to health professionals as provided in Article 7.2.

Therefore, no hospital, maternity ward, health centre or nursery[18] can be used for promoting any of those products. Accordingly, no publicity, giving of samples, posters, brochures, gifts and so on can take place in a health care facility, irrespective of who the promoter may be. This prohibition constitutes part of the policy of the Code to ban the advertising and other form of promotion of the products covered by it. As has been seen earlier, Article 5 bans these practices to the general public and at the retail level, while Article 6.2 does the same at the level of the health care facility, and thus covers another theatre for such practices.

However, Article 6.2 is not intended to prevent relevant information from reaching facilities of the health care systems. It does allow the dissemination of scientific and factual information to health professionals, as provided for in Article 7.2. In other words, the intent of the provision is to prevent promotion and not scientific and factual information about the products covered by the Code, which the health professionals may need in order to exercise their functions.

4. BAN ON SPECIFIC ASPECTS OF PROMOTION IN THE HEALTH CARE SYSTEM

Article 6.3 adds other specific types of promotional activities relating to products covered by the Code, which are not allowed in any part of the health care system. It reads as follows:

> Facilities of health care systems should not be used for the display of products within the scope of this Code, for placards or posters concerning such products, or for the distribution of material provided by a manufacturer or distributor other than that specified in Article 4.3.

---

17 For details see above pp. 101-102.
18 See the definition of "health care system" under Article 3 of the International Code.

Thus, the provision bans the use of any health care facility for the display, in any form or manner, of breast-milk substitutes, feeding bottles and teats, placards or posters promoting them, or the distribution of material provided by manufacturers or distributors, which is not educational or informational regulated by Article 4.3. It is well-known that hospitals and maternities are often used by manufacturers or distributors of breast-milk substitutes or other products covered by the Code, for promotional purposes of such products. This practice takes the form of displaying posters showing healthy-looking infants, other pictures or charts, with the name of the manufacturer, in maternity wards, waiting rooms near doctors' offices or other parts of the health care system. The author has himself seen, in a Member State in the Gulf in 1996, in a maternity hospital well-known for its policy of promoting breast-feeding, such posters and charts displayed in a nursery and maternity ward. When the matter was drawn to the attention of those responsible for the hospital, they were surprised that such posters and charts had not been removed. The IGBM researchers found posters promoting breast-milk substitutes in some of the health care facilities of all the four countries where the research was carried out.[19]

The purpose of the ban contained in Article 6.3 is to prevent the temptation to use such products, to remove a source of anxiety for mothers and would-be mothers and to remove any possible influence in favour of breast-milk substitutes, which may arise from this practice. It has been said that

> the distribution of infant formula,...by hospital personnel, also conveys the clear message that it is the preferred mode of feeding.[20]

Kaplan and Graff, commenting on the use by hospitals in the USA of early formula supplementation to feed infants, quoted four groups of Latina women in New York City, as saying:

> the message they are sending is to bottle-feed-there are a whole bunch of bottles that are out there – ones that look like your nipple, ones with characters like Mickey Mouse, bottles to stop gas. There is less information on the breast milk.[21]

Furthermore, the ban may also serve to remove any association, which a mother may perceive, between the health care system and the producers of breast-milk substitutes. Such an association could give the impression that the use

---

19 See *Cracking the Code*, op. cit., pp.19-20. It has also been reported that Chicco (which is one of the world's largest bottle and teat companies) gives free sample bottles to mothers in hospitals in South Africa and advertises in magazines distributed in the health care system. Chicco is said to advertise on banners and posters in Indonesian hospitals. See *Breaking the Rules*, op.cit., p.11. Violations of Article 6.3 have recently been reported in China, Hungary, Lebanon, Swaziland and the United Arab Emirates, to give but a few examples. See *Breaking the rules-Stretching the Rules*, op.cit, pp. 5, 9, 13, 48 and 94.

20 See *Breast-feeding – The technical basis and recommendations*, op.cit., p.22.

21 See above note 5, p. 13.

of breast-milk substitutes of that producer, or of others in general, is normal, otherwise there would not be any charts or posters in a facility of the health care system. It is to be noted, however, that Article 6.3 deals with some specific aspects of promotion of products within the scope of the Code, at the level of the health care facility. Thus, it is intended to complete the other aspects of promotion dealt with in Article 5 of the Code.

Article 6.3 does not interfere with the donation of informational and educational materials allowed by Article 4.3. There is a clear exception in favour of such materials in Article 6.3. Of course, this is subject to the conditions laid down in Article 4.3.[22]

5. PERSONNEL PROVIDED OR PAID FOR BY MANUFACTURERS OR DISTRIBUTORS

Article 6.4 of the International Code does not allow the use of personnel, provided either by the manufacturers or distributors of products covered by the Code, or paid for by them, in the health care system. It reads as follows:

> The use by the health care system of 'professional service representatives', 'mothercraft nurses' or similar personnel, provided or paid for by manufacturers or distributors, should not be permitted.

It is known that manufacturers or distributors of breast-milk substitutes provide women dressed like nurses, ("mothercraft nurses"), who are not in fact nurses, to hospitals, paediatric wards and maternities. Their main function is to contact mothers and would-be mothers, in order to promote the products of their employers. Manufacturers and distributors of products within the scope of the Code also employ persons, who are sent to facilities of the health care systems, as their representatives ("professional service representatives"), whose main function is to sell breast-milk substitutes to health workers, and inform and advise them about new products in this area, explaining the benefits derived from the use of such products. In other words, they promote the use of breast-milk substitutes. The provision bans the use of such personnel, in any part of the health care system.[23]

The rational for this ban is that such personnel, by their deceptive appearance, could give the impression that they are employed by the health care facility concerned, and as such could exert influence in favour of the use of breast-

---

22 For these conditions see above pp. 105-107.

23 The term "professional service representatives" and "similar personnel" were added to the Fourth Draft, by the Drafting Committee, in the light of the discussions at the August and September Consultations, 1980. See the proposal of the Swedish Delegate to add the words "all similar personnel", September Consultation 1980, tape 28, p.2. The French Delegate had a similar idea; ibid., p.3. See also the August Consultation 1980, p.11, paragraph 30.1.

milk substitutes in such facilities. A woman, dressed like a nurse, and telling a mother that bottle-feeding, or the use of breast-milk substitutes, is good for feeding her infant, could easily influence the mother, or would-be mother, who is hesitant, or unaware of the advantages of breast-feeding. How can the mother tell that such a woman is, in fact, not a nurse employed by that health care facility? Furthermore, such personnel, by their conduct, could influence health professionals and other health workers in the health care system, about the use of breast-milk substitutes. In addition, any similar personnel, it would seem, whatever their designation maybe, are not permitted to be used in the health care system. This category may include information officers, advisers and so on, provided or paid for by manufacturers or distributors of products within the scope of the Code. If such personnel, it would be reasonable to argue, are provided or paid for by the health care system, then their employment would not be incompatible with Article 6.4, provided that they are not promoting the use of breast-milk substitutes. Thus, the ban imposed by the provision on this practice constitutes a reasonable measure for the encouragement and promotion of breast-feeding.

6. DEMONSTRATION OF FEEDING WITH BREAST-MILK SUBSTITUTES

Article 6.5 of the International Code deals with the practice of demonstrating feeding with infant formula, whether home-made or manufactured, and restricts such demonstration to health workers, or other community workers only. It reads as follows:

> Feeding with infant formula, whether manufactured or home-prepared, should be demonstrated only by health workers, or other community workers if necessary; and only to the mothers or family members who need to use it; and the information given should include a clear explanation of the hazards of improper use.

Furthermore, the provision restricts such demonstration only to mothers or family members who need to use it. Such demonstration was known to be practised by manufacturers or distributors of breast-milk substitutes.[24] Therefore, it is in line with the policy of the Code to promote breast-feeding to permit the health worker, or the community worker alone, to carry out the demonstration of feeding with breast-milk substitutes. This restriction cuts a link and prevents contacts, which would otherwise exist, between manufacturers and distributors of breast-milk substitutes and the mother or members of her family. Thus, the risk of promoting such products can now be avoided, it being understood

---

24 It has been reported that Abbott representatives demonstrate how to use Similac and Isomil (both are breast-milk substitutes) in health care facilities in Chile, Colombia, Pakistan and South Africa. See *Breaking the Rules*, op.cit., p.8.

that the health worker or the community worker would not be interested in promoting bottle-feeding.

It is to be observed that the use of the term "infant formula", instead of the term "breast-milk substitutes" in Article 6.5 is, probably, due to an oversight by the drafters of the Code. Therefore, and in the light of the position taken by the WHA and the Executive Board,[25] Article 6.5 should be read to include *all* breast-milks substitutes. Furthermore, the health worker mentioned in the provision is intended to cover any health worker, as defined in Article 3 of the Code. However, the term "community workers" is not defined by the Code. Therefore, it should be given its ordinary meaning, i.e., any person providing any service to the community. The latter can demonstrate bottle-feeding only "if necessary", which implies that if there is a health worker, he or she has priority in carrying out such a task, perhaps because the health worker might be in a better position to explain the health hazards of the improper use of breast-milk substitutes.

The demonstration of bottle-feeding should be done to the mother or members of her family, "who need to use it". This should be understood in the sense of the absence of choice. That is to say, if the mother is ill, or has died, members of her family have to be taught how to use breast-milk substitutes for feeding the infant. The provision also requires that information should be provided about the health hazards of improper use of breast-milk substitutes. It could be inferred from the provision that this information should be provided by the person carrying out the demonstration, and, presumably, during it.

7. DONATIONS OR LOW-PRICE SALES OF SUPPLIES OF PRODUCTS COVERED BY THE INTERNATIONAL CODE

The donation of supplies of breast-milk substitutes, feeding bottles and teats, and the low-price sales thereof to the health care system, is one of the practices the Code is intended to regulate. Article 6.6 of the Code deals with this question and reads as follows:

> Donations or low-price sales to institutions or organizations of supplies of infant formula or other products within the scope of this Code, whether for use in the institutions or for distribution outside them, may be made. Such supplies should only be used or distributed for infants who have to be fed on breast-milk substitutes. If these supplies are distributed for use outside the institutions, this should be done only by the institutions or organizations concerned. Such donations or low-price sales should not be used by manufacturers, or distributors as a sales inducement.

The provision allows this practice to continue,[26] but only under certain condi-

---

25 See above pp. 54-55.

26 It would appear that the continuation of the practice of donations or low-price sales of supplies of breast-milk substitutes was insisted upon by one participant in the August

tions, presumably to permit Member States of WHO, which are not rich, to benefit from it, without harming breast-feeding. Therefore, the provision lays down the following conditions for its application:

(i)   The supplies should be made to institutions or organizations;
(ii) the supplies should only be used or distributed for infants who have to be fed on breast-milk substitutes;
(iii) if these supplies are distributed for use outside the institution, this should be done only by the institution or organization concerned;
(iv) such donations or low-price sales should not be used as a sales inducement; and
(v)   the supplies should be continued for as long as the infants concerned need them (Article 6.7).

Only if such conditions are met, a manufacturer or distributor of products within the scope of the Code can indulge in donations or low-price sales of such products.

Article 6.6 is one of the most controversial provisions of the International Code, for it is not clear as to what is meant by the terms "institutions" or "organizations". These last terms are not defined by the Code. Furthermore, the question of who are the "infants who have to be fed on breast-milk substitutes", proved to be problematic. And the provision can be abused, as a great deal of controversy has arisen with respect to the use of such supplies as a sales incentive. Therefore, these points shall be dealt with in the following pages.

(i) The supplies should be made to institutions or organizations

Article 6.6 of the Code allows donations or low-price sales of supplies of breast-milk substitutes or other products within the scope of the Code to be made to "institutions or organizations" as the first condition. But these terms are not defined by the Code. The question which arises then is this: are these "organizations" and "institutions" parts of the health care system, or are they something different? It is clear that Article 6.6 falls under the heading "health care systems". It could, therefore, be argued that these terms cover any institution or

---

Consultation 1980 namely, Dr Quaimina of Trinidad. She is reported to have said, though this recollection is from memory, that "...because of the poverty of government health systems: ...free supplies to hospitals" were needed. The infant food industry supported this position. See Douglas Johnson: "Dividing Charity from Promotion – A Brief History of the Supplies Debate Incorporated into Article 6, paragraphs 6 and 7, of the International Code of Marketing of Breast-milk Substitutes", 25 November 1985, p.1, paragraph 1 and p.3, paragraph 11. The Swiss Delegate at the September Consultation 1980 also felt that supplies of breast-milk substitutes "...to the health service should be made and that the health service would distribute these products to mothers who need the product". See September Consultation 1980, Transcription of Tapes, tape 28, p.4.

organization, which constitutes a part of the health care system, e.g., hospitals, maternity wards, paediatric departments and so on.

The late Sir Robert Jennings, the former Whewell Professor of International Law at Cambridge University, and a former President and Judge of the ICJ, is of the opinion that the terms "institutions" or "organizations" cover hospitals. He said that

> hospitals which are "health care systems" are no doubt included amongst the "institutions and organizations "to which certain kinds of donations and low-price sales are permitted to be made under Article 6.6.[27]

On the other hand, it could be argued that, although the provision falls under the heading "health care systems", the use of the terms "institutions" and "organizations" rather than facilities of the health care system, indicates a desire on the part of the drafters of the Code to make a distinction between the health care facilities and those "institutions" and "organizations". For had the intention been to cover health care facilities, the Code would have said so. Parts of Article 6 use the terms "facility of a health care system" (Art. 6.2), "facilities of health care systems" (Art. 6.3), and "the health care system" (Art. 6.4). The drafters could have used any of those terms, had they intended Article 6.6 to apply to parts of the health care system.

However, finally the WHA put an end to this uncertainty in 1994, when it urged Member States

> to ensure that there are no donations of free or subsidized supplies of breast-milk substitutes and other products covered by the International Code of Marketing of Breast-milk Substitutes in any part of the health care system.[28]

While no reference is made in the resolution to "institutions" or "organizations", it would be reasonable to suggest that the WHA has clarified the intent of the provision by urging Member States not to allow such supplies to be given to any "part of the health care system". Accordingly, any institution or organization which constitutes part of the health care system, i.e., an institution or organization "engaged directly or indirectly, in health care for mothers, infants, and pregnant women; and nurseries or child-care institutions"[29] can no longer receive such supplies. By contrast, any "institution" or "organization" which does not constitute part of the health care system such as welfare societies or orphanages, could still receive such supplies, provided that all the conditions laid down in the provision are met.

It is interesting to note that the 1985 WHO/UNICEF Consultation on in-

---

27 See an unpublished note by Sir Robert Jennings, November 1985, as a WHO Consultant on "the Meaning of Articles 6, paragraphs 6 and 7 of the International Code of Marketing of Breast-milk Substitutes", p.1, paragraph 4.

28 See Resolution WHA 47.5, operative paragraph 2(2).

29 See definition of "health care system" in Art.3 of the Code.

fants who have to be fed on breast-milk substitutes stated that

> maternity wards and hospitals should not be recipients of free or subsidized supplies of breast-milk substitutes.[30]

The same Consultation declared that

> in orphanages, refugee centres and disaster relief camps, for a variety of social and health reasons, there is likely to be a high proportion of infants who cannot be breast-fed. These institutions may require, and may receive, where necessary, free or subsidized supplies of breast-milk substitutes; they should, however, only be provided and used in a manner that, while ensuring that the infants in question are fed appropriately, do not interfere with the protection and promotion of breast-feeding on behalf of infants in general.[31]

Moreover, the Director-General of WHO wrote to a Member State (Finland), in 1985, in reply to its letter about Article 6.6, saying:

> ... the institutions and organizations mentioned in Article 6, paragraph 6, were intended to mean orphanages and similar social welfare agencies. They were not intended to refer to direct health care providers, that is to say health care facilities such as hospitals amd maternities....[32]

(ii) Infants who have to be fed on breast-milk substitutes

The second condition is that such supplies should only be used to feed, or distributed for, "infants who have to be fed on breast-milk substitutes." This phrase is not defined in the Code, and was the subject of controversy and differences of opinions. The NGOs and infant-food industry both requested WHO to provide some clarification of the meaning of the term.[33] And in May 1985, several delegates to the Thirty-eighth WHA called on the Director-General to convene a technical meeting for that purpose. The Swaziland Delegate (Dr. Tshabalala), referred to Article 6.6 of the Code and the widespread practice of donation of large quantities of breast-milk substitutes to hospitals for feeding new-born infants, which effectively undermined breast-feeding. She urged

> ...the Director-General to convene a meeting involving WHO, UNICEF, scientific

---

30 See Report of a Joint WHO/UNICEF Consultation Concerning "Infants who have to be Fed on Breast-milk Substitutes", WHO, Geneva, 17-18 December 1985, *WHO Doc. WHO/MCH/NUT/86.1*, (April 1996), p.5, paragraph 19.

31 See ibid., p.5, paragraph 24.

32 See letter of Dr Mahler, dated 29 August 1985, to the Minister of Social Affairs and Health, Finland, p.1, third paragraph. The Indian Infant Milk Substitutes Act 1992 permits the giving of supplies of breast-milk substitutes to orphanages; see Sec. 5(a) thereof. The draft Syrian Code 1993 does the same for orphanages and welfare societies; see Art. 7(b), (2). On the question of supplies in emergencies, see above pp. 62-63.

33 See letter from Nestlé to Dr. Tejada, ADG, dated 12 March 1984; and a letter from Infant Formula Action Coalition to the Director-General of WHO, dated 20 November 1985, attachment, p.3.

authorities and non-governmental organizations, so as to clarify the scope of the Articles of the Code relating to that practice.[34]

This call was supported by a number of delegates[35]. The Zimbabwe Delegate (Mrs. Tagwireyi) expressed the hope that

> ...WHO would collaborate with Member States and other relevant agencies in developing appropriate criteria or guidelines concerning infants needing breast-milk substitutes.[36]

It would seem that the Director-General had already decided, in collaboration with UNICEF, to convene such a meeting later in 1985, to develop guidelines for use by Member States in defining the phrase "infants who have to be fed on breast-milk substitutes".[37] In December 1985, a joint WHO/UNICEF Consultation Concerning "Infants who Have to Be Fed on Breast-milk Substitutes" was held in WHO, Geneva. The report of the Consultation was published in April 1986.[38]

The phrase in question, i.e., "infants who have to be fed on breast-milk substitutes", is capable of two interpretations. The first may be to the effect that the phrase covers infants who *need* to be fed on breast-milk substitutes, irrespective of whether this need arises from the wish of the mother not to breast-feed, or for compelling reasons. According to this interpretation, when a mother, who is healthy and capable of breast-feeding her infant, decides not to breast-

---

34 See *WHO Doc .WHA 38/1985/REC/3*, p.68.

35 See the statements by the Delegates of the then Yugoslavia, ibid., p.71, Malawi, ibid., p.76, Uganda, ibid., p.77, Canada, ibid., p.78, Bulgaria, ibid., p.79, and Mauritius, ibid., p.80.

36 Ibid., p.75.

37 See statement by Dr. Petros-Barvazian, the then Director, FHE, ibid., p.82.

38 See *WHO/MCH/NUT/86.1 (April 1986)*. The participants at the Consultation were: Professor C. Arneil, University of Glasgow, UK, Dr B. Coyaji, Director, King Edward Memorial Hospital, Pune, India, Dr M.K. Fathalla, Dean, Faculty of Medicine, University of Assiut, Egypt, Dr D Habte, Head, Department of Paediatrics and Child Health, Tikur Anbessa Hospital, Addis Ababa, Ethiopia, Professor F.E. Hytten, Clinical Research Centre, Harrow, UK, Mrs M.Kyenyka, Breast-feeding Information Group, Nairobi, Kenya, Dr M.E. Latham, Cornell University, New York, USA, Dr Chen Mei-Pu, The International Peace Maternity and Child Health Hospital, Shanghai, China, Dr M. Rea, Director of Infant and Maternal Health, Institute of Health, Sao Paulo, Brazil, and Dr M. Béhar (Temporary Adviser), former Chief, Nutrition Unit, WHO, Geneva. Those from WHO were: Dr A. Petros-Barvazian, Director, FHE, Dr M. Belsey, Chief, MCH, Dr A. Pradilla, Chief, NUT, Dr M. Carballo, MCH, Dr S. Shubber, Senior Legal Officer, Office of the Legal Counsel, Dr K. Edström, Senior Medical Liaison Officer with Operational UN Agencies, WHO, New York, and Mr J. Akré, NUT. Those from UNICEF were: Ms K. Gravero, Project Officer, UNICEF, New York, and Ms M. Newman-Black, NGO Liaison Officer, UNICEF, Geneva. See also the statement of the IOCU representative, Mrs Allain, at the Thirty-ninth WHA, 1986: "As had been observed...around the world, the availability of free supplies of powdered milk in hospitals led to routine bottle-feeding of a great many more infants than was necessary, a practice which directly undermined breast-feeding". See *WHO Doc. WHA39/1986/REC/3, p.102.*

feed because, for example, she is under a misconception of spoiling her appearance, then her infant is one who has to be fed on breast-milk substitutes, which is covered by Article 6.6.

This interpretation is in line with the position taken by IFM. In a paper submitted to the WHO/UNICEF Consultation 1985, IFM took the following position : Referring to the WHO/UNICEF Notes on the International Code 1982, relating to Article 6.6, where it was said that donations or low-price sales of breast-milk substitutes "...should only be used when necessary, for example on medical, economic or social grounds", IFM stated :

> It therefore seems that the definition of "infants who have to be fed on breast-milk substitutes" must relate back to the preamble of the Code, which states: "Considering that when mothers do not breast-feed or only do so partially, there is a legitimate market for infant formula..." thus the definition of an infant who has to be *fed on a breast-milk substitute is one whose mother does not breast-feed, or only does so partially.*[39]

The second interpretation is to the effect that the purpose and the intent of the phrase in question is to apply to situations where there is *compulsion* to use breast-milk substitutes, and not to situations when the mother chooses not to breast-feed for convenience's sake or for other considerations. This standpoint is supported by the interpretation of Article 6.6, by the late Sir Robert Jennings, who was consulted by WHO, before the holding of the above Consultation, on the interpretation of the phrase in question. Referring to the phrase "infants who have to be fed on breast-milk substitutes", he said:

> this means infants who, for clinical reasons cannot be breast-fed and for whom, therefore, there is no option other than the use of substitutes. "Have to" is a phrase indicating an absence of any choice in the matter. Of course the wrongful use of substitutes for infants who do not "have to be" thus fed, will change them into infants that do. But this is precisely what the Code seeks to prevent. This is apparent from the whole intent and purpose of the Code, and if any doubt on this point can be imagined, it must be dispelled by a reading of the Code as a whole, including its preamble.[40]

Moreover, WHO and UNICEF, commenting on Article 6.6, have said that the supplies covered by the provision

> should only be used when necessary, for example on medical, economic or social grounds.[41]

Furthermore, the principal part of the aim of the Code is the promotion of breast-feeding. But the easy availability of breast-milk substitutes in any part of the health care system is likely to lead to their use, without the necessity for

---

39 See information document prepared by IFM for the WHO/UNICEF Consultation 1985, p.4 (emphasis in the original).

40 See above note 27, p.1, paragraph 5.

41 See WHO/UNICEF NOTES 1982, p. 6, paragraph 24.

doing so. As stated in the Report of the WHO/UNICEF Consultation

> ...the routine availability of breast-milk substitutes, which are not only unnecessary but potentially dangerous because they could increase the likelihood of their being used to the detriment of breast-feeding, should not be permitted in maternity wards and hospitals.[42]

Therefore, the second interpretation should be preferred and the first one be rejected, as the former is in line with the aim of the Code and its policy. As the participants in the said Consultation pointed out: the aim of the Code

> ... was the base on which any discussion concerning "infants who have to be fed on breast-milk substitutes" should be built.[43]

Accordingly, the phrase "infants who have to be fed on breast-milk substitutes" applies to infants who are in situations where there is no alternative but to use breast-milk substitutes for survival. Such situations include the case of the mother being dead, or critically ill, the abandonment of the child, extreme poverty of the mother, the separation of mother and child due to natural disaster or man-made disaster, infants who are unable to suck, for example, those suffering from severe cardiac, respiratory or nervous-system disorder and so on.[44] By contrast, as the report of the WHO/UNICEF Consultation concluded

> ... infants of mothers who are physiologically able, but who choose not to breast-feed, should not be eligible to receive free or subsidized supplies of breast-milk substitutes.[45]

The interpretation of Sir Robert Jennings and both the report of the Consultation and the WHO Guidelines, it would appear, have clarified the meaning and intent of the phrase "infants who have to be fed on breast-milk substitutes", in Article 6.6. For when the WHA considered the report of the Director-General on the Code, in conformity with Article 11.6, as well as the report of the Consultation and the WHO Guidelines, no questions were raised as to the precise meaning of that phrase. Moreover, the WHA endorsed the Director-General's report.[46] It was also well received by the great majority of delegates at the Thirty-ninth session of the WHA[47]. The only objection raised in this connection

---

42 See Report of a Joint WHO/UNICEF Consultation concerning "Infants who Have to be Fed on Breast-milk Substitutes", above note 30, p.5, paragraph 19

43 See ibid., p.2, paragraph 4.

44 For details see ibid., pp.3-4; see also WHO Guidelines concerning the Main Health and Socio-economic Circumstances in which Infants have to be Fed on Breast-milk Substitutes, *WHO Doc. WHA39/1986/REC/1*, Annex 6, pp.125-127.

45 See above note 30, p.5, paragraph .23.

46 See Resolution WHA39.28, operative paragraph 1.

47 For example, see the statements of the Delegates of Brazil, Swaziland, Sweden, Liberia, China, Finland, Kuwait, the Netherlands, Ethiopia, Peru, Egypt, and Surinam. See *WHO Doc. WHA39/1986/REC/3*, pp.98, 102, 103, 104, 105, 107, 108, 110, 112 and 117.

was that of the US.[48] Consequently, the controversy surrounding the phrase "infants who have to be fed on breast-milk substitutes" appears to have come to an end. Of course, ultimately, it will be for each Member State implementing the International Code to define the categories of infants to whom Article 6.6 applies, in the light of their social and legal circumstances.[49]

(iii) Distribution of supplies for outside use by the institutions or organizations

Article 6.6 envisages the distribution of donations or low-price sales of supplies of breast-milk substitutes or other products within the scope of the Code, for use outside the institution or organization concerned. This is presumably intended to provide such supplies to "infants who have to be fed on breast-milk substitutes", to families where the mother has died, or is critically ill, or is taking care of abandoned children and so on.[50] However, the provision requires that such distribution should be done only by the institution or organization concerned, e.g., a welfare institution. This requirement, it would seem, is intended to prevent the distribution by other entities, which may use the occasion for promoting breast-milk substitutes, or other products covered by the Code, which is not allowed by the Code.

Moreover, Article 6.7 lays down another requirement in this respect, namely, the supplies should remain available for "as long as the infants concerned need them". This requirement places a responsibility on the shoulder of the distributing institution or organization to ensure this availability. For the provision states that where donated supplies are distributed outside an institution or organization

> the institution or organization should take steps to ensure that supplies can be continued as long as the infants concerned need them.

This is, probably, intended to avoid the situation where a family with an orphan infant may receive such supplies, for example, for one week, then it would have to buy the substitutes itself, which may not be possible, or may be very costly for the family. As the French Delegate to the September Consultation 1980, put it

---

48 The US Delegate (Mr Boyer) said that "the request that maternity wards and hospitals should not use free or subsidized supplies of breast-milk substitutes appeared to be an unnecessary folly, the imposition of a new and expensive burden on the hospitals of developing countries, which could ill afford the supplies they needed". He went on "the intervention at the seventh meeting by the Deputy Chief Delegate of his country had indicated substantial objections to those guidelines....In his view, the guidelines did not represent the reality of infant feeding practices". He also opposed the draft resolution under consideration. Ibid., p.208.

49 See WHO Guidelines, above note 44, p.130, paragraph 59, and Report of the Consultation, above note 30, p.5, paragraph 21.

50 See above, p. 144.

> ... when you place at the disposal of a mother a substitute product, if you started this,
> then you must be able to continue, otherwise it is very dangerous for the infant.[51]

If the continuity of supplies is not ensured, then the institution or organization would not be acting in conformity with Article 6, paragraphs 6 and 7. The donors of such supplies, it would seem clear from the wording of the provision, are also under an obligation to continue the donated supplies, for as long as the infants need them. This responsibility appears to be intended as a warning to the donors, in that they should be prepared to donate the supplies for the whole period required to feed infants on breast-milk substitutes . If otherwise, then the donors' action would not be compatible with Article 6.7. Therefore, there is dual responsibility here, that of the distributing institution or organization and that of the donor.

It is to be noted that Article 6.7 of the Code speaks of the "donors", as far as the responsibility for the continuation of supplies is concerned. But what about the sellers of low-price supplies? There may be situations where such sales amount to donations except in name. The IGBM report discloses that some health care facilities in Thailand have said that

> companies sometimes forget to demand payment for their regular procurement of
> baby milk.[52]

In situations where the price of products covered by the Code (Article 6.7) is too low, two possible interpretations can be advanced: First, if a price paid for the supplies, even though is too low, then the transaction might not be considered a "donation", and as such it would not be covered by Article 6.7. For a price has been paid for the supplies, and the provision does not specify a particular level of price. The countervailing argument could be to the effect that, if the price for the supplies is artificially too low, or if the company providing them "forgets" to claim the price, then this may amount to an attempt to avoid the application of Article 6.7 of the Code through the low price, or no claim of payment. Such cases, it is submitted, appear to be, for all intents and purposes, as cases of "donations", and as such they would be subject to Article 6.7 of the Code. It is submitted that the second interpretation is the preferred one, because it is in line with the intent and spirit of the Code in the promotion of breast-feeding.

The above treatment covers conditions (3) and (5) mentioned above, as it seems more appropriate to deal with them simultaneously because of the close link between them.

---

51 See above note 23, tape 28, p.6; see also the position with respect to HIV, p.58.
52 See below p.149.

(iv) Supplies should not be used as sales inducement

The Code allows the donation or low-price sales of supplies of breast-milk substitutes or other products within its scope, to institutions and organizations, provided that, *inter alia*, they are not used as a sales inducement by manufacturers or distributors of such products. In other words, if a manufacturer gives supplies of breast-milk substitutes to an institution, which is not part of the health care system, with the intention of using such a donation for the purpose of inducing that institution to buy more of these breast-milk substitutes from him, this conduct is contrary to Article 6.6 of the Code. It is well-known, however, that this practice exists for the purpose of inducing sales of such products, and not for "social purposes".[53] The then Nigerian Minister of Health said so eloquently, some years ago

> free and subsidized supplies [of breast-milk substitutes] are not charity; rather they are a well-known and effective marketing practice which should not be allowed to interfere with efforts to actively promote breast-feeding.[54]

Furthermore, the Liberian Delegate (Dr. Camanor) to the Thirty-ninth WHA: stated that

> the practice of free donations of breast-milk substitutes to hospitals and maternity wards encouraged mothers not to breast-feed and promoted the use of breast-milk substitutes by mothers who could normally breast-feed their babies.[55]

There is no escaping the fact that the infant-food industry finds the donation or low-price sales of supplies of breast-milk substitutes an attractive tool to penetrate the health care system in any country. For any manager of a health care system would find it advantageous to accept them, from a financial point of view. Such supplies can be a means of influence by the donor on the donee. There is force in the statement of the Swedish Delegate at the September 1980 Consultation that

> donation is one way of influencing people whom you want to influence, whether it is some prospective buyers or making head personnel more favourable to your plans....[56]

In conclusion, it must be stated that any donation or low-price sale of supplies of breast-milk substitutes and other products within the scope of the Code must comply with *all* the conditions laid down in Article 6, paragraphs 6 and 7. Any failure to comply with any of those conditions will render the conduct of a manufacturer or distributor incompatible with the International Code, even in

---

53 See definition of supplies in Art. 3 of the Code.

54 See Statement of Intent Concerning Resolution WHA39.28 by the late Professor Ransome-Kuti, the then Minister of Health of Nigeria, dated 16 May 1989.

55 See above note 38, p. 104.

56 See WHO September Consultation 1980, tape 28, p.3.

times of emergency. It is significant that the WHA, in the resolution it adopted in 1994 on infant and young child nutrition, urged Member States :

> to exercise extreme caution when planning, implementing or supporting emergency relief operations, by protecting, promoting and supporting breast-feeding for infants, and ensuring that donated supplies of breast-milk substitutes or other products covered by the International Code are given only if all the following conditions apply:
> (a) infants who have to be fed on breast-milk substitutes, as outlined in the guidelines concerning the main health and socio-economic circumstances in which infants have to be fed on breast-milk substitutes;
> (b) the supply is continued for as long as the infants need it;
> (c) the supply is not used as a sales inducement.[57]

As Marion Kelly, commenting on the effect of the Gulf War 1991 on breast-feeding in Iraq said :

> contrary to what was widely believed, the Gulf War had little impact on women's ability to breastfeed; what did change was the level of risk associated with artificial feeding. Widely practiced before the war, artificial feeding became much more dangerous in 1991 as a result of displacement of families to squalid camps, damage to water and electricity supplies, reduced access to markets and rising prices for imports.[58]

8. SUPPLIES AND THE INFANT-FOOD INDUSTRY

The infant food industry, implicitly, admitted the promotional nature of the practice of donation or low-price sales of supplies of breast-milk substitutes when, on 14 May 1991, IFM representatives met, at a working luncheon at the Palais des Nations, the Director-General of WHO and the Executive Director of UNICEF, in Geneva, to discuss the issue of supplies.[59] The discussions covered the issue of the ending of donations or low-price sales of supplies of breast-milk substitutes to maternity wards and hospitals in developing countries by the end of 1992. Subsequently, IFM announced that it agreed with WHO and UNICEF on the goal of ending donations or low-price supplies of infant formula to maternity wards and hospitals in developing countries by the end of

---

57 See Resolution WHA 47.5, operative paragraph 3; in a footnote, the WHA referred to *WHO Doc. WHA39/1986/REC/1*, Annex 6, part 2; for this document see above note 38.

58 See "Infant Feeding in Emergencies", *Disasters* (1993), Vol.17, p.113. On the use of breast-milk substitutes in emergencies, see above p.62.

59 The following persons took part in the working lunch: from UNICEF: the late Mr. J. Grant, Executive Director, Dr. S. Basta, Director, Geneva Office, Ms. Margaret Kyenkya-Isabirye, Adviser, Infant and Young Child Feeding, and Mr. Michael Shower, Counsellor to the Executive Director; from WHO, Dr. H. Nakajima, Director-General, Dr. Hu Ching-li, Assistant Director-General, Mrs. I. Breggeman, Director, Liaison Office with the UN, Dr M. Belsey, Programme Manager MCH, and the author; from the infant-food industry, American Home Products, Ms. Carol Emerling, Corporate Secretary, IFM, Mr. G. Borasio, President, and Nestlé, Mr. Geoffrey Fooks, Vice-President and Issues Manager for Corporate Affairs. See WHO Note for the Record (14.5.91).

1992. [60] IFM appears to have required that measures be taken by governments in this connection, and that it is

> ... essential that the measures taken by governments be clear and unambiguous, and that they engage the responsibility not only of all manufacturers, but also of all concerned in the health care system.[61]

In announcing the Baby-Friendly Hospital Initiative (BFHI) to all Member States in September 1991, the Director-General of WHO and the Executive Director of UNICEF referred to IFM's pledge on the issue of supplies and

> ... called on all heads of State to lend their leadership and authority to ensure that this requirement is met before the end of 1992, through the promulgation of relevant legislation or appropriate administrative action.[62]

So far as the developed countries are concerned, it would seem that June 1994 was set by IFM as the target date for the end of supplies of breast-milk substitutes. This date had been set in order

> ... to coincide with the entry into force of the European Directive on Infant Formulae and Follow-on Formulae...,[63]

adopted on 14 May 1991.

It would seem that, according to information available to WHO and UNICEF,

> ... as of February 1993 this practice [donation or low-price sales of supplies] either did not exist, or governments had taken action to end it, in 122 countries; in only eight developing countries had no such action been initiated. [64]

This practice is also reported to have ceased in some European countries, through voluntary agreements between the countries and the infant-food industry. [65]Presumably, WHO was relying on information provided by IFM.

Of course, neither the WHO Secretariat, nor the UNICEF secretariat, have the authority to verify the information in question under the International Code. For neither has the authority under the Code to monitor compliance

---

60 See Report of the Director-General to the Forty-fifth World Health Assembly, 4-14 May 1992, *WHO Doc. WHA45/1992/REC/1*, p.233, paragraph 137.

61 Ibid.

62 Ibid., pp. 233 and 234, paragraph 138. The BFHI is a WHO/UNICEF initiative launched in Ankara, June 1991, and is designed to promote breast-feeding in the health care system; for details see *1995 Progress Report, Baby-Friendly Hospital Initiative, UNICEF, New York*.

63 See Report of the Director-General on Infant and Young Child Nutrition to the Forty-seventh WHA, *WHO Doc. A47/6* (23 March 1994), p. 41, paragraph 146. The report is also to be found in *WHO Doc. WHA47/1994/REC/1*, Annex 1, pp.41-81.The, No.2175, 4 July 1991, pp. 35-49. European Communities (now the European Union) Directive (91/321/CCE) is to be found in *Official Journal of the European Communities*

64 See *WHA Doc. A 47/6*, p.41, paragraph 145.

65 Ibid., paragraph 148.

with it, in whole or in part. Furthermore, the WHO secretariat has not been authorized by the WHA to carry out such a function. It is also believed that the UNICEF secretariat has not been authorized by its competent organs to do so.

However, there is reason to believe that some manufacturers of breast-milk substitutes have continued the practice of donation of supplies of breast-milk substitutes. When the author was on a mission to a Member State in the Gulf in 1995, some officials of some of the hospitals visited there intimated to him that they had received offers of donations of supplies of breast-milk substitutes from several manufacturers of those products, even though the Ministry of Health of the Member State had banned the donation of such supplies. Furthermore, the IGBM researchers found that in Thailand, 35% of the health care facilities obtained free or low cost supplies.

> Two of these facilities stated that companies sometimes forget to demand payment for their regular procurement of baby milk.[66]

Nestlé's reply to the IGBM report appears to accept the finding of the report, at least by implication. It repeats its policy that

> free or low cost supplies may not be donated to maternity wards and hospitals for use by healthy new-born babies except in exceptional social circumstances.[67]

It is submitted that Nestlé's policy is not in conformity with Resolution WHA47.5, which speaks of "any part of the health care system", and not only "maternity wards or hospitals." Furthermore, Nestlé's policy refers to "healthy new-born babies", which could be considered as introducing a qualification on the general reference to "infants" in the Code. Thus, Nestlé accepts to give supplies of breast-milk substitutes to "non-healthy", new-born babies, which is different from the notion of "infants who have to be fed on breast-milk substitutes" in Article 6.6. Finally, Nestlé's policy contains an exception, namely, "exceptional social circumstances", for free or low cost supplies, which is not necessarily the same as the notion of "infants who have to be fed on breast-milk

---

66 See *Cracking the Code*, op. cit., p. 15. The following companies were said to be involved in this practice: Mead Johnson, Nestlé, Dumex, All, Snow, Wyeth, Abbott and Meiji. See ibid. It has also been reported that Abbott-Ross has given free supplies of infant formula to hospitals in Canada, Chile, Costa Rica, Ecuador, Egypt, El Salvador, Honduras, Malaysia, Morocco, Nicaragua, Oman, Pakistan, Peru, Singapore, South Africa and the USA; Meiji gives free supplies of breast-milk substitutes to hospitals in Pakistan and Thailand; Milupa gives free supplies of breast-milk substitutes in Argentina, Bangladesh, Bolivia, Côte d' Ivoire, France, Malaysia, Morocco, the Netherlands and Uganda; Nestlé does the same to hospitals in Bolivia, Brazil, Chile, Colombia, Côte d'Ivoire, Egypt, Gabon, Indonesia, Republic of Korea, Malaysia, Mexico, Pakistan, Peru, South Africa, Thailand; to give but a few examples. See *Breaking the Rules*, op. cit., pp. 9, 22, 25 and 28. It has been reported recently that donations of supplies of breast-milk substitutes have been given to hospitals in Lebanon, Hungary, Indonesia, to give but a few examples. See *Breaking the Rules-Stretching the Rule,,*op. cit., pp. 47, 53 and 92.
67 See *"A Missed Opportunity"*, op. cit., p.12.. See above pp.142-146.

substitutes".

It is worthwhile recalling that the WHA, in a resolution adopted in May 1986 urged Member States

> to ensure that the small amounts of breast-milk substitutes needed for the minority of infants who require them in maternity wards and hospitals are made available through the normal procurement channels and not through free or subsidized supplies.[68]

It would follow from this pronouncement of the WHA and the finding of the WHO/UNICEF Consultation 1985 and the WHO Guidelines that only a small minority of infants need such products, which should be bought by governments. So far as the Guidelines are concerned, they provide that

> Only small quantities of breast-milk substitutes are ordinarily required to meet the needs of a minority of infants in [maternity wards and hospitals], and they should only be available in ways that do not interfere with the protection and promotion of breast-feeding for the majority.

They go on to say that

> there will, of course, always be a small number of infants in [maternity wards and hospitals] who will need to be fed on breast-milk substitutes.[69]

On the other hand, the Consultation declared that

> the number of infants who need to be fed on breast-milk substitutes for absolute physiopathological or socioeconomic reasons is very small. In maternity wards and hospitals this number is smaller still since some of the conditions on which this need is based only manifest themselves after a mother and her infant have been discharged.[70]

Therefore, the continuation of the practice of free or subsidized supplies of breast-milk substitutes must indicate the promotional nature of the practice and the intent to use it as a sales inducement. Such a state of affairs, if continued, would offend against Article 6.6 of the International Code. Pending the implementation of the Code at the national level, manufacturers and distributors of breast-milk substitutes remain responsible "for taking steps to ensure that their conduct at every level conforms" to the principles and aim of the Code, as required by its Article 11.3.

---

68 See Resolution WHA39.28, operative paragraph 2(6).
69 See paragraphs 47 and 50 of the Guidelines, note 44 above, pp.128 and 129.
70 See above note 30, p.4, paragraph 19.

9. DONATIONS OF EQUIPMENT AND MATERIALS

Article 6.8 of the International Code allows the donation of equipment and materials to the health care system, by manufacturers and distributors of products within the scope of the Code. It reads as follows

> Equipment and materials, in addition to those referred to in Article 4.3, donated to a health care system may bear a company's name or logo, but should not refer to any proprietary product within the scope of this Code.

It is to be noted that the provision uses the term "company", whereas in other parts of the Code the term "manufacturer or distributor" of product within its scope is used. While the "company" can be any entity, it would be reasonable to suggest that it is probably meant to include those involved in the marketing of products within the scope of the Code. The provision does not permit reference "to any proprietary product within the scope of this Code". This wording, it is submitted, is a clear indication that the provision is probably intended to apply to a "company" which produces, or distributes, any product within the scope of the Code.

The equipment and materials allowed to be donated could include medical equipment, such as X-ray machines, incubators, refrigerators, video machines and so on; whereas materials could include towels, blankets, diapers and so on. Such equipment and materials are allowed to be given, in addition to informational and educational equipment mentioned in Article 4.3 of the Code. The rationale for the provision is, probably, to enable the health care system of poor countries, which cannot afford to buy such equipment and materials, to accept them, without compromising breast-feeding, from companies which produce products within the scope of the Code. For there is a safeguard against the use of such a practice for promotional purposes, which is this: the donated equipment may bear the name or the logo of the donor company, "but should not refer to any proprietary product within the scope of this Code." For example, if company X, *which produces breast-milk substitutes*, donates incubators to the teaching hospital in State Y, the incubators can bear the name of that company, but there can be no reference on those incubators to any of the breast-milk substitutes produced by company X, or for that matter, any other products covered by the Code, such as feeding bottles, even if they are produced by another company. The provision speaks of "any proprietary products", it does not say *any of its* proprietary products.

However, a problem could arise if the logo of the donor company is also the trade-mark of its products. For example, company Y, which produces feeding bottles, has a logo which is a rabbit, but at the same time it uses the rabbit as its trade-mark, on its feeding bottles. So, in practice people associate the rabbit with the feeding bottles. Supposing company Y donates incubators to hospital Z in State A, with the rabbits on this equipment, would this be considered as promotion or a practice authorized by Article 6.8?[71] It is submitted that it is not easy to answer this question, for, on the one hand, it could be argued that the rabbit is the logo of company Y, and as such, its use is allowed by Article 6.8 of the Code. On the other hand, it could be argued that since the rabbit identifies the feeding bottles of company Y, its appearance on the incubators could amount to advertising of its feeding bottles. However, bearing in mind the policy of the Code, and its primary aim, i.e., the promotion of breast-feeding, preference should be given to the argument which considers the putting of such a logo (i.e., the rabbit), as a form of promotion of a product within the scope of the Code. Since the Code bans any form of promotion, the use of the logo on the incubators, in our example, would not be compatible with the Code. A liberal interpretation in this respect could lead to abuse, and thus would be harmful to the promotion of breast-feeding.

It seems that there have been some violations of Article 6.8 of the Code by some manufacturers of breast-milk substitutes. The IGBM researchers have found that in all the countries where the research was carried out, the health care facilities received materials from companies which carried a brand name.[72]

---

71 It would seem that there are some companies whose names and the baby milk brand names they produce are the same, e.g., Farley's Snow Brand, Meiji, Cow & Gate. See *Breaking the Rules,* op. cit., p.5.

72 See *Cracking the Code,* op. cit., p. 16. The companies involved in this practice are: All, Coberco, Gerber, Hipp, Infacare, J&J, Mead Johnson, Milco, Nestlé, Nutrica, Snow and Wyeth. Ibid.

CHAPTER IX

THE POSITION OF HEALTH WORKERS UNDER THE INTERNATIONAL CODE

The health worker is defined in the International Code as follows:

> a person working in a component of ...a health care system, whether professional or non-professional, including voluntary, unpaid workers.[1]

He or she can play a very important role in the promotion of breast-feeding. He or she can also play a negative role in prescribing breast-milk substitutes when they are not necessary. The health worker has also certain responsibilities under the Code. The preamble of the International Code succinctly describes the position of the health worker as follows: Member States of WHO

> affirming that health care systems, and the health professionals and other health workers serving in them, have an essential role to play in guiding infant feeding practices, encouraging and facilitating breast-feeding, and providing objective and consistent advice to mothers and families about the superior value of breast-feeding, or, where needed, on the proper use of infant formula....[2]

The role of the health worker, his responsibility and other aspects related thereto are dealt with in Article 7 of the Code, which reads as follows:

> 7.1 Health workers should encourage and protect breast-feeding; and those who are concerned in particular with maternal and infant nutrition should make themselves familiar with their responsibilities under this Code, including the information specified in Article 4.2.

> 7.2 Information provided by manufacturers and distributors to health professionals regarding products within the scope of this Code should be restricted to scientific and factual matters, and such information should not imply or create a belief that bottle-feeding is equivalent or superior to breast-feeding. It should also include the information specified in Article 4.2.

> 7.3 No financial or material inducements to promote products within the scope of this Code should be offered by manufacturers or distributors to health workers or members of their families, nor should these be accepted by health workers or members of their families.

> 7.4 Samples of infant formula or other products within the scope of this Code, or

---

1   See Art.3 of the Code.
2   See tenth preambular paragraph of the International Code.

of equipment or utensils for their preparation or use, should not be provided to health workers except when necessary for the purpose of professional evaluation or research at the institutional level. Health workers should not give samples of infant formula to pregnant women, mothers of infants and young children, or members of their families.

7.5 Manufacturers and distributors of products within the scope of this Code should disclose to the institution to which a recipient health worker is affiliated any contribution made to him or on his behalf for fellowships, study tours, research grants, attendance at professional conferences, or the like. Similar disclosures should be made by the recipient.

Article 7 of the Code had its origin in Article 4 of the First Draft. The latter was improved in the Second Draft (Article 5), repeated in the Third Draft (Article 4) and expanded in the Fourth Draft to its present form. The following aspects of the provision shall be dealt with:

1. ENCOURAGEMENT AND PROTECTION OF BREAST-FEEDING

Article 7.1 of the Code places on the shoulders of the health worker the responsibility for the encouragement and protection of breast-feeding. It reads as follows:

Health workers should encourage and protect breast-feeding; and those who are concerned in particular with maternal and infant nutrition should make themselves familiar with their responsibilities under this Code, including the information specified in Article 4.2

This is a reasonable approach, for the health worker, wherever he or she works, is bound to come across pregnant women, or mothers, be it at paediatric units, gynaecological units or any health care centre or clinic. Furthermore, the pregnant woman, or the mother, will probably be more prepared to accept the advice, explanation, guidance and so on relating to breast-feeding and its superiority on any other form of feeding, from a health worker than from anyone else. Thus, the health worker could influence the decision of the mother one way or the other, i.e.– either in favour of breast-feeding or in favour of breast-milk substitutes. Kaplan and Graff point out that

most women decide how they will feed their baby by the last trimester of pregnancy. Information given during prenatal care is extremely influential, and it is well documented that . . . provider attitudes influence women's choice of infant-feeding methods.

They go on to say that

a health provider who distributes materials that are ultimately designed to maximize formula sales is inadvertently strengthening the formula promotions message, potentially at the expense of patients' plans to breastfeed.[3]

---

3   See Kaplan and Graff, op. cit, p. 12.

Moreover, it has been said that

> ... the extent to which hospital personnel and hospital routines foster or discourage breast-feeding among new mothers is one of the principal determinants of the rate of initiation of breast-feeding. Although in many countries only a minority of births may occur in a medical centre, the direct and indirect messages given to the mothers in this setting and the mode of feeding there will be highly regarded and frequently emulated.[4]

The responsibility of the health worker covers two elements : the encouragement of breast-feeding, and the protection of breast-feeding. Encouragement of breast-feeding can take the form, as pointed out earlier, of offering advice, explanation, and education to mothers before breast-feeding starts, while the protection may take the form of urging mothers to continue breast-feeding, lactation management, explaining the harm to breast-feeding from the introduction of bottle-feeding and so on. Of course, this responsibility is in line with the aim of the Code. The Swiss Delegate (Dr. Cornaz) to the Thirty-ninth WHA clearly described the health worker's role in this respect, when she said:

> experience showed that the promotion of breast-feeding hinged on health personnel, particularly on the medical profession. They were particularly well placed to inform mothers and to encourage them to breast-feed, and to influence both the family and the professional milieu. The information should be given during pregnancy, the stay in the maternity hospital, and the weeks following delivery. Doctors were also best qualified to encourage the authorities, the hospitals and the employers and professional organizations to take measures to promote breast-feeding.[5]

Article 7.1 also calls on "those concerned with maternal and infant nutrition" to make themselves familiar with their responsibilities under the Code. But who are those people who are so concerned? Are they health workers, or are other persons, such as nutritionists and community workers, intended to be covered by the provision? The wording is not very clear, but it would be reasonable to suggest that health workers, only, are meant to be covered by the provision. This standpoint can be supported by the heading of the provision "health workers" and the reference to the responsibilities of those persons under the Code. The main responsibilities contained in the Code, in the area of promotion and protection of breast-feeding, are those of health workers only. For example, health workers are not allowed to receive financial or material inducements from manufacturers or distributors of products within the scope of the Code (Article 7.3), and breast-milk substitutes should be used only on the advice of the health worker (Article 9.2(c)). Therefore, the health workers who are particularly concerned with maternal and infant nutrition are required, besides the encouragement and protection of breast-feeding, to familiarize themselves

---

4   See *Promotion of Breast-feeding Through MCH Services and Primary Health Care, loc.cit.,* p.22.

5   See *WHO Doc. WHA39/1986/REC/3*, p.113.

with their responsibilities under the Code, including the information specified in Article 4.2, i.e., the information contained in written, audio or visual materials dealing with infant feeding and intended to reach pregnant women and mothers of infants and young children.[6] The purpose of this requirement is to prepare the health worker for the promotion and protection of breast-feeding, and to enable him or her to avoid the practices that might compromise his or her task, which are regulated by the Code.

It might be interesting to point out that in some Member States implementing the International Code, the encouragement and protection of breast-feeding is formulated as an obligation imposed on the health worker, and non-compliance would expose him to the penalty provided by the law.[7] This approach seems to be intended as an incentive to the health worker to protect and promote breast-feeding, and a means of accountability, if he fails to carry out his obligation.

In order to carry out his task of encouraging and protecting breast-feeding, the health worker needs to be trained, educated and sensitized about breast-feeding, in general, and the International Code in particular. Ighogboja, Odumodu and Olarewaju say that

> women should be encouraged to use health facilities during pregnancy and delivery as this has been shown to positively influence breast-feeding patterns. Those providing maternal and child health services should be trained and sensitized to give simple, consistent, and objective breast-feeding education with practical demonstrations to expectant and nursing mothers.[8]

There is also another element in support of this position in Article 6.1 of the Code, which calls, in general terms, on Member States to take appropriate measures to encourage and protect breast-feeding. As has been pointed out earlier, such measures could include the incorporation of the subject of breast-feeding and lactation management in the curricula of physicians, nurses, midwives and other health workers.[9] Furthermore, health workers, as defined in the Code, cover professional and non-professional persons. The latter category of persons includes people who may not have any professional training or knowledge about breast-feeding, its health benefits to mother and child, e.g., community workers, hence the need to train and educate them in this area. So far as familiarity with the International Code is concerned, the author has been on missions for WHO in several countries, and has had contacts with senior officials in ministries of health and health care systems in those countries. It was surprising for him to see that only very few of those officials were aware of the

---

6   For details, see above Chapter VI.
7   For example see the draft Omani Code 1995, Arts. 8(1) and 18(3); see also the draft Syrian Code 1993, Arts. 8(1) and 18(3).
8   See "Breast-feeding Patterns in Jos, Nigeria, before Baby-Friendly Hospital Initiative", 42 *Journal of Tropical Paediatrics* 1996, p.179.
9   See above p.131.

existence of the Code, let alone its contents. Hence, the need for educating the health worker on the International Code becomes rather significant.

2. SCIENTIFIC AND FACTUAL INFORMATION RELATING TO PRODUCTS COVERED BY THE INTERNATIONAL CODE

In order to allow the flow of relevant information on products covered by the Code, Article 7.2 gives manufacturers and distributors of such products the facility to provide health professionals with scientific and factual information.[10] It reads as follows:

> Information provided by manufacturers and distributors to health professionals regarding products within the scope of this Code should be restricted to scientific and factual matters, and such information should not imply or create a belief that bottle-feeding is equivalent or superior to breast-feeding. It should also include the information specified in Article 4.2.

As the Swiss Delegate put it at the September Consultation 1980: commenting on Article 4.1 of the Third Draft, which is similar to Article 7.2, he said:

> ... the health workers must be given sufficient information as to the value of breast-milk and the advantages of breast-feeding, the risks that can result from artificial feeding, ways in which the mother can be helped to prepare for breast-feeding and continue breast-feeding, as well as the way in which one can help mothers who have to use breast-milk substitutes.[11]

However, the provision lays down the following condition for its application:

(1) The information has to be limited to "scientific and factual matters".
(2) Such information can be communicated to "health professionals" only.
(3) Such information "should not imply or create a belief that bottle-feeding is equivalent or superior to breast-feeding".
(4) Such information should include the information specified in Article 4.2.

So far as condition (1) is concerned, it is intended to allow the relevant information that is of concern to the health professional, namely, the scientific and factual information relating to such products. Information on scientific matters may cover information relating to the composition of the product, its characteristics, risks which may arise during its use and so on. Information relating to factual matters may cover the question of the storage of the product, its correct preparation for use, and the quantities to be used and so on. Therefore, any information which goes outside this field, be it promotional, educational

---

10 In the First Draft of the International Code, the expression "factual and ethical information" was used. See Art. 4, Sec.4.1.
11 See September Consultation 1980, Transcription of Tapes, tape 28, p.7. This position was supported by Brazil, ibid., Denmark, ibid., tape 29, p.1.

or public relations, would not be compatible with Article 7.2. For example, if company X, which produces breast-milk substitutes, sends to paediatricians brochures on their products, containing some scientific information, as well as matters which amount to advertising of those products, then this action offends against Article 7.2, because the brochures are not "restricted to scientific and factual matters." Of course, what is factual or scientific information has to be determined by objective criteria, in the relevant context.

The IGBM researchers found that in all the countries where the research was carried out, health workers received information that violates Article 7.2 of the Code. The report gives as an example the practice in Bangladesh, where companies, e.g., Nestlé and Mead Johnson, provide health workers with a pad of small leaflets, which feature products covered by the Code.[12] Nestlé's reply to the IGBM report finding does not appear to deny the existence of this practice. It merely states that

> apart from Poland, the allegations are at an extremely low level. Only 23 incidents in total were reported from 165 health facilities included in the research.[13]

Whether or not only 23 incidents had occurred is immaterial, for the fact remains that that practice is not compatible with the International Code.

As regards condition (2), the category of health workers, who can receive such information, is "health professionals". The latter term is not specially defined under the Code, but is covered by the definition of "health worker" in Article 3. That definition covers both "professional" and "non-professional" workers in a component of a health care system. Therefore, it is clear that the intention is to exclude the possibility of providing scientific and factual information to the "non-professional" health worker. The latter term is, also, undefined in the Code. What is meant by "health professionals" is probably those health workers "... belonging to, connected with, a profession...."[14] This covers doctors, specialists or otherwise, nurses, midwives and so on, that is to say, any health worker who belongs, or is connected, with a profession. Any health worker, who is not so connected, such as an auxiliary worker, or traditional birth attendant, does not qualify to receive the scientific and factual information covered by Article 7.2. This distinction appears to be intentional and is reasonable, for

---

12 See *Cracking the Code*, op. cit., pp.10 and 11. The following companies are also involved: Fasska, Mead Johnson, Coberco, Lyemph, Nestlé, Nutricia, Hipp, Humana, Snow and Wyeth, to give but a few examples. It has also been reported that some manufacturers of breast-milk substitutes send literature to health workers not limited to scientific and factual information: for example, Abbott-Ross sends such literature to health workers in Brazil, Colombia, Mexico, Pakistan, the Philippines and South Africa, see *Breaking the Rules*, op. cit. p.9, the same holds true for Mead Johnson, in Colombia, Mexico, Pakistan, Peru, the Philippines and Spain, ibid., p.21.

13 See "*A Missed Opportunity*," op.cit, p.10.

14 See *The Concise Oxford Dictionary* 9th edn, p.1092. See also the definitions of "health professional" and "health worker", in IBFAN's Model Law, Sec. 2, (9) and (10).

only the professional health worker can appreciate the nature, relevance and implication of such information to the health of the infant. Therefore, the provision of scientific and factual information to non-professional health workers would not be in conformity with Article 7.2 of the Code.

So far as condition (3) is concerned, the intention here is, probably, to avoid the use of this type of information for promoting breast-milk substitutes. For example, statements like "how close to Nature can you get?",[15] the description of a product as "an excellent alternative to breast-feeding",[16] and "comes very close to the composition of mother's milk"[17] can be considered as statements implying, or, at least, creating a belief, that the products in question are equivalent to breast-milk and breast-feeding. "How close to Nature can you get?" can easily be interpreted as suggesting, implying or creating a belief that the infant formula in question is very close to mother's milk. The same applies to the other statements mentioned above, which are even more suggestive of equality of those breast-milk substitutes with mother's milk and breast-feeding. The use of the expression "imply or create a belief" by the drafters of the Code indicates that they have considered even that hinting, or leading someone to believe, that bottle-feeding is equivalent to breast-feeding in the information in question is not permissible under the Code. Therefore, the statements above amount to a breach of condition (3) of Article 7.2.

As regards condition (4), it refers to a requirement laid down in Article 4.2 of the Code relating to particulars that have to be incorporated in informational and educational materials dealing with infant feeding, and intended to reach pregnant women and mothers of infants and young children. Those particulars cover both scientific and factual matters, e.g., benefits and superiority of breast-feeding and the health hazards of improper use of breast-milk substitutes, besides social and economic factors and a ban on the use of pictures or texts, which may idealize the use of breast-milk substitutes.[18] The requirement to incorporate such particulars in the scientific and factual information to health professionals indicates a persistence, on the part of the drafters of the Code, to deny any possibility of the use of Article 7.2 as a means of advertising or promoting breast-milk substitutes.

All the conditions laid down in Article 7.2 must be met before the information allowed by the provision can be distributed to health professionals, because the facility provided by the provision lends itself to abuse.

---

15 This is reported to have been stated in a pamphlet for Cow & Gate infant formula, addressed to health workers in the UK; see *Breaking the Rules*, op.cit. p.31.

16 This is reported to have been stated in brochures given by Cow & Gate to doctors, in Pakistan, for Nutrilon Soya and Premium; ibid.

17 This is reported to have been stated in an advertisement by Nutricia for Nutrilon premium in a health worker magazine in the Netherlands; ibid.

18 For details see above Chapter VI.

3. FINANCIAL OR MATERIAL INDUCEMENTS TO HEALTH WORKERS OR THEIR FAMILIES

Article 7.3 of the International Code does not allow offers of financial or material inducements by manufacturers or distributors of products covered by the Code to health workers or members of their families, intended to promote the products covered by the Code. It reads as follows:

> No financial or material inducements to promote products within the scope of this Code should be offered by manufacturers or distributors to health workers or members of their families, nor should these be accepted by health workers or members of their families.

The provision is intended to curb the well-known practice, by manufacturers and distributors of breast-milk substitutes, of offering health workers gifts, financial advantages and travel expenses, in order to influence them, compromise their objectivity or buy their goodwill, for the purpose of promoting their products. In the words of the Swedish Delegate to the September Consultation 1980,

> we know that handing out a gift is an age-old way of influencing people and health workers are no exceptions.[19]

Furthermore, the Yemeni Delegate to the September Consultation 1980 said that

> ... the manufacturers [of breast-milk substitutes] will never give anything for the benefit of the health worker, in such a way that it will work to give the importance of defending breast-milk.[20]

It has been said that

> ... when one man receives a gift from another, he loses his independence.[21]

The Jelliffes wrote some years ago that

> the medical and nursing profession can sometimes be very naive in their interactions with commercial companies, so that mixtures of 'manipulation by assistance' (free sample; assistance with research funds; hospitality at meetings)...are very frequently and successfully used promotional methods, usually unperceived, minimized, or tolerated as such by the physicians, nurses, and nutritionists concerned.[22]

---

19 See above note 11, tape 29, p.1

20 Ibid., p. 4.

21 See Swami Vivekamanda, Raja-Yoga, 1992, quoted by R.K. Anand, in his article "Health Workers and the baby food industry", 312 *British Medical Journal*, 22 June 1996, p.1557.

22 See D.B. Jelliffe and E.F.P. Jelliffe, *Human milk in the modern world* 1986, quoted by Anand, ibid., p.1556. The Jelliffes said the following before the US Senate Subcommittee on Health and Scientific Research: "Promotional activities [on breast-milk substitutes] have also been directed through the health services....In addition, a great deal of low-cost, often tax-free in-

The representative of the International Confederation of Midwives (Miss Ashton) clearly stated at the WHA in 1996 that financial support from manufacturers of products covered by the Code could undermine breast-feeding. Commenting on the draft resolution on infant feeding before Committee A, which included a paragraph on financial support from producers of those products, she said:

> efforts to meet the essential needs of mothers for the professional support of midwives in achieving successful breast-feeding could be undermined because of pressures associated with the offer and acceptance of financial and other support from manufacturers involved in the infant formula industry, including the manufacturers of bottles and teats.[23]

And it seems that some producers of breast-milk substitutes acknowledge the use of health workers in this way, for promotional purposes. Dr Anand says

> that companies strive to use health professionals to promote their product is no secret. Describing *Abbott Topics*, a medical magazine sent to health workers, the company says 'as the voice of Abbott, *Abbott Topics* can be a positive force in moulding the physician's opinion of Abbott. In effect we are striving to make the physician a lowpressure salesman of Abbott.[24]

Indeed, the WHA, at its Forty-ninth session, 1996, urged Member States

> to ensure that the financial support for professionals working in infant and young child health does not create conflicts of interest, especially with regard to the WHO/UNICEF Baby Friendly Hospital Initiative.[25]

It might be interesting to mention that in the area of pharmaceuticals, it has been reported in the press that a pharmaceutical company in the UK (Fisons) has offered financial and material inducements to doctors, so that they prescribe its products. It has been reported that Fisons has

> offered doctors under-the-counter cash payments in return for prescribing its asthma drugs; offered more than 100 doctors expensive free foreign trips on the understanding that they would promise to put new patients on the drugs; set up a secret slush fund to reward GPs who regularly prescribe the drugs. The fund was established to pay for luxury goods, theatre and ballet tickets and golfing breaks.[26]

---

direct promotion and opinion moulding has been undertaken by lavish assistance to professionals in the forms of social entertainment at conferences, travel and fellowships, and of funds for research". See *US Senate Hearing*, op. cit., p.73.

23 See *Forty-ninth World Health Assembly*, Geneva, 20-25 May 1996, *WHO Doc. WHA49/1996/REC/3* (hereinafter referred to as "*WHO Doc. WHA49/1996/REC/3*"), p.100.

24 See above note 21, p. 1556; Anand was quoting an INFACT publication of 1981, on Abbotts' *Direct Mail and Mail Order Handbook*, 1981.

25 See Resolution WHA49.15,(25 May 1996), operative paragraph 3(2); for the text of the resolution, see *WHO Doc. WHA49/1996/REC/1*, pp.15-16.

26 See *The Sunday Times* (7 November 1993), p.1.

Mention may also be made of a European Union Directive, which bans the giving, offering or promising, of gifts, pecuniary advantages or benefits in kind, to persons qualified to prescribe or supply medicinal products (i.e. doctors or chemists), unless they are inexpensive and related to the practice of medicine or pharmacy.[27] The Directive also prohibits persons qualified to prescribe or supply medicinal products from soliciting or accepting any such inducement.[28] The Council of the European Communities states, in the preamble of the Directive,

> ...persons qualified to prescribe medicinal products must be able to carry out these functions objectively without being influenced by direct or indirect financial inducements.[29]

The UK has gone further, in its attempts to curb the practice of giving financial or material inducements to health professionals. Baroness Jay, the then Health Minister, it has been reported in the press, announced new measures on 28 July 1997, making it a criminal offence for drug manufacturers to offer GPs and chemists subsidized holidays, cheap drinks or free gifts ranging from television sets and garden machinery to filing cabinets and mobile telephones, in return for the prescription of certain drugs.[30] It is also an offence for the GPs and chemists to accept such inducements. The penalty for offering such gifts and inducements by drug manufacturers is a fine of up to £5,000 or two years imprisonment; and the penalty for the GP or chemist is a fine of a maximum of £5,000.[31]

If such an approach and measures can be applied to gifts and inducements in the drug area, then it is submitted that a similar approach and measures can be adopted and applied to gifts and inducements to health workers, who promote or encourage the use of breast-milk substitutes or other products covered by the Code. After all, the harm that can arise from the use of such products is a serious one that can affect society as a whole, and as such, justifies making the offering of gifts and inducements, and their acceptance, as an offence punishable by a heavy fine or imprisonment or both.

The ban contained in Article 7.3 of the Code constitutes one of the most important principles in the fight against promotional practices by manufacturers of breast-milk substitutes. What is worthy of note is that the obligation on the part of manufacturers and distributors of breast-milk substitutes *not to offer* financial or material inducements is coupled with the obligation imposed

---

27 See Council Directive 92/28/EEC of 31 March 1992 on advertising of medicinal products for human use, Art. 9, paragraph (3). For the text of the Directive, see L 113 *Official Journal of the European Communities* (30.4.92), pp.13-18.

28 Ibid., paragraph (3).

29 Ibid., p.13.

30 See *The Sunday Times* (27 July 1997), p.24, *The Times* (28 July 1997), p.9, and the press release of the U.K. Department of Health, 28 July 1997.

31 See *The Sunday Times*, loc.cit

on the part of the health worker and members of his family *not to accept* such offers. This becomes significant when the International Code is implemented at the national level, in a legal instrument. For, in this case, both the offerors and the offerees can be made accountable before the law, either for offering, or for accepting, such financial or material inducements. The former, or the latter, constitutes a breach of the law of the country concerned.

The idea of including in the ban, contained in Article 7.3, the non-acceptance of financial or material inducement by the health worker or members of his family, came from the proposal of the Swiss Delegate at the September Consultation 1980. Referring to Article 4.2 of the Third Draft (the origin of Article 7.3 of the Code) he said:

> ... I would like to add the idea that on the one hand it must be forbidden to give gifts and on the other hand it must also be forbidden to accept them.[32]

However, Article 7.3 of the Code does not define the term "inducement", it would appear, intentionally. Therefore, the ordinary meaning of the term should be applied. To "induce", according to *The Concise Oxford Dictionary*, means "prevail on; persuade".[33] Accordingly, any offer of financial benefits, be they gifts, travel funds, calendars, watches, pens, attendance at meetings or conferences, research funds and so on, whether personal or professional, falls under the heading "inducement", be it financial or material. And as such, they are not allowed by Article 7.3 to be offered to the health worker or to a member of his family, nor to be accepted by them. But, according to the IGBM report, in all the countries where the research was carried out, health workers received gifts from companies to promote products within the scope of the Code. [34] Other violations of the Code in this respect have also been reported.

Nestlé's reply to the IGBM' report finding is that

---

32 See above note 11, tape 29, p2.

33 See op. cit., p.693.

34 See *Cracking the Code*, op. cit, pp. 15-16. The companies involved are: Abbott, All, Mead Johnson, Milco and Nestlé, to give but a few examples. Further, the Zimbabwe Delegate to the Forty-ninth WHA (Dr. Stamps) told Committee A that a number of violations of the International Code had occurred in his country by food manufacturers and retail outlets, for example, the distribution of free gifts to health workers. See above note 23, p.96. It has also been reported that Abbott Ross provides doctors in the Philippines with car services during conventions and gives telephone mats, cuddly toy bears, utility bags and baby books to health workers. It gives similar gifts in Australia, Canada, Colombia, Mexico, Pakistan and South Africa. See *Breaking the Rules*, op.cit, pp.8-9. Mead Johnson is said to give health workers gifts of pens, clocks, prescription pads with logos, key rings in Australia, Egypt, Pakistan and the Philippines. See ibid., p.21. Nestlé is said to give health workers pens, calendars, desk sets and prescription pads, in Chile, Colombia, Costa Rica, Indonesia, Côte d'Ivoire, India, the Republic of Korea, Malaysia, Mexico, Pakistan, the Philippines, South Africa and Spain. It is also said that Nestlé sponsors, in the Philippines, doctors attending conferences. See ibid, p.28. It has been reported recently that such practices are continued by the infant food industry in Argentina, Lebanon, Russia and the United Arab Emirates, see *Breaking the Rules-Stretching the Rules,* op. cit., pp. 5 and 93.

Nestlé's policy on this is absolutely clear. In 1984 Nestlé agreed to end non-professional gifts. It was also agreed with WHO and UNICEF that "inexpensive materials of professional utility" were in line with the Code, and could be given to health professionals. Subsequently, a list of 16 items was produced and sent to UNICEF and WHO.[35]

Nestlé's statement calls for the following comments: First, Nestlé says that it agreed in 1984 "to end non-professional gifts". But Article 7.3 of the Code makes no distinction between professional and non-professional gifts. Any financial or material inducement is not allowed by the Code. Secondly, Nestlé says that it agreed with WHO and UNICEF that "inexpensive materials of professional utility" were in line with the Code, and could be given to health professionals, and that a list of 16 items was sent to WHO and UNICEF. There is no evidence of this alleged agreement. Furthermore, assuming that such an agreement exists, it would be very interesting to know who in WHO agreed with Nestlé about the "inexpensive" gifts? Was it the Director-General, the ADG concerned or the Director of FHE? Was the WHO agreement given by an authorized official? The author was responsible for the legal aspects of the Code from February 1980 until February 1997, when he retired from the service of WHO. He does not recall seeing any such proposal from Nestlé, or the list of 16 items sent by Nestlé to WHO, even though he had had occasions to deal with matters relating to Nestlé. Moreover, the statement those "inexpensive" gifts were in line with the Code and could be given to health professionals amounts to an interpretation of Article 7.3 of the Code, in that it interprets the expression "financial or material inducements." According to this interpretation, "expensive" gifts are not in line with the Code, but "inexpensive" ones are. This position is contrary to the declared policy of the Director-General, and the well-known position of the WHO Secretariat, to the effect that they have no authority under the Code, or subsequent resolutions of the WHA, to interpret the Code. Therefore, Nestlé's statement above, it is submitted, is open to question and highly dubious.

Article 7.3 applies to any kind of financial or material inducement, provided that it is designed "to promote products" within the scope of the Code. This applies to both direct and indirect promotion. Therefore, any offer of financial inducement, which could reasonably be related to the promotion, direct or indirect of, for example, a breast-milk substitute, is caught by the provision. By contrast, any such offer, which is completely unrelated to the promotion of any product covered by the Code, would not be caught by the provision. After all, the Code was not intended to interfere with the activities of manufacturers, or distributors, of products covered by it, if they are not related to the promotion, or other practices, not allowed by the Code.

But how can one determine whether a certain gift or material inducement is meant for the promotion of a particular product covered by the Code? The

---

35 See *A Missed Opportunity*, op. cit., p. 12.

answer may be to the effect that one has to take into account all relevant circumstances of such a gift, in order to determine whether or not it is intended for promotional purposes. For example, if company X offers the wife of a health worker from a Middle Eastern State a trip to Switzerland, to attend a so-called scientific meeting, assuming, for the sake of argument, that the wife in question is neither a scientist, nor has any other qualifications that can render her eligible to attend that meeting, it would then be reasonable to characterize this trip as a material inducement to the wife of a health worker, presumably for the purpose of influencing her husband, the health worker, indirectly. The influence here would be to promote the products of company X. As has been said earlier, such offers are resorted to by manufacturers and distributors, not for social reasons but for promotional ones. By contrast, if company X invites the wife of a university teacher of French literature, who is not herself a health worker, in the same country for the same meeting, Article 7.3 of the Code, indeed the whole Code, has no relevance here, because the persons concerned are not health workers.

4. BAN ON SAMPLES, EQUIPMENT AND UTENSILS TO HEALTH WORKERS

It may be recalled that Article 5.2 of the Code bans the giving of samples of products within its scope to pregnant women, mothers or members of their families.[36] Article 7.4 completes the picture by banning the giving of samples of such products, or equipment or utensils for their preparation or use, to health workers. It reads as follows:

> Samples of infant formula or other products within the scope of this Code, or of equipment or utensils for their preparation or use, should not be provided to health workers except when necessary for the purpose of professional evaluation or research at the institutional level. Health workers should not give samples of infant formula to pregnant women, mothers of infants and young children, or members of their families.

However, Article 7.4 contains an exception to the ban, and a safeguard against abuse. The exception is that samples of products within the scope of the Code, or equipment or utensils for their preparation or use, can be provided to the health worker "when necessary for the purpose of professional evaluation or research at the institutional level." Therefore, if company X, which produces breast-milk substitutes, brings out a new product on the market, and wishes to have it evaluated by a health worker, at a university or hospital laboratory, for its efficacy and composition, it can do so under the Code. The same applies if company X wants the health worker to carry out scientific research on the new

---

36 See above p.119.

product, for the purpose of professional evaluation or research at the institutional level. This exception, it would appear, was intended to keep the door open for cooperation between companies, producing products covered by the Code and equipment and tools for their use or preparation, and health workers, in the area of evaluation and research relating to such products and equipment and utensils. Such cooperation would be in favour of improving the quality of such products, and thus benefit infants and child health. And this is in line with the policy of the Code on cooperation between governments, NGOs, consumer groups and industry "in activities aimed at the improvement of maternal, infant and young child health and nutrition."[37] This area of cooperation is another proof that the Code was not intended against the infant-food industry.

The safeguard provided in Article 7.4 is that the health worker, who receives such samples of breast-milk substitutes for professional evaluation or research, cannot give any of them "to pregnant women, mothers of infants and young children or members of their families." The rationale here is that, if the health worker gives such samples, he or she would be carrying out promotional activities, contrary to the policy of the Code and Article 5.1 thereof. Furthermore, Article 5.2 does not allow manufacturers and distributors of breast-milk substitutes to give samples, *inter alia*, of breast-milk substitutes, to pregnant women, mothers or members of their families. It would be illogical, and contrary to the Code's policy and intent, to allow the health worker to give such samples to those persons. Therefore, it would be reasonable to suggest that the drafters of the Code intended to stop the practice of giving samples of breast-milk substitutes, at the health worker's level, in order to avoid creating a gap in the Code. Moreover, the evaluation or research has to be at the institutional level, thus involving the collectivity of the institution in that activity. This collective involvement could guard against abuse.

It may be asked: can the health worker give samples provided under Article 7.4 to members of *his own* family? The provision speaks of members of families of pregnant women and mothers of infants and young children. Therefore, according to a literal interpretation of the provision, the health worker may not be precluded from giving samples of breast-milk substitutes to members of his own family. A countervailing argument may be advanced to the effect that, although the provision does not, expressly, refer to the family members of the health worker, they may be covered by implication. The policy and intent of the Code, as has been pointed out, is against the practice of giving samples of breast-milk substitutes, and it bans it, expressly, in Article 5.2, when exercised by manufacturers or distributors. Moreover, Article 5.1 bans advertising and any other form of promotion to the general public, *inter alia*, of breast-milk substitutes. The giving of such samples by the health worker to members of his family would be a violation of the principle laid down in Article 5. Moreover, the spirit of Article 7.4 would not allow the health worker to do so. Finally,

---

37 See thirteenth preambular paragraph of the Code.

further support can derived from the WHO/UNICEF Comment on Article 7.4 thus:

> This prohibition of the giving of samples also applies to the *health worker's own family.*[38]

Therefore, it may be concluded that the health worker cannot give samples of breast-milk substitutes, provided under Article 7.4, to members of his own family. The second interpretation is to be preferred, as it is in line with the aim and intent of the Code.

According to the IGBM report, staff at the health care facilities in all the countries, where the research was carried out, received free samples from companies, contrary to Article 7.4 of the Code.[39] Nestlé's reply to the report finding is that

> the number of health workers who said they had received samples was insignificant.

It goes on to say in the footnote:

> In Thailand, there is a strict and open Nestlé policy. No samples are ever given direct to mothers and will only be given to health facilities for professional evaluation....[40]

Whether or not the number of health workers receiving samples is "insignificant" is immaterial, for the giving of prohibited samples even to one health worker amounts to a violation of Article 7.4 of the Code.

5. DISCLOSURE OF CONTRIBUTIONS TO FELLOWSHIPS, STUDY TOURS, RESEARCH GRANTS AND CONFERENCE ATTENDANCE

It is well-known that manufacturers and distributors of breast-milk substitutes sometimes offer health workers fellowships to study abroad, or arrange a study tour for them, or invite them to attend professional conferences, either entirely, or partly, at the expense of the manufacturer or distributor. This question is dealt with in Article 7.5 of the Code, which reads as follows:

---

38 See the WHO/UNICEF Notes on the International Code 1982, p.8, paragraph 35. (the emphasis is in the original). It might be interesting to point out that, some of the countries implementing the International Code, have provided, expressly, for the ban on the health worker giving samples of breast-milk substitutes to his own family. For examples, see Art. 8(6) of the draft Moroccan Code 1993; Art. 8(4) of the draft Omani Code1995; and Art. 8 (6) of the draft Syrian Code 1993.

39 See *Cracking the Code*, op. cit., p.14. The companies involved are Nestlé, Nutricia, Infacare, Dumex, Wyeth, to give but a few examples. See ibid. It has been recently reported that this practice is continuing; see for examples, Australia, Germany, Guatemala and Indonesia. See *Breaking the Rules-Stretching the Rules,*op. cit., pp. 47, 69 and 92.

40 See *A Missed Opportunity*, op. cit., p.11.

> Manufacturers and distributors of products within the scope of this Code should disclose to the institutions to which a recipient health worker is affiliated any contribution made to him or on his behalf for fellowships, study tours, research grants, attendance at professional conferences, or the like. Similar disclosures should be made by the recipient.

This is a useful means of affording opportunities to health workers from developing countries, who otherwise would not be able to take part in, or attend such professional activities, or benefit from such participation. As Dr. Behar, former Chief of Nutrition at WHO pointed out, at the February Consultation 1980:

> ... There are some practices which companies do which we cannot and should not try to prevent. For instance, I know of a large company [which] sponsors fellowships for training physicians in paediatrics in good places, [and] are doing good training.[41]

However, there is a risk in such participation for the health worker, in that he or she, may be influenced by the company, or entity, which bears the expenses for such participation, or may feel indebted to it. In such a situation, the health worker may be in a position of conflict of interest, as he or she may intentionally or unintentionally, promote the use of breast-milk substitutes, generally, and the products of that company or entity, in particular, instead of promoting breast-feeding.

The drafters of the International Code wanted to maintain this practice of offering fellowships, study tours, and so on, and at the same time try to remove the source of the risk just mentioned. To achieve that end, Article 7.5 allows manufacturers and distributors of products within the scope of the Code to continue to offer such tours, fellowships and so on, but on one condition, namely, there should be a disclosure by the manufacturer or distributor "to the institution to which the recipient health worker is affiliated any contribution made to him or on his behalf" for such fellowships, study tours and so on. The recipients also should disclose the contribution. This requirement was included in the provision upon the proposal of the US Delegate to the September Consultation 1980. He suggested that "the burden of disclosures should be on both sides."[42]

This disclosure appears to be intended to bring the whole matter of the fellowship or the study tour to the open, so that the institution concerned and those responsible for it become aware of the contribution. When the matter becomes public knowledge, it is assumed that the chances of bringing pressure to bear, by the donor on the recipient, would be reduced. Furthermore, if the recipient is found to be promoting the products of the donor, people will make a link between this behaviour and the donor company and would, probably,

---

41 See Consultation on Code of Ethics, Infant and Young Child Feeding, Geneva, 14-15 February 1980, p. 86.
42 See above note 11, tape 29, p.5.

expose his behaviour. This would not be possible if the contribution from the company remains publicly unknown, as was the case before the adoption of the International Code.

It might be interesting to point out that during the August Consultation 1980, the representative of ICIFI stated

> their disagreement with the obligation for donors to make public disclosure of their contributions.[43]

By contrast, the representative of the International Union of Nutritional Sciences (IUNS) stated that

> ... "public disclosure" meant that the information was available in the public domain and was therefore not hidden or concealed.[44]

However, at the September Consultation 1980, there was no particular objection to the provision. The French Delegate went so far as to say that

> I do not think we should be too pessimistic and consider that all manufacturers and distributors are gangsters....I can very easily see that manufacturers might give a donation or gift for a congress or international meeting, that is quite current, which will be dealing with paediatrics.[45]

It is to be observed that Article 7.5 speaks only of disclosure to the institution, and does not seem to require the agreement of the institution before the health worker can accept. Therefore, it can be argued that whether the institution to which the health worker is affiliated agrees or not, the recipient is not barred from accepting such a contribution. However, non-disclosure by either the manufacturer or distributor, or the recipient, amounts to a breach of Article 7.5. Furthermore, non-disclosure might be considered as a piece of evidence of a "financial or material inducement" to the health worker, by implication, to promote a product within the scope of the Code. As such, it would be caught by Article 7.3, which bans such a practice. Furthermore, the contributions covered by Article 7.5 can be direct to the health worker, or to a third party, on his behalf, e g., payment of travel expenses to the airlines or the payment of attendance fees to the conference organizers. Finally, the contribution can be made to the activities mentioned in the provision, i.e., fellowships, study tours and so on, "or the like", i.e., similar activities.

Nevertheless, the WHA, at its Forty-ninth session in 1996, was concerned about the question of contributions made by the infant food industry to health institutions, ministries of health and health professionals. It adopted a resolution expressing its concern

---

43 See August Consultation 1980, p. 13, paragraph 37.1.
44 Ibid.
45 See above note 11, tape 29, pp.4-5.

that health institutions and ministries may be subject to subtle pressure to accept, in-appropriately, financial or other support for professional training in infant and child health.[46] It urged Member States to ensure that the financial support for professionals working in infant and young child health does not create conflicts of interest, especially with regard to the WHO/UNICEF Baby Friendly Hospital Initiative.[47]

Therefore, the WHA has, for the first time since the adoption of the International Code, expressed its concern in relation to the substance of Article 7.5 of the Code. This concern covers the "subtle pressure to accept, inappropriately" financial contributions for training health professionals, as well as "conflicts of interest" which may arise from financial support for health workers. This concern by the WHA is a clear indication that the risk, for the health work-er, mentioned earlier, does exist and is serious, and Member States should do something about it.

It may be interesting to point out that some national and international health professional associations have refused to accept financial contributions from the infant food industry to their meetings or congresses, it would appear, in order to avoid being subjected to such pressures or influence. For example,

> the Indian Academy of Paediatrics has been moving towards independence from the baby food industry...[and] the Indian Medical Association (with 100,000 members) has also decided not to take any support from the baby food industry.[48]

The International Confederation of Midwives took a decision in 1986

> not to accept sponsorship from infant formula manufacturers at any of its meetings and it had encouraged its constituent organizations to take a similar stand.[49]

However, Member States implementing the International Code can decide, within their social and legal framework, how Article 7.5 of the International Code and the resolution adopted by the WHA, in 1996, should be implement-ed. A State may allow contributions made for the purposes mentioned in Ar-ticle 7.5, with certain conditions, such as their being made to institutions, as is the case in Brazil,[50] and requires approval from the competent authorities,

---

46 See Resolution WHA49.15, fourth preambular paragraph. The US Delegate (Ms Vogel) at the Forty-ninth WHA 1996, stated that "the fourth preambular paragraph of the amended version of the draft resolution [Resolution WHA49.15] was so vaguely worded that it might be taken to mean that any financial support for professional training in infant and child health was inappropriate. Surely, that was not the Committee's intention ?". See above note 23, pp. 96-97.

47 See Resolution WHA49.15, operative paragraph 3(2).

48 See Anand, loc.cit., p.1556.

49 See statement by Miss Ashton at the Forty-ninth WHA 1996; above note 23, p.100.

50 See for examples: the Brazilian Marketing Regulations 1992 permit manufacturers and distributors of products covered by the Regulations to give financial and/or material support only to scientific institutions or associations of medical doctors or nutritionists that are nationally accredited, while any and all forms of incentive to individuals are forbidden (Art. 18 ot the Regulations). The Guatemalan Law of 1983 requires disclosure

before acceptance. This requirement would, probably, satisfy the concern of the provision, as well as that of the WHA. Or, equally, a State may not allow any such contribution at all.[51]

---

of contributions by manufacturers and distributors, and requires health workers to obtain permission from their superiors and, where appropriate, the Ministry of Public Health and Social Welfare or the Guatemalan Social Security Institute (Art. 11 of the Law).

51 The draft Moroccan Code 1993 permits financial contributions to the health worker, on condition that they are disclosed by the donor and recipient, in writing to the ministry of health. If such a contribution is made to a facility of a health care system, the agreement of the Minister of Health must be obtained before acceptance. See Art. 9, paragraphs (1) and (2). See to the same effect Art. 9 of the draft Syrian Code 1993. The draft Omani Code 1995 requires the written agreement of the minister of health, before a health worker can accept such a contribution. The same applies to any contribution to a facility of the health care system. See Art.9, paragraphs (1) and (2). Some national codes are silent on the matter, therefore, it might be assumed that they do not permit contributions from manufacturers and distributors of products covered by the Code to health workers, for examples, see the Bahraini Law 1995, the Iranian Law 1996, and the Tunisian Code 1983.

CHAPTER X

COMPANY EMPLOYEES

One of the practices the drafters of the International Code intended to regulate is the aggressive marketing of products within the scope of the Code, by company personnel, which can have harmful effects on breast-feeding. This aggressive marketing is motivated by sales incentives, which drive those personnel to sell more products, in order to gain more money, to the detriment of breast-feeding. Another practice which the drafters of the Code intended to curb is the use of marketing personnel for educational functions in relation to pregnant women or mothers of infants and young children, in the health care system. There is a risk that such personnel, being employed by companies to market breast-milk substitutes, feeding bottles or teats, are more likely to promote these products than breast-feeding. Naturally, they stand to gain more from the use of breast-milk substitutes than from the promotion of breast-feeding. However, the Code is not intended to interfere with the relations between manufacturers and distributors of products within its scope and their employees.[1] Its main concern is the promotion and protection of breast-feeding.

Article 8 of the Code deals with these two practices, and reads as follows:

> 8.1 In systems of sales incentives for marketing personnel, the volume of sales of products within the scope of this Code should not be included in the calculation of bonuses, nor should quotas be set specifically for sales of these products. This should not be understood to prevent the payment of bonuses based on the overall sales by a company of other products marketed by it.

> 8.2 Personnel employed in marketing products within the scope of this Code should not, as part of their job responsibilities, perform educational functions in relation to pregnant women or mothers of infants and young children. This should not be understood as preventing such personnel from being used for other functions by the health care system at the request and with the written approval of the appropriate authority of the government concerned.

Article 8 had its origin in Article 5 of the First Draft of the Code, which was

---

1   The representatives of ICIFI and Mead-Johnson felt that Article 5.1 of the Third Draft (the origin of Article 8.1) "...constituted interference in the employer/employee relationship". See August Consultation 1980, p.13, paragraph 38. On the other hand, one expert and the representatives of INFACT and Ross Laboratories were in agreement with the paragraph. See ibid.

subsequently amended in the Second Draft (Article 6) and the Third Draft (Article 5), and was finally refined in Article 8 of the Fourth Draft.

The following aspects of the provision shall be dealt with:

1. SALES INCENTIVES

In line with its policy to promote and protect breast-feeding, the Code aims at reducing the aggressive marketing of products within its scope by the marketing personnel of companies involved in the production or distribution of such products. This takes the form of a ban, laid down in Article 8.1, which reads as follows:

> In systems of sales incentives for marketing personnel, the volume of sales of products within the scope of this Code should no be included in the calculation of bonuses, nor should quotas be set specifically for sales of these products. This should not be understood to prevent the payment of bonuses based on the overall sales by a company of other products marketed by it.

Accordingly, it is not permissible for manufacturers or distributors of products covered by the Code to include the volume of sales in the calculation of bonuses for their personnel, as a sales incentive. Nor does the provision allow the setting of quotas, specifically, for the sales of products covered by the Code by such personnel. The term "marketing personnel" is defined in Article 3 of the Code as

> any persons whose functions involve the marketing of a product or products coming within the scope of this Code.

What Article 8.1 means is this: if Company X gives a bonus, as an incentive, for each employee selling large quantities of breast-milk substitutes, (for example for every three hundred kilograms), this system would be contrary to Article 8.1 of the Code. The same applies, if company X sets a quota, shall we say, of 1,000 tins of breast-milk substitutes per week, for each of its employees to sell. The rationale is that in such marketing systems, the marketing employees would feel under pressure to meet such targets for sale, in order to earn more money. Therefore, they will try to follow an aggressive approach to persuade any mother of an infant, or would-be mother, to buy those products, whether or not they are necessary for infant feeding. This conduct is bound to have harmful effects on breast-feeding.

During the discussion of the provision at the September Consultation 1980, the US Delegate pointed out that

> if corporation policies encourage employees to market these products too aggressively, then their activities can have the effect of discouraging breast-feeding.[2]

---

2   See the September Consultation 1980, Transcription of Tapes, tape 29, p.6.

The Swedish Delegate to the September Consultation 1980 put it thus:

> if the salary is based on the volume of sale then I think this is a very, very strong inducement for increasing the sales. And I think, there is enough experience in this field and the field of pharmaceutics to say that there is a lot of misuse in this field....[3]

It would not be an exaggeration to say that the more such products are sold the less there are mothers who breast-feed. The Dutch Delegate to the September Consultation 1980 made the following apt comment:

> ... breast-milk substitutes are products that should not be sold by inducing somebody to buy them but [they] should be bought on demand .... They should be sold on a totally different basis to other articles. They should only be sold when the need is there, expressed by the mother, and not by inducing to increase sale.[4]

The Code is not intended to prevent the systems of sales incentives by companies to their marketing personnel. The Code is against the systems of volume of sales and quotas, as incentives to marketing personnel, for the sale of products covered by the Code, because of the harmful effect on breast-feeding from these systems. Article 8.1 clearly states that the ban imposed

> should not be understood to prevent the payment of bonuses based on the overall sales by a company of other products marketed by it.

It should be stated that "marketing" in the term "marketing personnel" should be understood to mean marketing in the sense of the definition of that term in Article 3 of the Code, i.e., "product promotion, distribution, selling, advertising, product public relations, and information services."

2. EDUCATIONAL FUNCTIONS BY MARKETING PERSONNEL

Article 8.2 of the Code does not permit the employees of companies involved in the marketing of products within the scope of the Code to carry out educational functions. It reads as follows:

> Personnel employed in marketing products within the scope of this Code should not, as part of their job responsibilities, perform educational functions in relation to pregnant women or mothers of infants and young children. This should not be understood as preventing such personnel from being used for other functions by the health care system at the request and with the written approval of the appropriate authority of the government concerned.

Accordingly, any person employed by a company, or an entity, to market any product covered by the Code, cannot perform such educational functions.

---

3   Ibid., p.7.
4   See ibid., tape 30, p.1.

However, it is not clear whether the ban on "educational functions" in Article 8.2 applies to any area of education, or is limited to education relating to the products covered by the Code. Therefore, two interpretations may be advanced.

The first is to the effect that the "educational functions" which company personnel are banned by the provision from exercising are those relating to the products covered by the Code, only, i.e., those relating to breast-milk substitutes, feeding bottles and teats. Therefore, it could be argued that since such personnel are responsible for the sale, and promotion, *inter alia*, of such products to pregnant women and mothers of infants and young children, then the education intended to be covered by the Code would be limited to those products only. The context within which the term "educational functions" falls could support this interpretation.

The second interpretation is to the effect that the ban imposed by Article 8.2 vis-à-vis marketing personnel applies, generally, to any field of education. Therefore, it could be argued that the ban applies to any function intended for the instruction of pregnant women or mothers of infants and young children, *in any field*, be it in the field of breast-feeding, use of breast-milk substitutes, public health, hygiene and so on. Support for this standpoint can be derived from the wording of the provision, which contains no qualifications with respect to the educational functions in question. Furthermore, the *travaux préparatoires* indicate that the ban was intended to be general. The Pakistani Delegate to the September Consultation 1980 attempted to limit the ban to

> educational functions in relation to the promotion [of breast-milk substitutes or bottle-feeding][5],

but the attempt failed.

The Indian Delegate to the September Consultation did not want company marketing personnel to be associated with any educational function. He said :

> ...[such] personnel should not be involved in any sort of education functions, because they may start by talking about the importance of breast-feeding but invariably end up by giving some samples and inducing [mothers]... to start breast-milk substitutes. So they should not...talk about any educational aspects.... [6]

Furthermore, questions of conflict of interests may also be relevant here. For on the one hand, the International Code aims, basically, at the promotion of breast-feeding, therefore, any educational function, in relation to pregnant women or mothers of infants and young children, should be directed towards that aim. On the other hand, the main aim of employees of manufacturers or distributors of products within the scope of the Code is to promote and sell those products. If those employees are allowed to educate mothers or pregnant women in any health area, it is likely that the employees would promote the products they

---

5   See ibid., p.2.
6   Ibid., p.3.

are employed to sell. Therefore, conflict of interest between the promotion of breast-feeding and bottle-feeding would arise. This state of affairs did not escape the notice of the Swedish Delegate to the September Consultation 1980, who made a reference to the Recommendations of the October Meeting 1979, regarding the risk of conflict of interest, when marketing personnel are working in the health care system.[7] The Recommendation in question does not allow personnel paid by companies producing or selling breast-milk substitutes, to work in the health care system even if they are assigned general responsibilities.[8] He suggested that the Consultation stick to that recommendation.[9]

It is submitted that the second interpretation, namely that Article 8.2 bans generally any educational function by marketing personnel, is preferred, because it is in line with the aim and intent of the Code.

Article 8.2 does not state, clearly, whether the ban on educational functions applies to the health care system only, or elsewhere. It would be reasonable to argue that the ban is probably intended to apply to the health care system, alone. The second sentence of the provision refers to the possibility of the health care system using company personnel "for other functions". Therefore, this implies that the "educational functions", in the first sentence of the provision, were not allowed to be carried out at the same place, i.e., at the facilities of the health care system. Furthermore, Article 5.5 of the Code bans marketing personnel, in their business capacity, from seeking any contact, generally, with pregnant women or with mothers of infant and young children.[10] And one can deduce from the discussion at the September Consultation 1980, that the ban was envisaged to apply to the health care system alone.[11]

It should be stated that the term "marketing" in Article 8.2 should be given the meaning in its definition in Article 3, i.e., "product promotion, distribution, selling, advertising, product public relations, and information services." This stand of the Code on the "educational functions" of company marketing personnel is logical and reasonable, and in line with its policy and aim. It may be recalled that Article 4.1 of the Code puts the responsibility for the provision of objective and consistent information on infant and young child feeding on the shoulder of governments. Moreover, Article 6.5 of the Code limits the demonstration of bottle-feeding to health workers, only, or other community workers, when necessary. In addition, Article 5.5 does not allow marketing personnel, in their business capacity, to seek direct or indirect contact of any kind with

---

7   See ibid., tape 31, p.1.
8   The relevant part of the Recommendation reads as follows: "No personnel paid by companies producing or selling breast-milk substitutes should be allowed to work in the health care system, even if they are assigned more general responsibilities that do not directly include the promotion of formulas, in order to avoid the risk of conflict of interest". See *Joint WHO/UNICEF Meeting, Geneva, 9-12 October 1979*, loc.cit., pp.29-30.
9   See above note 2, tape 31, p.1.
10   See above p.126.
11   See for example the statement of the Swedish Delegate, above note 7.

pregnant women or with mothers of infants and young children. Therefore, Article 8 provides yet another measure to prevent contact between such personnel and those women, in the field of education. All these measures, it is submitted, have one aim in mind, namely, to prevent such personnel from exercising any influence or pressure on, or creating doubt in the minds of those women about breast-feeding under whatever guise, to the detriment of breast-feeding.
It should be pointed out that Article 8.2 of the Code permits the use of marketing personnel by the health care system in functions other than educational ones. Article 8.2 states clearly that the ban on the educational functions

> should not be understood as preventing such personnel from being used for other functions by the health care system at the request and with the written approval of the appropriate authority of the government concerned.

Accordingly, such personnel can be used for example, as chemists or administrators in a health care facility, provided that it is done at the request and with the written approval of the appropriate authority of the government concerned. The latter could be a department of the ministry of health, or another ministry, a teaching hospital and so on, but always subject to the two conditions laid down by the provision, namely, a request of the appropriate health authority, and its written approval of the request
In the implementation of the Code at the national level, some Member States have followed the approach of Article 8 of the Code completely,[12] while some others have either imposed a ban on the use of sales incentives in the calculation of remuneration for company employees,[13] or banned the latter from carrying out educational functions vis-à-vis pregnant women or mothers of infants.[14]

---

12 For examples see sec.10 of the Indian Infant Milk Substitutes Act 1992, Art. VI of the Sri Lankan Code for the Promotion of Breast-feeding 1983, Art.11 of the draft Syrian Code 1993, Art.11 of the draft Moroccan Code 1993, Art.11 of the draft Omani Code 1995, and Art.11 of the draft UAE Code 1995.
13 For example, see sec. 11 of the Kenyan Code 1983.
14 For example, see sec. 9 of the Philippine Code 1988.

CHAPTER XI

LABELLING

The labelling of any product is an important means of providing the consumer with the pertinent information about the product, in order to enable him to know what he is buying. The International Code follows the same principle, insofar as breast-milk substitutes are concerned. In the words of the Algerian Delegate to the September Consultation 1980, certain things should be printed on the label

> ... so that we can educate people to read what they are consuming, or giving to their children.[1]

Moreover, because of the special circumstances surrounding the use and marketing of breast-milk substitutes, i.e.,

> the vulnerability of infants in the early months of life and the risks involved in inappropriate feeding practices, including the unnecessary and improper use of breast-milk substitutes,[2]

the Code has its own requirements for labelling of those products. These requirements are laid down in Article 9, which reads as follows:

> 9.1 Labels should be designed to provide the necessary information about the appropriate use of the product, and so as not to discourage breast-feeding.
>
> 9.2 Manufacturers and distributors of infant formula should ensure that each container has a clear, conspicuous, and easily readable and understandable message printed on it, or on a label which cannot readily become separated from it, in an appropriate language, which includes all the following points:
>
> > (a) the words "Important Notice" or their equivalent;
> > (b) a statement of the superiority of breast-feeding;
> > (c) a statement that the product should be used only on the advice of a health worker as to the need for its use and the proper method of use;
> > (d) instructions for appropriate preparation, and a warning against the health hazards of inappropriate preparation. Neither the container nor the label should have pictures of infants, nor should they have other pictures or text which may idealize

---

1   See September Consultation 1980, Transcription of Tapes, tape 21, p.2.
2   See seventeenth preambular paragraph of the International Code.

the use of infant formula. They may, however, have graphics for easy identification of the product as a breast-milk substitute and for illustrating methods of preparation. The terms "humanized", "maternalized" or similar terms should not be used. Inserts giving additional information about the product and its proper use, subject to the above conditions, may be included in the package or retail unit. When labels give instructions for modifying a product into infant formula, the above should apply.

9.3 Food products within the scope of this Code, marketed for infant feeding, which do not meet all the requirements of an infant formula, but which can be modified to do so, should carry on the label a warning that the unmodified product should not be the sole source of nourishment of an infant. Since sweetened condensed milk is not suitable for infant feeding, nor for use as a main ingredient of infant formula, its label should not contain purported instructions on how to modify it for that purpose.

9.4 The label of food products within the scope of this Code should also state all the following points:
(a) the ingredients used;
(b) the composition/analysis of the product;
(c) the storage conditions required; and
(d) the batch number and the date before which the product is to be consumed,
taking into account the climatic and storage conditions of the country concerned.

Article 9 of the Code came out in its present form in the Fourth Draft of the Code (Article 9). Only parts of the present provision were contained in the First Draft (Article 1.6), the Second Draft (Article 2.4) and the Third Draft (Article 1.3).The following aspects of the provision shall be dealt with:

1. POINTS TO BE INCLUDED IN THE LABEL

Article 9.2 requires manufacturers and distributors of breast-milk substitutes to label their products in a particular form. It reads as follows:

Manufacturers and distributors of infant formula should ensure that each container has a clear, conspicuous, and easily readable and understandable message printed on it, or on a label which cannot readily become separated from it, in an appropriate language, which includes all the following points:
(a) the words "Important Notice";
(b) a statement of the superiority of breast-feeding;
(c) a statement that the product should only be used on the advice of a health worker as to the need for its use and the proper method of use;
(d) instructions for appropriate preparation, and a warning against the health hazards of inappropriate preparation. Neither the container nor the label should have pictures of infants, nor should they have other pictures or text which may idealize the use of infant formula. They may, however, have graphics for easy identification of the product as a breast-milk substitute and for illustrating methods of preparation. The terms "humanized", "maternalized" or similar terms should not be used. Inserts giving additional information about the product and its proper use, subject to the above conditions, may be included in the package or retail unit. When labels give instructions for modifying a product into infant formula, the above should apply.

Accordingly, each container of such of such products, or each label attached to a container,[3] should include all the specific points mentioned in subparagraphs (a) to (d) of the provision. Furthermore, these points have to be clear, conspicuous, easily readable and in an appropriate language. It is not unknown that, at times, certain labels of products, be they breast-milk substitutes or otherwise, contain information which may be important but is either in very tiny print, not easily understandable, or tucked away inside the container. So the result is that the consumer has no access to such information and, consequently, he or she is not appropriately informed about what he or she is buying. During the discussion of Article 1.3 of the Third Draft (the origin of Article 9), at the September Consultation 1980, the Swiss Delegate made the following apt observation with respect to the type of print sometimes used on labels

> ... I would like to propose...that in the final wording of this text we say that the label should mention clearly and obviously, quite often we have information which is important but printed in such small letters that no one can read them.[4]

Furthermore, the language used on the label is very important, for one may have all the pertinent information and warnings, but in a language unknown to the consumer in the country where the breast-milk substitute is being sold.[5] This is useless; hence the Code requires the information to be given in "an appropriate language".[6] It may be asked: who decides whether a given language is an "appropriate language" or not ?[7] It is submitted that the decision has to be based on the requirement of the national measures giving effect to the Code. In the absence of such measures, the decision has to be based on objective criteria, in the light of the aim and intent of the Code, and not on the subjective determination of the producer concerned.

---

3   For the definition of "container" and "label", see Art.3 of the Code.

4   See above note 1, p.3.

5   It has been reported that some manufacturers of products covered by the Code use a language on the label which is unknown in the country of sale: Chicco is a very large producer of bottles and teats, and is reported to have sold its products, with the label in Italian, in Bolivia, Chile and Mauritius. See *Breaking the Rules*, op.cit, p.11. Wyeth is reported to have sold its formula with English only labels in Mauritius, where the majority of the population speak French or Creole. Ibid, p.37. Nestlé's infant formulas are reported to have been sold with the text of the label not in the local language in Ghana, India, Indonesia, Pakistan, the Philippines, Zimbabwe and Uganda. Ibid, p.27. See more recent examples in Georgia, Indonesia and Saudi Arabia, see *Breaking the Rules – Stretching the Rules*, op.cit, pp. 32, 54 and 123.

6   Art. 1.3 of the Third Draft contained the term "appropriate local language". This term was the subject of some discussion at the September Consultation 1980. The French Delegate suggested the replacement of "local" by "appropriate". He said: "I am not sure that the national language [is] always the appropriate language. If we say appropriate then each State is sovereign and can assume its responsibilities appropriately". See above note 1, p.5. The Indian Delegate supported the French proposal. Ibid.

7   The Pakistani Delegate at the September Consultation 1980 asked: "who is going to decide the question of appropriate language? It will be appropriate in the eyes of one country and it may not be appropriate in the eyes of another country". Ibid, tape 23, p.1.

Furthermore, it is the responsibility of the manufacturers and distributors to ensure that the container, or label, of a breast-milk substitute should be in the form stated in the provision. During the deliberation of the provision at the September Consultation 1980, it was suggested by the Algerian Delegate that it should be the responsibility of governments to ensure that the container, or label, is in the required form. He said:

> I think it is much more practical to ask governments to ensure that there is some sort of regulation of the matter rather than ask distributors to do it.[8]

On the other hand, the Swedish Delegate stated that

> ... we do wish to avoid in the Code a language which would as it were exonerate the industry altogether.[9]

It is, probably, reasonable and practical to make the labelling of breast-milk substitutes the responsibility of manufacturers and distributors, as is the case under the Code. For, the industry has more means to meet this requirement than some developing countries. Furthermore, the industry would be accountable for any failure to comply with the Code requirements on labelling. This would not be the case if the burden had been shifted to Member States. However, when the products are imported, this may not be possible. As was pointed out by the Pakistani Delegate, referring to the Algerian suggestion, he said:

> I am afraid this is ...not possible in the developing countries, where almost 100 per cent of the infant formula are imported from abroad.[10]

So far as the specific points that have to be mentioned are concerned, we shall deal with them one by one.

(a) Important Notice

Article 9.2(a) requires the words "Important Notice" or their equivalent, to be put on the label. The purpose of this requirement is to draw attention, for when these words, or their equivalent, are seen by the purchaser, be it a mother or a member of her family, then her attention would be drawn to the label, which contains besides other important points to be read.

(b) Superiority of breast-feeding

Article 9.2(b) requires a statement of the superiority of breast-feeding. This

---

8   Ibid, tape 21, p.1. The Swiss Delegate supported the Algerian Delegate on this point. See ibid., p.3; so did the Canadian Delegate, ibid., p.6.
9   Ibid, tape 22, p.1.
10 Ibid, tape 23, p.1.

point is an important reminder to the purchaser of the superiority of breast-feeding over bottle feeding.[11] However, if the labelling of a breast-milk substitute container says "breast milk is the ideal food for your baby" but goes on to say "however if you cannot or do not wish to breastfeed, your doctor will recommend you to use a formula based on milk adapted to the nutritional requirements of your child as of birth", as has been reported to have been used on "Important Notice" for Gallia, a breast-milk substitute produced by Danone in Burkina Faso.[12] Is this label compatible with Article 9.2(b)? Two answers may be given. The first could be in the positive, in that the label shows "the superiority of breast-feeding" in saying "breast-milk is the ideal food for your baby". The second answer could be in the negative, in that while the label praises breast-feeding, it takes away, or at least, throws doubt on the validity of this praise when it says "if you cannot or do not wish to breast-feed, your doctor will recommend you to use a formula based on milk adapted to the nutritional requirements of your child as of birth". Such wording amounts to an attempt to induce the mother, or would-be mother, to believe that Gallia would fulfil the same function as mother's milk. Therefore, it could be argued that the label in question is not compatible with Article 9.2(b) of the International Code. It is submitted that the second answer is the preferred one, because it is in line with the aim and intent of the Code.

(c) Use of the breast-milk substitute on health worker's advice

Article 9.2(c) requires a statement that the product should be used only on the advice of a health worker as to the need for its use and the proper method of use. This requirement seems to be intended to discourage the routine buying of breast-milk substitutes at will. The statement warns the purchaser that the use of breast-milk substitutes is not like any other food item, and resort to it has to be made *only* on the advice of a health worker as to the need for its use and the proper method of use. The involvement of the health worker is an assurance that the health of the mother and child are taken into account in the decision-making.

It may be interesting to mention a case, which has actually arisen, involving WHO. A manufacturer of breast-milk substitutes asked WHO, some years ago, whether an instructional material prepared by it was compatible with the International Code. The material in question contained the statement "consult a health professional before introducing anything other than breast-milk". The Office of the Legal Counsel of WHO said: this statement

---

11 Some producers of breast-milk substitutes are reported to have on the label of their product the statement "sound nutritious substitute for breast-milk"; see some Mead Johnson's labels, *Breaking the Rules*, op.cit., p.20. Also Nestlé's statement "breast-feeding...is preferred whenever possible". See ibid, p.27.

12 See *Breaking the Rules – Stretching the Rules*, op.cit, p.19.

... is not, in our opinion, the same as the requirement of Article 9.2(c) of the International Code, which specifically requires "a statement that the product should be used only on the advice of a health worker *as to the need for its use* and the proper method of use" (emphasis added). The statement in [the instructional materials] is deficient in that it does not refer to the purpose of consultation, i.e., as to the *need* to use the product and the proper use of it. In order to be in line with Article 9.2(c) of the International Code, the statement in question must be amended along the following lines: "Therefore always consult a health worker as to the need for breast-milk substitutes and the proper method of their use.[13]

When the health worker's advice is sought about the use of breast-milk substitutes, it is expected that he, or she, would take the opportunity of explaining to the mother the health benefits of breast-feeding to her and to her infant. He or she could also encourage the mother to start, or restart breast-feeding. It is possible that there might be mothers who would breast-feed, as the result of the health worker's advice. And if the health worker sees the need for the mother to use breast-milk substitutes, then he can advise her about the quantities needed and the proper method of use, e.g., the necessity of cleaning the feeding bottle and the use of clean water and so on. This is another piece of evidence that the Code is not against the use of breast-milk substitutes, as such.[14]

(d) Instructions for appropriate preparation and warning of health hazards from inappropriate preparation

Article 9.2(d) requires instructions for appropriate preparation of a breast-milk substitute, and a warning against the health hazards of inappropriate preparation, to be on the label. This is a safety measure for the protection of the infant, in that the manufacturer, or distributor, is required to explain to the mother how to prepare the product, correctly, presumably indicating the quantity to be used and the periods of feeding and so on. Equally, the manufacturer or distributor should warn the mother against the health hazards, if the product is not prepared correctly. For example, the mother should be warned against using unclean water or dirty feeding bottles, for the preparation of a breast-milk substitute, or about the minimum quantities to use, and that if the mother acts otherwise, her infant could be sick or malnourished.

It is to be noted that Article 9.2 allows "inserts giving additional information about the product and its proper use" to be included in the package or retail unit. But in this case, all the conditions laid down in the provision apply to such inserts. The same applies to labels giving instructions for modifying a product, which is not a breast-milk substitute, into a breast-milk substitute. For in this case, the modified product is considered as a breast-milk substitute, and,

---

13 See an internal memorandum from the Office of the Legal Counsel to Chief, MCH, dated 28 June 1985, p. 1, paragraph 2.

14 For more details see Chapter II above.

as such, it will fall within the scope of the provision and, indeed, the scope of the Code.

If all the points mentioned in Article 9.2(a) to (d) are included in the label of a breast-milk substitute, then this constitutes compliance with the provision. If any one of them is missing, then there will be a breach of the provision. Of course, it is possible that a country importing breast-milk substitutes may require a manufacturer to put a particular label on the imported product, or no label at all. In this case, there would be no breach of the Code, for in this case the manufacturer would be complying with the request of the country concerned, which request may be based on the local legal requirements, or the health policy of that country. Moreover, a country implementing the Code has the right to add other requirements to those mentioned in Article 9.2, if it deems fit. This is so because the Code was adopted as a minimum requirement.[15] However, the points mentioned in the provision are for information only, therefore, there cannot be any advertising or promotion, express or implied, in the label.

2. THE USE OF THE TERM "INFANT FORMULA"

Attention must be drawn to the use of the term "infant formula" in Article 9.2, instead of the term "breast-milk substitutes". This reference must not be understood to mean that the labelling requirements in the provision apply only to "infant formula". The requirements laid down in the provision are intended to apply to all breast-milk substitutes. For Article 2 of the International Code clearly states that the Code applies to all breast-milk substitutes including "infant formula":

> The Code applies to the marketing, and practices related thereto, of the following products: breast-milk substitutes, including infant formula; other milk products, foods and beverages, including bottle-fed complementary foods, when marketed or otherwise represented to be suitable, with or without modification, for use as a partial or total replacement of breast-milk......

Therefore, it could well be argued that the reference in Article 9.2 to "infant formula" is due to an oversight on the part of the drafters of the International Code. This standpoint derives support from the wording of Article 9, paragraphs 3 and 4, which clearly refer to "food products within the scope of this Code." It is not logical to say that the Code applies to all products considered as breast-milk substitutes, according to its Article 2, but then on a very important issue, namely labelling of such products, the application is restricted to one kind of breast-milk substitute, i.e., "infant formula". Article 9.2 has to be read in conjunction with Article 2 of the Code, and the aim of the Code. Therefore, it is submitted that the requirements of Article 9.2 apply to the labelling of *all*

---

15 See above p.43.

breast-milk substitutes and not only to "infant formula". And this interpretation is in line with the aim and intent of the Code.

3. BAN ON PICTURES OR TEXTS IN THE LABEL

Article 9.2 of the Code does not allow the use of "pictures of infants", or "other pictures or text which may idealize the use of infant formula", on a container or a label of breast-milk substitutes. It may be recalled that Article 4.2 of the Code, also, does not allow the "use of any picture or text which may idealize the use of breast-milk substitutes" on any informational and educational materials.[16] The provision applies to any *picture or text*, which *may* have that effect, irrespective of the form or wording used. The rationale for this ban is that such pictures or texts may act as a temptation for mothers to use the product in question. They may also mislead the mother into believing that bottle-feeding may be equivalent or superior to, her own milk. It is well-known that labels, or containers of breast-milk substitutes, have pictures of healthy-looking babies, often with red cheeks, bears or feeding bottles.[17] A pregnant woman, or a mother of an infant, may see, perceive, or believe that such pictures give an indication that their use would have a good effect on the health of their babies,[18] as well as an invitation to use them. Therefore, they buy them under such misconception. The same applies to texts praising the use of such products to such an extent that the mother, or pregnant woman, might be persuaded to buy them. The result would be to the detriment of breast-feeding. Moreover, the presentation of such attractive pictures, or texts, is more akin to promotion of such products, rather than to the information the provision is intended to provide. This standpoint can further be supported by the statement in the provision that the container,

---

16 See above Chapter VI.

17 Some manufacturers of products within the scope of the Code are reported to have the following on their labels: Chicco's labels of bottles contain the statement "a Chicco bottle is an 'ideal substitute for mother's breast-milk when she is unable to breastfeed'...". These are said to have been found in South Africa. These labels also contain a photograph of a baby bottle-feeding itself. See above note 5, p.11. Farley's breast-milk substitutes containers show a picture of a cuddly toy bear; ibid, p.13. Hipp has removed the baby picture from the label of its breast-milk substitutes, in Germany, but has replaced it with a cartoon of a cow and a duck along with a feeding bottle, ibid, p.18. Mead Johnson's infant formula sold in the USA, Ghana and Bermuda, are said to have labels with pictures of Peter Rabbit, a children's story book character, being bottle-fed by his mother, ibid, p.20. Recently, similar labels have been used by some manufacturers of breast-milk substitutes, see *Breaking the Rules – Stretching the Rules,* op.cit pp. 6, 19 and 94, to give but a few examples.

18 The Codex International General Standard for the Labelling of Prepackaged Foods provides the following general principle on labelling: "Prepackaged food shall not be described or presented on any label or in any labelling in a manner that is false, misleading or deceptive or is likely to create an erroneous impression regarding its character in any respect." See Codex Alimentarius Commission, *CAC/RS 1-1969*, p.5, paragraph 2.1.

or label, may "have graphics for easy identification of the product as a breast-milk substitute and for illustrating methods of preparation". Such graphics are allowed by the provision, because their purpose would be to inform the user, rather than promote the product. It is to be recalled that advertising and any other form of promotion to the general public[19] is banned by Article 5.1 of the Code. It follows that a disguised form of promotion under labelling (Article 9.2) cannot be allowed under the Code.

What is the test that can be applied to a picture or text "which may ideal-ize the use of infant formula"? It is submitted that objective criteria have to be applied, taking into account the social, economic, and legal contexts of the country concerned, in order to determine whether or not a given picture or text "may idealize" the use of bottle-feeding or breast-milk substitutes, always bear-ing in mind the aim and intent of the Code. The term "idealize" is wide enough to cover a variety of representations. And according to *The Concise Oxford Dictionary*, to "idealize" means

> regard or represent (a thing or person) in ideal form or character; exalt in thought to ideal perfection or excellence.[20]

The picture of an infant, a bear, or a rabbit can have such an effect, if it is rep-resented "in ideal form" or if it exalts "in thought to ideal perfection or excel-lence", and shows, or implies, a link between the looks, the power or the growth of the subject in the picture and the product in question. It is to be noted that the drafters used the term "may idealize" and *not "idealize"*, thus indicating that if a picture or text may *express the possibility*[21] of idealizing the use of breast-milk substitutes, then it would be subject to the Code, which bans such use.

Article 9.2 also bans the use of the terms "humanized", "maternalized" or similar terms. Similar terms may include terms such as "equivalent to breast-milk" and "sound nutritious substitute for breast-milk".[22] This ban is probably intended to prevent the creation of an impression that the product in question (i.e., the breast-milk substitute) has been prepared "to resemble human milk",[23] or is related to the mother.[24] The ban also applies to any similar terms designed to create such an impression.

---

19 On advertising and promotion see above Chapter VII.

20 See 9th edn. (1995) p.674.

21 "May" according to *The Concise Oxford Dictionary* means "expressing possibility (it be true...)". Ibid, p.752.

22 See Art. 13 of the Guatemalan Law 1983. See also Mead Johnson's labels mentioned in note 11 above.

23 "Humanized milk" means "cow's milk prepared to resemble human milk". Ibid., 5th edn (1969), p.592.

24 "Maternal" means "of mothers; motherly". Ibid, p.750. It has been reported that Nestlé uses the term "maternalized" on the label of some of its breast-milk substitutes in Spain. See above note 5, p.27. Wyeth is reported to use the same terms on the label of some of its breast-milk substitutes in Gabon and Côte d'Ivoire. Ibid., p.37.

It might be interesting to point out that WHO was asked by a producer of breast-milk substitutes, some years ago, to comment on some instructional material produced by it, and whether or not it would be compatible with the International Code if that material were given to mothers, after a decision had been made not to breast-feed. The instructional material in question was envisaged under Article 4.2 of the Code and contained instructions about the use of breast-milk substitutes, and an illustration of a smiling and cheerful-looking mother, bottle-feeding her infant. As has been mentioned earlier, Article 4.2 of the Code uses the expression "any pictures or text which may idealize the use of breast-milk substitutes". The Office of the Legal Counsel of WHO took the view that the illustration in that context "may idealize" the use of breast-milk substitutes. It said:

> broadly speaking, the expression on the face of the mother, together with the wording used in the context of the instructions, would seem to represent, or could represent, bottle-feeding as an ideal way of infant feeding. It should be stated that Article 4, paragraph 2, uses the term "may idealize" the use of breast-milk substitutes. Therefore,...that illustration...would not be compatible with Article 4, paragraph 2, of the International Code.[25]

Such claims appear to be intended to put breast-milk substitutes on a footing of equality with breast-milk, which is contrary to the whole intent and spirit of the International Code. It may be recalled that the Code does not permit scientific and factual information from manufacturers or distributors to health professionals to "imply or create a belief that bottle-feeding is equivalent or superior to breast-feeding".[26] At any rate, the use of the terms in question on the label could create confusion in the mind of the would-be users, to say the least.

According to the IGBM report, in all the countries where the research was carried out, violations of Article 9 of the Code were found. The report gives an example of a label on a carton of breast-milk substitutes, which omits the notice on the superiority of breast-feeding and uses a term similar to "humanized".[27]One of these companies was Nestlé, which replied to the report to the effect that its

> ...policy on labels of all its products is very strict, and on formula milks includes all the essential items mentioned in the WHO Code.[28]

But it would seem that the statement does not refute the accusation in question.

---

25 See an internal memorandum from the Office of the Legal Counsel to Chief, MCH, dated 24 September 1985, p.1, paragraph 2.

26 See Art. 7.2 of the Code. See also above p.159 *et seq.*

27 See *Cracking the Code*, op. cit., p.20 .The companies involved are: Nestlé, Nutricia, Cannon, Gerber, to give but a few examples; also recently similar practices have been reported, see *Breaking the Rules – Stretching the Rules*, op.cit,pp. 6, 19 and 94 .

28 See *A Missed Opportunity*, op. cit., p. 13.

4. FOOD PRODUCTS NOT SUITABLE AS BREAST-MILK SUB-STITUTES

Article 9.3 of the International Code provides that

> food products within the scope of this Code, marketed for infant feeding, which do not meet all the requirements of an infant formula, but which can be modified to do so, should carry on the label a warning that the unmodified product should not be the sole source of nourishment of an infant.

The wording of the provision is a bit complicated, and one delegate at the September Consultation 1980 had some difficulty in understanding its predecessor in the Third Draft,[29] (Article 1.5). What the provision seems to be saying is that there are certain food products within the scope of the Code, which are not suitable as breast-milk substitutes, because they do not meet all the requirements of an infant formula. However, those products can be modified, in order to meet all the requirements of an infant formula. Those products are required by the provision to carry a special warning on the label to the effect that the "unmodified product should not be the sole source of nourishment of an infant". The purpose of the warning is to alert the mother not to use the "unmodified product", as a breast-milk substitute, because of its inadequacy for the nourishment of an infant. These requirements of infant formula, prepared industrially, are those contained in the applicable Codex Alimentarius standards, namely, the Codex Standard for Infant Formula, 1981.[30] The Code defines "infant formula", in its Article 3 as

> a breast-milk substitute formulated industrially in accordance with applicable Codex Alimentarius standards, to satisfy the normal nutritional requirements of an infant...[31]

If some of these requirements are missing, presumably, the product would not be suitable as a sole source of nourishment of an infant, hence the required warning.

It should be pointed out that Article 9.3 of the Code does not, expressly, refer to the Codex Alimentarius standard in question. But this can be inferred from the wording of its predecessor, which referred to the provision dealing with Codex standards under the Code.[32] Moreover, the Code definition of in-

---

29 See the statement of the Swiss Delegate at the September Consultation 1980, above note 1, tape 24, p.1.

30 See Codex STAN 72 – 1981 (amended 1983, 1985, 1987), formerly CAC/RS 72 – 1976. The text of the standard is to be found in Vol.4, *Codex Alimentarius*, 2nd ed. (1994), pp.15-24. See also the definition in the revised standard, Standard for Infant Formula and Formulas for Special Medical Purposes Intended for Infants, *CODEX STAN 72*, Sec. 2.1.1,1981

31 For details, see below Chapter XII.

32 See Art. 1.5 of the Third Draft of the Code: "a breastmilk supplement that does not meet the

fant formula, as has been mentioned earlier, refers to applicable Codex standards. The requirements laid in the Codex Standard are those related to the essential composition of infant formula, the level of vitamins, minerals, protein, food additives and so on. If these requirements are not complied with, then the nutritional value of the product in question would be seriously affected, and the health of the infant would be impaired as a result of the use of the product.

Article 9.3 goes on to single out "sweetened condensed milk" as not suitable for infant feeding, nor for use as a main ingredient of infant formula. Consequently, it does not allow the label of "sweetened condensed milk" to contain purported instructions for the purpose of modifying it for use for infant feeding. The Indian Delegate to the September Consultation 1980 felt it

> ...best to indicate clearly that sweetened condensed milk should not be used as a breast-milk substitute.[33]

The Algerian Delegate added:

> ...it seems to me to be extremely dangerous to consider encouraging [sweetened condensed milk] in developing countries. In my country sweetened condensed milk has been banished from the market.[34]

The Swedish Delegate added his support in saying that

> sweetened condensed milk is probably the most dangerous stuff and certainly responsible for a lot of under-nutrition.[35]

The warnings required by Article 9.3 are clearly intended to protect the health of infants and to prevent their malnutrition.

5. COMPOSITION, STORAGE, BATCH NUMBER AND EXPIRY DATE OF BREAST-MILK SUBSTITUTES

In addition to the requirements laid down in Article 9.2 of the Code, Article 9.4 requires the label of products within the scope of the Code, to state all the following points:

> (a) the ingredients used; (b) the composition/analysis of the product; (c) the storage conditions required for the product; and (d) the batch number and the date before which the product is to be consumed...

---

nutritional standards set for infant formula referred to in Article 7 [Codex standard]...etc".

33 See above note 1, tape 23, p.4.

34 Ibid., tape 24, p.2.

35 Ibid., p.3. There was one attempt at the September Consultation 1980 to treat corn starch, cassava flour and cereal like sweetened condensed milk, but without success. See the intervention by the French Delegate, ibid., p.1, the intervention by the Australian Delegate, ibid., p.2, and the intervention by the Swedish Delegate, ibid., p.3.

These details on the label are intended to show the buyer what product he or she is buying, its suitability for consumption, how to store it and when not to use it. These elements are very important to protect the health of the consumer (the infant), and they show the concern of the drafters of the Code to safeguard his health. Furthermore, it is important for the mother to be aware of these elements and to have them on the label of containers, for example, of breast-milk substitutes, because the latter are imported in many developing countries, and their quality and soundness may deteriorate during their transport, which can harm the health of the infant. The same applies to other products covered by the Code. The Burundi Delegate (Dr. Mpitabakana) to the Thirty-third WHA, 1980, pointed out in Committee A that

> since powdered milk was imported it was extremely costly, and it frequently deteriorated in transit so that its quality was poor and it was even dangerous. As a consequence, the number of cases of gastroenteritis had increased.[36]

It is interesting to note that the requirements of Article 9.4 come, directly, from the Codex Standard for Infant Formula 1981,[37] and delegates at the September Consultation 1980 were aware of that. It suffices to refer to the statement of the Canadian Delegate. Referring to the discussion of what the label of a breast-milk substitute should contain, he said:

> it was just to draw attention to the fact that the Codex standard for infant formulae covers practically all the points that have been raised including contents,...storage and handling...including the fact that the composition must be on the label.[38]

It is significant that the Codex Standard for Infant Formula requires, under "Optional Labelling" that Article 9 of the International Code "should be duly taken into account".[39] Furthermore, the Codex Committee on General Principles proposed an amendment to Codex Code of Ethics for International Trade in Food to the effect that

> The labelling of foods for infants and children should be in accordance with relevant provisions of the International Code of Marketing for Breast-milk Substitutes (Article 9), World Health Assembly resolutions ....[40]

It may be worthwhile mentioning that some Member States implementing the Code, through national measures, have followed Article 9 of the Code, with

---

36 See *WHO Doc. WHA33/1980/REC/3*, p.75.

37 See Secs. 3, 6, and 9.2-9.4 of the Codex standard.

38 See above note 1, tape 21, p.5. See also the statements of the French Delegate, ibid, p.5, and the Swiss and Algerian Delegates, ibid, tape 32, pp.1 and 2.

39 See Sec. 9.6 of the Codex standard: "An indication that Infant Formula is intended to replace or supplement breast-feeding, where breast-feeding is not possible or is insufficient, may be given on the label. In this case, the provisions of Article 9 of the International Code of Marketing of Breast-milk Substitutes of the World Health Organization should be duly taken into account."

40 See Art. 5.10 CAC Doc. CX/GP 00/8, p. 7.

some variations.[41] This shows the importance attached by those States to the information which manufacturers or distributors of products within the scope of the Code should provide on the label to the mothers of infants or pregnant women, regarding those products and their relationship and effect on breast-feeding.

---

41 For examples: see Art. 4 of the Bahraini Law 1995; Arts. 8-12 of the Brazilian Marketing Regulations; Art.11 of the Guatemalan Rules for the Marketing of Breast-milk Substitutes 1987; Sec.6 of the Indian Infant Milk Substitutes Act 1992; Art.12 of the draft Omani Code 1995; Arts. 10-11 of the Tunisian Law 1983; and Art. 12 of the draft UAE Code 1995. See also Art.7 of the EEC Directive 1991; and secs.6-10 of IBFAN's Model Law.

CHAPTER XII

QUALITY OF FOOD PRODUCTS COVERED BY THE INTERNATIONAL CODE

Since the International Code recognizes that there are situations when the use of breast-milk substitutes becomes necessary, it requires that such products must be of a high quality, in order to protect the health of the consumer (i.e., the infant). Therefore, the Code requires that when breast-milk substitutes are being sold or otherwise distributed, they should meet internationally recognized and elaborated standards. Article 10 of the Code deals with this question, and reads as follows:

> 10.1 The quality of products is an essential element for the protection of the health of infants and therefore should be of a high recognized standard.

> 10.2 Food products within the scope of this Code should, when sold or otherwise distributed, meet applicable standards recommended by the Codex Alimentarius Commission and also the Codex Code of Hygienic Practice for Foods for Infants and Children.

All the drafts of the Code contained a provision on the quality of breast-milk substitutes, be it under the heading "standards" (Article 7 of the Third Draft), or "quality" (Article 6 of the First Draft, Article 8 of the Second Draft and Article 10 of the Fourth Draft). The following aspects of the provision shall be dealt with.

CODEX STANDARDS AND THE CODE OF HYGIENIC PRACTICE FOR FOODS FOR INFANTS AND CHILDREN

The Codex Alimentarius Commission[1] (CAC) is an international body established by WHO and FAO, in 1963, to implement the Joint FAO/WHO Food Standards Programme. The purpose of the latter Programme is to protect the health of consumers and to ensure fair practices in the food trade.[2] Member-

---

1   On the Codex Alimentarius Commission, see the late J.P. Dobbert, «Le Codex Alimentarius: vers une nouvelle méthode de règlementation internationale», *Annuaire français de droit international*, 15 (1969), p. 679; see also Shubber, "The Codex Alimentarius under International Law", *International and Comparative Law Quarterly 21 (1972), p.631.*

2   See Art. 1 (a) of the Statutes of CAC, *Codex Alimentarius Commission, Procedural Manual,*

ship in the CAC is open to States Members of WHO or FAO and Associate Members of FAO and WHO.[3] The CAC adopts food standards which contain requirements for food aimed at ensuring for the consumer a sound, wholesome food product free from adulteration, correctly labelled and presented.[4] The Codex standards go through detailed discussions and exchanges of views among members of the Commission, which may last for some years, before final adoption. The CAC has adopted the Codex Standard for Infant Formula in 1981.[5] It has also adopted the Codex International Code of Hygienic Practice for Foods for Infants and Children in 1979.[6]

The Codex Standard for Infant Formula, as we have seen earlier, contains requirements relating to the essential composition of infant formula, for example, it specifies what the base for it should be, what it should contain in terms of calories, the minimum and maximum levels of vitamins, minerals, protein and so on.[7] Furthermore, the Standard specifies what food additives are permitted to be used in the preparation of infant formula and their levels.[8] It also deals with many other issues such as contaminants, hygiene, ingredients, date marking, storage instructions, information on utilization [9] and so on. On the other hand, the Codex Code of Hygienic Practice for Infants and Children contains the minimum hygienic requirements for the handling, production, preparation, packaging, etc. of infant foods.[10]

These two Codex instruments are intended to ensure that infant formula is produced and prepared in a safe and sound way, in order to protect the health of the consumer. Therefore, their application to breast-milk substitutes covered by the International Code is aimed at securing a high quality for those products, and a large measure for the protection of infants. This is in line with the aim of the Code, when the necessity arises for the use of breast-milk substitutes. It may be recalled that in 2004 powdered infant formula was contaminated by Enterobacter sakazaki and salmonella, which caused infection and illness in infants.[11] Moreover, in China in 2008, 50,000 children were admitted to hospital suffering from a contaminant of infant formula, with some deaths.[12]

It should be stated that Article 10.2 makes applicable to food products covered by the Code, present and future Codex standards. This is clear from the

---

8th edn. (1993), p.5; see also the 15th edn. (2005).

3　See Art. 2 of the Statutes of CAC, ibid.

4　See General principles of the Codex Alimentarius, paragraph 3, ibid., p.31.

5　See Codex STAN 72-1981 (amended 1983, 1985, 1987), for text see Vol. 4 *Codex Alimentarius*, pp.15-24.

6　See *CAC/RCP 21-1979*.

7　See Sec.3.1 of the Codex Standard for Infant formula.

8　Ibid., Sec.4.

9　See ibid., Secs.5, 6, 9, 9.2, 9.4 and 9.5.

10　See above note 6, p.1, paragraph.1.

11　See above Chapter IV, p. 76.

12　Ibid, pp. 76-77.

wording of the provision; for while it referred specifically to the Codex Code of Hygienic Practice, it made no such specific reference to the Codex Infant Formula standard. The provision merely referred to "applicable standards recommended by the Codex Alimentarius Commission". Therefore, it would be reasonable to interpret this phrase to cover existing, and future standards, which may be adopted by the CAC.

Therefore, the CAC must exercise caution that, if it develops standards relevant to breast-milk substitutes, not only the provisions of the Code should be taken into account, but also their spirit and the subsequent relevant WHA resolutions. It would be pertinent to mention that the WHA requested the CAC to give full consideration, when carrying out its functions,

> to improve the quality standards of infant foods, and to support and promote the implementation of the International Code.[13]

In the absence of the requirements laid down in Article 10.2 of the Code, it would be free for all to judge what is, and what should be, the quality of breast-milk substitutes, particularly bearing in mind that most of these products are exported to developing countries. There may be differences of standards between the exporting and importing countries in this respect. A member of the Executive Board, Dr. Al-Ghassany, pointed to the assumption that

> ...the products referred to in the international code would be manufactured to the same standards for use in the (developed) producing country as for use abroad. In fact, certain products were exported by manufacturers but not marketed in their own countries[14]

Furthermore, during the September Consultation 1980, the Swiss Delegate, commenting on the quality of breast-milk substitutes, proposed that

> ... measures should be taken to ensure that the quality of products is guaranteed.[15]

The Algerian Delegate, commenting on the application of Codex standards, said:

> ... because governments do not always appear to grant all interest that should be granted to these matters as to what is going to become of the products [breast-milk substitutes] that have been manufactured in their countries, and which will be sold in other countries.[16]

He went on to suggest that governments of the manufacturing and exporting

---

13 See Resolution WHA34.22, operative paragraph 4, for the text of the resolution see *WHO Handbook*, Vol. II, pp.91-92.
14 See *WHO Doc. EB67/1981/REC/2*, p.315.
15 See September Consultation 1980, Transcription of Tapes, tape 32, p.1.
16 Ibid., p.2.

firms should give sufficient guarantees as to the quality of these products.[17]

It may be asked: what is the legal nature of Codex food standards and codes of practice? So far as the standards are concerned, the answer may be to the effect that these standards are recommendations to Members of CAC, and as such they are not binding *per se*. Members of CAC become bound by such standards only when they accept them.[18] In this case, they could be incorporated in the national legislation of the accepting country. It might be interesting to point out that some of the States implementing the International Code apply their national standards[19] to breast-milk substitutes, while others apply both national standards and Codex standards.[20] As regards the Codex Codes of Practice, they are advisory in nature, and are adopted by CAC to assist in achieving the purpose of the Codex Alimentarius.[21] They constitute advice from CAC to its Members, and they appear to require no particular action on their part. At any rate, the reference to their application to breast-milk substitutes in Article 10 of the International Code does not alter their legal nature. After all, the Code itself is a recommendation of WHA,[22] therefore, it cannot give those instruments a binding character. Nevertheless, their applicability to breast-milk substitutes can provide sufficient health protection for the infants who use them.

However, given the technical expertise that is involved in the preparation of Codex standards and codes of practice, the length of time taken in the process, and the moral and professional weight of the parent organizations of the CAC (WHO and FAO), these standards and codes provide a reasonable yardstick against which the quality of breast-milk substitutes can be measured. However, it may be interesting to point out those Codex standards and other related advisory texts can be used by the World Trade Organization (WTO) as "reference points or benchmarks in international trade disputes."[23]

---

17 Ibid., p.3.

18 Under the old Codex regime, acceptance may be full acceptance or acceptance with specified deviations. See General Principles of the Codex Alimentarius, 8ᵗʰ edn. above note 2, p.40, paragraph 4.A.(i), and p.41, paragraph (ii). But the General Principles have been amended and there is no longer any need to accept them. The Codex Standards are now published and issued to all Member States and Associate Members of FAO and/or WHO and to the International Organizations concerned. See above note 2, 15ᵗʰ edn., p.26.

19 See for examples, Sec.11 (1) of the Indian Infant Milk Substitutes Act 1992, which applies the national standards specified under the Prevention of Food Adulteration Act, 1954, and the standards specified by the Bureau of Indian Standards. See also Art. 13 of the draft Omani Code 1995, which applies Omani national standards, and Art. 13 of the draft UAE Code 1995, which applies UAE national standards.

20 See for examples, Art. 3 of the Bahraini Law 1995, and Art. 6 of the Brazilian Marketing Regulations, which apply Codex standards and internal laws and standards.

21 See above note 2, 15ᵗʰ edn., p.31, paragraph 1.

22 See above Chapter II, p.42.

23 See *CAC Doc. ALINORM 95/7*, Part 2, 13, paragraph 77. The Codex Alimentarius has long served as a reference for GATT with respect to technical barriers to trade, and "Codex food safety standards will be recognized in GATT as providing sufficient justification for trade restrictions and will become the reference or "measuring stick" of national requirements".

It might appropriate to conclude this chapter by the call of the WHA, at its 58th session in 2005 to the CAC

> to establish standards, guidelines and recommendations on foods for infants and young children formulated in a manner that ensures the development of safe and appropriately labelled products that meet their known nutritional and safety needs, thus reflecting WHO policy, in particular...the International Code of Marketing of Breast-milk Substitutes and other relevant resolutions of the Health Assembly.[24]

See Relation between the Codex Alimentarius Commission and the General Agreement on Tariffs and Trade, *WHO Doc. A46/25*, (1993), Annex, p. 18. GATT has been replaced by WTO, a collection of relevant agreements have been published by WTO in 2007 in *The Legal Texts of WTO*.

24 See Resolution WHA58.32, 25 May 2005, second operative paragraph (2).

CHAPTER XIII

IMPLEMENTATION OF
THE INTERNATIONAL CODE

The implementation of the International Code is a very crucial process for the promotion of breast-feeding, the proper use of breast-milk substitutes when they are necessary, and for the regulation of the marketing practices relating thereto. The Swedish Delegate to the September Consultation 1980 probably expressed the feeling of all participants when he said that

> ... the implementation-monitoring process will be the crucial one in this whole process [i.e., the preparation of the International Code].[1]

The Thirty-ninth WHA has also recognized that

> ... the implementation of the International Code of Marketing of Breast-milk Substitutes is one of the important actions required in order to promote healthy infant and young child feeding.[2]

Indeed, this is very true, because without implementation of the Code at the national level, nothing can happen, from a legal point of view. The Code has no direct effect at the national level, therefore, action by the national authorities to implement it is essential.

The various aspects of implementation are dealt with in Article 11 of the Code, which reads as follows:

> 11.1 Governments should take action to give effect to the principles and aim of this Code, as appropriate to their social and legislative framework, including the adoption of national legislation, regulations or other suitable measures. For this purpose, governments should seek, when necessary, the cooperation of WHO, UNICEF and other agencies of the United Nations system. National policies and measures, including laws and regulations, which are adopted to give effect to the principles and aim of this Code should be publicly stated, and should apply on the same basis to all

---

1   See September Consultation 1980, Transcription of Tapes, tape 34, p.1.

2   See Resolution WHA37.30, (May 1984) second preambular paragraph; see also a similar paragraph in Resolution WHA39.28, (May 1986), third preambular paragraph; for the text of these resolutions see *WHO Handbook*, Vol. II, p. 93, and Vol. III, pp. 61-62. The Innocenti Declaration on the Protection, Promotion and Support of Breast-feeding of 1990, called on all governments to give effect to the International Code of Marketing of Breast-milk Substitutes and subsequent relevant WHA resolutions in their entirety, by the year 1995.The same call was made in the Innocenti Declaration of 2005.

those involved in the manufacture and marketing of products within the scope of this Code.

The Third and Fourth Drafts of the International Code, alone, contained a provision on implementation.[3] The following aspects of implementation shall be dealt with:

1. IS IMPLEMENTATION OF THE INTERNATIONAL CODE COMPULSORY?

In accordance with Article 11.1 of the International Code, governments should take action to give effect to its principles and aims. Moreover, the WHA urged in 1981 all Member States

> to give full and unanimous support to the implementation...of the provisions of the International Code in its entirety as an expression of the collective will of the membership of the World Health Organization; [and] to translate the International Code into national legislation, regulations or other suitable measures.[4]

The WHA appealed, in all its subsequent resolutions on infant feeding, directly and indirectly, to Member States to implement the Code and the WHA's subsequent relevant resolutions; it also requested the Director-General, in some resolutions, to provide technical assistance to Member States in the implementation process.[5] The Innocenti Declarations of 1990 and 2005 also called on governments to implement the International Code. Therefore, it is legitimate to ask: are Member States under an obligation to implement the Code and subsequent relevant resolutions of WHA? The answer depends on what legal effect resolutions of WHA have. Are they to be considered as mere recommendations devoid of any binding effect? Or can one attribute a certain binding effect to some recommendations of the WHA? The International Code was adopted as a recommendation under Article 23 of the WHO Constitution, as has been seen earlier, therefore,[6] these questions may be answered by analogy with the legal effect of resolutions of the UN General Assembly, which have been the subject of considerable discussions by international lawyers.[7]

---

3   See Art. 8.1 of the Third Draft and Art. 11.1 of the Fourth Draft.
4   See Resolution WHA34.22, operative paragraph 2(1) and (2); for the text, see above note 2, Vol. II, pp. 91-92.
5   See for examples Resolution WHA35.26, operative paragraph 1, Resolution WHA37.30, second preambular paragraph, see ibid, pp 92-93; Resolution WHA41.11, operative paragraph 3 (6), ibid., Vol. III, pp. 62-63, and Resolution WHA49.15, operative paragraph 2, see *WHO Doc. WHA49/1996/REC/1*, pp. 15-16.
6   For details, see above Chapter II.
7   For examples, see D.H.N. Johnson, "The Effects of Resolutions of the General Assembly of the United Nations" 32 *British Yearbook of International Law* (1955-56), p. 97 et seq.; R.A. Falk, "On the Quasi-Legislative Competence of the General Assembly" 60 *American Journal*

Let us see what a recommendation is:

Castañeda considers that, in normal usage, the term "recommendation" covers

> ... only the acts that the great majority of their authors have characterized as such. From this point of view, there is no doubt that the prevailing meaning is that of 'invitation'; hence recommendations are only the resolutions adopted with no intention of binding their addressees. It would be necessary to exclude from the concept of recommendation, consequently, decisions that carry the legal obligation to execute their content ....[8]

Schermers and Blokker say

> the term "recommendation" is most frequently used to describe non-binding suggestions of international organs .... Many organizations use "resolution" in the same context as "recommendation" for non-binding invitations to their members.[9]

Some writers are of the view that resolutions of the UN General Assembly have binding effect only in the internal matters and working of the UN,[10] e.g., admission of new members. For example, MacGibbon says that

> ...General Assembly resolutions possess the legal force of recommendations only: they neither make law for, nor operate with binding effect upon, any State – with the well-known exceptions...of those resolutions on a number of "internal" United Nations matters (approval of the budget, apportionment of expenses, adoption of rules of procedure, establishment of subsidiary organs ...) where the Charter has empowered the Assembly to take decisions which have full legal force and effect with regard to Members.[11]

Others maintain that, besides the resolutions which concern the internal matters and working of the UN, certain resolutions of the General Assembly have a binding effect.[12] For example, Castañeda says

---

of *International Law* (1966), p. 782 et seq.; H.G. Schermers and N.M. Blokker, *International Institutional Law* (1995), pp. 755-757; D.W. Bowett, *The Law of International Institutions*, 4th edn. (1982), pp. 45-47; I. MacGibbon, "Means for the Identification of International Law – General Assembly Resolutions: Customs, Practice and Mistaken Identity", in Cheng ed., *International Law: Teaching and Practice* (1982), p. 10 et seq.; and J.Castañeda, *Legal Effects of United Nations Resolutions* (1969).

8   See Castañeda, op.cit., pp.8-9.
9   See Schermers and Blokker, op.cit., p.755, sec. 1217.
10 See Bowett, op. cit., pp.45-46; Johnson, op. cit., pp.121-122; and MacGibbon, op.cit., p.10.
11 Ibid. Schermers and Blokker, in relation to General Assembly resolutions are of the view that "lawyers...usually require that one of two...conditions be satisfied before a rule will be deemed legally binding: either the states must officially accept a rule as legally binding, or there must be an accepted legally binding rule (such as the constitution of an international organization) which expressly provides that particular rules will be legally binding. In this more narrow view, recommendations do not bind the members legally". Op.cit., p.756, sec. 1219.
12 See Castañeda, op.cit., pp.111, 117, 150, and 171; see also O. Schachter, "Towards a Theory of International Obligations", in S.M. Schwebel ed., *The Effectiveness of International Decisions* (1971), p.371.

United Nations organs, in the performance of their functions, also make pronouncements as to the existence or non-existence of certain facts or legal situations. Sometimes the stand taken by an organ in these matters is nothing but the expression of
a point of view or opinion from which no legal consequence flows. But on occasion,
these pronouncements or estimations have a special characteristic: they are "deter-
minations" from which may derive under certain circumstances – difficult to formulate in a general manner...- legal consequences that cannot be opposed in a juridically
significant way by the members.[13]

Yet another view is to the effect that resolutions of the General Assembly constitute evidence of accepted practice of international customary rules,[14] or form
elements creating rules of international customary law, in certain circumstances.[15] The late Sir Robert Jennings says

... the possible effect of a generally acclaimed General Assembly resolution falls easily
into place in the orthodox scheme of things....It is surprising how long it has taken
to appreciate and evaluate the unanimously adopted General Assembly resolution as
evidence of accepted practice ....[16]

Professor Cheng, discussing the effect of General Assembly resolutions in relation to international customary law, says:

Indeed, it may be permissible to...say that the role of usage in the establishment of
rules of international customary law is purely evidentiary: it provides evidence on
the one hand of the contents of the rule in question and on the other hand of the
opinio juris of the States concerned. Not only is it unnecessary that the usage should
be prolonged, but there need also be no usage at all in the sense of repeated practice, provided that the *opinio juris* of the States concerned can be established. Consequently, international customary law has in reality only one constitutive element,
the *opinio juris*.[17]

Another view is that of Schachter, who, commenting on the legal effect of General Assembly resolutions, said:

... in some cases you may have a single expression of a consensus in a resolution
which will be accepted for a long time as a statement of obligatory requirements. If
we place our sole emphasis on UN practice as customary law, it does not quite cover
those situations which did not involve repetition and continued usage but nonetheless
involved an understanding that a specific obligation resulted from a resolution ....[18]

Dame Rosalyn Higgins (formerly Judge and President of the International
Court of Justice) is of the view that

---

13 See Castañeda, op.cit., p.117.

14 See Sir Robert Jennings, "General Course on Principles of International Law", The Hague
Academy, 121 *Recueil des Cours*, Vol. II (1967), p.335.

15 See B. Cheng, "United Nations Resolutions on Outer Space: "Instant" International
Customary Law?" 5 *Indian Journal of International Law* (1965), p.38.

16 See Sir Robert Jennings, loc.cit.

17 See Cheng, op.cit., p.37.

18 See Schwebel ed., op.cit., p.371.

it is now fairly widely accepted that United Nations resolutions, under certain conditions, can be treated as sources of international law. (Those conditions would be that
the resolutions are clear, and represent a repeated practice over a sufficient length of
time by the great majority of nations).[19]

So far as resolutions of the WHA are concerned, some relate to the internal matters and working of the Organization, such as the admission of new
Members,[20] the establishment of certain organs,[21] and the approval of the budget estimates,[22] which are binding on Member States. This category of resolutions resembles those adopted by the General Assembly for similar questions.
As regards the WHA resolutions on relations between the Organization and
Member States, e.g. the adoption of the International Code, the position may
be expressed as follows:

The WHA resolution adopting the Code, and its subsequent relevant resolutions on infant and young child feeding, contain certain declarations and
findings with respect to the importance of breast-feeding and its effect on the
healthy growth and development of infants, as well as the role the governments
of Member States can play in the protection of breast-feeding.[23] The WHA in
these resolutions, expressed its conviction that the protection and promotion of
infant feeding, including the regulation of the marketing of breast-milk substitutes, affect infant and young child health directly and profoundly;[24] it went on
to urge all Member States to give full and unanimous support to the implementation of the Code, which contains a number of principles as an expression of
the collective will of the Organization's membership. The WHA also urged the
translation of the Code into national legislation, regulations, or other suitable
measures.

The WHA also recognized that the implementation of the Code is an important contribution to healthy infant and young child feeding in all countries.[25] The WHA urged Member States to protect and promote breast-feeding,
as an essential component of their overall food and nutrition policies and programmes on behalf of women and children; and to ensure that the principles
and aim of the Code are given full expression in national health and nutrition
policy and action.[26]In 1996 the WHA stressed the continued need to implement the International Code and subsequent relevant resolutions of the Assembly.[27] In 2001, twenty years after the adoption of the International Code,

---

19 See R. Higgins, "The Identity of International Law", in Cheng ed., op.cit., p.28.
20 20 See Art. 6 of the WHO Constitution.
21 Ibid., Art. 18(e).
22 Ibid., Art. 56.
23 See for example Resolution WHA34.22, the first, second and third preambular paragraphs,
   WHO Handbook, Vol. II, p.91, and Resolution WHA35.26, operative paragraph 1, ibid., p.92.
24 See Resolution 34.22, fifth preambular paragraph, ibid., p.92.
25 See Resolution WHA39.28, third preambular paragraph, ibid., Vol. III, p.61.
26 See Resolution WHA43.3, operative paragraph 2(1) and (6), ibid., pp.63 and 64.
27 See Resolution WHA49.15, operative paragraph 2, for text, see *WHO Doc. WHA49/1, 1996/*

the WHA urged Member States to strengthen national mechanisms to ensure global compliance with the International Code.[28] And lastly, in 2010 the Executive Board of WHO recommended to the WHA the adoption of a resolution urging Member States

> (2) to strengthen and expedite the implementation of the Golbal Strategy for Infant and Young Child Feeding with emphasis on giving effect to the International Code of Marketing of Breast-milk Substitutes, adopted in resolution WHA 34.22.[29]

The WHA in the resolution it adopted in 2010, urged Member States

> (2) to strengthen and expedite the sustainable implementation of the global strategy for infant and young child feeding including emphasis on giving effect to the aim and principles of the International Code of Marketing of breast-milk Substitutes...,

> (3) to develop and /or strengthen legislative, regulatory and /or other effective measures to control the marketing of breast-milk substitutes in order to give effect to the International Code of Marketing of Breast-milk Substitutes and relevant resolutions adopted by the World Health Assembly.[30]

It would be relevant to mention that all the resolutions of the WHA, in this respect, were adopted by overwhelming majorities,[31] by consensus[32] or by unanimity.[33]

The various views mentioned earlier, concerning the effect of resolutions of the UN General Assembly, probably apply by analogy to resolutions of the WHA. Accordingly, those international lawyers who consider General Assembly resolutions as non-binding would likely take the same view of resolutions of the WHA.[34] According to this position, Member States of WHO are under no obligation to implement the International Code. This position can be further supported by the choice made by the WHA of adopting the Code as a recommendation under Article 23 of the WHO Constitution, in contrast with regulations under Article 22 of the WHO Constitution. [35] Regulations adopted by the WHA are binding vis-à-vis Member States, unless they reject them or attach reservations to them, whereas recommendations do not have such an effect.

On the other hand, Castañeda would probably take the same stand on Gen-

---

REC/1 pp.15-16.

28 See Resolution WHA 54.2, operative paragraph 2 (9).
29 See EB 126.R.5, p.2, paragraph 1 (2), 21 January 2010.
30 See Resolution WHA 63.23, 21 May 2010, operative paragraph 1, *WHA63/2010/REC/1*, p.47.
31 The WHA resolution adopting the International Code (WHA34.22) was opposed by one Member State (the US), with three abstentions; see above p.42. See also Resolution WHA39.28, which was adopted by a great majority, with one member State against and six abstentions. See *WHO Doc. WHA39/1986/REC/3*, p.210.
32 See for example Resolution WHA47.5, see WHO Doc. *WHA47/1994/REC/3*, p.46.
33 See Resolution WHA49.15, *WHO Doc. WHA49/1996/REC/3*, p.101.
34 See for example MacGibbon, loc.cit. and Schermers and Blokker, loc.cit.
35 For details see above pp. 26-29.

eral Assembly resolutions as on the WHA resolutions in question. According to this position, Member States may be said to be unable to escape the "legal consequences"[36] arising from those WHA resolutions in relation to the implementation of the International Code. Those writers who consider some General Assembly resolutions as evidence of international customary rules,[37] or elements creating such rules,[38] would, probably, take the same stand on the WHA resolutions in question. According to this position then, such resolutions may develop into customary law, and thus bind Member States in relation to implementation of the Code, or they may already express the *opinio juris* of the Member States. The ICJ regards the attitude of States to certain General Assembly resolutions, and resolutions of other fora, as evidence of the existence of *opinio juris*. In the case concerning *Military and Paramilitary Activities in and against Nicaragua, (Merits)* 1986, the ICJ, referring to the requirement of the existence of *opinio juris* said:

> this *opinio juris* may...be deduced from, *inter alia*, the attitude of the Parties and the attitude of States towards certain General Assembly resolutions, and particularly resolution 2625 (XXV) entitled "Declaration on Principles of International Law concerning Friendly Relations and Co-operation among States in accordance with the Charter of the United Nations". The effect of consent to the text of such resolutions... may be understood as an acceptance of the validity of the rule or set of rules declared by the resolution by themselves. The ICJ went on to say it would therefore seem apparent that the attitude referred to expresses an *opinio juris* respecting such rule (or set of rules).... [39]

The ICJ also referred to the support of the US to a resolution of the Sixth International Conference of American States condemning aggression (18 February 1928), and its acceptance of the principle of the prohibition of the use of force contained in the declaration on principles governing the mutual relations of States participating in the Conference on Security and Cooperation in Europe (Helsinki, 1 August 1975) and said:

> acceptance of a text in these terms confirms the existence of an *opinio juris* of the participating States ....[40]

Professor Cheng considers *opinio juris* as the only element necessary to create an international custom. Therefore, according to this standpoint, it would seem there is already an international custom binding Member States to implement the Code.

Schachter would, probably, apply his view on General Assembly resolutions[41] to the resolutions of the WHA in question. Accordingly, such resolu-

---

36 See above p.202.
37 See ibid.
38 See ibid.
39 See ICJ Rep. (1986), pp. 99-100, paragraph. 188.
40 Ibid., p. 100, paragraph 189.
41 See above p. 202.

tions may be accepted as "a statement of obligatory requirements", and as such, they could be said to bind Member States to implement the Code. Dame Rosalyn Higgins' conditions with respect to resolutions of the General Assembly[42] could easily apply to the resolutions of the WHA in question, in that they are clear, repeated over nearly 30 years at the WHA and adopted by great majorities[43] of the Member States. Therefore, Member States could be said to be bound to implement the Code.

Further support for this position may be found in the advisory opinion of the ICJ on the *Legal Consequences for States of the Continued Presence of South Africa in Namibia (South West Africa) notwithstanding resolution 276 (1970) of the Security Council.* The ICJ said:

> ... It would not be correct to assume that, because the General Assembly is in principle vested with recommendatory powers, it is debarred from adopting, in specific cases within the framework of its competence, resolutions which make determinations or have operative design.[44]

And, again, the ICJ said in its advisory opinion on the *Legality of the Threat or Use of Nuclear Weapons:*

> The Court notes that General Assembly resolutions, even if they are not binding, may sometimes have normative value. They can, in certain circumstances, provide evidence important for establishing the existence of a rule or the emergence of an *opinio juris*. To establish whether this is true of a given General Assembly resolution, it is necessary to look at its content and the conditions of its adoption; it is also necessary to see whether an *opinio juris* exists as to its normative character. Or a series of resolutions may show the gradual evolution of the *opinio juris* required for the establishment of a new rule.[45]

The action of Member States may support the view that the WHA resolutions in question have legal effect. In 1994, more than 160 Member States and territories had notified the Director-General of WHO of the adoption of national

---

42 See above p.202-203.
43 Professor Virally maintains: "...A State which has not declared its acceptance of a recommendation is not bound by it, though it may be fairly asked whether the principle of good faith will permit a State to disregard a recommendation which it has formally approved by its affirmative vote". See Virally, "The Sources of International Law", in Sørensen ed. *Manual of Public International Law*, p. 161. See Dame Rosalyn Higgins' comment on voting: "...There are really three options available to a State: it can vote against, it can abstain, or vote for, making a collateral statement indicating that it does not believe the statement to be a correct enunciation of the law or one that requires action from it. So that if it declines to exercise any of these three options and votes for, with adequate time for consultation at home, having gone through the *ad referendum* process, it is then arguable that it is bound". She goes on: "my point went to the acceptance really by vote of States of a recommendation... It is not the recommendation that binds, but the acceptance of the States through the vote". See: Schwebel, op.cit., pp. 398 and 399. For a contrary view, see MacGibbon, op.cit., p. 13.
44 See ICJ Rep. (1971), p.50, paragraph. 105.
45 See ICJ Rep. (1996), p. 26, paragraph 70.

measures to implement the Code,[46] and in 2008 the number had risen to 196.[47]

These measures have taken various forms: administrative measures,[48] with either partial or full implementation,[49] the drafting of implementing legislation,[50] or the enactment of such legislation[51]. This may well indicate that these Members feel under a legal obligation to implement the Code, otherwise they need not have done so.

It might be appropriate to conclude this discussion by quoting Schermers and Blokker, who make the following apt comment:

> As was mentioned above, recommendations do not legally bind the members. However, this does not mean that they have no effect on them. The existence of a legal obligation provides merely one of many reasons for observing a rule and indeed, in international law, where sanctions often prove to be illusory, the legal obligation may not even be the prime motivation behind norm compliance. A number of factors can be seen to plead in favour of giving effect to recommendations. There are several examples of decisions recognizing such effect.

They go on to give the example of IAEA, and say

> another example is the recommendation of the World Health Assembly pursuant to which the International Code of Marketing of Breast-milk Substitutes was adopted. According to Article 11.1 of this Code, "Governments should take action to give effect to the principles and aim of this Code ...". In practice, most governments have given effect to at least portions of the Code through legally enforceable measures.[52]

---

46 See report of the Director-General on Infant and Young Child Nutrition (progress and evaluation report; and status of implementation of the International Code of Breast-milk Substitutes, 23 March 1994, WHO Doc. WHA47/1994/REC/1, Annex 1, p. 63 et seq.

47 See IBFAN's *State of the Code by Country* 2009.

48 See for examples the order of the Ministry of Public Health and Population of Gabon, 1991, banning the distribution of supplies of breast-milk substitutes to health care institutions, note 46, p.64, paragraph 74; the prohibition imposed by the Côte d'Ivoire government on 1 February 1992 on the donations of breast-milk substitutes to health services; ibid., paragraph 73; in Ecuador, a code of behaviour, disallowing the free distribution of breast-milk substitutes, was signed in 1993 by the First Lady, ibid, p.66, paragraph 87; in Pakistan, a notification by the Ministry of Health was issued prohibiting or controlling advertising and distribution of free or low-cost supplies of breast-milk substitutes; ibid., p.69, paragraph 113; and Saudi Arabia accepted the Muscat Declaration of January 1993 by the Arab Ministers of Health on the promotion of breast-feeding, ibid., p.70, paragraph 114.

49 IBFAN's *State of the Code by Country*.

50 See for examples draft legislations prepared in the following Member States with legal assistance from WHO: Iraq, Jordan, Morocco, Syria, Oman and the United Arab Emirates; see also draft regulations of February 1992 of the United Republic of Tanzania; see above note 27, pp. 64-65, paragraph 77.

51 See for examples, the Burkina Faso national code of 26 July 1993, see ibid., p. 64, paragrah 71; the Guatemalan Law 1983, ibid., p. 66, paragraph 88; the Indian Infant Milk Substitutes Act 1992, ibid, p. 67, paragraph 97; the Nepalese Breast-milk Susbstitution Act ibid., p. 68, paragraph 99; the following countries have adopted laws, Bahrain, China, Iran and Nigeria, and Viet Nam adopted a Ministerial Decree.

52 See Schermers and Blokker, op.cit., pp. 756-757, sec. 1220.

This writer subscribes to the view that the resolutions of the WHA in question must have been intended to have more than a moral effect, insofar as the implementation of the International Code is concerned. For these resolutions contain repeated calls to Member States for the implementation of the Code and references to its relevance to the promotion of breast-feeding. Moreover, as has been seen above, those resolutions were adopted by huge majorities, or by consensus, and as such, they express the position of more than 190 States.[53] Therefore, it is submitted that they should "have operative design", to borrow the ICJ words,[54] vis-à-vis Member States. This "operative design" could take the form of an obligation to implement the International Code.

It may be interesting to refer to a decision of the Supreme Court of the Philippines in 2007, in a case involving the claim of some manufacturers of breast-milk substitutes that the Philippine Milk Code of 2006 implementing the International Code was unconstitutional. The Supreme Court quoted the writer on the legal effect of WHA resolutions to the effect that

> WHA recommendations are generally not binding, but they carry moral and political weight as the constitute the judgment on a health issue of the collective membership of the highest international body in the field of health.[55]

The Supreme Court considered WHA resolutions as "soft law" and went on to say

> The provisions of the WHA Resolutions cannot be considered as part of the law of the land that can be implemented by the executive agencies without the need of a law to be enacted by the legislature.[56]

It is submitted with respect that the Supreme Court of the Philippines only referred to one part of the description of this writer of the WHA resolutions, and even then, it omitted the term *"per se"* in the quotation in question. The Supreme Court should have referred to the detailed discussion of the legal effect of WHA resolutions in Chapter XIII of this work, if it wanted to assess the situation appropriately.

However, whether or not there is a legal obligation to implement the International Code in legislation, regulations or other suitable measures, it is submitted that the decisive factor for the implementation of the Code is the political commitment in a given Member State to promote and protect breast-feeding and the healthy growth and development of infants. It is not surprising that a meeting, held under WHO's auspices in The Hague in 1991, recommended that

---

53 The membership of WHO stands now at 191 Member States and two Associate Members, see *WHO Basic Documents*, 45th edn., pp. 169-172.

54 See above p.206.

55 See Decision of the Supreme Court of the Republic of the Philippines, EN BANC, G.R. No. 173034, October 9, 2007, p. 12.

56 See ibid., p. 16.

governments should make a political commitment to give effect to the principles and aim of the International Code *in its entirety*, as a minimum measure. Political commitment implies monitoring of compliance with national measures, imposition of sanctions, and availability of adequate human and other resources to follow up.[57]

If there is such a commitment, the process of implementation of the Code becomes a reality, but in the absence of such a commitment, the State concerned is not likely to do anything, even if the Code were a binding treaty. But the State which neglects the health of its infants commits a big mistake. A former Director-General of WHO (Dr Mahler) had said that

> ... children are a priceless resource, and that any nation which neglects them does so at its peril.[58]

2. THE EXTENT OF IMPLEMENTATION OF THE INTERNATIONAL CODE

When a Member State decides to implement the International Code, what is the extent of this implementation? The first point to be made is that the Code is to be implemented as "a minimum requirement" and in "its entirety", as declared by the WHA.[59] Furthermore, when the Code was under preparation some members of the Executive Board considered it as "the bare minimum of measures", "minimum international requirements" and "minimum requirement",[60] while it was described as "a minimum compromise"[61] at the WHA. The implications of those descriptions of the Code are that Member States implementing the Code can go beyond its provisions, and expand them, add to them and so on, according to their social and legislative framework and their overall development objectives. However, they cannot go below the "minimum requirements". Moreover, since the provisions of the International Code are like a series of parts, which complete each other, if any part is omitted, there would be a gap

---

57 See Review and Evalution of National Action Taken to Give Effect to the International Code of Marketing of Breast-milk Substitutes: Report of a Technical Meeting, The Hague, 30 September-3 October 1991, *WHO Doc WHO/MCH/NUT/91.2*, p. 4, paragraph 9. The following States and organizations participated in that meeting: Sweden, Norway, Yemen, The Netherlands, Poland, U.K., Philippines, Egypt, Finland, Guatemala, Iran, Kenya, Papua New Guinea, Brazil and Nigeria; IOCU, IPA, IFGO, ICM, IFM, SIDA, and UNICEF. See ibid., Annex 2, pp. 23, 24.

58 See message from the Director-General of WHO for World Health Day, 1984, "Children's health – tomorrow's wealth", *World Health*, January-February 1984, p. 5.

59 See Resolution WHA34.22, last preambular paragraph and operative paragraph 2(1), for the text of the resolution see *WHO Handbook*, Vol. II, pp. 91-92.

60 See the statements of Dr Yaqoub, Dr Alvarez and Dr Mork, at the Executive Board, Sixty-seventh Session, Geneva, 14-30 January 1981. *WHO Doc. EB67/1981/REC/2*, pp. 306 and 307.

61 See the statement of the Swedish Delegate (Dr Alsén) at the Thirty-fourth WHA 1981, *WHO Doc. WHA34/1981/REC/3*, p. 190.

that would leave the rest of it hanging in the air. For example, if Article 5.5 of the Code is left out in a national measure giving effect to the Code, there would be a gap that would enable marketing personnel, in their business capacity, to contact pregnant women or mothers of infants and young children freely, to the detriment of breast-feeding. It would also affect the elements the drafters wanted to cover in that provision, namely, the practices that have, or can have, adverse effects on breast-feeding. It is worthwhile mentioning again the decision of the Supreme Court of the Philippines in this context. In their efforts to implement the International Code, the Philippines health authorities omitted to impose an absolute ban on advertising and promotion of products covered by the International Code, as required by Article 6.1 of the Code, in the Philippines Milk Code. The latter expressly provided that

> ... advertising, promotion or other marketing materials may be allowed if such material are duly authorized or approved by the Inter-Agency Committee (IAC), (Sec.6).

Some manufacturers of breast-milk substitutes in the Philippines went to court claiming the Milk Code contained provisions that were not constitutional. One of these provisions is Section 6 (a) of the Milk Code. The Supreme Court held that

> The Milk Code is almost a verbatim reproduction of the ICMBS [the International Code] but it is well to emphasize ... that the Code did not adopt the provision of the ICMBS absolutely prohibiting advertising or other forms of promotion to the general public of products within the scope of the ICMBS. Instead, the Milk Code expressly provides that advertising, promotion or other marketing materials may be allowed if such materials are duly authorized or approved by the ...IAC.[62]

The Supreme Court held that the provision of the Milk Code imposing total prohibition on advertising and promotion was invalid.[63]

So far as the expansion of the provisions of the International Code is concerned, it may be necessary because of certain developments in marketing practices, or the appearance of some new products in the market, since the adoption of the International Code in 1981, e.g., follow-up milks. Expansion of some provisions of the International Code may also be justified in order to clarify the intent of some provisions, and provide for concrete measures thereunder. For example, Article 6.1 of the International Code provides that

> the health authorities in Member States should take appropriate measures to encourage and protect breast-feeding and promote the principles of this Code, and should give appropriate information and advice to health workers in regard to their responsibilities....

The provision does not spell out what those "appropriate measures" might be, nor does it specify what "appropriate information and advice" should be given

---

62 See Supreme Court of the Republic of the Philippines, op. cit., p. 8.
63 See ibid., p.40.

by the health authorities to the health worker. Here is an opportunity for Member States to provide expressly and clearly what they consider necessary and relevant in this context.[64]

Another pertinent point in this respect is that, when a Member State implements the Code, it would be advisable to have a provision in its national measure which would enable its competent authorities to keep up with changes in marketing practices or other areas relevant to the Code. Such a provision would be outside the existing Code's provisions, and yet would provide a legal basis for future action, at the national level, should the need arise for the protection of breast-feeding. Moreover, in addition to the articles of the Code, the WHA has requested Member States to include the relevant resolutions adopted by it, in their national measures.[65] This is a very interesting development, for there are certain issues which were not included in the Code, but the WHA requested Member States to do something about them. For example, the question of maternity protection in the work-place and its implication for breast-feeding,[66] the enactment of legislation for the protection of breast-feeding rights of working women, cooperation between the ILO and WHO in this connection,[67] the ban on the donations, or low-price sales, of supplies of breast-milk substitutes and other products covered by the Code to the health care system, were among the questions included in those resolutions. The question of the Baby-Friendly Hospital Initiative in Member States was another issue not covered by the Code, but included in some of the Assembly resolutions.[68] These questions should be included in any national action giving effect to the Code, because of their relevance and importance to the promotion of breast-feeding.

3. PARTIAL IMPLEMENTATION OF THE INTERNATIONAL CODE

As has been pointed out earlier, the Code was adopted as "a minimum require-

---

64 It might be interesting to point out that some Member States included, in the implementation of Article 6.1, the expansion of teaching of breast-feeding and lactation management at medical schools, the provision of maternity leave for working mothers, and the provision of breast-feeding facilities at the work place. For examples see Art. 7, paragraphs 1-3 of the draft Jordanian Code 1994, and Art. 7, paragraphs 1-3 of the draft Omani Code 1995; see also Arts. 3 and 4 of the Iranian Law 1996.

65 See Resolution WHA45.34 (May 1992), operative paragraph 2.1 (c); Resolution WHA47.5 (9 May 1994), operative paragraph 3(5); and Resolution WHA49.1(25 May 1996), operative paragraph 2, for texts see *WHO Handbook*,Vol. III, pp. 64-66, *WHO Doc. WHA47/1994/ REC/1*, pp. 3-5, and above note 4.

66 See Resolution WHA47.5, operative paragraph 2(4).

67 See Resolution WHA45.34, operative paragraphs 2(1)(d), and 3(5). WHO and the ILO have a cooperation agreement in areas of common interest to the two Organizations, concluded in 1948. See *WHO Basic Documents*, 45th edn., p. 50

68 See Resolution WHA45.34, operative paragraph 2(2) and Resolution WHA47.5, operative paragraph 3(4).

ment" and the WHA urged Member States to implement it "in its entirety". Therefore, the question may be raised: is partial implementation of the Code a proper implementation? If a Member State intending to implement the Code adopts national measures banning only advertising and promotion of breast-milk substitutes, would this constitute the implementation described in Article 11.1 of the Code? The answer must be in the negative, because Article 11.1 requires governments to take action to give effect to the principles and aim of the Code. The principles and aim, it is submitted, cover all the provisions of the Code. Furthermore, the resolution adopted by the WHA, to which the Code was annexed, expressly urged all Member States

> to give full and unanimous support to the implementation of...the provisions of the International Code in its entirety....[69]

Moreover, as has been seen above, subsequent resolutions of the WHA urged Member States to implement not only the Code but also subsequent relevant resolutions of the Assembly. Therefore, partial implementation is not tantamount to proper implementation as intended by the drafters of the Code. It should be pointed out that in some Member States, the ministry of health has issued a circular applying some parts of the Code,[70] or issued directives concerning nutrition and education,[71] or issued memoranda to health personnel with copies of the International Code,[72] or laid down requirements relating to the labelling of breast-milk substitutes,[73] or issued instructions dealing with some aspects of the International Code.[74] Such measures, it is submitted, would not be considered as a proper implementation of the Code, because they do not cover all the provisions of the Code, nor do they reflect the relevant resolutions of the WHA.

However, it must be pointed out that the Code contains certain provisions, which are intended to provide some options and flexibility to Member States, in the national context. If in the process of implementation of the Code, a Member State chooses not to exercise this option, or flexibility, this would not seem to detract from proper implementation. For example, Article 4.3 of the Code affords the appropriate government authorities, be they the health authorities or other authorities, the possibility of requesting donations of informational or educational equipment from manufacturers and distributors of products covered by the Code. Now if a government does not wish to have this possibility,

---

69 See Resolution WHA34.22, operative paragraph 2 (1).

70 See Botswana's report to the Director-General, The International Code of Marketing of Breast-milk Substitutes: Synthesis of Reports on Action Taken (1981-1990), WHO Doc. WHO/MCH/NUT/90.1, p. 4, paragraph 15.

71 See Madagascar's report to the Director-General, ibid., p. 6, paragraph 29.

72 See WHO Doc. WHO/HLE/NUT/92.1, p. 19, paragraph 65 (1). According to IBFAN's State of the Code by Country, 2009, 75 countries have implemented the Code in part.

73 See Hungary's report to the Director-General, above note 70, p. 22, paragraph 112.

74 See Djibouti's report to the Director-General, ibid., p. 30, paragraph 151.

and in implementing the Code in national legislation it does not include Article 4.3 in that legislation, this would not render its action as partial implementation of the Code. This is so, because the intention of the drafters was not to impose an obligation on governments in that provision, but rather to give them an option, which they can choose to include or to ignore, at their discretion. The same applies to Article 6.6 of the Code.[75] This kind of provision is different from those which are intended to impose certain obligations and restraint, for the purpose of curbing certain marketing practices and thus promote and protect breast-feeding, such as Article 4.1 or Article 5, to give but some examples. The non-inclusion of these provisions in any national measures would constitute partial implementation of the Code, and as such it would be incompatible with Article 11.1 and WHA resolutions.

4. MODES OF IMPLEMENTATION OF THE INTERNATIONAL CODE

Article 11.1 of the Code gives governments three means of implementing the Code: 1) legislation, 2) regulations, and 3) other suitable measures, as appropriate to their social and legislative framework. This is a reasonable approach and affords Member States the flexibility to choose from these three means of implementation, as appropriate, from the point of view of the national context.

(1) Legislation

Legislation is defined as

> the process of deliberate law-making or law-changing by an expression of the will of a person or body recognized by a particular legal system as having power and authority validly to declare law. The term is also used of the products of the legislative process, of the body of rules laid down thereby. In this sense it is equivalent to statute-law.[76]

Accordingly, the Code may be implemented by the legislature in a Member State as a statute, a national code or an act of parliament. It could also be implemented as an amendment of an existing statute, code or an act of parliament.

Legislation would be the best means of implementing the Code, in that it

---

75 In fact, some of the Member States implementing the International Code have not included any provision relating to Article 6.6 of the International Code; or the giving of such supplies is forbidden or restricted. For example the Iranian Law 1996, does not contain a provision on supplies, whereas the Brazilian Regulations for Infant's Foods 1992, forbid the giving of such supplies (Art.19); the same applies to the draft Jordanian Code 1994 (Art. 7(b) and the draft Omani Code 1995 (Art. 7(7). The Indian Infant Milk Substitutes Act 1992, restricts the giving of such supplies to orphanages only (Sec. 5(a)).

76 See D.M. Walker, *The Oxford Companion to Law* (1980), p.757.

could provide a new law, with its own structure, definitions, monitoring system and so on. However, legally speaking, the same could be achieved through the amendment of an existing law, although this option might be more complicated than straight legislation. Some delegates to the WHA expressed their preference for legislation as the means of implementing the Code. The Gambian Delegate to the Forty-seventh WHA (Dr. George) observed that

> the promotion of breast-feeding could succeed only where legislation was passed to create the environment in which women could breast-feed their children without fear of penalties from employers, as more working women entered the formal sector in the developing world.[77]

This was echoed by the Dutch Delegate (Dr. Van Etten), who said :

> The Netherlands considered that greater emphasis should be placed on legislation as the most important mechanism for implementing the Code.[78]

It might be interesting to mention that the US took the position, as early as July 1980, that the Code should provide the basis for national legislation. In its comments on the Second Draft of the Code, the US said the following:

> A code taking the formulation of recommendations under Article 23 [of the WHO Constitution] could serve not only as a statement of principles to guide all those in infant feeding, but also as a detailed basis for national legislation.[79]

The Code has been implemented in legislation in a small number of countries.[80]

(2) Regulations

A regulation is defined as

> in a broad sense any prescription intended to govern conduct. More specifically the term is commonly used of subordinate legislation issued by Departments of State in pursuance of statutory powers.[81]

Accordingly, the Code may be given effect to in a set of rules issued by the ministry of health or another competent authority, based on existing statutory powers, such as a public health law or food law. Regulations are subordinate

---

77 See Forty-seventh World Health Assembly, 1994, *WHO Doc. WHA47/1994/REC/3*, p.33.

78 Ibid. p. 35.

79 See a letter from Dr. J.B. Richmond, Assistant Secretary for Health and Surgeon General, Department of Health and Human Services, to the Director-General of WHO, dated 31 July 1980, p.4, third paragraph. Also as early as 1980, some delegates to the Thirty-third WHA envisaged national legislation or regulations for the implementation of the Code. See statements by the Delegates of Niger, Togo and Switzerland, *WHO Doc. WHA33/1980/REC/3*, pp.75, 79 and 87.

80 See below p.222.

81 See Walker, op. cit, p.1053. For regulations under the WHO Constitution, see above pp.27-29.

to those legal instruments that can be adopted under the heading "legislation", but they are sufficient, from a legal point of view, for the implementation of the Code, and might be easier to adopt under some legal systems than legislation. In fact, the Code has been implemented in some Member States as regulations.[82]

(3) Other suitable measures

The third means of implementing the Code is by the adoption of "other suitable measures". While there would be no difficulty in identifying the legal instrument used for implementing the Code as legislation or regulations, there may be some difficulty with the term "other suitable measures", particularly with reference to "voluntary agreements". The term "other suitable measures" is not defined in the Code, nor does it have any special definition, therefore, it may be interpreted in two ways:

First, according to a literal interpretation of the term, "other suitable measures" covers any measure or action taken by a competent authority in a State to give effect to the Code, be they legally binding or not. According to this interpretation then, the term covers instructions by the ministry of health, a ministerial decree, a declaration, a voluntary agreement between manufacturers or distributors of breast-milk substitutes and the government concerned and so on. Therefore, voluntary agreements could be considered as a proper implementation of the Code. During the consideration of the report of the Director-General, on the implementation of the Code, by the Executive Board in 1994, one member (Dr Milan) stated that

> ... in cases where the implementation of legislation was unsatisfactory, other voluntary means should be explored.[83]

The second interpretation of the term "other suitable measures" may be to the effect that they cover any action or measure taken by a competent authority in a State and intended to be *legally binding*, such as a cabinet decision or a decree by a minister of health. Therefore, any measure which is taken to implement the Code, which lacks a legally binding effect, e.g., voluntary agreements, cannot be considered as one of the "other suitable measures" mentioned in Article 11.1. The bases for this interpretation are: first, Article 11.1 speaks of "legislation, regulations or other suitable measures", thus, it appears to put the three categories, i.e., "legislation, regulations or other suitable measures" on a footing of equality. The same is true of Article 11.7 of the Code, which says that the Director-General

---

82 For examples, see the Brazilian Marketing Regulations 1992, the Guatemalan Rules for the Marketing of Breast-milk Substitutes 1987 and the Tanzanian Regulations 1994.

83 See *Executive Board, Ninety-third Session, Geneva, 17-26 January 1994, WHO Doc. EB93/1994/REC/2*, (hereinafter referred to as "WHO Doc. EB93/1994/REC/2"), p. 112.

... shall, on request, provide technical support to Member States preparing national legislation or regulations, or taking other appropriate measures in implementation and furtherance of the principles and aim of this Code.

Therefore, it could be argued that since the first two categories are legally binding in nature, it follows that the third category should also be of the same nature. Furthermore, in its advisory opinion on the *Competence of the ILO to Regulate Agricultural Labour and Production* 1922, the PCIJ summarized the activities specified in the preamble to Part XIII (Labour) of the Treaty of Versailles as means of improving conditions of labour and doing away with injustice, hardship and privation; the preamble concludes with the expression "and other measures". In relation to the latter expression, the PCIJ said:

and, as the Treaty says, 'other measures' which must mean measures to improve the conditions of labour and to do away with injustice, hardship and privation.

McNair says that this ruling

... illustrates the ejusdem generis doctrine by confining the 'measures' to the category of measures previously specified in the preamble.[84]

Moreover, the Code is intended, primarily, to protect and promote breast-feeding, and this purpose can be achieved only by a proper legal instrument, enacted at the national level, laying down specific obligations vis-à-vis those to whom it is addressed. This is not the case with non-binding measures, e.g., voluntary agreements, which are, by their nature, non-binding.[85] Therefore, it is submitted that the literal interpretation should be rejected and the second interpretation is to be preferred, as it is more inline with the aim and intent of the Code.[86]

5. VOLUNTARY AGREEMENTS

The question may be raised: can voluntary agreements be considered as a mode of proper implementation of the International Code? According to *The Concise Oxford Dictionary* "voluntary" means

done, acting or able to act at one's own free will; not constrained or compulsory....[87]

---

84 See McMair *The Law of Treaties* (1961), p. 394. See also PCIJ Series, B, Nos 2 and 3, cited in McNair, ibid. The term "*ejusdem generis*" means "of the same kind or nature". See *Osborn's Concise Law Dictionary*, 6th edn., (1976), p.128.

85 See below, note 87.

86 See also Shubber "The Code-Legal Aspects of Implementation in a Changing World", 1 *N U* (1996), pp.12-13. The *N U* is published by the Unit of International Child Health, Department of Paediatrics, Uppsala University, Sweden.

87 See 9th edn. (1995), p. 1570.

Accordingly, a voluntary agreement does not possess a binding nature and the parties thereto may withdraw from it, at their own will, any time, without being in breach of any obligation. This cannot be in line with the aim and intent of the Code, which is intended to regulate the marketing of products covered by it, with the banning and restricting of certain marketing practices. One writer, commenting on voluntary agreements in the area of tobacco between the tobacco industry and government, said:

> voluntary agreements are weak means of controlling tobacco promotion; they are complex and difficult to monitor, and are subject to differences of interpretation which can hinder implementation. They...leave the industry free to find loopholes to evade the restrictions ....[88]

Moreover, any measure implementing the Code must contain penalties, in order to enforce compliance with it. Voluntary agreements, for example, cannot contain such penalties.

Thirdly, some parts of the resolutions of the WHA may also provide some support to the above point of view. For example, in 1981, the WHA requested the Director-General of WHO to give all possible support to Member States, for the implementation of the International Code,

> and in particular in the preparation of national legislation and other measures related thereto.[89]

The WHA, again, in 1988, requested the Director-General of WHO to provide legal and technical assistance to Member States

> in the drafting and /or the implementation of national codes of marketing of breast-milk substitutes, or other similar instruments.[90]

The references in these resolutions to "national legislation and other measures related thereto", and to "national codes of marketing of breast-milk substitutes, or other similar instruments", is an indication of what the Member States had in mind when adopting those resolutions. It would seem that what they had in mind is probably a *binding legal instrument*.

It might be interesting to mention that the question of the use of voluntary agreements as a means of implementing the Code drew strong reactions from the Executive Board. Some members of the Executive Board expressed concern about the reference to voluntary agreements in the report of the Director-General on the International Code in 1994. Dr Okware (alternate to Dr Makumbi),

---

88 See Ruth Roemer, Legislative action to combat the world tobacco epidemic (1993), p. 15.

89 See Resolution WHA34.22, operative paragraph 5 (1); for text see above note 2, Vol. II, pp. 91-92.

90 See Resolution WHA41.11, operative paragraph 3 (6); for text see above note 2, Vol. III, pp. 62-63.

... expressed concern that certain voluntary arrangements mentioned elsewhere in the report went beyond the mandate given to the Director-General by the [World] Health Assembly.

He referred to paragraph 131 of the report and said, with regard to paragraph 131, he was

concerned about the many countries that were adopting voluntary arrangements rather than legislation and regulations required by the Code. A new dimension had apparently been added without the authority of the Health Assembly,...since it was his understanding that the Code had originally been intended to be binding, with no provision for voluntary arrangements. If that was in fact the case, paragraph 131 should be amended accordingly....[91]

Another member of the Executive Board, Dr. Al-Jaber, also drew attention to paragraph 131 of the Director-General's report and stated that

it was important to avoid abuse or misinterpretation of the International Code.[92]

Other members of the Executive Board expressed preference for legislation, as a method of implementation of the International Code.[93]

The WHO secretariat, in reply, assured members of the Executive Board that the Director-General's report on the issue of voluntary agreements would be revised, and that such agreements were not mentioned in the Code, nor in the WHA resolutions. Dr. Antezana, ADG, stated that

the [WHO] Secretariat would take care of the concerns clearly expressed by Dr. Ok-ware.[94]

Dr. Belsey, FHE, stated that

the preamble to the Code called on governments to take action appropriate to the social and legislative framework... and to give effect to the principles and aim of the Code, including the enactment of legislation, regulations or other suitable measures. It was true that voluntary agreements were not specifically mentioned either in the Code or any of the resolutions [of the WHA].[95]

The Director-General's report was finally revised in accordance with the wishes of the members of the Executive Board and the offending parts were deleted.

It is worthwhile mentioning that the WHA itself does not seem to consider

---

91 See above note 83, p. 112. The representative of IOCU, Ms Peck pointed out that "...the Code stated that governments should take action, including the adoption of national legislation, regulations or other suitable measures, and thus clearly gave legislation priority over voluntary measures, which had in fact never been mentioned as being part of the "other appropriate measures"". See ibid. p. 114. The Director-General's report was, finally revised, and the offending parts were deleted.

92 See ibid., p.112.

93 See statements of Mrs Herzog, Dr Milan, and Dr Okware. See ibid., pp. 111 and 112.

94 Ibid., p.115.

95 I bid., p.116.

voluntary agreements as an appropriate measure for the implementation of the International Code. For in the resolution it adopted in 2010, it expressed

> ... concern over reports of the ineffectiveness of measures, particularly voluntary measures, to ensure compliance with the International Code of Marketing of Breast-milk Substitutes in some countries.[96]

It might be appropriate to conclude this discussion with a comment made in relation to voluntary agreements with the tobacco industry:

> A number of countries that once relied on voluntary agreements with the industry have rejected this arrangement and have replaced it with legislation as a more effective method of control.[97]

6. THE ADVANTAGES OF PROPER IMPLEMENTATION OF THE INTERNATIONAL CODE

There are, no doubt, advantages in the proper implementation of the International Code, for all concerned, be they health authorities, manufacturers or distributors of products covered by the Code, consumer groups or professional organizations.

First, the implementation of the Code enhances the role and prestige of WHO as the highest international authority in the area of health, generally, and infant health, in particular. Judge Weeramantry, in his Dissenting Opinion in the Advisory Opinion of the ICJ on the *Legality of the use by a State of Nuclear Weapons in Armed Conflict,* 1996, described WHO as the world's leading health authority, and is

> a body charged with the highest responsibilities in regard to the health of the global community.[98]

The Code is the first international instrument of this kind hitherto adopted by the WHA.

Secondly, the implementation of the Code constitutes a yardstick for judging the marketing practices of manufacturers and distributors, actions of health workers and the conduct of the health care system in the implementing State. For example, whether or not the giving of supplies of breast-milk substitutes to the health care system, free, or at a low price, is legal or otherwise, will be judged by the national measure implementing the Code, rather than the Code itself, which is not binding on Member States. This will provide a certainty in the law and avoid the subjective interpretation of the actions of manufacturers, distributors or health workers; for any dispute regarding compliance with such

---

96 See Resolution WHA 63, 21 May 2010, 11th preambular paragraph.
97 See Ruth Roemer, loc.cit.
98 See ICJ Reports (1996), p. 137.

a national measure will be decided by the competent authorities of the Member State concerned, be it a court of law or any similar body, according to the legal system of that State.

Thirdly, the implementation of the Code at the national level offers a good opportunity for the Member State to expand its provisions, and for laying down the framework for detailed formulation of its principles, as it deems fit.

Fourthly, a State implementing the Code will have the possibility of providing for a well-structured mechanism for monitoring compliance with its national measures, such as the designation of the competent body to do so, the procedures for complaint investigation, the role of the health worker, NGOs and individuals, in the monitoring scheme and so on.

Fifthly, a national legal measure implementing the Code will have some sanctions, which will constitute a deterrent against violations, and presumably, the drafters of the Code had intended that the matter of sanctions be left for each State to determine, when implementing the Code.

Finally, the implementation of the Code will ensure absence of any discrimination between local manufacturers or distributors and foreign ones, in that Article 11.1 of the Code provides that

> national policies and measures, including laws and regulations...should apply on the same basis to all those involved in the manufacture and marketing of products within the scope of this Code.

In the absence of a legal instrument implementing the Code, there could be discrimination, on a *de facto* basis, between nationals and foreigners, without, perhaps, the possibility of legal remedy. Incidentally, this constitutes a clear indication of the even-handedness of the Code, and that it is not intended as a trade barrier, nor is it contrary to the GATT. It would be relevant to quote what the Director-General has said on this point: referring to the concern expressed by some NGOs on the issue, he said:

> ... it appears reasonable to assume that the conclusion of the "Uruguay Round" of GATT negotiations will not weaken the capacity of Member States to adopt and enforce national measures, including laws and regulations, to give effect to the principles and aim of the International Code.[99]

It may be worthwhile mentioning that, in order to facilitate the implementation of the Code, and in view of the lack of the necessary expertise in some Member States in this respect, the drafters of the Code suggested in Article 11.1 that

> ... governments should seek, when necessary, the cooperation of WHO, UNICEF and other agencies of the United Nations system in the implementation process.

Moreover, the drafters also enjoined the Director-General of WHO in Article 11.7 to provide, on request

---

99 See above note 46, p.76, paragraph 141.

technical support to Member States preparing national legislation or regulations, or taking other appropriate measures in implementation and furtherance of the principles and aim of this Code.[100]

Indeed, the Director-General was requested by several Member States to provide legal assistance to them in the preparation of national legislation or regulations in the implementation of the Code.[101]

Another way of facilitating the process of implementation of the Code is the holding of regional or national workshops, to which Member States of the region are invited. WHO has held, in cooperation with UNICEF, three regional workshops.[102] In these workshops, the principles and aim of the Code were explained, and the importance, advantages and the necessity of implementation, and their consequences for the promotion of breast-feeding were emphasized. A great deal of guidance and advice were also rendered to participants, from the point of view of drafting, and drawing attention to the difficulties which might confront those working for the implementation of the Code. Such difficulties include the lack of political commitment, insufficient attention to intersectoriality, the scope of the Code, the erroneous assumption about the application of the Code to a particular age group, the negative impact of partial implementation.[103] The Baby-Friendly Hospital Initiative is another opportunity to draw attention to the implementation of the Code and the importance thereof to the promotion of breast-feeding.

The implementation of the International Code is very important for the protection and promotion of breast-feeding and the healthy growth and development of infants. Therefore, any implementation has to be done in a suitable legal instrument, be it a statute, regulations, a decree and so on, within the

---

100 Resolution WHA34.22, in which the WHA adopted the Code, as well as subsequent resolutions of the Assembly, also called on the Director-General "to give all possible support to Member States, as and when requested, for the implementation of the International Code." See operative paragraph 5.1 of the Resolution; see also for examples Resolution WHA 41.11, operative paragraph 3(6), and Resolution WHA 45.34, operative paragraph 3(3); for text of resolutions see above notes 89 and 90.

101 In November 1982, the Secretariat of the Caribbean Community (CARICOM) requested WHO's cooperation in connection with the implementation of the International Code in the countries of the Community; and in February 1983, the Secretariat of the Council of Arab Ministers of Health of the Gulf States made a similar request on behalf of its members. The following Member States have also requested WHO legal assistance in drafting national legislation and regulations: the Islamic Republic of Iran, Vietnam, Iraq, Morocco, Syria, Jordan, Oman and the United Arab Emirates. The author provided the requested legal assistance to those States. In the majority of the cases, it was possible for WHO to provide the legal assistance thanks to the generous financial support from the Dutch Government.

102 In 1993-94 three workshops were held by WHO, one in EMRO, Cairo, September 1993, one bi-regional, SEARO and WPRO, Manila, March 1994, and the third in AMRO, Guatemala, July 1994. All these workshops were held, again thanks to the generous donation from the Dutch Government.

103 See the WHO Hague Meeting, 1991, above note 57, p. 3, paragraph 8.

relevant national context. The implementation of the Code should be done in a reasonable, pragmatic and flexible manner, providing legal bases, in the instrument itself, to meet future changes and developments. Unfortunately, thirty years after the adoption of the Code by the WHA, very few Member States have implemented it as envisaged by the Assembly.[104]

There are, probably, several reasons for this delay, insofar as developing countries are concerned. First, it may be that breast-feeding has a low priority in the health programmes of many of those countries. This may be due to a mistaken under-estimation of the relevance of breast-feeding to these health programmes. Secondly, lack of resources and expertise in some developing countries may have contributed to their neglect to implement the International Code. Unawareness of the possibility of compensating for this deficiency from outside, be it from WHO, UNICEF or other UN agencies, or bilateral agencies, has added to the problem. Thirdly, manufacturers or distributors of products covered by the Code might have played a role in delaying, or stopping, any implementation of the Code. The Pakistani Delegate, Dr. Alsam, stated in Committee A of the 54th WHA that

> For the past 10 years, the government [of Pakistan] had been working towards the adoption of an ordinance for the protection of breast-feeding and young child nutrition, but it had met with considerable resistance from the manufacturers of breast-milk substitutes. He called upon WHO to mobilize public opinion and increase the pressure on those manufacturers to implement the International code....[105]

At the Hague Meeting 1991, it was stated that

> direct efforts by the infant-food industry or their local agents and distributors to weaken national measures or delay their adoption have been mentioned in a number of country reports. Another industry approach described has been the preparation of guidelines for, or provision of assistance in, developing national measures, which were weaker than the International Code. In *Kenya*, for example, a three-year review of the national code concluded in 1986 that many loopholes were present "as a result of the involvement of the manufacturers during the developmental stage."[106]

---

104 According to IBFAN's *State of the Code by Country*, 2009, only 30 countries have implemented all or nearly all provisions of the Code. If one examines the WHO Synthesis of Reports on Action Taken to give effect to the Code (1981-1990), by more than 150 countries and territories, one finds that no more than 20 States have actually implemented the International Code fully in legislation or regulations and 12 States have prepared draft laws or regulations for that purpose. See above note 70, pp. 4-40, paragraphs 13-207. Since then a handful of States have implemented the Code as legislation or regulations and about the same number have prepared draft legislation.

105 See *WHO DOC. A54/A/SR/3,*p. 7.

106 See above note 57, Annex 1, p.13, paragraph 14. It has been reported that in Pakistan, "a draft legislation has been pending with the Ministry of Health since 1992, but the pressure of the infant formula producers and distributors is hampering efforts to introduce this legislation in the Parliament." See *Society for the Protection of the Rights of the Child (SPARC)* September 1996, p.6.

Finally, a combination of some of these elements might have caused the delay in the implementation of the Code.

7. THE DISADVANTAGES OF NON-IMPLEMENTATION OF THE INTERNATIONAL CODE

The disadvantages of non-implementation of the International Code can be summarised as follows:

First, the marketing of products covered by the Code will be carried out without any special legal regime regulating it. Therefore, manufacturers and distributors of breast-milk substitutes are likely to carry out, with impunity, aggressive promotion of those products to the detriment of breast-feeding

Secondly, in the absence of implementation of the International Code, the practices which the Code is intended to regulate will be carried out with impunity. For, manufacturers and distributors could argue that they were not violating any legal rules in marketing their products. The cause of breast-feeding will be undermined.

Thirdly, in the absence of a national measure implementing the International Code, there is no possibility of monitoring the implementation of the Code, in spite of the rule on self-monitoring.

Fourthly, no sanctions can be imposed against any entity carrying our practices banned by the International Code. For there is no legal instrument that makes such practices illegal, and as such liable to be sanctioned

CHAPTER XIV

MONITORING OF THE INTERNATIONAL CODE

Monitoring the application of the International Code constitutes a very important step towards achieving its aim, particularly at the national level. For, without such monitoring, one cannot be sure whether a national measure giving effect to the Code is being observed or not. Several Member States have noted, in their reports to WHO on the review and evaluation of the action taken to give effect to the Code, that

> ... without effective monitoring and follow-up, previous achievements in restraining inappropriate marketing practices can be eroded.[1]

Furthermore, monitoring the application of the Code involves large sections of any society in the process. Therefore, there will be awareness and realization in the State concerned that some measures have been taken to protect and promote breast-feeding, and that it is important that those measures should be complied with, through the monitoring process.

Article 11 of the Code deals with monitoring and reads as follows:

- - -

> 11.2 Monitoring the application of this Code lies with governments acting individually, and collectively through the World Health Organization as provided in paragraphs 6 and 7 of this Article. The manufacturers and distributors of products within the scope of this Code, and appropriate non-governmental organizations, professional groups, and consumer organizations should collaborate with governments to this end.

> 11.3 Independently of any other measures taken for implementation of this Code, manufacturers and distributors of products within the scope of this Code should regard themselves as responsible for monitoring their marketing practices according to the principles and aim of this Code, and for taking steps to ensure that their conduct at every level conforms to them.

> 11.4 Non-governmental organizations, professional groups, institutions, and individuals concerned should have the responsibility of drawing the attention of manufacturers or distributors to activities which are incompatible with the principles and aim of this Code, so that appropriate action can be taken. The appropriate governmental authority should also be informed.

---

1   See The Hague Meeting 1991, above p.209, Annex 1, p. 16, paragraph. 34.

11.5 Manufacturers and primary distributors of products within the scope of this Code should apprise each member of their marketing personnel of the Code and of their responsibilities under it.

11.6 In accordance with Article 62 of the Constitution of the World Health Organization, Member States shall communicate annually to the Director-General information on action taken to give effect to the principles and aim of this Code.

11.7 The Director-General shall report in even years to the World Health Assembly on the status of implementation of the Code; and shall, on request, provide technical support to Member States preparing national legislation or regulations, or taking other appropriate measures in implementation and furtherance of the principles and aim of this Code.

All the drafts of the International Code contained provisions[2] on monitoring, but the Third and Fourth Drafts contained more detailed provisions than the First and Second Drafts. The following aspects of monitoring shall be dealt with:

1. STATE MONITORING

In accordance with Article 11.2 of the International Code,

> Monitoring the application of this Code lies with governments acting individually, and collectively through the World Health Organization as provided in paragraphs 6 and 7 of this Article. The manufacturers and distributors of products within the scope of this Code, and appropriate non-governmental organizations, professional groups, and consumer organization should collaborate with governments to this end.

The term "monitoring" is not defined in the Code, but its dictionary meaning is: to "maintain regular surveillance over."[3] So far as individual monitoring is concerned, each Member State decides for itself what is appropriate, in the light of its social framework, legal system and health conditions. For this purpose, a State may entrust the monitoring to a department of health, health inspectors[4] or a monitoring committee[5] established for the purpose. It is to

---

2 See Art. 7, paragraph 8, of the First Draft, Art. 9, paragraph 1, of the Second Draft, Art. 8 of the Third Draft and Art. 11 of the Fourth Draft.

3 See *The Concise Oxford Dictionary*, 9th edn., p. 879.

4 The Bahrain Law 1995, designates officials of the Ministry of Health, nominated by the Minister of Health, for monitoring purposes; see Art. 12 thereof. The Indian Infant Milk Substitutes Act 1992, designates "the food inspector" and "the authorized officer" for monitoring purposes; see Sec. 12 thereof. IBFAN Model Law gives inspectors monitoring rights, see Secs. 21-22 thereof. In Nigeria, monitoring the national code is given to the Food and Drugs Administration.

5 See Art. 5 of the Iranian Law 1996. The participants at the Hague Meeting 1991 recommended that the monitoring of national measures adopted to give effect to the International Code be undertaken "through existing mechanisms, e.g., those relating to food inspection, health

be observed that individual monitoring can be carried out only within the territory of a Member State, in conformity with the territorial principle of international law. Furthermore, it presupposes the implementation of the Code by one of the means mentioned in Article 11.1 of the Code. For the Code, being a recommendation of the WHA, has no direct application in the territories of Member States.[6] Finally, the Code calls on manufacturers and distributors of products within the scope of the Code, appropriate NGOs, professional groups and consumer organizations to collaborate with governments for the purpose of monitoring the application of the Code. As will be seen shortly, each one of these groups has been given a role in monitoring.

The situation concerning monitoring, and the difficulties encountered by Member States in the process, have been clearly summed up by the participants at the Hague Meeting 1991, as follows :

> several countries have encountered difficulties in establishing mechanisms for monitoring the implementation of national measures [giving effect to the Code]. Self-monitoring by the infant-food industry has in some cases been found to be inadequate or unsatisfactory. In others national codes have failed to designate a responsible monitoring authority. Elsewhere the authorized institution lacks the personnel or resources to engage in effective monitoring.[7]

The participants also observed that

> in many countries national measures have not included specific sanctions or penalties that are strong enough to force uncooperative companies to comply.[8]

This is not surprising, as many countries, particularly the developing ones, lack the experience and expertise in this area. Thus, the WHA has requested the Director-General of WHO

> to advise Member States on a framework which they may use in monitoring[9] the application of national measures implementing the International Code; and to ensure that monitoring the application of the International Code and subsequent relevant resolutions is carried out in a transparent, independent manner, free from commercial influence.[10]

It might be interesting to note that the WHA has not only referred to the moni-

---

service practices and trade regulations". See above note 1, p.7, paragraph 33.

6   Regulations and Directives adopted by the Council and Commission of the European Economic Community (now the European Union) are binding upon Member States of the Union. See Art. 189 of the Rome Treaty. Under the WHO Constitution, regulations adopted by the WHA are binding on Member States, except for those Members who reject them or attach reservations to them. See Art. 22 of the WHO Constitution.

7   See above note 1, p. 16, paragraph 36.

8   Ibid., p. 17, paragraph 39.

9   See Resolution WHA47.5, operative paragraph 3(5); for the text of the resolution, see *WHO Doc. WHA47/1994/REC/1*,pp.3-5.

10 See Resolution WHA49.15,operative paragraph 3(3); for the text of the resolution, see *WHO Doc.. WHA49/1996/REC/1*, pp.15-16.

toring of the Code, but also to its subsequent relevant resolutions. This implies that those resolutions should be relevant to the implementation of the Code at the national level.[11] Furthermore, the WHA urged Member States to ensure that the process of monitoring should be transparent, independent and free from commercial influences. This call is clearly intended to render the monitoring process objective and credible; for the monitoring process could be flawed by manipulation by those with commercial interests, by the absence of transparency or the absence of independence for those carrying out monitoring. It is submitted that an example of an independent and an objective monitoring is the one commissioned by a group of NGOs, academic institutions and churches in the UK in 1997 (IGBM).[12]

2. COLLECTIVE MONITORING

So far as collective monitoring is concerned, this is described in Article 11, paragraphs 6 and 7, which read as follows:

> 11.6 In accordance with Article 62 of the Constitution of the World Health Organization, Member States shall communicate annually to the Director-General information on action taken to give effect to the principles and aim of this Code.

> 11.7 The Director-General shall report in even years to the World Health Assembly on the status of implementation of the Code; and shall, on request, provide technical support to Member States preparing national legislation or regulations, or taking other appropriate measures in implementation and furtherance of the principles and aim of this Code.

Accordingly, the WHA is the forum for collective monitoring. The annual reporting requirement in Article 11.6 already exists under Article 62 of the WHO Constitution, which enjoins Member States to report, annually, on action taken with respect to, *inter alia*, recommendations made to Member States by the Organization. This requirement is made expressly applicable to the Code, which is a recommendation of the WHA. When annual reports are received by the Director-General, he examines them in order to ascertain what measures have been taken by the reporting State concerning the implementation of the Code. He then prepares his biennial report to the WHA,[13] describing the action taken by Member States, at the national level, for the implementation of the Code, and the status of implementation in general. However, according to the practice of WHO, the Director-General does not evaluate the reports from Member States. But there is nothing in law, nor in the Code, that prohibits the Director-General from evaluating the action of Members States, in order to ascertain whether or

---

11 See above p.209.

12 See *Cracking the Code*, op. cit., p.1.

13 Only once did the Director-General report to the WHA within one year, i.e. in 1982, one year after the adoption of the Code.

not these actions are in compliance with the criterion laid down by the WHA, namely the implementation of the International Code "in its entirety".[14]

During the discussion of the Director-General's report to the WHA, any Member State can raise questions on the measures taken to implement the Code by any other Member State. Furthermore, any Member State may comment on, criticize and make suggestions vis-à-vis the attitude of other Member States which have not taken any action to implement the Code, or whose action is not adequate in this respect. The raising of questions, the making of suggestions or criticism does not constitute an intervention in the internal affairs of Member States under international law. The late Sir Robert Jennings and the late Sir Arthur Watts describe the concept of intervention in international law as follows:

> although states often use the term 'intervention' loosely to cover such matters as criticism of another state's conduct, in international law it has a stricter meaning, according to which intervention is forcible or dictatorial interference by a state in the affairs of another state, calculated to impose certain conduct or consequences on that other state. Intervention is thus a form of interference by one state in the affairs, internal or external, of another; and intervention may affect those affairs either directly or indirectly.[15]

Through such discussions, it is hoped that Member States may be embarrassed, incited or encouraged to implement, or complete or expedite the implementation of the Code. It might be interesting to refer to a remark made by a delegate at the Forty-seventh WHA 1994, relating to the mode of voting, but may reveal, or allude to, a desire to embarrass, or identify States that may have attitudes not favourable to the implementation of the Code. The remark was made by the Kenyan Delegate (Professor Okelo) in connection with a draft resolution, which was under consideration by Committee A of the WHA. He supported the draft resolution and

> requested that, if voting became necessary, a roll-call vote should be taken, so that *any Members favouring unsafe practices could be identified.*[16]

This collective monitoring of the implementation of the International Code may be compared with that prevailing in the ILO, where ILO Members are required to submit reports to it on the legal position and practices in their territories, with respect to conventions and recommendations adopted by the General Conference of the ILO. The Director-General of the ILO submits to the General Conference a summary of the reports and information submitted by the Members on the measures taken to give effect to such conventions and recommendations.[17]

---

14 See Resolution WHA 34.22, operative paragraph 2 (1) 21 May 1981.
15 See Oppenheim, *International Law*, 9th edn. (1992), Vol. I, Part 1, p. 430.
16 See *WHO Doc. WHA47/1994/REC/3*, p. 40, emphasis added.
17 See Arts. 19, 22 and 23 of the ILO Constitution.

It may be observed that the collective monitoring at the WHA lacks any legal force, but it could be considered as a kind of political or moral pressure on, or encouragement, to Member States to take action to implement and apply the Code. Any observer of the debates of the WHA will see the seriousness, attention and importance given by Member States to the reports of the Director-General on the implementation of the Code[18].

It may be interesting to point out that an attempt was made in 1994 to dispense with the biennial reporting by the Director-General and leave it both to his discretion, and when significant new information became available;[19] but it was withdrawn at the end.[20] However, in January 1996, the Executive Board decided that

> ...biennial reporting should continue as required in WHA33.32, but that every second report should be a comprehensive report, starting in 1998.[21]

A last remark in this connection is that Article 11.2 of the Code requires manufacturers, distributors, appropriate NGOs and consumer organizations to collaborate with governments in the monitoring process. This is a requirement imposed on such groups and organizations to do so, and is not an obligation imposed on governments to seek such collaboration. Therefore, if a government does not call on such organizations and groups in the process of monitoring the implementation of national measures giving effect to the Code, that government would not be in breach of Article 11.2. But any of these entities is entitled to draw the attention to any violation of the Code. It is worth mentioning that the Indian Law of 1992 has given NGOs the right to sue any manufacturer or distributor who violates that Law. (Section 21 (c)).

---

18 For example, in 1996, even though the Director-General's report was short, and the duration of the WHA was short (20 to 25 May 1996), Committee A of the Assembly spent a considerable time on the debates of the report and the draft resolution related thereto. Twenty-six delegates and four representatives of NGOs addressed Committee A, and an informal consultation was held in order to work out the formulation of the resolution. See *WHO Doc. WHA49/1996/REC/3*, pp. 94-101. See also Resolution WHA49.15, *WHO Doc. WHA49/1996/REC/1*, pp.15-16. And in 2010, the WHA session was also short (17-21 May 2010) during the discussions of Committee A of what became Resolution WHA63.23, a large number of delegates intervened in the discussion and a drafting committee was established to finalize the text of the resolution. See WHO Doc. *WHA63/2010/REC/1*.

19 See the proposal made by the US Delegate (Dr Sumaya), concerning the resolution proposed by the Executive Board. See above note 16, p. 36. The proposal was opposed by a number of delegates, and was finally withdrawn by the US Delegate.

20 See ibid., p. 39.

21 See Resolution EB97.R13, operative paragraph 3; the text of the resolution is to be found in *WHO Doc.EB97/1996/REC/1*, p. 14. The reporting cycle in Resolution WHA33.32 is laid down in operative paragraph 6 (7) thereof.

3. SELF-MONITORING BY INDUSTRY

Article 11.3 of the International Code provides a mechanism for self-monitoring by manufacturers and distributors of products within the scope of the Code, of their marketing practices. It reads as follows:

> Independently of any other measures taken for implementation of this Code, manufacturers and distributors of products within the scope of this Code should regard themselves as responsible for monitoring their marketing practices according to the principles and aim of this Code, and for taking steps to ensure that their conduct at every level conforms to them.

This is a very interesting feature of the Code, as it is essentially addressed to Member States for action. And yet manufacturers and distributors are asked to do something, irrespective of whether or not action has been taken at the national level by the government concerned to give effect to the Code. The following observations may be made:

The first point to be made here is that the responsibility for monitoring lies with manufacturers and distributors of products within the scope of the Code. This responsibility applies to the monitoring of their marketing practices. The criterion for monitoring is the Code, its aim and principles. Any other criterion used for self-monitoring cannot be considered as conforming with Article 11.3 of the Code. It is worthwhile mentioning one example where a very large producer of breast-milk substitutes, namely Nestlé, claimed compliance with the International Code and self-monitoring, in a report it submitted to the Director-General of WHO in 1999. Nestlé did not use Article 11.3 as the criterion for its self-monitoring, but used another criterion. It says in its Report:

> In accordance with the International Code, the criterion used for self-monitoring in the current report is the International Code, as applied and defined by each country. In other words, the criterion is what the government endorses and accepts as the interpretation of the Code in that country.... This is in accordance with the International Code itself....[22]

But Article 11.3 of the International Code speaks of self-monitoring in "accordance with the principles and aim of this Code." There is nothing in Article 11.3 to suggest that the Code can be monitored as applied, defined, endorsed or accepted by a government as its interpretation thereof. If a Member State enacts a decree which does not implement the Code in its entirety, then Nestlé will use that decrees as its criterion for self-monitoring. It is submitted that this position cannot be considered as conforming to Article 11.3, and as such, it cannot amount to self-monitoring as envisaged under Article 11.3 of the Code.

Moreover, the responsibility for self-monitoring is engaged "independently of any other measures taken for implementation" of the Code. Accordingly, if company X is a producer of breast-milk substitutes, and it operates in State

---

22 See the Nestlé Report, op. cit., p. 2.

A, which, let us assume, has not taken any action to implement the Code, X is required by Article 11.3 to maintain regular surveillance over the marketing practices of its branches, personnel and agents, in order to ascertain their compliance with the provisions of the Code, even though State A has no law, regulations or other legal instrument implementing the Code. If X fails to do so, it would be considered in breach of its responsibility under Article 11.3 of the Code. It should be emphasized that any monitoring process has to be carried out on the basis of the criteria laid down by the WHA, namely, transparency, independence, and freedom from commercial influence. These criteria were laid down by the WHA in 1996, when it urged Member States

> to ensure that monitoring the application of the International Code and subsequent relevant resolutions is carried out in a transparent, independent manner, free from commercial influence.[23]

Secondly, the question may be raised: What is the nature of this responsibility? Is it a legal responsibility or a moral one? The Philippine Delegate to the September Consultation 1980, drew attention to this question. Referring to the word "compliance" in the origin of Article 11.3, he said:

> again we come here into the question whether there is a legal obligation or a moral obligation.[24]

It is possible to advance two answers to this question. The first may be to the effect that such a responsibility is a moral one, in that the Code is addressed to Member States, which are expected to implement it into laws, regulations or other suitable measures. Therefore, companies involved in the marketing of the products covered by the Code are not expected to have any legal responsibility, in the absence of a national legal instrument implementing the Code. The Code, being a recommendation of the WHA, cannot create direct legal obligations for such companies, even though the Code attributes a certain role for them. According to this interpretation then, Article 11.3 imposes a moral obligation, only, on such manufacturers and distributors.

The second answer may be to the effect that Article 11.3 imposes a legal obligation on manufacturers and distributors to ensure compliance with the Code. This position can be supported by the wording of the provision. It starts with the expression

> independently of any other measures taken for implementation of this Code, manufacturers and distributors...should regard themselves as responsible for monitoring their marketing practices.

Therefore, there is a responsibility, independently of any national implementation of the Code. The US Delegate to the September Consultation 1980 drew

---

23 See Resolution WHA 49.15, 25 May 1996, operative paragraph 3 (3).
24 See September Consultation 1980, loc.cit., tape 34, p. 5.

attention to the wording of Article 8, paragraph 2, of the Third Draft, which is the same as in Article 11.3, and said:

> in point 2, it says that manufacturers of products covered by this code should regard themselves as under the obligation to monitor their own compliance with it. The obligation part there has a legal meaning....Where a company is to regard itself as bound by the code, that has the possibility of a legal meaning of being binding.[25]

It is significant to note that in 2010 the WHA called upon the

> ... infant food manufacturers and distributors to comply fully with their responsibilities under the International Code of Marketing of Breast-milk Substitutes and subsequent relevant World Health Assembly resolutions.[26]

Furthermore, the provision requires steps to be taken by manufacturers and distributors to "ensure that their conduct at every level conforms to them". Moreover, Article 11.5 enjoins manufacturers and primary distributors of products within the scope of the Code to

> apprise each member of their marketing personnel of the Code and of their responsibilities under it.

Therefore, there is an added obligation to inform each member of such personnel, of what they can do, and what they cannot do under the Code.

In addition, the practice of some companies may be invoked in support of this interpretation. In 1982, Nestlé, the Swiss-based multinational company, which is one of the largest producers of breast-milk substitutes in the world, if not the largest, declared its intention to comply with the International Code and issued instructions to that effect to all its companies, agents and distributors of breast-milk substitutes. It also requested WHO to comment on those instructions, which was done by WHO. Furthermore, it set up the Nestlé Infant Formula Commission (NIFAC), headed by a lawyer, the late Senator Edmund Muskie, to examine complaints of non-compliance by Nestlé's companies, agents and distributors with the provisions of the Code. Nestlé's executive vice-president, Dr. C. Angst, stated that

> ... the Muskie Commission [NIFAC] plays a vital role in evaluating our policies and ensuring that our infant formula marketing practices are in conformity with the WHO Code. The Commission also provides a channel of communication with all concerned people through which legitimate questions about our policies can be raised and which guarantees serious consideration of all reasonable criticism.[27]

---

25 See ibid., p.3. The U.K. Delegate associated himself with the remarks made by the US Delegate. Ibid. The Philippines Delegate observed that "compliance would mean a state of obligation or rule of law, legal obligation". See ibid., p.5.

26 See Resolution WHA63.23, 21 May 2010, operative paragraph 2.

27 The statement is cited by Sethi in *Multilateral Corporations and the Impact of Public Advocacy on Corporate Strategy*, p.263; for details concerning NIFAC, its mandate and work, see ibid., pp.263-288.

While NIFAC is now defunct and Nestlé's Report does not comply with Article 11.3 of the Code, Nestlé's attitude shows that, at least, it considered that there is a legal obligation in Article 11.3 with respect to self-monitoring. However, it has to be stated that this legal responsibility could be said to be limited to applying the internal rules and regulations of the manufacturers and distributors to the offending party. In other words, all that a company can do to one of its personnel or agents, who has violated the provisions of the Code, is to terminate his employment or contract. Logically, it cannot do more than that, in the absence of a national law, regulations or other legal measures in the State concerned providing for different penalties. After all, a company is not a State, even though it may have, at times, more resources than a State, and its powers are limited.

Finally, it may be concluded that it is probable that Article 11.3 applies only where no legal measures have been adopted at the national level to implement the Code. If national legislation has been adopted in a given country, providing for a mechanism for its monitoring, with certain functions given to that mechanism, then this will be the governing rule for monitoring the marketing practices of any manufacturer or distributor of any product covered by the Code in that country. However, this does not affect the power of such a manufacturer or distributor to take certain contractual measures, internally, against the offending person, as described above. At any rate, self-monitoring cannot be very effective, unless the criteria laid down by the WHA are fully applied. As has been seen earlier, some countries have found out that, in some cases, self-monitoring is inadequate or unsatisfactory.[28] In addition, there is a possible conflict of interest, in that the main interest of infant-food manufacturers is to market their products, (marketing in the sense of the Code definition) and if they take a strict attitude towards compliance with the International Code, this might lead to discouragement of their personnel and companies from achieving that aim.

4. THE ROLE OF NGOS, GROUPS, INSTITUTIONS AND INDIVIDUALS IN MONITORING

Article 11.4 of the International Code gives NGOs, professional groups, institutions and individuals

> the responsibility of drawing the attention of manufacturers or distributors to activities which are incompatible with the principles and aim of this Code.

Accordingly, such organizations, institutions and individuals have a role to play

---

28 See above p.226-227. See also the reported violations of the International Code by some companies, for examples, Abbott-Ross, Bagel, Gerber, Lyempf, Mead-Johnson, Milupa and Nestlé. See *Breaking the Rules*, op. cit., pp. 8, 10, 17, 19, 21,23 and 27.

in the monitoring, in that they are made responsible for drawing the attention of manufacturers or distributors to activities not compatible with the provisions of the Code, so that appropriate action is taken to correct the situation. While this role may not seem significant in theory, it can be quite effective in practice. Individuals, professional groups, consumer's organizations and other organizations of the civil society, constitute a large section of any society and are therefore likely to observe any marketing activity of companies, which is incompatible with the provisions of the Code. For example, a health worker may become aware of the giving of supplies of breast-milk substitutes by company X to a health care facility. In this case, it is his responsibility to draw X's attention to this practice, and to inform the appropriate governmental authorities, in order to stop it. An ordinary citizen may see an advertisement for breast-milk substitutes in a remote shop, so he can draw the attention of the manufacturer, or distributor concerned to this violation of the Code, as well as informing the competent health authority about it. Consumer organizations would certainly be on the look out for any marketing activity that may infringe any provision of the Code, in order to protect the interests of the consumer. The Swedish Delegate to the September Consultation 1980, drew attention to the importance of the involvement of consumer and professional groups in the monitoring process of the Code. He said:

> ... we believe that the monitoring of the implementation of whatever we finally agree upon, will be exceedingly important and we would therefore wish to and we presume that an effective implementation of the code will have to involve very closely... [consumer and professional groups]. We would therefore wish to say, not that they should also be involved, but that consumer and professional groups should be closely involved in the monitoring process.[29]

It may be observed that the responsibility imposed by Article 11.4 is limited to drawing the attention of manufacturers and distributors concerned, as well as informing the competent authorities, of violations of the Code. Such groups, individuals and institutions have no power to take any measure, be it legal or otherwise, against the offending person, in the absence of any national legal measures implementing the Code giving them such a power. It is interesting to point out that under the Indian legislation giving effect to the Code, "voluntary organizations engaged in the field of child welfare and development and child nutrition", have been given the right to bring an action before the competent courts, against the offending person or company.[30] The national measures may also authorize such groups and individuals to report the violation of the national legal measures to the police, or other competent authorities.[31] In order to be

---

29 See above note 24, tape 34, p. 1.
30 See the Indian Infant Milk Substitutes Act 1992, Sec. 21(1)(c).
31 See the draft Jordanian Code 1994, Art.16(1), which gives the right to women's organizations and individuals to inform the Monitoring Committee of any violation of the national Code. See also to the same effect, Art. 16(1) of the draft Omani Code 1995, and Art. 16 (1) of the

effective, monitoring has to be coupled with sanctions,[32] otherwise it would not be effective. Some countries have encountered difficulties in enforcing national measures, because of the absence of sanctions, inadequate sanctions or inability to apply them in practice.[33]

It may be asked: Is monitoring limited to national NGOs and other organizations? Or could NGOs and other organizations from outside the country concerned do so? Two interpretations are possible: The first could be to the effect that such outside NGOs and other organizations could carry out monitoring in the territory of a Member State of WHO. This interpretation would be based on the wording of Article 11.4, which does not appear to prohibit such a role. The second interpretation could be to the effect that the monitoring role given by Article 11.4 of the Code to NGOs, professional groups, institutions and individuals concerned seems to be limited to national organizations, groups, institutions and individuals. In other words, it would appear that no foreign NGO, professional group, institution or individual can go to the territory of a Member State to carry out monitoring the implementation of the International Code in its territory. This interpretation can be based on the following grounds:

First of all, the wording of the provision does not seem to allow such a role to any foreign element mentioned in it. Furthermore, a foreign NGO going to a health care facility, for the purpose of inspecting whether or not it is receiving free or subsidized supplies of breast-milk substitutes might be interfering in the running of that health care facility, and might even be infringing the national law or regulations in force. Such an action may also constitute an infringement of the sovereignty of the State concerned. It may be recalled that the International Code was adopted as a recommendation, to be implemented at the national level. Therefore, any monitoring role must be assumed to be intended for the nationals of the Member State concerned, be they individuals, groups, organizations or institutions. However, the Member State concerned is fully entitled in law to invite, or give its consent to, any foreign NGO, group, institution or individuals to come to its territory, in order to help that State to carry out any monitoring activity related to the Code.[34] An example of such a monitoring exercise is the one carried out by the IGBM in 1996 in Bangladesh, Poland,

---

draft UAE Code 1995.

32 For examples, see Art. 13 of the Bahraini Law 1995, Art. 9 of the Iranian Law 1996, and Secs. 13(1), 14 and 15(1) of the Indian Infant Milk Substitutes Act 1992.

33 See above note 1, p. 7, paragraph 32.

34 During the discussions of the Executive Board of the Director-General's report on the implementation of the International Code, in 1994, the representative of Save the Children Fund (Ms Rundall) stated that "...monitoring by UNICEF and IBFAN showed that companies still continued the practice [of the provision of free supplies], despite clear resolutions by WHO and action by many governments". See Executive Board – Ninety-third Session, 1994, *EB93/1994/REC/2*, p.115. It is not clear from the statement of Ms Rundall whether the monitoring in question had been carried out with the consent of the States concerned or not. If there was consent on the part of those States, then the monitoring was carried out properly, but in the absence of consent, the legality of monitoring becomes highly questionable.

South Africa and Thailand, where the consent of those States was, apparently, obtained, and permission to visit health care facilities had to be obtained in advance.[35] It would appear that the persons who carried out the monitoring enjoyed complete independence from the infant-food industry and IBFAN.[36]

Finally, it should be stated that neither WHO, nor UNICEF, has any monitoring role under the International Code. Nevertheless, any Member State may request their cooperation, insofar as monitoring at the national level is concerned. But in the absence of a request from a Member State, neither WHO, nor UNICEF, can, on its own initiative, go to the territory of any Member State for monitoring the implementation of the International Code. There is no legal basis for such a role under the Constitution of WHO, nor under the constitutive instrument of UNICEF, nor under general international law.

However, it is possible, from a legal point of view, for the WHA to attribute such a role to the Organization. This standpoint could be justified on the basis that WHO was the organization which adopted the Code in 1981, and that the WHA is the policy organ of WHO.[37] Therefore, it could be possible to alter the policy of WHO in this context, and give such a role to the Organization, always bearing in mind the promotion, protection and encouragement of breast-feeding.

---

35 See *Cracking the Code*, op. cit., pp.3 and 4.
36 Ibid., p.3.
37 See Art. 18, paragraph (a)

CHAPTER XV

CONCLUSIONS

Breast-feeding, while it is a decision for the mother to make, has become an international issue, because of its importance to the development of healthy infants, and its relevance to the social and economic development of any society. The use of breast-milk substitutes to replace mother's milk has also become an international issue, because of the harm that can be caused to the health of infants, when the conditions for the proper use of those substitutes are not met, as well as the financial burden arising from such use.

When the frequency of the use of breast-milk substitutes had become alarming, and the ill-health effects of such use had become glaring and substantive, voices at the international level were raised, and the WHA raised the alarm, as early as 1974. From then onwards, efforts to protect and promote breast-feeding began to move forward, culminating in the adoption of the International Code in 1981 by the WHA.

The adoption of the International Code is a historical event which constitutes a significant step for the protection and promotion of breast-feeding and the healthy development of infants at a crucial stage in their life. After all, the Code is "an expression of the collective will of the membership of the World Health Organization"[1]. Under the regime of the Code, breast-feeding is the rule, while the use of breast-milk substitutes is the exception to be resorted to only when necessary. Furthermore, the adoption of the Code was a clear recognition, at the international level, that the use of breast-milk substitutes, and the marketing of such products is not a normal commercial operation. Such marketing and the practices related to it, which existed before the adoption of the Code, and unfortunately still exist, have, or are likely to have, an effect, directly or indirectly, on the decision of the mother as to whether to breast-feed her infant or use breast-milk substitutes.

Marketing practices, such as the giving of samples of breast-milk substitutes to mothers or pregnant women, and the promotion of those products, can influence the mother not to breast-feed her infant, with the resulting harm from improper use and the financial burden on families, especially in developing countries. However, the Code does not ban the use of breast-milk substitutes

---

1   See Resolution WHA34.22, operative paragraph 2(1).

and other products covered by it, nor was it intended as a measure against the infant-food industry. It recognizes that there are situations where breast-milk substitutes are necessary for feeding infants. It also recognizes the important and constructive role of the infant-food industry in this respect. Nevertheless, it imposes certain obligations on the latter industry. The Code leaves the mother, alone, to decide how to feed her infant, but insists that such a decision should be made on the basis of objective information provided to the mother and her education on the benefits of breast-feeding to her and her infant. The Code, also, calls on the health workers, NGOs and society to encourage and help the mother to breast-feed and to continue to do so, for as long as possible. But unfortunately the promotion of products within the scope of the Code continues until today. The WHA at its 63rd session in 2010 expressed

> ... deep concern over persistent reports of violation of the International Code of Marketing of Breast-milk Substitutes by some infant food manufacturers and distributors with regard to promotion targeting mothers and health-care workers.[2]

The International Code has its own definitions of certain terms and commercial practices, which are probably wider than the ordinary meaning of those terms and practices. However, this is justified for the special needs of the Code. For it is the first time that such a legal instrument has been adopted by the WHA, in order to regulate certain commercial practices that are, or can be, harmful to the health of infants. Moreover, those definitions apply only for the purposes of the International Code, and do not necessarily have general application to other areas of health.

The Code lays down certain obligations on the health care system, the health worker and governments to promote and to protect breast-feeding, because of its importance to the development of healthy societies. Every person in society can help to promote breast-feeding, directly or indirectly, for the benefit of society. Health workers have a very important role to play in this respect, because of their knowledge of the subject, their contact with the mother or pregnant woman, and their influence on their decision as to whether to breast-feed or use breast-milk substitutes. Therefore, they can play a positive role in the promotion of breast-feeding, or a negative role in the promotion of the use of breast-milk substitutes.

The International Code is the first original instrument at the international level, dealing specifically with the promotion and protection of breast-feeding, and the use of breast-milk substitutes when their use is necessary. The Director-General of WHO, described it, twenty years later as

> a pioneering instrument and as the basic platform for action to improve infant and young child nutrition.[3]

---

2   See Resolution WHA 63., 21 May 2010, 10th preambular pargraph.
3   See Report of the Directory-General to the 54th WHA, 2001, *WHO Doc.A54/sr/2*, p. 19.

It was the result of a compromise at the international level, and was envisaged as a minimum requirement. However, the Code has to be implemented at the national level, *in its entirety*, by a proper legal instrument, in order to achieve its aim. As a recommendation of the WHA, the Code is not *per se* binding, therefore it needs to be given effect to by Member States, with possible expansion here and there in its provisions, as necessary to the relevant jurisdiction. Without proper implementation, the Code cannot achieve what its drafters intended it to achieve, i.e., basically the promotion and protection of breast-feeding. Even though the International Code was adopted as a recommendation by the WHA, the resolution adopting it, as well as subsequent relevant resolutions of the WHA, have created a legal obligation for Member States to implement it in its entirety, including relevant subsequent WHA resolutions.

Unfortunately, the implementation of the Code at the national level is not very encouraging. Thirty years after the adoption of the Code, only some thirty Members States have adopted it in full or substantially. There is an absolute need to have a proper legal instrument regulating the marketing practices of manufacturers and distributors of breast-milk substitutes and other products covered by the Code, in both developed and developing countries. For the existence of such an instrument will provide certainty in the law, and protect the interests of all concerned, be they consumers, producers of products covered by the Code, and professional groups.

Member States concerned about their population and the health, economic and social development of their societies should have the political will to implement the Code, in its entirety, and preferably with some expansion of some of its principles. Such implementation constitutes a sound measure for the protection and promotion of breast-feeding in the interest of society.

Monitoring the application of the International Code is another important process, which is left to Member States, the WHA and self-monitoring by the manufacturers of products covered by the Code. However, neither WHO nor UNICEF has any role in monitoring the application of the Code.

The adoption of the International Code at the national level requires a political decision and a serious commitment to the protection of the health of infants and mothers. Each Member State that is concerned about its human wealth, namely the health of its population, has to give serious consideration to the implementation of the International Code in its entirety. The WHA declared in 2010 that

> Implementation of the global strategy for infant and young child feeding and its operational targets requires strong political commitment and a comprehensive approach....[4]

The WHA also urged Member States

---

4   See Resolution WHA 63, above note 2, 14th preambular paragraph.

to increase political commitment in order to prevent and reduce malnutrition in all its forms.[5]

It is hoped that in the not too distant future all the Members States of WHO will adopt the International Code in its entirety, as required by the WHA. This hope could receive strong impetus from the recent position of the WHO Secretariat, which identified six areas for action in the intensification of support to Member States for the implementation of the International Code, in conformity with the request of WHA to the Director-General in Resolution WHA.61.20. These areas are:

> ... advocacy; operational research, including research on the evidence of the effect that implementation of the Code is having on infant and young child nutrition in countries with Code-related national legislation, and research to describe good practices for implementation of the Code and the global strategy for infant and young child feeding; training; technical assistance in policy development and in legislative reform, including assistance in the proper interpretation of the Code and subsequent relevant Health Assembly resolutions, so as to avoid possible ambiguities; and monitoring ....[6]

---

5 See ibid., operative paragraph 1 (1).
6 See Infant and young child nutrition-Report by the Secretariat, WHO Doc. A63/9, 1 April 2010, p 4, paragraph 19.

PART III

APPENDICES

1. INTERNATIONAL CODE OF MARKETING OF BREAST-MILK SUBSTITUTES

The Member States of the World Health Organization:

Affirming the right of every child and every pregnant and lactating woman to be adequately nourished as a means of attaining and maintaining health;

Recognizing that infant malnutrition is part of the wider problems of lack of education, poverty, and social injustice;

Recognizing that the health of infants and young children cannot be isolated from the health and nutrition of women, their socio-economic status and their roles as mothers;

Conscious that breast-feeding is an unequalled way of providing ideal food for the healthy growth and development of infants; that it forms a unique biological and emotional basis for the health of both mother and child; that the anti-infective properties of breast milk help to protect infants against disease; and that there is an important relationship between breast-feeding and child-spacing;

Recognizing that the encouragement and protection of breast-feeding is an important part of the health, nutrition and other social measures required to promote healthy growth and development of infants and young children; and that breast-feeding is an important aspect of primary health care;

Considering that when mothers do not breast-feed, or only do so partially, there is a legitimate market for infant formula and for suitable ingredients from which to prepare it; that all these products should accordingly be made accessible to those who need them through commercial or non-commercial distribution systems; and that they should not be marketed or distributed in ways that may interfere with the protection and promotion of breast-feeding;

Recognizing further that inappropriate feeding practices lead to infant malnutrition, morbidity and mortality in all countries, and that improper practices in the marketing of breast-milk substitutes and related products can contribute to these major public health problems;

Convinced that it is important for infants to receive appropriate complementary foods, usually when the infant reaches four to six months of age, and that every effort should be made to use locally available foods; and convinced, nevertheless, that such complementary foods should not be used as breast-milk substitutes;

Appreciating that there are a number of social and economic factors affecting breast-feeding, and that, accordingly, governments should develop social support systems to protect, facilitate and encourage it, and that they should create an environment that fosters breast-feeding, provides appropriate family and community support, and protects mothers from factors that inhibit breast-feeding;

Affirming that health care systems, and the health professionals and other health workers serving in them, have an essential role to play in guiding infant feeding practices, encouraging and facilitating breast-feeding, and providing objective and consistent advice to mothers and families about the superior value of breast-feeding, or, where needed, on the proper use of infant formula, whether manufactured industrially or home-prepared;

Affirming further that educational systems and other social services should be involved in the protection and promotion of breast-feeding, and in the appropriate use of complementary foods;

Aware that families, communities, women's organizations and other non-governmental organizations have a special role to play in the protection and promotion of breast-feeding and in ensuring the support needed by pregnant women and mothers of infants and young children, whether breast-feeding or not;

Affirming the need for governments, organizations of the United Nations system, nongovernmental organizations, experts in various related disciplines, consumer groups and industry to cooperate in activities aimed at the improvement of maternal, infant and young child health and nutrition;

Recognizing that governments should undertake a variety of health, nutrition and other social measures to promote healthy growth and development of infants and young children, and that this Code concerns only one aspect of these measures;

Considering that manufacturers and distributors of breast-milk substitutes have an important and constructive role to play in relation to infant feeding, and in the promotion of the aim of this Code and its proper implementation;

Affirming that governments are called upon to take action appropriate to their social and legislative framework and their overall development objectives to give effect to the principles and aim of this Code, including the enactment of legislation, regulations or other suitable measures;

Believing that, in the light of the foregoing considerations, and in view of the vulnerability of infants in the early months of life and the risks involved in inappropriate feeding practices, including the unnecessary and improper use of breast-milk substitutes, the marketing of breast-milk substitutes requires special treatment, which makes usual marketing practices unsuitable for these products;

THEREFORE:

The Member States hereby agree the following articles which are recommended as a basis for action.

Article 1. Aim of the Code

The aim of this Code is to contribute to the provision of safe and adequate nutrition for infants, by the protection and promotion of breast-feeding, and by ensuring the proper use of breast-milk substitutes, when these are necessary, on the basis of adequate information and through appropriate marketing and distribution.

Article 2. Scope of the Code

The Code applies to the marketing, and practices related thereto, of the following products: breast-milk substitutes, including infant formula; other milk products, foods and beverages, including bottle-fed complementary foods, when marketed or otherwise represented to be suitable, with or without modification, for use as a partial or total replacement of breast-milk; feeding bottles and teats. It also applies to their quality and availability, and to information concerning their use.

Article 3. Definitions

For the purposes of this Code:

"Breast-milk substitute" means any food being marketed or otherwise represented as a partial or total replacement for breast-milk, whether or not suitable for that purpose.

"Complementary food" means any food, whether manufactured or locally prepared, suitable as a complement to breast-milk or to infant formula, when either becomes insufficient to satisfy the nutritional requirements of the infant. Such food is also commonly called "weaning food" or "breast-milk supplement".

"Container" means any form of packaging of products for sale as a normal retail unit, including wrappers.

"Distributor" means a person, corporation or any other entity in the public or private sector engaged in the business (whether directly or indirectly) of marketing at the wholesale or retail level a product within the scope of this Code. A "primary distributor" is a manufacturer's sales agent, representative, national distributor or broker.

"Health care system" means governmental, nongovernmental or private institutions or organizations engaged, directly or indirectly, in health care for mothers, infants and pregnant women; and nurseries or child-care institutions. It also includes health workers in private practice. For the purposes of this Code, the health care system does not include pharmacies or other established sales outlets.

"Health worker" means a person working in a component of such a health care system, whether professional or non-professional, including voluntary, unpaid workers.

"Infant formula" means a breast-milk substitute formulated industrially in accordance with applicable Codex Alimentarius standards, to satisfy the normal nutritional requirements of infants up to between four and six months of age, and adapted to their physiological characteristics. Infant formula may also be prepared at home, in which case it is described as "home-prepared".

"Label" means any tag, brand, mark, pictorial or other descriptive matter, written, printed, stencilled, marked, embossed or impressed on, or attached to, a container (see above) of any products within the scope of this Code.

"Manufacturer" means a corporation or other entity in the public or private sector engaged in the business or function (whether directly or through an agent or through an entity controlled by or under contract with it) of manufacturing a product within the scope of this Code.

"Marketing" means product promotion, distribution, selling, advertising, product public relations, and information services.

"Marketing personnel" means any persons whose functions involve the marketing of a product or products coming within the scope of this Code.

"Samples" means single or small quantities of a product provided without cost.

"Supplies" means quantities of a product provided for use over an extended period, free or at a low price, for social purposes, including those provided to families in need.

Article 4. Information and education

4.1   Governments should have the responsibility to ensure that objective and consistent information is provided on infant and young child feeding for use by families and those involved in the field of infant and young child nutrition. This responsibility should cover either the planning, provision, design and dissemination of information, or their control.

4.2   Informational and educational materials, whether written, audio, or visual, dealing with the feeding of infants and intended to reach pregnant women and mothers of infants and young children, should include clear information on all the following points: (a) the benefits and superiority of breast-feeding; (b) maternal nutrition, and the preparation for and maintenance of breast-feeding; (c) the negative effect on breast-feeding of introducing partial bottle-feeding; (d) the difficulty of reversing the decision not to breast-feed; and (e) where needed, the proper use of infant formula, whether manufactured industrially or home-prepared. When such materials contain information about the use of infant formula, they should include the social and financial implications of its use; the health hazards of inappropriate foods or feeding methods; and, in particular, the health hazards of unnecessary or improper use of infant formula and other breast-milk substitutes. Such materials should not use any pictures or text which may idealize the use of breast-milk substitutes.

4.3   Donations of informational or educational equipment or materials by manufacturers or distributors should be made only at the request and with the written approval of the appropriate government authority or within guidelines given by governments for this purpose. Such equipment or materials may bear the donating company's name or logo, but should not refer to a proprietary product that is within the scope of this Code, and should be distributed only through the health care system.

Article 5. The general public and mothers

5.1   There should be no advertising or other form of promotion to the general public of products within the scope of this Code.

5.2   Manufacturers and distributors should not provide, directly or indirectly, to pregnant women, mothers or members of their families, samples of products within the scope of this Code.

5.3   In conformity with paragraphs 1 and 2 of this Article, there should be no point-of-sale advertising, giving of samples, or any other promotion device to induce sales directly to the consumer at the retail level, such as special displays, discount coupons, premiums, special sales, loss-leaders and tie-in sales, for products within the scope of this Code. This provision should not restrict the establishment of pricing policies and practices intended to provide products at lower prices on a long-term basis.

5.4   Manufacturers and distributors should not distribute to pregnant women or mothers of infants and young children any gifts of articles or utensils which may promote the use of breast-milk substitutes or bottle-feeding.

5.5   Marketing personnel, in their business capacity, should not seek direct or indirect contact of any kind with pregnant women or with mothers of infants and young children.

Article 6. Health care systems

6.1 The health authorities in Member States should take appropriate measures to encourage and protect breast-feeding and promote the principles of this Code, and should give appropriate information and advice to health workers in regard to their responsibilities, including the information specified in Article 4.2.

6.2 No facility of a health care system should be used for the purpose of promoting infant formula or other products within the scope of this Code. This Code does not, however, preclude the dissemination of information to health professionals as provided in Article 7.2.

6.3 Facilities of health care systems should not be used for the display of products within the scope of this Code, for placards or posters concerning such products, or for the distribution of material provided by a manufacturer or distributor other than that specified in Article 4.3.

6.4 The use by the health care system of «professional service representatives», «mothercraft nurses» or similar personnel, provided or paid for by manufacturers or distributors, should not be permitted.

6.5 Feeding with infant formula, whether manufactured or home-prepared, should be demonstrated only by health workers, or other community workers if necessary; and only to the mothers or family members who need to use it; and the information given should include a clear explanation of the hazards of improper use.

6.6 Donations or low-price sales to institutions or organizations of supplies of infant formula or other products within the scope of this Code, whether for use in the institutions or for distribution outside them, may be made. Such supplies should only be used or distributed for infants who have to be fed on breast-milk substitutes. If these supplies are distributed for use outside the institutions, this should be done only by the institutions or organizations concerned. Such donations or low-price sales should not be used by manufacturers or distributors as a sales inducement.

6.7 Where donated supplies of infant formula or other products within the scope of this Code are distributed outside an institution, the institution or organization should take steps to ensure that supplies can be continued as long as the infants concerned need them. Donors, as well as institutions or organizations concerned, should bear in mind this responsibility.

6.8 Equipment and materials, in addition to those referred to in Article 4.3, donated to a health care system may bear a company's name or logo, but should not refer to any proprietary product within the scope of this Code.

Article 7. Health workers

7.1　Health workers should encourage and protect breast-feeding; and those who are concerned in particular with maternal and infant nutrition should make themselves familiar with their responsibilities under this Code, including the information specified in Article 4.2.

7.2　Information provided by manufacturers and distributors to health professionals regarding products within the scope of this Code should be restricted to scientific and factual matters, and such information should not imply or create a belief that bottle-feeding is equivalent or superior to breast-feeding. It should also include the information specified in Article 4.2.

7.3　No financial or material inducements to promote products within the scope of this Code should be offered by manufacturers or distributors to health workers or members of their families, nor should these be accepted by health workers or members of their families.

7.4　Samples of infant formula or other products within the scope of this Code, or of equipment or utensils for their preparation or use, should not be provided to health workers except when necessary for the purpose of professional evaluation or research at the institutional level. Health workers should not give samples of infant formula to pregnant women, mothers of infants and young children, or members of their families.

7.5　Manufacturers and distributors of products within the scope of this Code should disclose to the institution to which a recipient health worker is affiliated any contribution made to him or on his behalf for fellowships, study tours, research grants, attendance at professional conferences, or the like. Similar disclosures should be made by the recipient.

Article 8. Persons employed by manufacturers and distributors

8.1　In systems of sales incentives for marketing personnel, the volume of sales of products within the scope of this Code should not be included in the calculation of bonuses, nor should quotas be set specifically for sales of these products. This should not be understood to prevent the payment of bonuses based on the overall sales by a company of other products marketed by it.

8.2　Personnel employed in marketing products within the scope of this Code should not, as part of their job responsibilities, perform educational functions in relation to pregnant women or mothers of infants and young children. This should not be understood as preventing such personnel from being used for other functions by the health care system at the request and with the written approval of the appropriate authority of the government concerned.

Article 9. Labelling

9.1 Labels should be designed to provide the necessary information about the appropriate use of the product, and so as not to discourage breast-feeding.

9.2 Manufacturers and distributors of infant formula should ensure that each container has a clear, conspicuous, and easily readable and understandable message printed on it, or on a label which cannot readily become separated from it, in an appropriate language, which includes all the following points: (a) the words "Important Notice" or their equivalent; (b) a statement of the superiority of breast-feeding; (c) a statement that the product should be used only on the advice of a health worker as to the need for its use and the proper method of use; (d) instructions for appropriate preparation, and a warning against the health hazards of inappropriate preparation. Neither the container nor the label should have pictures of infants, nor should they have other pictures or text which may idealize the use of infant formula. They may, however, have graphics for easy identification of the product as a breast-milk substitute and for illustrating methods of preparation. The terms "humanized", "maternalized" or similar terms should not be used. Inserts giving additional information about the product and its proper use, subject to the above conditions, may be included in the package or retail unit. When labels give instructions for modifying a product into infant formula, the above should apply.

9.3 Food products within the scope of this Code, marketed for infant feeding, which do not meet all the requirements of an infant formula, but which can be modified to do so, should carry on the label a warning that the unmodified product should not be the sole source of nourishment of an infant. Since sweetened condensed milk is not suitable for infant feeding, nor for use as a main ingredient of infant formula, its label should not contain purported instructions on how to modify it for that purpose.

9.4 The label of food products within the scope of this Code should also state all the following points: (a) the ingredients used; (b) the composition/analysis of the product; (c) the storage conditions required; and (d) the batch number and the date before which the product is to be consumed, taking into account the climatic and storage conditions of the country concerned.

Article 10. Quality

10.1   The quality of products is an essential element for the protection of the health of infants and therefore should be of a high recognized standard.

10.2   Food products within the scope of this Code should, when sold or otherwise distributed, meet applicable standards recommended by the Codex Alimentarius Commission and also the Codex Code of Hygienic Practice for Foods for Infants and Children.

Article 11. Implementation and monitoring

11.1   Governments should take action to give effect to the principles and aim of this Code, as appropriate to their social and legislative framework, including the adoption of national legislation, regulations or other suitable measures. For this purpose, governments should seek, when necessary, the cooperation of WHO, UNICEF and other agencies of the United Nations system. National policies and measures, including laws and regulations, which are adopted to give effect to the principles and aim of this Code should be publicly stated, and should apply on the same basis to all those involved in the manufacture and marketing of products within the scope of this Code.

11.2   Monitoring the application of this Code lies with governments acting individually, and collectively through the World Health Organization as provided in paragraphs 6 and 7 of this Article. The manufacturers and distributors of products within the scope of this Code, and appropriate nongovernmental organizations, professional groups, and consumer organizations should collaborate with governments to this end.

11.3   Independently of any other measures taken for implementation of this Code, manufacturers and distributors of products within the scope of this Code should regard themselves as responsible for monitoring their marketing practices according to the principles and aim of this Code, and for taking steps to ensure that their conduct at every level conforms to them.

11.4   Nongovernmental organizations, professional groups, institutions, and individuals concerned should have the responsibility of drawing the attention of manufacturers or distributors to activities which are incompatible with the principles and aim of this Code, so that appropriate action can be taken. The appropriate governmental authority should also be informed.

11.5   Manufacturers and primary distributors of products within the scope of this Code should apprise each member of their marketing personnel of the Code and of their responsibilities under it.

11.6   In accordance with Article 62 of the Constitution of the World Health

Organization, Member States shall communicate annually to the Director-General information on action taken to give effect to the principles and aim of this Code.

11.7 The Director-General shall report in even years to the World Health Assembly on the status of implementation of the Code; and shall, on request, provide technical support to Member States preparing national legislation or regulations, or taking other appropriate measures in implementation and furtherance of the principles and aim of this Code.

2. RELEVANT RESOLUTIONS OF THE WORLD HEALTH ASSEMBLY

WHA27.43

The Twenty-seventh World Health Assembly,

Reaffirming that breast-feeding has proved to be the most appropriate and successful nutritional solution for the harmonious development of the child;

Noting the general decline in breast-feeding, related to socio-cultural and environmental factors, including the mistaken idea caused by misleading sales promotion that breast-feeding is inferior to feeding with manufactured breast-milk substitutes;

Observing that this decline is one of the factors contributing to infant mortality and malnutrition, in particular in the developing world; and

Realizing that mothers who feed their babies with manufactured foods are often unable to afford an adequate supply of such foods and that even if they can afford such foods the tendency to malnutrition is frequently aggravated because of lack of understanding of the amount and correct and hygienic preparation of the food which should be given to the child,

1. RECOMMENDS strongly the encouragement of breast-feeding as the ideal feeding in order to promote harmonious physical and mental development of children;

2. CALLS THE ATTENTION of countries to the necessity of taking adequate social measures for mothers working away from their homes during the lactation period, such as arranging special work timetables so that they can breast-feed their children;

3. URGES Member countries to review sales promotion activities on baby foods and to introduce appropriate remedial measures, including advertisement codes and legislation where necessary;

4. URGES the Director-General to intensify activities relevant to the promotion of breast-feeding, to bring those matters to the notice of the medical profession and health administrators and to emphasize the need for health personnel, mothers and the general public to be educated accordingly; and

5. REQUESTS the Director-General to promote and further support activities related to the preparation and use of weaning foods based on local products.

May 1974

WHA31.47

The Thirty-first World Health Assembly,

Having considered the Director-General's report on the role of the health sector in the development of national and international food and nutrition policies and plans;

Recalling resolutions WHA27.43, WHA28.42 and WHA30.51;

Convinced that malnutrition is one of the major impediments in attaining the goal of health for all by the year 2000, and that new approaches based on clearly defined priorities and maximum utilization of local resources are needed for a more effective action to combat malnutrition;

Noting with concern the continued decline in breast-feeding in many countries, while in certain countries it has been possible to arrest or reverse this trend;

Recognizing that during the first months of life breast-feeding is the safest and most appropriate way to feed infants and that it should be maintained as long as possible, with timely supplementation and weaning which ideally should be done with locally available and acceptable foods;

1. THANKS the Director-General for this report;

2. ENDORSES the functions of the health sector in this field, as described in the report of the Director-General;

3. RECOMMENDS that Member States give the highest priority to stimulating permanent multisectoral coordination of nutrition policies and programmes and to preventing malnutrition in pregnant and lactating women, infants and young children by:

   (1) supporting and promoting breast-feeding by educational activities among the general public; legislative and social action to facilitate breast-feeding by working mothers; implementing the necessary promotional and facilitating measures in the health services; and regulating inappropriate sales promotion of infant foods that can be used to replace breast milk;

   (2) ensuring timely supplementation and appropriate weaning practices and the feeding of young children after weaning with the maximum utilization of locally available and acceptable foods; carrying out, if necessary, action-oriented research to support this approach; and training personnel for its promotion;

4. REQUESTS the Director-General:

   (1) to develop, in cooperation with Member States, a programme of research and development in nutrition, oriented primarily to the needs of developing countries, and aimed initially at the prevention of malnutrition in pregnant and lactating women and in young chil-

dren by promoting adequate nutrition of the mother and by encouraging breast-feeding and timely supplementation and appropriate weaning practices, with the maximum utilization of locally available and acceptable foods;

(2) to take any necessary measures to coordinate international activities designed to promote breast-feeding, and especially to work in close collaboration with other United Nations agencies active in this field;

(3) to cooperate with national institutions in their problem-solving research and training programmes so as to strengthen their capacity to combat malnutrition, and to stimulate technical cooperation among developing countries in this field;

(4) to collaborate with multilateral and bilateral organizations and agencies and with other intergovernmental and nongovernmental organizations in programmes of technical cooperation with countries for the development and implementation of national food and nutrition policies, plans and programmes;

(5) to stimulate the mobilization of scientific and financial resources in support of a global effort to eliminate malnutrition;

5. URGES governments, multilateral and bilateral organizations and agencies to support the proposed programme of research and development in nutrition through their technical and scientific institutions and workers and by financial contributions.

May 1978

WHA33.32

The Thirty-third World Health Assembly,

Recalling resolutions WHA27.43 and WHA31.47 which in particular reaffirmed that breastfeeding is ideal for the harmonious physical and psychosocial development of the child, that urgent action is called for by governments and the Director-General in order to intensify activities for the promotion of breastfeeding and development of actions related to the preparation and use of weaning foods based on local products, and that there is an urgent need for countries to review sales promotion activities on baby foods and to introduce appropriate remedial measures, including advertisement codes and legislation, as well as to take appropriate supportive social measures for mothers working away from their homes during the lactation period;

Recalling further resolutions WHA31.55 and WHA32.42 which emphasized maternal and child health as an essential component of primary health care, vital to the attainment of health for all by the year 2000;

Recognizing that there is a close interrelationship between infant and young child feeding and social and economic development, and that urgent action by governments is required to promote the health and nutrition of infants, young children and mothers, *inter alia* through education, training and information in this field;

Noting that a joint WHO/UNICEF Meeting on Infant and Young Child Feeding was held from 9 to 12 October 1979, and was attended by representatives of governments, the United Nations system and technical agencies, nongovernmental organizations active in the area, the infant food industry and other scientists working in this field;

1.   ENDORSES in their entirety the statement and recommendations made by the joint WHO/UNICEF Meeting, namely on the encouragement and support of breastfeeding; the promotion and support of appropriate weaning practices; the strengthening of education, training and information; the promotion of the health and social status of women in relation to infant and young child feeding; and the appropriate marketing and distribution of breastmilk substitutes. This statement and these recommendations also make clear the responsibility in this field incumbent on the health services, health personnel, national authorities, women's and other nongovernmental organizations, the United Nations agencies and the infant-food industry, and stress the importance for countries to have a coherent food and nutrition policy and the need for pregnant and lactating women to be adequately nourished; the joint Meeting also recommended that "There should be an international code of marketing of infant formula and other products used as breastmilk substitutes. This should be supported by both exporting and importing countries and observed by all manufacturers. WHO and UNICEF are requested to organ-

ize the process for its preparation, with the involvement of all concerned parties, in order to reach a conclusion as soon as possible";

2. RECOGNIZES the important work already carried out by the World Health Organization and UNICEF with a view to implementing these recommendations and the preparatory work done on the formulation of a draft international code of marketing of breastmilk substitutes.

3. URGES countries which have not already done so to review and implement resolutions WHA27.43 and WHA32.42:

4. URGES women's organizations to organize extensive information dissemination campaigns in support of breastfeeding and healthy habits;

5. REQUESTS the Director-General:

   (1) to cooperate with Member States on request in supervising or arranging for the supervision of the quality of infant foods during their production in the country concerned, as well as during their importation and marketing;

   (2) to promote and support the exchange of information on laws, regulations, and other measures concerning marketing of breastmilk substitutes;

6. FURTHER REQUESTS the Director-General to intensify his activities for promoting the application of the recommendations of the joint WHO/UNICEF Meeting and, in particular:

   (1) to continue efforts to promote breastfeeding as well as sound supplementary feeding and weaning practices as a prerequisite to healthy child growth and development;

   (2) to intensify co-ordination with other international and bilateral agencies for the mobilization of the necessary resources for the promotion and support of activities related to the preparation of weaning foods based on local products in countries in need of such support and to collate and disseminate information on methods of supplementary feeding and weaning practices successfully used in different cultural settings;

   (3) to intensify activities in the field of health education, training and information on infant and young child feeding, in particular through the preparation of training and other manuals for primary health care workers in different regions and countries;

   (4) to prepare an international code of marketing of breastmilk substitutes in close consultation with Member States and with all other parties concerned including such scientific and other experts whose collaboration may be deemed appropriate, bearing in mind that:

       (a) the marketing of breastmilk substitutes and weaning foods must be viewed within the framework of the problems of infant and young child feeding as a whole;

(b) the aim of the code should be to contribute to the provision of safe and adequate nutrition for infants and young children, and in particular to promote breastfeeding and ensure, on the basis of adequate information, the proper use of breastmilk substitutes, if necessary;

(c) the code should be based on existing knowledge of infant nutrition;

(d) the code should be governed *inter alia* by the following principles:

(i) the production, storage and distribution, as well as advertising, of infant feeding products should be subject to national legislation or regulations, or other measures as appropriate to the country concerned;

(ii) relevant information on infant feeding should be provided by the health care system of the country in which the product is consumed;

(iii) products should meet international standards of quality and presentation, in particular those developed by the Codex Alimentarius Commission, and their labels should clearly inform the public of the superiority of breastfeeding;

(5) to submit the code to the Executive Board for consideration at its sixty-seventh session and for forwarding with its recommendations to the Thirty-fourth World Health Assembly, together with proposals regarding its promotion and implementation, either as a regulation in the sense of Articles 21 and 22 of the Constitution of the World Health Organization or as a recommendation in the sense of Article 23, outlining the legal and other implications of each choice;

(6) to review the existing legislation in different countries for enabling and supporting breastfeeding, especially by working mothers, and to strengthen the Organization's capacity to cooperate on the request of Member States in developing such legislation;

(7) to submit to the Thirty-fourth World Health Assembly, in 1981, and thereafter in even years, a report on the steps taken by WHO to promote breastfeeding and to improve infant and young child feeding, together with an evaluation of the effect of all measures taken by WHO and its Member States.

23 May 1980

WHA34.22

International Code of Marketing of Breast-milk Substitutes

The Thirty-fourth World Health Assembly,

Recognizing the importance of sound infant and young child nutrition for the future health and development of the child and adult;

Recalling that breast-feeding is the only natural method of infant feeding and that it must be actively protected and promoted in all countries;

Convinced that governments of Member States have important responsibilities and a prime role to play in the protection and promotion of breast-feeding as a means of improving infant and young child health;

Aware of the direct and indirect effects of marketing practices for breast-milk substitutes on infant feeding practices;

Convinced that the protection and promotion of infant feeding, including the regulation of the marketing of breast-milk substitutes, affect infant and young child health directly and profoundly, and are a problem of direct concern to WHO;

Having considered the draft International Code of Marketing of Breast-milk Substitutes prepared by the Director-General and forwarded to it by the Executive Board;

Expressing its gratitude to the Director-General and to the Executive Director of the United Nations Children's Fund for the steps they have taken in ensuring close consultation with Member States and with all other parties concerned in the process of preparing the draft International Code;

Having considered the recommendation made thereon by the Executive Board at its sixty-seventh session;

Confirming resolution WHA33.32, including the endorsement in their entirety of the statement and recommendations made by the joint WHO/UNICEF Meeting on Infant and Young Child Feeding held from 9 to 12 October 1979;

Stressing that the adoption of and adherence to the International Code of Marketing of Breast-milk Substitutes is a minimum requirement and only one of several important actions required in order to protect healthy practices in respect of infant and young child feeding;

1.   ADOPTS, in the sense of Article 23 of the Constitution, the International Code of Marketing of Breast-milk Substitutes annexed to the present resolution;

2.   URGES all Member States:

(1) to give full and unanimous support to the implementation of the recommendations made by the joint WHO/UNICEF Meeting on Infant and Young Child Feeding and of the provisions of the International Code in its entirety as an expression of the collective will of

the membership of the World Health Organization;

(2) to translate the International Code into national legislation, regulations or other suitable measures;

(3) to involve all concerned social and economic sectors and all other concerned parties in the implementation of the International Code and in the observance of the provisions thereof;

(4) to monitor the compliance with the Code;

3. DECIDES that the follow-up to and review of the implementation of this resolution shall be undertaken by regional committees, the Executive Board and the Health Assembly in the spirit of resolution WHA33.17;

4. REQUESTS the FAO/WHO Codex Alimentarius Commission to give full consideration, within the framework of its operational mandate, to action it might take to improve the quality standards of infant foods, and to support and promote the implementation of the International Code;

5. REQUESTS the Director-General:

(1) to give all possible support to Member States, as and when requested, for the implementation of the International Code, and in particular in the preparation of national legislation and other measures related thereto in accordance with operative subparagraph 6(6) of resolution WHA33.32;

(2) to use his good offices for the continued cooperation with all parties concerned in the implementation and monitoring of the International Code at country, regional and global levels;

(3) to report to the Thirty-sixth World Health Assembly on the status of compliance with and implementation of the Code at country, regional and global levels;

(4) based on the conclusions of the status report, to make proposals, if necessary, for revision of the text of the Code and for the measures needed for its effective application.

21 May 1981

WHA35.26

The Thirty-fifth World Health Assembly,

Recalling resolution WHA33.32 on infant and young child feeding and resolution WHA34.22 adopting the International Code of Marketing of Breast-milk Substitutes;

Conscious that breast-feeding is the ideal method of infant feeding and should be promoted and protected in all countries;

Concerned that inappropriate infant feeding practices result in greater incidence of infant mortality, malnutrition and disease, especially in conditions of poverty and lack of hygiene;

Recognizing that commercial marketing of breast-milk substitutes for infants has contributed to an increase in artificial feeding;

Recalling that the Thirty-fourth World Health Assembly adopted an international code intended, *inter alia*, to deal with these marketing practices;

Noting that, while many Member States have taken some measures related to improving infant and young child feeding, few have adopted and adhered to the International Code as a "minimum requirement" and implemented it "in its entirety", as called for in resolution WHA34.22;

1. URGES Member States to give renewed attention to the need to adopt national legislation, regulations or other suitable measures to give effect to the International Code;

2. REQUESTS the Director-General:

    (1) to design and coordinate a comprehensive programme of action to support Member States in their efforts to implement and monitor the Code and its effectiveness;

    (2) to provide support and guidance to Member States as and when requested to ensure that the measures they adopt are consistent with the letter and spirit of the International Code;

    (3) to undertake, in collaboration with Member States, prospective surveys, including statistical data of infant and young child feeding practices in the various countries, particularly with regard to the incidence and duration of breast-feeding.

14 May 1982

WHA37.30

The Thirty-seventh World Health Assembly,

Recalling resolutions WHA27.43, WHA31.47, WHA33.32, WHA34.22 and WHA35.26, which dealt with infant and young child feeding;

Recognizing that the implementation of the International Code of Marketing of Breast-milk Substitutes is one of the important actions required in order to promote healthy infant and young child feeding;

Recalling the discussion on infant and young child feeding at the Thirty-sixth World Health Assembly, which concluded that it was premature to revise the International Code at that time;

Having considered the Director-General's report, and noting with interest its contents;

Aware that many products unsuitable for infant feeding are being promoted for this purpose in many parts of the world, and that some infant foods are being promoted for use at too early an age, which can be detrimental to infant and young child health;

1.   ENDORSES the Director-General's report;

2.   URGES continued action by Member States, WHO, non-governmental organizations and all other interested parties to put into effect measures to improve infant and young child feeding, with particular emphasis on the use of foods of local origin;

3.   REQUESTS the Director-General:

   (1) to continue and intensify collaboration with Member States in their efforts to implement and monitor the International Code of Marketing of Breast-milk Substitutes as an important measure at the national level;

   (2) to support Member States in examining the problem of the promotion and use of foods unsuitable for infant and young child feeding, and ways of promoting the appropriate use of infant foods;

   (3) to submit to the Thirty-ninth World Health Assembly a report on the progress in implementing this resolution, together with recommendations for any other measures needed to further improve sound infant and young child feeding practices.

17 May 1984

WHA39.28

The Thirty-ninth World Health Assembly,

Recalling resolutions WHA27.43, WHA31.47, WHA33.32, WHA34.22, WHA35.26 and WHA37.30 which dealt with infant and young child feeding;

Having considered the progress and evaluation report by the Director-General on infant and young child nutrition;

Recognizing that the implementation of the International Code of Marketing of Breast-milk Substitutes is an important contribution to healthy infant and young child feeding in all countries;

Aware that today, five years after the adoption of the International Code, many Member States have made substantial efforts to implement it, but that many products unsuitable for infant feeding are none the less being promoted and used for this purpose; and that sustained and concerted efforts will therefore continue to be necessary to achieve full implementation of and compliance with the International Code as well as the cessation of the marketing of unsuitable products and the improper promotion of breast-milk substitutes;

Noting with great satisfaction the guidelines concerning the main health and socioeconomic circumstances in which infants have to be fed on breast-milk substitutes, in the context of Article 6, paragraph 6, of the International Code;

Noting further the statement in the guidelines, paragraph 47; "Since the large majority of infants born in maternity wards and hospitals are full term, they require no nourishment other than colostrum during their first 24-48 hours of life – the amount of time often spent by a mother and her infant in such an institutional setting. Only small quantities of breast-milk substitutes are ordinarily required to meet the needs of a minority of infants in these facilities and they should only be available in ways that do not interfere with the protection and promotion of breast-feeding for the majority";

1.   ENDORSES the report of the Director-General;

2.   URGES Member States:

    (1)   to implement the Code if they have not yet done so;

    (2)   to ensure that the practices and procedures of their health care systems are consistent with the principles and aim of the International Code;

    (3)   to make the fullest use of all concerned parties-health professional bodies, nongovernmental organizations, consumer organizations, manufacturers and distributors-generally, in protecting and promoting breast-feeding and, specifically, in implementing the Code and monitoring its implementation and compliance with its provisions;

(4) to seek the cooperation of manufacturers and distributors of products within the scope of Article 2 of the Code, in providing all information considered necessary for monitoring the implementation of the Code;

(5) to provide the Director-General with complete and detailed information on the implementation of the Code;

(6) to ensure that the small amounts of breast-milk substitutes needed for the minority of infants who require them in maternity wards and hospitals are made available through the normal procurement channels and not through free or subsidized supplies;

3. REQUESTS the Director-General:

(1) to propose a simplified and standardized form for use by Member States to facilitate the monitoring and evaluation by them of their implementation of the Code and reporting thereon to WHO, as well as the preparation by WHO of a consolidated report covering each of the articles of the Code;

(2) to specifically direct the attention of Member States and other interested parties to the following:

(a) any food or drink given before complementary feeding is nutritionally required may interfere with the initiation or maintenance of breast-feeding and therefore should neither be promoted nor encouraged for use by infants during this period;

(b) the practice being introduced in some countries of providing infants with specially formulated milks (so-called «follow-up milks») is not necessary.

16 May 1986

WHA41.11

The Forty-first World Health Assembly,

Having considered the report by the Director-General on infant and young child nutrition;

Recalling resolutions WHA33.32, WHA34.22 and WHA39.28 on infant and young child feeding and nutrition, and resolutions WHA37.18 and WHA39.31 on the prevention and control of vitamin A deficiency and xerophthalmia, and of iodine deficiency disorders;

Concerned at continuing decreasing breast-feeding trends in many countries, and committed to the identification and elimination of obstacles to breast-feeding;

Aware that appropriate infant and young child nutrition could benefit from further broad national, community and family interventions;

1.   COMMENDS governments, women's organizations, professional associations, consumer and other nongovernmental groups, and the food industry for their efforts to promote appropriate infant and young child nutrition, and encourages them, in cooperation with WHO, to support national efforts for coordinated nutrition programmes and practical action at country level to improve the health and nutrition of women and children;

2.   URGES Member States:

(1) to develop or enhance national nutrition programmes, including multisectoral approaches, with the objective of improving the health and nutritional status of their populations, especially that of infants and young children;

(2) to ensure practices and procedures that are consistent with the aim and principles of the International Code of Marketing of Breast-milk Substitutes, if they have not already done so;

3.   REQUESTS the Director-General to continue to collaborate with Member States, through WHO regional offices and in collaboration with other agencies of the United Nations system, especially FAO and UNICEF:

(1) in identifying and assessing the main nutrient and dietary problems, developing national strategies to deal with them, applying these strategies, and monitoring and evaluating their effectiveness;

(2) in establishing effective nutritional status surveillance systems in order to ensure that all the main variables which collectively determine nutritional status are properly addressed;

(3) in compiling, analyzing, managing and applying information that they have gathered on the nutritional status of their population;

(4) in monitoring, together with other maternal and child health in-

dicators, changes in the prevalence and duration of full and sup-plemented breast-feeding with a view to improving breast-feeding rates;

(5) in developing recommendations regarding diet, including timely complementary feeding and appropriate weaning practices, which are appropriate to national circumstances;

(6) in providing legal and technical assistance, upon request from Member States, in the drafting and/or the implementation of na-tional codes of marketing of breast-milk substitutes, or other similar instruments;

(7) in designing and implementing collaborative studies to assess the impact of measures taken to promote breast-feeding and child nu-trition in Member States.

11 May 1988

WHA43.3

The Forty-third World Health Assembly,

Recalling resolutions WHA33.32, WHA34.22, WHA35.26, WHA37.30, WHA39.28 and WHA41.11 on infant and young child feeding and nutrition;

Having considered the report of the Director-General on infant and young child nutrition;

Reaffirming the unique biological properties of breast milk in protecting against infections, in stimulating the development of the infant's own immune system, and in limiting the development of some allergies;

Recalling the positive impact of breast-feeding on the physical and emotional health of the mother, including its important contribution to child-spacing;

Convinced of the importance of protecting breast-feeding among groups and populations where it remains the infant-feeding norm, and promoting it where it is not, through appropriate information and support, as well as recognizing the special needs of working women;

Recognizing the key role in protecting and promoting breast-feeding played by health workers, particularly nurses, midwives and those in maternal and child health/family planning programmes, and the significance of the counselling and support provided by mothers' groups;

Recognizing that, in spite of resolution WHA39.28, free or low-cost supplies of infant formula continue to be available to hospitals and maternities, with adverse consequences for breast-feeding;

Reiterating its concern over the decreasing prevalence and duration of breast-feeding in many countries;

1.   THANKS the Director-General for his report;

2.   URGES Member States:

   (1)   to protect and promote breast-feeding, as an essential component of their overall food and nutrition polices and programmes on behalf of women and children, so as to enable all infants to be exclusively breast-fed during the first four to six months of life;

   (2)   to promote breast-feeding, with due attention to the nutritional and emotional needs of mothers;

   (3)   to continue monitoring breast-feeding patterns, including traditional attitudes and practices in this regard;

   (4)   to enforce existing, or adopt new, maternity protection legislation or other suitable measures that will promote and facilitate breast-feeding among working women;

   (5)   to draw the attention of all who are concerned with planning and providing maternity services to the universal principles affirmed in the joint WHO/UNICEF statement on breast-feeding and maternity

services that was issued in 1989;

(6) to ensure that the principles and aim of the International Code of Marketing of Breast-milk substitutes and the recommendations contained in resolution WHA39.28 are given full expression in national health and nutrition policy and action, in cooperation with professional associations, women's organizations, consumer and other nongovernmental groups, and the food industry;

(7) to ensure that families make the most appropriate choice with regard to infant feeding, and that the health system provides the necessary support;

3. REQUESTS the Director-General, in collaboration with UNICEF and other international and bilateral agencies concerned:

(1) to urge Member States to take effective measures to implement the recommendations included in resolution WHA39.28;

(2) to continue to review regional and global trends in breast-feeding patterns, including the relationship between breast-feeding and child-spacing;

(3) to support Member States, on request, in adopting measures to improve infant and young child nutrition, *inter alia* by collecting and disseminating information on relevant national action of interest to all Member States; and to mobilize technical and financial resources to this end.

14 May 1990

WHA45.34

The Forty-fifth World Health Assembly,

Having considered the report of the Director-General on infant and young child nutrition;

Recalling resolutions WHA33.32, WHA34.22, WHA35.26, WHA37.30, WHA39.28, WHA41.11 and WHA43.3 concerning infant and young child nutrition, appropriate feeding practices and related questions;

Reaffirming that the International Code of Marketing of Breast-milk Substitutes is a minimum requirement and only one of several important actions required in order to protect healthy practices in respect of infant and young child feeding;

Recalling that products that may be promoted as a partial or total replacement for breast-milk, especially when these are presented as suitable for bottle-feeding, are subject to the provisions of the International Code;

Reaffirming that during the first four to six months of life no food or liquid other than breast milk, not even water, is required to meet the normal infant's nutritional requirements, and that from the age of about six months infants should begin to receive a variety of locally available and safely prepared foods rich in energy, in addition to breast milk, to meet their changing nutritional requirements;

Welcoming the leadership of the Executive Heads of WHO and UNICEF in organizing the "baby-friendly" hospital initiative, with its simultaneous focus on the role of health services in protecting, promoting and supporting breast-feeding and on the use of breast-feeding as a means of strengthening the contribution of health services to safe motherhood, child survival, and primary health care in general, and endorsing this initiative as a most promising means of increasing the prevalence and duration of breast-feeding;

Expressing once again its concern about the need to protect and support women in the workplace, for their own sakes but also in the light of their multiple roles as mothers and care-providers, *inter alia*, by applying existing legislation fully for maternity protection, expanding it to cover any women at present excluded or, where appropriate, adopting new measures to protect breast-feeding;

Encouraged by the steps being taken by infant-food manufacturers towards ending the donation or low-price sale of supplies of infant formula to maternity wards and hospitals, which would constitute a step towards full implementation of the International Code;

Being convinced that charitable and other donor agencies should exert great care in initiating, or responding to, requests for free supplies of infant foods;

Noting that the advertising and promotion of infant formula and the presentation of other products as breast-milk substitutes, as well as feeding-bottles and teats, may compete unfairly with breast-feeding which is the safest and lowest-cost method of nourishing an infant, and may exacerbate such competition and favour uninformed decision-making by interfering with the advice and guidance to be provided by the mother's physician or health worker;

Welcoming the generous financial and other contributions from a number of Member States that enabled WHO to provide technical support to countries wishing to review and evaluate their own experiences in giving effect to the International Code,

1.   THANKS the Director-General for his report;

2.   URGES Member States:

  (1) to give full expression at national level to the operational targets contained in the Innocenti Declaration, namely:

    (a) by appointing a national breast-feeding coordinator and establishing a multisectoral breast-feeding committee;

    (b) by ensuring that every facility providing maternity services applies the principles laid down in the joint WHO/UNICEF statement on the role of maternity services in protecting, promoting and supporting breast-feeding;

    (c) by taking action to give effect to the principles and aim of the International Code of Marketing of Breast-milk Substitutes and subsequent relevant Health Assembly resolutions in their entirety;

    (d) by enacting legislation and adopting means for its enforcement to protect the breast-feeding rights of working women;

  (2) to encourage and support all public and private health facilities providing maternity services so that they become "baby-friendly":

    (a) by providing the necessary training in the application of the principles laid down in the joint WHO/UNICEF statement;

    (b) by encouraging the collaboration of professional associations, women's organizations, consumer and other nongovernmental groups, the food industry, and other competent sectors in this endeavour;

  (3) to take measures appropriate to national circumstances aimed at ending the donation or low-priced sale of supplies of breast-milk substitutes to health care facilities providing maternity services;

  (4) to use the common breast-feeding indicators developed by WHO, with the collaboration of UNICEF and other interested organizations and agencies, in evaluating the progress of their breast-feeding programmes;

  (5) to draw upon the experiences of other Member States in giving ef-

fect to the International Code;

3.   REQUESTS the Director-General:

(1) to continue WHO's productive collaboration with its traditional international partners, in particular UNICEF, as well as other concerned parties including professional associations, women's organizations, consumer groups and other nongovernmental organizations and the food industry, with a view to attaining the Organization's goals and objectives in infant and young child nutrition;

(2) to strengthen the Organization's network of collaborating centres, institutions and organizations in support of appropriate national action;

(3) to support Member States, on request, in elaborating and adapting guidelines on infant nutrition, including complementary feeding practices that are timely, nutritionally appropriate and biologically safe and in devising suitable measures to give effect to the International Code;

(4) to draw the attention of Member States and other intergovernmental organizations to new developments that have an important bearing on infant and young child feeding and nutrition;

(5) to consider, in collaboration with the International Labour Organization, the options available to the health sector and other interested sectors for reinforcing the protection of women in the workplace in view of their maternal responsibilities, and to report to a future Health Assembly in this regard;

(6) to mobilize additional technical and financial resources for intensified support to Member States.

14 May 1992

WHA47.5

The Forty-seventh World Health Assembly,

Having considered the report by the Director-General on infant and young child nutrition;

Recalling resolutions WHA33.32, WHA34.22, WHA35.26, WHA37.30, WHA39.28, WHA41.11, WHA43.3, WHA45.34 and WHA46.7 concerning infant and young child nutrition, appropriate feeding practices and related questions;

Reaffirming its support for all these resolutions and reiterating the recommendations to Member States contained therein;

Bearing in mind the superiority of breast-milk as the biological norm for the nourishment of infants, and that a deviation from this norm is associated with increased risks to the health of infants and mothers,

1. THANKS the Director-General for his report;

2. URGES Member States to take the following measures:

   (1) to promote sound infant and young child nutrition, in keeping with their commitment to the World Declaration and Plan of Action for Nutrition, through coherent effective intersectoral action, including:

      (a) increasing awareness among health personnel, nongovernmental organizations, communities and the general public of the importance of breast-feeding and its superiority to any other infant feeding method;

      (b) supporting mothers in their choice to breast-feed by removing obstacles and preventing interference that they may face in health services, the workplace, or the community;

      (c) ensuring that all health personnel concerned are trained in appropriate infant and young child feeding practices, including the application of the principles laid down in the joint WHO/UNICEF statement on breast-feeding and the role of maternity services;

      (d) fostering appropriate complementary feeding practices from the age of about six months, emphasizing continued breast-feeding and frequent feeding with safe and adequate amounts of local foods;

   (2) to ensure that there are no donations of free or subsidized supplies of breast-milk substitutes and other products covered by the International Code of Marketing of Breast-milk Substitutes in any part of the health care system.

   (3) to exercise extreme caution when planning, implementing or sup-

porting emergency relief operations, by protecting, promoting and supporting breast-feeding for infants, and ensuring that donated supplies of breast-milk substitutes or other products covered by the scope of the International Code are given only if all the following conditions apply:

    (a) infants have to be fed on breast-milk substitutes, as outlined in the guidelines concerning the main health and socio-economic circumstances in which infants have to be fed on breast-milk substitutes;

    (b) the supply is continued for as long as the infants concerned need it;

    (c) the supply is not used as a sales inducement;

(4) to inform the labour sector, and employers' and workers' organizations, about the multiple benefits of breast-feeding for infants and mothers, and the implications for maternity protection in the workplace;

3.   REQUESTS the Director-General:

(1) to use his good offices for cooperation with all parties concerned in giving effect to this and related resolutions of the Health Assembly in their entirety;

(2) to complete development of a comprehensive global approach and programme of action to strengthen national capacities for improving infant and young child feeding practices, including the development of methods and criteria for national assessment of breast-feeding trends and practices;

(3) to support Member States, at their request, in monitoring infant and young child feeding practices and trends in health facilities and households, in keeping with new standard breast-feeding indicators;

(4) to urge Member States to join in the Baby-friendly Hospital Initiative and to support them, at their request, in implementing this Initiative, particularly in their efforts to improve educational curricula and in-service training for all health and administrative personnel concerned;

(5) to increase and strengthen support to Member States, at their request, in giving effect to the principles and aim of the International Code and all relevant resolutions, and to advise Member States on a framework which they may use in monitoring their application, as appropriate to national circumstances;

(6) to develop, in consultation with other concerned parties and as part of WHO's normative function, guiding principles for the use in emergency situations of breast-milk substitutes or other products

covered by the International Code which the competent authorities in Member States may use, in the light of national circumstances, to ensure the optimal infant-feeding conditions;

(7) to complete, in cooperation with selected research institutions, collection of revised reference data and the preparation of guidelines for their use and interpretation, so as to assess the growth of breast-fed infants;

(8) to seek additional technical and financial resources for intensifying WHO's support to Member States in infant feeding and in the implementation of the International Code and subsequent relevant resolutions.

9 May 1994

WHA49.15

The Forty-ninth World Health Assembly,

Having considered the report by the Director-General on infant and young child nutrition;

Recalling resolutions WHA33.32, WHA34.22, WHA39.28, and WHA45.34 among others concerning infant and young child nutrition, appropriate feeding practices and other related questions;

Recalling and reaffirming the provisions of resolution WHA47.5 concerning infant and young child nutrition, including the emphasis on fostering appropriate complementary feeding practices;

Concerned that health institutions and ministries may be subject to subtle pressure to accept, inappropriately, financial or other support for professional training in infant and child health;

Noting the increasing interest in monitoring the application of the International Code of Marketing of Breast-Milk Substitutes and subsequent relevant Health Assembly resolutions,

1.   THANKS the Director-General for his report;

2.   STRESSES the continued need to implement the International Code of Marketing of Breast-Milk Substitutes, subsequent relevant resolutions of the Health Assembly, the Innocenti Declaration, and the World Declaration and Plan of Action for Nutrition;

3.   URGES Member States:

    (1) to ensure that complementary foods are not marketed or used in ways that undermine exclusive and sustained breast-feeding;

    (2) to ensure that the financial support for professionals working in infant and young child health does not create conflicts of interest, especially with regard to the WHO/UNICEF Baby Friendly Hospital Initiative;

    (3) to ensure that monitoring the application of the International Code and subsequent relevant resolutions is carried out in a transparent, independent manner, free from commercial influence;

    (4) to ensure that the appropriate measures are taken, including health information and education in the context of primary health care, to encourage breast-feeding;

    (5) to ensure that the practices and procedures of their health care systems are consistent with the principles and aim of the International Code;

    (6) to provide the Director-General with complete and detailed information on the implementation of the Code;

4.   REQUESTS the Director-General to disseminate as soon as possible to

Member States the "Guiding principles for feeding infants and young children during emergencies".

25 May 1996

WHA 51st session 1998

No resolution on the International Code was adopted.

WHA 53rd session 2000

No resolution on the International Code was adopted.

WHA 54.2

The Fifty-fourth World Health Assembly,

Recalling resolutions WHA33.22, WHA34.22, WHA35.26, WHA37.30, WHA39.28, WHA41.11, WHA43.3, WHA45.34, WHA46.7 and WHA49.15 on infant and young child nutrition, appropriate feeding practices and related questions;

Deeply concerned to improve infant and young child nutrition and to alleviate all forms of malnutrition in the world, because more than one-third of under-five children are still malnourished-whether stunted, wasted or deficient in iodine, vitamin A, iron or other micronutrients- and because malnutrition still contributes to nearly half of the 10.5 million deaths each year among preschool children worldwide;

Deeply alarmed that malnutrition of infants and young children remain one of the most severe global public health problems, at once a major cause and consequence of poverty, deprivation, food insecurity and social inequality, and that malnutrition is a cause not only of increased vulnerability to infection and other diseases, including growth retardation, but also of intellectual, mental, social and development handicap, and of increased risk of disease throughout childhood, adolescence and adult life;

Recognizing the right of everyone to have access to safe and nutritious food, consistent with the right to adequate food and the fundamental right of everyone to be free from hunger, and that every effort should be made with a view to achieving progressively the full realization of this right;

Acknowledging the need for all sectors of society – including governments, civil society, health professional associations, nongovernmental organizations, commercial enterprises and international bodies – to contribute to improved nutrition for infants and young children by using every possible means at their disposal, especially by fostering optimal feeding practices, incorporating a comprehensive multisectoral, holistic and strategic approach;

Noting the guidance of the Convention on the Rights of the Child, in particular Article 24, which recognizes, *inter alia*, the need for access to and availability of both support and information concerning the use of basic knowledge of child health and nutrition, and the advantages of breastfeeding for all segments of society, in particular parents and children;

Conscious that despite the fact that the International Code of Marketing of Breast-milk Substitutes and relevant, subsequent Health Assembly resolutions state that there should be no advertising or other forms of promotion of products within its scope, new modern communication methods, including electronic means, are currently increasingly being used to promote such products; and conscious of the need for the Codex Alimentarius Commission to take the International Code and subsequent relevant Health Assembly resolutions into consideration in dealing with health claims in the development of food standards and guidelines;

Mindful that 2001 marks the twentieth anniversary of the adoption of the International Code of Marketing of Breast-milk Substitutes, and that the adoption of the present resolution provides an opportunity to reinforce the International Code's fundamental role in protecting, promoting and supporting breastfeeding;

Recognizing that there is a sound scientific basis for policy decisions to reinforce activities of Member States and those of WHO; for proposing new and innovative approaches to monitoring growth and improving nutrition; for promoting improved breastfeeding and complementary feeding practices, and sound culture-specific counselling; for improving the nutritional status of women of reproductive age, especially during and after pregnancy; for alleviating all forms of malnutrition; and for providing guidance on feeding practices for infant of mothers who are HIV-positive;

Noting the need for effective systems for assessing the magnitude and geographical distribution of all forms of malnutrition, together with their consequences and contributing factors, and of foodborne diseases; and for monitoring food security;

Welcoming the efforts made by WHO, in close collaboration with UNICEF and other international partners, to develop a comprehensive global strategy for infant and young child feeding, and to use the ACC Sub-Committee on Nutrition as an interagency forum for coordination and exchange of information in this connection;

1. THANKS the Director-General for the progress report on the development of a new global strategy for infant and young child feeding;

2. URGES Members States:

   (1) to recognize the right of everyone to have access to safe and nutritious food, consistent with the right to adequate food and the fundamental right of everyone to be free from hunger, and that every effort should be made with a view to achieving progressively the full realization of this right and to call on all sectors of society to cooperate in efforts to improve the nutrition of infants and young children;

   (2) to take necessary measures as States Parties effectively to implement the Convention on the Rights of the Child, in order to ensure every child's right to the highest attainable standard of health and health care;

   (3) to set up or strengthen interinstitutional and intersectoral discussion forums with all stakeholders in order to reach national consensus on strategies and policies including reinforcing, in collaboration with ILO, policies that support breastfeeding by working women, in

order substantially to improve infant and young child feeding and to develop participatory mechanisms for establishing and implementing specific nutrition programmes and projects aimed at new initiatives and innovative approaches;

(4) to strengthen activities and develop new approaches to protect, promote and support exclusive breastfeeding for six months as a global public health recommendation, taking into account the findings of the WHO expert consultation on optimal duration of exclusive breastfeeding,[1] and to provide safe and appropriate complementary foods, with continued breastfeeding for up to two years of age or beyond, emphasizing channels of social dissemination of these concepts in order to lead communities to adhere to these practices;

(5) to support the Baby-friendly Hospital Initiative and to create mechanisms, including regulations, legislation or other measures, designed, directly and indirectly, to support periodic reassessment of hospitals, and to ensure maintenance of standards and the Initiative's long-term sustainability and credibility;

(6) to improve complementary foods and feeding practices by ensuring sound and culture-specific nutrition counselling to mothers of young children, recommending the widest possible use of indigenous nutrient-rich foodstuffs; and to give priority to the development and dissemination of guidelines on nutrition of children under two years of age, to the training of health workers and community leaders on this subject, and to the integration of these messages into strategies for health and nutrition information, education and communication;

(7) to strengthen monitoring of growth and improvement of nutrition, focusing on community-based strategies, and to strive to ensure that all malnourished children, whether in a community or hospital setting, are correctly diagnosed and treated;

(8) to develop, implement or strengthen sustainable measures including, where appropriate, legislative measures, aimed at reducing all forms of malnutrition in young children and women of reproductive age, especially iron, vitamin A and iodine deficiencies, through a combination of strategies that include supplementation, food fortification and diet diversification, through recommended feeding practices that are culture-specific and based on local foods, as well as through other community-based approaches;

(9) to strengthen national mechanisms to ensure global compliance

---

1 As formulated in the conclusions and recommendations of the expert consultation (Geneva, 28 to 30 March 2001) that completed the systematic review of the optimal duration of exclusive breastfeeding (see document A54/INF.DOC/4).

with the International Code of Marketing of Breast-milk Substitutes and subsequent relevant Health Assembly resolutions, with regard to labelling as well as all forms of adverting, and commercial promotion in all types of media, to encourage the Codex Alimentarius Commission to take the International Code and relevant subsequent Health Assembly resolutions into consideration in developing its standards and guidelines; and to inform the general public on progress in implementing the Code and subsequent relevant Health Assembly resolutions;

(10) to recognize and assess the available scientific evidence on the balance of risk of HIV transmission through breastfeeding compared with the risk of not breastfeeding, and the need for independent research in this connection; to strive to ensure adequate nutrition of infants of HIV-positive mothers; to increase accessibility to voluntary and confidential counselling and testing so as to facilitate the provision of information and informed decision-making; and to recognize that when replacement feeding is acceptable, feasible, affordable, sustainable and safe, avoidance of all breastfeeding by HIV-positive women is recommended; otherwise, exclusive breastfeeding is recommended during the first months of life; and that those who choose other options should be encouraged to use them free from commercial influences;

(11) to take all necessary measures to protect all women from the risk of HIV infection, especially during pregnancy and lactation;

(12) to strengthen their information systems, together with their epidemiological surveillance systems, in order to assess the magnitude and geographical distribution of malnutrition, in all its forms, and of foodborne disease;

3. REQUEST the Director-General:

(1) to give greater emphasis to infant and young child nutrition, in view of WHO's leadership in public health, consistent with and guided by the Convention on the Rights of the Child and other relevant human rights instruments, in partnership with ILO, FAO, UNICEF, UNFPA and other competent organizations both within and outside the United Nations system;

(2) to foster, with all relevant sectors of society, a constructive and transparent dialogue in order to monitor progress towards implementation of the International Code of Marketing of Breast-milk substitutes and subsequent relevant Health Assembly resolutions, in an independent manner and free from commercial influence, and to provide support to Members States in their efforts to monitor imple-

mentation of the Code;

(3) to provide support to Member States in the identification, implementation and evaluation of innovative approaches to improving infant and young child feeding, emphasizing exclusive breastfeeding for six months as a global public health recommendation, taking into account the findings of the WHO expert consultation on optimal duration of exclusive breastfeeding,[2] the provision of safe and appropriate complementary foods, with continued breastfeeding up to two years of age or beyond, and communist-based and cross-sector activities;

(4) to continue the step-by-step country- and region-based approach to developing the new global strategy on infant and young child feeding, and to involve the international health and development community, in particular UNICEF, and other stakeholders as appropriate;

(5) to encourage and support further independent research on HIV transmission through breastfeeding and on other measures to improve the nutritional status of mothers and children already affected by HIV/AIDS;

(6) to submit the global strategy for consideration to the Executive Board at its 109th session in January 2002 and to the Fifty-fifth World Health Assembly (May 2002).

18 May 2001

---

2 As formulated in the conclusions and recommendations of the expert consultation (Geneva, 28 to 30 March 2001) that completed the systematic review of the optimal duration of exclusive breastfeeding (see document A54/INF.DOC/4).

WHA55.25

The Fifty-fifth World Health Assembly,

Having considered the draft global strategy for infant and young-child feeding;

Deeply concerned about the vast numbers of infants and young children who are still inappropriately fed and whose nutritional status, growth and development, health and very survival are thereby compromised;

Conscious that every year as much as 55% of infant deaths from diarrhoeal disease and acute respiratory infections may be the result of inappropriate feeding practices, that less than 35% of infants worldwide are exclusively breastfed for even the first four months of life, and that complementary feeding practices are frequently ill-time, inappropriate and unsafe;

Alarmed at the degree to which inappropriate infant and young-child feeding practices contribute to the global burden of disease, including malnutrition and its consequences such as blindness and mortality due to vitamin A deficiency, impaired psychomotor development due to iron deficiency and anaemia, irreversible brain damage as a consequence of iodine deficiency, the massive impact on morbidity and mortality of protein-energy malnutrition, and the later-life consequences of childhood obesity;

Recognizing that infant and young-child mortality can be reduced through improved nutritional status of women of reproductive age, especially during pregnancy, and by exclusive breastfeeding for the first six months of life, and with nutritionally adequate and safe complementary feeding through introduction of safe and adequate amounts of indigenous foodstuffs and local foods while breastfeeding continues up to the age of two years or beyond;

Mindful of the challenges posed by the ever-increasing number of people affected by major emergencies, the HIV/AIDS pandemic, and the complexities of modern lifestyles coupled with continued promulgation of inconsistent messages about infant and young-child feeding;

Aware that inappropriate feeding practices and their consequences are major obstacles to sustainable socioeconomic development and poverty reduction;

Reaffirming that mothers and babies form an inseparable biological and social unit, and that the health and nutrition of one cannot be divorced from the health and nutrition of the other;

Recalling the Health Assembly's endorsement (resolution WHA33.32), in their entirety, of the statement and recommendations made by the joint WHO/UNICEF Meeting on Infant and Young Child Feeding held in 1979; its adoption of the International Code of Marketing of Breast-milk Substitutes (resolution WHA34.22), in which it stressed that adoption of and adherence to the Code were a minimum requirement; its welcoming of the Innocenti Declaration on the Protection, Promotion and Support of Breastfeeding as a basis for international health policy and action (resolution WHA44.33); its urging encouragement and support for all public and private health facilities providing maternity services so that they become "baby-friendly" (resolution WHA45.34); its urging ratification and implementation of the Convention on the Rights of the Child as a vehicle for family health development (resolution WHA46.27); and its endorsement, in their entirety, of the World Declaration and Plan of Action for Nutrition adopted by the International Conference on Nutrition (resolution WHA46.7);

Recalling also resolutions WHA35.26, WHA37.30, WHA39.28. WHA41.11, WHA43.3, WHA45.34, WHA46.7, WHA47.5, WHA49.15 and WHA54.2 on infant and young-chid nutrition, appropriate feeding practices and related questions;

Recognizing the need for comprehensive national policies on infant and young-child feeding, including guidelines on ensuring appropriate feeding of infants and young children in exceptionally difficult circumstances;

Convinced that it is time for governments to renew their commitment to protection and promoting the optimal feeding of infants and young children,

1. ENDORSES the global strategy for infant and young-child feeding;
2. URGES Member States, as a matter of urgency;

    (1) to adopt and implement the global strategy, taking into account national circumstances, while respecting positive local traditions and values, as part of their overall nutrition and child health policies and programmes, in order to ensure optimal feeding for all infants and young children, and to reduce the risks associated with obesity and other forms of malnutrition;

    (2) to strengthen existing, or establish new, structures for implementing the global strategy through the health and other concerned sectors, for monitoring and evaluating its effectiveness, and for guiding resource investment and management to improve infant and young-child feeding;

    (3) to define for this purpose, consistent with national circumstance:

        (a) national goals and objectives,

        (b) a realistic timeline for their achievement,

        (c) measurable process and output indicators that will permit; accurate monitoring and evaluation of action taken and a rapid response to identified needs;

    (4) to ensure that the introduction of micronutrient interventions and the marketing of nutritional supplements do not replace, or undermine support for the sustainable practice of, exclusive breastfeeding and optimal complementary feeding;

    (5) to mobilize social and economic resources within society and to en-

gage them actively in implementing the global strategy and in achieving its aims and objectives in the sprit of resolution WHA49.15;

3. CALLS UPON other international organization and bodies, in particular ILO, FAO, UNICEF, UNHCR, UNFPA and UNAIDS, to give high priority, within their respective mandates and programmes and consistent with guidelines on conflict of interest, to provision of support to governments in implementing this global strategy, and invites donors to provide adequate funding for the necessary measures;

4. REQUESTS the Codex Alimentarius Commission to continue to give full consideration, within the framework of its operational mandate, to action it might take to improve the quality standards of processed foods for infants and young children and to promote their safe and proper use at an appropriate age, including through adequate labelling, consistent with the policy of WHO, in particular the International Code of Marketing of Breastmilk Substitutes, resolution WHA54.2, and other relevant resolutions of the Health Assembly;

5. REQUESTS the Director-General:

   (1) to provide support to Member States, on request, in implementing this strategy, and in monitoring and evaluating its impact;

   (2) to continue, in the light of the scale and frequency of major emergencies worldwide, to generate specific information and develop training materials aimed at ensuring that the feeding requirements of infants and young children in exceptionally difficult circumstances are met;

   (3) to strengthen international cooperation with other organizations of the United Nations system and bilateral development agencies in promoting appropriate infant and young-child feeding;

   (4) to promote continued cooperation with and among all parties concerned with implementing the global strategy.

18 May 2002

18 May 2002

WHA 57th session 2004

No resolution on the International Code was adopted.

WHA58.32

The Fifty-eighth World Health Assembly,

Recalling the adoption by the Health Assembly of the International Code of Marketing of Breast-milk Substitutes annexed to resolution WHA34.22, resolutions WHA39.28, WHA41.11, WHA46.7, WHA47.5, WHA49.15, WHA54.2 on infant and young child nutrition, appropriate feeding practices and related questions, and particularly resolution WHA55.25, which endorses the global strategy for infant and young child feeding;

Having considered the report on infant and young child nutrition;[1]

Aware that the joint FAO/WHO expert meeting on *Enterobacter sakazakii* and other microorganisms in powdered infant formula (2004) concluded that intrinsic contamination of powdered infant formula with *E. sakazakii* and *Salmonella* had been a cause of infection and illness, including severe disease in infants, particularly preterm, low birth-weight or immunocompromised infants, and could lead to serious developmental sequelae and death;[2]

Noting that such severe outcomes are especially serious in preterm, low birth-weight and immunocompromised infants, and therefore are of concern to all Member States;

Bearing in mind that the Codex Alimentarius Commission is revising its recommendation on hygienic practices for the manufacture of foods for infants and young children;

Recognizing the need for parents and caregivers to be fully informed of evidence-based public-health risks of intrinsic contamination of powdered infant formula and the potential for introduced contamination, and the need for safe preparation, handling and storage of prepared infant formula;

Concerned that nutrition and health claims may be used to promote breast-milk substitutes as superior to breastfeeding;

Acknowledging that the Codes Alimentarius Commission plays a pivotal role in providing guidance to Member States on the proper regulation of foods, including foods for infant and young children;

Bearing in mind that on several occasions the Health Assembly has called upon the Commission to give full consideration, within the framework of its operational mandate, to evidence-based action that it might take to improve the health standards of foods, consistent with the aims and objectives of relevant public health strategies, particularly WHO's global strategy, for infant and young child feeding (resolution WHA55.25) and Global Strategy on Diet, Physical Activity and Health (resolution WHA57.17);

---

1 Document A58/5.
2 FAO/WHO Expert Meeting on *E. sakazakii* and other Microorganisms in Powered Infant Formula ; Meeting Report, Microbiological Risk Assessment Series No. 6, 2004, p.37.

Recognizing that such action requires a clear understanding of the respective roles of the Health Assembly and the Codex Alimentarius Commission, and that of food regulation in the broader context of public health policies;

Taking into account resolution WHA56.23 on the joint FAO/WHO evaluation of the work of the Codex Alimentarius Commission, which endorsed WHO's increased direct involvement in the Commission and requested the Director-General to strengthen WHO's role in complementing the work of the Commissions with other relevant WHO activities in the areas of food safety and nutrition, with special attention to issues mandated in Health Assembly resolutions,

1. URGES Member States

    (1) to continue to protect, promote and support exclusive breastfeeding for six months as a global public-health recommendation, taking into account the findings of the WHO Expert Consultation on optimal duration of exclusive breastfeeding,[1] and to provide for continued breastfeeding up to two years of age or beyond, by implementing fully the WHO global strategy on infant and young child feeding that encourages the formulation of a comprehensive national policy, including where appropriate a legal framework to promote maternity leave and a supportive environment for six months' exclusive breastfeeding, a detailed plan of action to implement, monitor and evaluate the policy, and allocation of adequate resources for this process;

    (2) to ensure that nutrition and health claims are not permitted for breast-milk substitutes, except where specifically provided for in national legislation;[2]

    (3) to ensure that clinicians and other health-care personnel, community health workers and families, parents and other caregivers, particularly of infants at high risk, are provided with enough information and training by health-care providers, in a timely manner on the preparation, use and handling of powdered infant formula in order to minimize health hazards, are informed that powdered infant formula may contain pathogenic microorganisms and must be prepared and used appropriately; and where applicable, that this information is conveyed through an explicit warning on packaging;

    (4) to ensure that financial support and other incentives for programmes and health professionals working in infant and young child health

---

1   As formulated in the conclusions and recommendations of the Expert Consultation (Geneva 28-30 March 2001) that completed the systematic review of the optimal duration of exclusive breastfeeding (see document A54/INF.DOC./4).

2   The reference to national legislation also applies to regional economic integration organizations.

do not create conflicts of interest;

(5) to ensure that research on infant and young child feeding, which may form the basis for public policies, always contains a declaration relating to conflicts of interest and is subject to independent peer review;

(6) to work closely with relevant entities, including manufacturers, to continue to reduce the concentration and prevalence of pathogens, including *Enterobacter sakazakii*, in powdered infant formula;

(7) to continue to ensure that manufacturers adhere to Codex Alimentarius or national food standards and regulations:

(8) to ensure policy coherence at national level by stimulating collaboration between health authorities, food regulators and food standard-setting bodies;

(9) to participate actively and constrictively in the work of the Codex Alimentarius Commission;

(10) to ensure that all national agencies involved in defying national positions on public health issues for use in all relevant international forums, including the Codex Alimentarius Commission, have a common and consistent understanding of health policies adopted by the Health Assembly, and to promote these policies;

2. REQUESTS the Codex Alimentarius Commission:

(1) to continue to give full consideration, when elaborating standards, guidelines and recommendations, to those resolutions of the Health Assembly that are relevant in the framework of its operational mandate;

(2) to establish standards, guidelines and recommendations on foods for infants and young children formulated in a manner that ensures the development of safe and appropriately labelled products that meet their known nutritional and safety needs, thus reflecting WHO policy, in particular the WHO global strategy for infant and young child feeding and the International Code of Marketing of Breast-milk Substitutes and other relevant resolutions of the Health Assembly;

(3) urgently to complete work currently under way on addressing the risk of microbiological contamination of powdered infant formula and establish appropriate microbiological criteria or standards related to *E. sakazakii* and other relevant microorganisms in powdered infant formula; and to provide guidance on safe handling and on warning messages on product packaging;

3. REQUESTS the Director-General:

(1) in collaboration with FAO, and taking into account the work under-
     taken by the Codex Alimentarius Commission, to develop guide-
     lines for clinicians and other health-care providers, community
     health workers and family, parents and other caregivers on the prep-
     aration, use, handling and storage of infant formula so as to mini-
     mize risk, and to address the particular needs of Member States in
     establishing effective measures to minimize risk in situations where
     infants cannot be, or are not, fed breast-milk;

(2) to take the lead in supporting independently reviewed research,
     including by collecting evidence from different parts of the world,
     in order to understand better the ecology, taxonomy, virulence and
     other characteristics of *E. sakazakii*, in line with the recommenda-
     tions of the FAO/WHO Expert Meeting on *E. sakazakii* and other
     Microorganisms in Powdered Infant Formula, and to explore means
     of reducing the level in reconstituted powdered infant formula;

(3) to provide information in order to promote and facilitate the contri-
     bution of the Codex Alimentarius Commission, within the frame-
     work of its operational mandate, to full implementation of interna-
     tional public-health policies;

(4) to report to the Health Assembly each even year, along with the re-
     port on the status of implementation of the International Code of
     Marketing of Breast-milk Substitutes and the relevant resolutions
     of the Health Assembly, on progress in the consideration of matters
     referred to the Codex Alimentarius Commission for its action.

25 May 2005

WHA59.21

The Fifty-ninth World Health Assembly,

Having considered the report on infant and young child nutrition which highlights the contribution of optimal infant feeding practices to achievement of the internationally agreed health-related development goals, including those contained in the Millennium Declaration;[1]

Recalling the adoption by the Health Assembly of the International Code of Marketing of Breast-milk Substitutes (Resolution WHA34.22) resolutions WHA35.26, WHA37.30, WHA39.28, WHA41.11, WHA43.3, WHA47.5, WHA49.15, WHA54.2 and WHA58.32 on infant and young child nutrition, appropriate feeding practices and related questions;

Reaffirming in particular resolutions WHA44.33 and WHA55.25 which respectively welcomed the 1990 Innocenti Declaration on the Protection, Promotion and Support of Breastfeeding and endorsed the Global Strategy for Infant and Young Child Feeding as the foundations for action in the protection, promotion and support of breastfeeding;

Welcoming the Call for Action contained in the Innocenti Declaration 2005 on Infant and Young Child Feeding;

Mindful that 2006 marks the twenty-fifth anniversary of the International Code of Marketing of Breast-milk Substitutes, and recognizing its increased relevance in the wake of the HIV/AIDS pandemic, rising frequency of complex human and natural emergencies, and concerns about the risks of intrinsic contamination of powdered infant formula,

1. REITERATES its support for the Global Strategy for Infant and Young Child Feeding;

2. WELCOMES the Call for Action made in the Innocenti Declaration 2005 on Infant and Young Child Feeding as a significant step towards achievement of the fourth Millennium Development Goal to reduce child mortality;

3. URGES Member States to support activities on this Call for Action and, in particular, to renew their commitment to policies and programmes related to implementation of the International Code of Marketing of Breast-milk Substitutes and subsequent relevant Health Assembly resolutions and to revitalization of the Baby-Friendly Hospital Initiative to protect, promote and support breastfeeding;

4. CALLS on multilateral and bilateral donor arrangements and international financial institutions to direct financial resources for Member States to carry out these efforts;

5. REQUESTS the Director-General to mobilize technical support for Mem-

---

1   Document A59/13.

ber States in the implementation and independent monitoring of the International Code of Marketing of Breast-milk Substitutes and subsequent relevant Health Assembly resolutions

27 May 2006

WHA61.29

The Sixty-first World Health Assembly,

Having considered the report on infant and young child nutrition: biennial progress report;[1]

Reaffirming the significance of the adoption by the Health Assembly of the International Code of Marketing of Breast-milk Substitutes (resolution WHA34.22), and resolutions WHA35.26, WHA37.30, WHA39.28, WHA41.11, WHA43.3, WHA45.34, WHA47.5, WHA49.15, WHA54.2, WHA55.25, WHA58.32 and WHA59.21 on infant and young child nutrition;

Reaffirming, in particular, resolutions WHA54.2, WHA55.25 and WHA58.32, which recognize the importance of exclusive breastfeeding for the first six months of life, the Global Strategy for Infant and Young Child Feeding, and the evidence-based public health risks of intrinsic contamination of powdered infant formula, the potential for introduced contamination and the need for safe preparation, handling and storage of prepared infant formula;

Recalling resolution WHA49.15 on infant and young child nutrition, which recognizes the need to ensure that the commitment and support for breastfeeding and optimal infant and young child nutrition are not undermined by conflicts of interest;

Affirming that early initiation and exclusive breastfeeding is the natural and optimal means to achieve food security and optimal health for infants and young children, and concerned that the rates have remained low;

Welcoming the biennial progress report and noting the salient points that need further consideration, specifically persistent malnutrition-one of the most severe public health problems, as indicated by the alarmingly high rates of under-five mortality;

Noting further the need to improve implementation and monitoring the International Code of Marketing of Breast-milk Substitutes;

Aware that powdered infant formula is not a sterile product and that it can contain pathogenic bacteria, and welcoming the WHO/FAO guidelines on safe preparation, storage and handling of powdered infant formula;[2]

Encouraged by the work of FAO and WHO through the Codex Alimentarius Commission on the revised proposed draft Code of Hygienic Practice for powdered Formulae for Infants and Young Children;

1. URGES Member States :

    (1) to strengthen implementation of the International Code of Market-

---

1   Document A61/17 Add.1.
2   World Health Organization in collaboration with the Food and Agriculture Organization of the United Nations. *Safe preparation, storage and handling of powdered infant formula*, Geneva, World Health Organization, 2007.

ing of Breast-milk Substitutes and subsequent relevant Health Assembly resolutions by scaling up efforts to monitor and enforce national measures in order to protect breastfeeding while keeping in mind the Health Assembly resolutions to avoid conflicts of interest;

(2) to continue action on the Global Strategy for Infant and Young Child Feeding and the Innocenti Declaration of 2005 on infant and young child feeding and to increase support for early initiation and exclusive breastfeeding for the first six months of life, in order to reduce the scourge of malnutrition and its associated high rates of under-five morbidity and mortality;

(3) to implement, through application and wide dissemination, the WHO/FAO guidelines on safe preparation, storage and handling of powdered infant formula in order to minimize the risk of bacterial infection and, in particular, ensure that the labelling of powdered formula conforms with the standards, guidelines and recommendations of the Codex Alimentarius Commission and taking into account resolution WHA58.32;

(4) to investigate, as a risk-reduction strategy, the possible use and, in accordance with national regulations, the safe use of donor milk through human milk banks for vulnerable infants, in particular premature, low-birth-weight and immunocompromised infants, and to promote appropriate hygienic measures for storage, conservation, and use of human milk;

(5) to take action through food-safety measures, including appropriate regulatory measures, to reduce the risk of intrinsic contamination of powdered infant formula by *Enterobacter sakazakii* and other pathogenic microorganisms during the manufacturing process as well as the risk of contamination during storage, preparation and handling, and to monitor the effectiveness of these measures:

2. REQUESTS the Director-General:

(1) to continue monitoring progress through reports to the Health Assembled each even year, along with the report on the status of implementation of the International Code of Marketing of Breast-milk Substitutes and the relevant resolutions of the Health Assembly, on progress in the consideration of matters referred to the Codex Alimentarius for its action;

(2) to continue to promote breastfeeding and infant and young child nutrition as essential for achieving the Millennium Development Goals, in particular those relating to the eradication of extreme poverty and hunger and to the reduction of child mortality;

(3) to intensify support for the implementation of the International

Code of Marketing of Breast-milk Substitutes;

(4) to provide support urgently for research on the safe use of expressed and donated breast milk, owing to the current challenges facing countries in the implementation of safe infant feeding practices, mindful of the national rules and regulations and cultural and religious beliefs;

(5) to provide support for strengthening of national information systems in order to improve the evidence base for policies in this area;

(6) to review the global current situation of infant and child nutrition including nutrition and HIV, and submit a report to the Sixty-third World Health Assembly.

24 May 2008

WHA63.23

The Sixty-third World Health Assembly,

Having considered the report on infant and young child nutrition;[1]

Recalling resolutions WHA33.32, WHA34.22, WHA35.26, WHA37.30, WHA39.28, WHA41.11, WHA43.3, WHA45.34, WHA46.7, WHA47.5, WHA49.15 and 54.2, WHA55.25, WHA58.32, WHA59.21, WHA61.20 on infant and young child nutrition, and on nutrition and HIV/AIDS and the Codex Allimentarius Guidelines for use of nutrition and health claims;[2]

Conscious that achieving the Millennium Development Goals will require the reduction of maternal and child malnutrition;

Aware that worldwide malnutrition accounts for 11% of the global burden of disease, leading to long-term poor health and disability and poor educational and developmental outcomes; that worldwide 186 million children are stunted[3] and 20 million suffer from the most deadly form of severe acute malnutrition each year, and that nutritional risk factors, including underweight, suboptimal breastfeeding and vitamin and mineral deficiencies, particularly of vitamin A, iron, iodine and zinc, are responsible for 3.9 million deaths (35% of total deaths) and 144 million disability-adjusted life years (33% of total disability-adjusted life years) in children less than five years old;

Aware that countries are faced with increasing public health problems posed by the double burden of malnutrition (both undernutrition and overweight), with its negative later-life consequences;

Acknowledging that 90% of stunted children live in 36 countries and that children under two years of age are most affected by undernutrition;

Recognizing that the promotion of breast-milk substitutes and some commercial foods for infants and young children undermines progress in optimal infant and young child feeding;

Mindful of the challenges posed by the HIV/AIDS pandemic and the difficulties in formulating appropriate policies for infant and young child feeding, and concerned that food assistance does not meet the nutritional needs of young children infected by HIV;

Concerned that in emergencies, many of which occur in countries not on track to attain Millennium Development Goal 4 and which include situations created by the effects of climate change, infants and young children are particularly vulnerable to malnutrition, illness and death;

Recognizing that national emergency preparedness plans and international emergency responses do not always cover protection, promotion and support of optimal infant and young child feeding;

---

1 Document A61/9.
2 Document CAC/GL/23.
3 World Health Statistics, 2010. *World Health Organisation*, Geneva, 2010.

Expressing deep concern over persistent reports of violations of the International Code of Marketing of Breast-milk Substitutes by some infant food manufacturers and distributors with regard to promotion targeting mothers and health-care workers;

Expressing further concern over reports of the ineffectiveness of measures, particularly voluntary measures, to ensure compliance with the International Code of Marketing of Breast-Milk Substitutes in some countries;

Aware that inappropriate feeding practices and their consequences are major obstacles to attaining sustainable socioeconomic development and poverty reduction;

Concerned about the vast numbers of infants and young children who are still inappropriately fed and whose nutritional status, growth and development, health and survival are thereby compromised;

Mindful of the fact that implementation of the global strategy for infant and young child feeding and its operation targets requires strong political commitment and a comprehensive approach, including strengthening of health systems and communities with particular emphasis on the Baby-friendly Hospital Initiative, and careful monitoring of the effectiveness of the interventions used;

Recognizing that the improvement of exclusive breastfeeding practices, adequate and timely complementary feeding, along with continued breastfeeding for up to two years or beyond, could save annually the lives of 1.5 million children under five years of age;

Aware that multisectoral food and nutrition policies are needed for the successful scaling up of evidence-based safe and effective nutrition interventions;

Recognizing the need for comprehensive national policies on infant and young child feeding that are well integrated within national strategies for nutrition and child survival;

Convinced that it is time for governments, civil society and the international community to renew their commitment to promoting the optimal feeding of infants and young children and to work together closely for this purpose;

Convinced that strengthening of national nutrition surveillance is crucial in implementing effective nutrition policies and scaling up interventions,

1. URGES Member States:

    (1) to increase political commitment in order to prevent and reduce malnutrition in all its forms;

    (2) to strengthen and expedite the sustainable implementation of the global strategy for infant and young child feeding including emphasis on giving effect to the aim and principles of the International Code of Marketing of Breast-milk Substitutes, and the implementation of the Baby-friendly Hospital Initiative;

(3) to develop and/or strengthen legislative, regulatory and/or other effective measures to control the marketing of breast-milk substitutes in order to give effect to the International Code of Marketing of Breast-milk Substitutes and relevant resolutions adopted by the World Health Assembly;

(4) to end inappropriate promotion of food for infants and young children and to ensure that nutrition and health claims shall not be permitted for foods for infants and young children except, where specifically provided for, in relevant Codex Alimentarius standards or national legislation;

(5) to develop or review current policy frameworks addressing the double burden of malnutrition and to include in the framework childhood obesity and food security and allocate adequate human and financial resources to ensure implementation of those policies;

(6) to scale up interventions to improve infant and young child nutrition in an integrated manner with the protection, promotion and support of breast-feeding and timely, safe and appropriate complementary feeding as core interventions; the implementation of interventions for the prevention and management of severe malnutrition; and the targeted control of vitamin and mineral deficiencies;

(7) to consider and implement, as appropriate, the revised principles and recommendations on infant feeding in the context of HIV, issued by WHO in 2009[1], in order to address the infant feeding dilemma for HIV-infected mothers and their families while ensuring protection, promotion and support of exclusive and sustained breast-feeding for the general population;

(8) to ensure that national and international preparedness plans and emergency responses follow the evidence-based Operational Guidance for Emergency Relief Staff and Programme Managers[2] on infant and young child feeding in emergencies, which includes the protection, promotion and support for optimal breastfeeding, and the need to minimize the risks of artificial feeding, by ensuring that any required breast-milk substitutes are purchased, distributed and used according to strict criteria;

(9) to include the interventions referred to in subparagraph 1(6) above in comprehensive maternal and child health services and support the aim of universal coverage and principles of primary health care, including strengthening health systems as outlined in resolution WHA62.12;

---

1 *Rapid advice: revised principles and recommendations in the context of HIV,* November 2009. Geneva, World Health Organisation, 2009.

2 Available online at hmp://www.ennonline.net/resources/6.

(10) to strengthen nutrition surveillance systems and improve use and reporting of agreed Millennium Development Goals indicators in order to monitor progress;

(11) to implement the WHO Child Growth Standards by their full integration into child health programmes;

(12) to implement the measures for prevention of malnutrition as specified in the WHO strategy for community-based management of severe acute malnutrition,[1] most importantly improving water and sanitation systems and hygiene practices to protect children against communicable disease and infections;

2. CALLS UPON infant food manufacturers and distributors to comply fully with their responsibilities under the International Code of Marketing of Breast-milk Substitutes and subsequent relevant World Health Assembly resolutions;

3. REQUESTS the Director-General:

(1) to strengthen the evidence base on effective and safe nutrition actions to counteract the public health effects of the double burden of malnutrition, and to describe good practices for successful implementation;

(2) to mainstream nutrition in all WHO's health policies and strategies and confirm the presence of essential nutrition actions, including integration of the revised principles and recommendations on infant feeding in the context of HIV, issued by WHO in 2009, in the context of the reform of primary health care;

(3) to continue and strengthen the existing mechanisms for collaboration with other United Nations agencies and international organizations involved in the process of ensuring improved nutrition including clear identification of leadership, division of labour and outcomes;

(4) to support Member States, on request, in expanding their nutritional interventions related to the double burden of malnutrition, monitoring and evaluating impact, strengthening or establishing effective nutrition surveillance systems, and implementing the WHO Child Growth Standards, and the Baby-friendly Hospital Initiative.

(5) to support Member States, on request, in their efforts to develop and/or strengthen legislative, regulatory or other effective measures to control marketing of breast-milk substitutes;

---

1 *Community-based management of severe acute malnutrition: a joint statement by the World Health Organization, the World Food Programme, the United Nations System Standing Committee on Nutrition and the United Nations Children's Fund,* Geneva, World Health Organisation, 2007.

(6) to develop a comprehensive implementation plan on infant and young child nutrition as a critical component of a global multisectoral nutrition framework for preliminary discussion at the Sixty-fourth World Health Assembly and for final delivery at the Sixty-fifth World Health Assembly, through the Executive Board and after broad consultation with Member States.

21 May 2010

BIBLIOGRAPHY

Books

Bowett, D.W. *The Law of International Institutions*, 4th edn. (1982), London.

Buffle, J.C. *Dossier N ...Comme Nestlé*, (1986), Paris.

Castañeda, J. *Legal Effects of United Nations Resolutions*, (1969), New York and London.

Cheng, B. *International Law : Teaching and Practice*, (1982), London.

Chetley, A. *The Politics of Baby Foods – Successful Challenges to an International Marketing Strategy* (1986), London.

Hafez, G.and Bagchi, K. *Promotion of Breast-feeding Through MCH Services and Primary Health Care* (1995), Alexandria.

IBFAN/GIFA *Does the Nestlé Report Comply with the International Code?* (2000), Geneva

Kelsen, H. *The Law of the United Nations* (1950), London.

McNair *The Law of Treaties* (1961), Oxford

Nestlé *Implementation of the WHO Code-Report to the Director-General of the World Health Organization* (1999), Geneva.

Oppenheim *International Law*, Vol. I, Parts 1 and 2, 9th edn., (1992) London.

Palmer, G. *The Politics of Breastfeeding*, 3rd edn., (2009), London.

Roemer, R. *Legislative Action to Combat the World Tobacco Epidemic* 2nd edn., (1993), Geneva.

Saadeh, R., Labbok, M., Cooney, K. and Koniz-Booker, P. *Breast-feeding – The Technical Basis and Recommendations for Action* (1993), Geneva.

Savage King, F. *Helping Mothers to Breast-feed*, Revised edn. (1992), Nairobi.

Schermers, H. G. and Blokker, N.M. *International Institutional Law* 3rd edn. (1995), The Hague/London/Boston.

Schwebel, S.M. *The Effectiveness of International Decisions* (1971), Leyden.

Sethi, S.P. *Multinational Corporations and the Impact of Public Advocacy on Corporate Strategy – Nestlé and the Infant Formula Controversy* (1994), Boston/Dordrecht/London.

Sokol, E. J. *The Code Handbook- A Guide to Implementing the International Code of Marketing of Breast-milk Substitutes* (1997), Penang.

Sorensen, M. *Manual of Public International Law* (1968), London, Melbourne and Toronto.

UNHCR *Guidance on Infant Feeding and HIV in the context of refugees and displaced populations* (2009).

UNICEF *1990–2005 Celebrating the Innocenti Declaration on the Protection, Promotion and support of Breastfeeding* (2006), Florence.

Walker, D. M. *The Oxford Companion to Law* (1980), Oxford.

Articles

Anand, R. K. "Health Workers and the Baby Food Industry", 312 *British Medical Journal* (22 June 1966), p.1556.

Cheng, B. "United Nations Resolutions on Outer Space: 'Instant' International Customary Law", 5 *Indian Journal of International Law* (1965), p.23.

Coutsoudis, A., Coovadia, H.M. and King. J. "The breastmilk brand: promotion of child survival in the face of Formula-milk marketing", *The Lancet*, vol. 374, (August 1, 2009), p.423.

Dobbert, J. P. "Le Codex Alimentarius: vers une nouvelle méthode de réglementation international," 15 *Annuaire français de droit international* (1969), p.679.

Falk, R. A. "On the Quasi-Legislative Competence of the General Assembly,» 60 *American Journal of International Law* (1966), p. 782.

Firebrace, J. *Infant Feeding in the Middle East* (March/April 1983).

FAO/WHO Codex Alimentarius Commission, *Procedural Manual*, 8th and 15th edn. (1993) (2005).

Greiner, T. "The Infant Food Industry – Why and How it Promotes its Products", *N U - News on Health Care in Developing Countries*Vol. 10 (1/96), p. 27.

IBFAN Breaking the Rules (1994).

IBFAN State of the Code by Country (1994).

IBFAN Breaking the Rules-Stretching the Rules (2007)

IBFAN State of the Code by Country (2009)

IGBM *Cracking the Code* (1997).

Ighogboja, I. S., Odumodu, C.U. and Olarewaju, R. S. "Breast-feeding Pattern in Jos, before Baby-friendly Hospital Initiative" 42 *Journal of Tropical Pediatrics* (June 1996), p. 178.

Jelliffe, D.B., and Jelliffe, E.F. P. "Feeding Young Infants in Developing Countries", *Marketing and Promotion of Infant Formula in Developing Nations, 1978, Hearing Before the Subcommittee on Health and Scientific Research of the Committee on Human Resources, United States Senate, Ninety-Fifth Congress, 23 May 1978*, p. 71.

Jennings, Sir Robert "General Course on Principles of International Law", *The Hague Academy, 121 Recueil des Cours,* Vol.II, (1967), p. 32.

Johnson, D.H.N. "The Effects of Resolutions of the General Assembly of the United Nations", 32 *British Yearbook of International Law* (1965-66), p.97.

Kaplan D.L. and Graff K.M. "Marketing Breastfeeding-Reversing Corporate Influence on Infant Feeding Practices", Journal of Urban Health: Bulletin of the New York Academy of Medicine (2008), doi:10.1007/S 11524-008-9279-6, p.1.

Kelly, M. "Infant Feeding in Emergencies", 17 *Disasters*, Vol.2 (1993), p.110.

Kylberg, E. "The Swedish Code ", *N U-News on Health Care in Developing Countries*, Vol.10 (1/96), p. 9.

Linnecar, A. "The International Breast-feeding Movement: Challenges for the Year 2000", *N U News on Health Care in Developing Countries*, Vol.10 (1/96), p.32.

Margulies, L. "Implementation and Monitoring under the International Code of Marketing of Breast-milk Substitutes", *N U – News on Health Care in Developing Countries*, Vol.10 (1/96), p.14.

Nashat, M. "Le Code International de Commercialisation des Substituts du Lait Maternel", 27 *Annuaire français de droit international* (1980), p.490.

Nestlé, U.K. "*A Missed Opportunity*" – *Nestlé Comments on the IGBM Report "Cracking the Code" (1997)*.

Post, J.E. "The International Infant Formula Industry", *Marketing and Promotion of Infant Formula in Developing Nations, 1978, Hearing Before the Subcommittee on Health and Scientific Research of the Committee on Resources, United States Senate, Ninety-Fifth*

Congress, 23 May 1978, p. 216.

Post, J.E. and Baer, E. "The International Code of Marketing of Breast-milk Substitutes: Consensus, Compromise and Conflict in the Infant Formula Controversy", 25 *The Review – International Commission of Jurists* (December 1980),p. 53.

Shubber, S. "The Codex Alimentarius under International Law", 21 *International and Comparative Law Quarterly* (1972), p. 631.

Shubber, S. "The International Code of Marketing of Breast-milk Substitutes", 36 *International Digest of Health Legislation* (1985), p. 879.

Shubber, S. "The Code- Legal Aspects of Implementation in a Changing World" *N U – News on Health Care in Developing Countries, Vol.10* (1/96), p.11.

Svensson, L. "The Role of the Infant Food Industry: Today and Tomorrow", *N U – News on Health Care in Developing Countries* (1/96), p.23.

UNICEF Baby Friendly Hospital Initiative – 1995 Progress Report.

UNICEF/WHO Joint WHO/UNICEF Meeting on Infant and Young Child Feeding, Geneva 9-12 October 1979 – Statement – Recommendations – List of Participants.

UNICEF/WHO Notes on the International Code of Marketing of Breast-milk Substitutes (July 1982).

UNICEF/WHO Report of a Joint WHO/UNICEF Consultation Concerning "Infants Who Have to be Fed on Breast-milk Substitutes", 17-18 December 1985 (WHO/MCH/NUT/86.1) April 1986.

Wallstrom, E. and Rubenson, B. "SIDA's Involvement in the Promotion of Breast-feeding – a Brief Account", *NU – News on Health Care in Developing Countries*, Vol. 10 (1/96), p. 19.

INDEX